Writing and Rewriting

Janet R. Mayes
Formerly The City College
of New York

The Macmillan Company, New York

Copyright © 1972, Janet R. Mayes
Printed in the United States of America
All rights reserved. No part of this book may be reproduced or transmitted in any form or by any means, electronic or mechanical, including photocopying, recording, or any information storage and retrieval system, without permission in writing from the Publisher.

The Macmillan Company
866 Third Avenue, New York, New York 10022
Library of Congress catalog card number: 74-165240
Printing: 1 2 3 4 5 6 7 8   Year: 2 3 4 5 6 7 8

Credits and Acknowledgments

Copyright works, listed in the order of their appearance, are reprinted in the United States, its possessions, and dependencies by permission of the following.

"Children of West Africa," by Alfred Acquaye. From *Children of West Africa* by Alfred Allotey Acquaye, © 1968 by Sterling Publishing Co., Inc., N.Y. 10016.

"The Fire Next Time," by James Baldwin. From *The Fire Next Time* by James Baldwin. Copyright © 1962, 1963 by James Baldwin. Reprinted by permission of the publisher, The Dial Press.

"Giovanni's Room," by James Baldwin. From *Giovanni's Room* by James Baldwin. Copyright © 1956 by James Baldwin. Reprinted by permission of the publisher, The Dial Press.

"Nobody Knows My Name," by James Baldwin. From *Nobody Knows My Name* by James Baldwin. Copyright © 1954, 1956, 1958, 1959, 1960, 1961 by James Baldwin. Reprinted by permission of the publisher, The Dial Press.

"Tell Me How Long the Train's Been Gone," by James Baldwin. From *Tell Me How Long the Train's Been Gone* by James Baldwin. Copyright © 1968 by James Baldwin. Reprinted by permission of the publisher, The Dial Press.

"Before the Mayflower," by Lerone Bennett, Jr. From *Before the Mayflower: A History of Black America* by Lerone Bennett, Jr. (Chicago: Johnson Publishing Company, Inc.), 1961, 1969.

"Soul on Ice," by Eldridge Cleaver. From *Soul on Ice* by Eldridge Cleaver. Copyright © 1968 by Eldridge Cleaver. Used with permission of McGraw-Hill Book Company.

"Flying Home," by Ralph Ellison. From *Cross Section* by Ralph Ellison (New York: L. B. Fischer, 1944).

"Invisible Man," by Ralph Ellison. From *Invisible Man* by Ralph Ellison. (New York: Random House, Inc., 1947).

"The Magus," by John Fowles. (Boston: Little, Brown and Company, 1965).

"Diary of a Harlem Schoolteacher," by Jim Haskins. Copyright © 1969 by Jim Haskins. Reprinted by permission of Grove Press, Inc.

Cynthia Dale

Writing and Rewriting

"Soon One Morning," by Herbert Hill. Introduction to *Soon One Morning, New Writing by American Negroes, 1940-1962* (edited by Herbert Hill). Copyright © 1963 By Alfred A. Knopf, Inc. (New York: Alfred A. Knopf, Inc., 1963).

"One Friday Morning," by Langston Hughes. From *Laughing to Keep from Crying* (Anthology of American Negro Literature, Sylvestre C. Watkins, ed.). (New York: Random House, Inc., 1944).

"American Sexual Reference," by LeRoi Jones. From *Home: Social Essays* by LeRoi Jones. Reprinted with omissions by permission of William Morrow and Company, Inc. Copyright © 1965, 1966 by LeRoi Jones.

"Blues People," by LeRoi Jones. From *Blues People* by LeRoi Jones. Reprinted with omissions by permission of William Morrow and Company, Inc. Copyright © 1963 by LeRoi Jones.

"Cold, Hurt, and Sorrow," by LeRoi Jones. From *Home: Social Essays* by LeRoi Jones. Reprinted with omissions by permission of William Morrow and Company, Inc. Copyright © 1962, 1966 by LeRoi Jones.

"To Be a Slave," by Julius Lester. From *To Be a Slave* (New York: The Dial Press, 1968).

"The Chief," by Albert Luthuli. From *I Will Still Be Moved: Reports from South Africa*, ed. by Marion Friedmann (London, Eng.: Amnesty International Ltd.; Quadrangle Books, Inc., 1963).

"An Outlaw," by Nelson Mandela. From *I Will Still Be Moved: Reports from South Africa*, ed. by Marion Friedmann (London, Eng.: Amnesty International Ltd.; Quadrangle Books, Inc., 1963).

"Daddy Was a Numbers Runner," by Louise Meriwether. (Englewood Cliffs, N.J.: Prentice-Hall, Inc., 1970).

"Black Drama," by Loften Mitchell. From the book *Black Drama* by Loften Mitchell. Copyright © 1967 by Hawthorne Books, Inc.

"The River Between," by James Ngugi. (New York: Humanities Press, Inc., 1965).

"Farm Jails," by Lewis Nkosi. From *I Will Still Be Moved: Reports from South Africa*," ed. by Marion Friedmann (London, Eng.: Amnesty International, Inc.; Quadrangle Books, Inc., 1963). Reprinted by permission of Lewis Nkosi c/o International Famous Agency. Copyright 1963 by Amnesty International.

"Challenge of the Congo," by Kwame Nkrumah. (New York: International Publishers Co., Inc., 1967).

"An African Barrister," by Duma Nokwe. From *I Will Still Be Moved: Reports from South Africa*, ed. by Marion Friedmann. (London, Eng.: Amnesty International, Inc.; Quadrangle Books, Inc., 1963).

"Ujamaa: Essays on Socialism," by Julius K. Nyerere. From *Essays on Socialism* by Julius K. Nyerere. (London, Eng.: Oxford University Press, 1968). Reprinted with the permission of the Office of the President, The United Republic of Tanzania.

"Macerio," by Juan Rulfo. From *The Burning Plain and Other Stories*. (Austin: University of Texas Press, 1967).

"On African Socialism," by Leopold Senghor. Trans. by Mercer Cook (New York: Frederic A. Praeger, Inc., 1964).

"The Development of the Black Revolutionary Artist," by James T. Stewart. Copyright © 1968 by James Stewart. Reprinted from *Black Fire*, ed. by LeRoi Jones & Larry Neal. (New York: William Morrow & Co., Inc.) Used with permission of the author and the Ronald Hobbs Literary Agency.

"Slaughterhouse-Five," by Kurt Vonnegut, Jr. From *Slaughterhouse-Five, or The Children's Crusade* by Kurt Vonnegut, Jr. Copyright © 1969 by Kurt Vonnegut, Jr. A Seymour Lawrence Book/Delacorte Press. Reprinted by permission of the publisher.

"Black Souls Are Not for Sale," by A. Cecil Williams. From *The Black Scholar* (December 1970).

"Black Boy," by Richard Wright. (About 870 words, *passim*) from *Black Boy* by Richard Wright (Harper & Row, Perennial Ed. 1966).

"Native Son," by Richard Wright. (About 590 words as scattered quotes) from *Native Son* by Richard Wright. Copyright, 1940 by Richard Wright; renewed, 1968 by Ellen Wright. Reprinted by permission of Harper & Row, Publishers, Inc.

"Uncle Tom's Children," by Richard Wright. (About 950 words as scattered quotes) from *Uncle Tom's Children* by Richard Wright. Copyright, 1936, 1937, 1938 by Richard Wright. Reprinted by permission of Harper & Row, Publishers, Inc.

"The Man Who Went to Chicago," by Richard Wright. Copyright 1945 by L. B. Fischer Publishing Corporation under the title "Early Days in Chicago." Reprinted by permission of Paul F. Reynolds, Inc., 559 Fifth Avenue, New York, N.Y. 10017

**To My Students
and to the memory of
Betty Rawls**

Preface

Writers rarely communicate complex ideas by worrying about so-called correctness while composing. Thus *Writing and Rewriting* encourages students to write freely <u>first</u> and to change or "edit" their writing to conform to the mechanical conventions of college writing—if they so choose—<u>afterwards</u>. To this end, the text provides a practical method of self-editing for students with sentence-level difficulties in American college writing. Most exercises in the book are composed of sentences and paragraphs to "edit" according to the mechanical writing conventions covered in the preceding lesson. Students can study one of these lessons—most lessons are self-contained—and then find practice material to edit before applying the concepts to their own writing. At various points in the book, passages are provided with cumulative editing "problems" for review purposes.

The text assumes that writers learn a convention by seeing it in action and by trying to use it in various ways. Most illustrations are taken from the works of many published authors. The exercises to edit are all excerpts from the same sources altered to provide practice in recognizing and changing words and phrases that do not conform to the mechanical conventions of college writing. The authors' original versions appear in the Bibliographic "Answer" Section in the back. In addition, several chapters instruct the student to complete or "add on" to a partial sentence using the particular mechanical convention discussed.

Some excerpts are by authors fairly well known in the United States. Many are from works that have yet to be appreciated and used as models by apprentice writers in this country. These include: African, Afro-American, American Indian, Mexican, Puerto Rican, and South American. Since these literatures tend to be badly in need of exposure, appreciation, and translation into English, it is the express intention of this text to encourage further reading and study in them. An extensive bibliography is provided for that purpose. Students and teachers who are unable to find some of these authors in standard libraries and book stores are urged to do what they can to have the works of these authors purchased.

Writing and Rewriting is designed to provide college students with the skill to switch easily into college writing conventions. Students need to be free to choose this mode of communication if it becomes necessary—for whatever personal or political reasons they may have. Indeed, writing within the conventions can not only be creative and inspiring but also well worth the sustained effort needed to master the technique, as the excerpts demonstrate. On the other hand, this text is not designed to uphold college writing standards as the only way to write. One uses writing to communicate and influence, and one communicates so that one's audience understands most clearly, whoever that audience happens to be at any particular moment. It should be self-evident that a variety of writing styles is appropriate in college and that the styles of college writing can be appropriate in other situations.

However, an "academic" or textbook tone of writing is not the subject of this book. Examples of this can be found in most college texts. What is of importance here are the principles that govern the mechanics of the "academic" tone. Most excerpts used for illustrations and exercises conform to these principles but not to the tone. The text encourages students to write freely in the styles they feel most creative and comfortable with. Then they can edit for the mechanical college conventions. This way, they do not have the double chore of writing in an academic tone and making sure they conform to the conventions. In future essays, if and when they select an "academic" or textbook tone, not only will they know the mechanical conventions, but they will also be able to infuse and improve it with their own creativity.

Grammatical or linguistic terminology is avoided as much as possible. People rarely learn a writing convention by putting labels on various words or parts of a sentence. At the same time, prescription is often unavoidable in a guidebook. But this text uses only those grammatical terms and "rules" absolutely necessary in teaching a particular writing device. An index of terms is provided for those who want to know traditional labels. Since no assumption is made about what students "should know" before using this text, very basic aspects of the conventions are covered thoroughly; and if students already know the content of particular sections, they should merely skim them to be able to recognize the definitions used in later chapters.

All excerpts chosen for exercises and illustrations were selected from material gathered by students and teachers of varied ethnic backgrounds, whose recommendations were based upon what excited them. I want to extend my gratitude to these dedicated researchers as well as to my students at The City College of New York, who are my teachers, and my friends, who in one way or another provided emotional, inspirational, and material support to the production of this text. Researchers: Jean Campbell, Grace Hunicutt, Rita Losch, Lucy Matos, Valerie Morley, Jenny Mulrenan, Elaine Schwager, Gail Stokes; Consultants: Bertha Doleman, College Skills Division, Department of Special Programs, The City College of New York, C.U.N.Y., and Supervisor, Reading Laboratory, Cooperative College Center of Westchester, Affiliate of the State University of New York at Purchase; Elizabeth Howell, Reading Consultant; William Jones, coordinator of English, Urban University Department, Newark College of Arts and Sciences, Rutgers University; George McDonald, Director of College Skills Division, Department of Special Programs, The City College of New York, C.U.N.Y.; Allene Marcus, associate, American Language Program, Columbia University; Cruz Martinez, Community Mental Health Worker, Lincoln Hospital, New York City; Maxine Morrin, George Washington High School, New York City; Irene G. Rabinowitz, Reading Specialist, Reading Skills Center, New York City Community College, The City University of New York; Mina P. Shaughessy, Director, Basic Writing Program, Department of English, The City College of New York, C.U.N.Y.; Jean K. Taylor, Newark College of Arts and Sciences, Rutgers University. Emotional, Inspirational, and Material Support: Kathryne Andrews, Marian

Arkin, Ellen Bernstein, Al Bryson, John Cates, Pat Cox, Michael Engl, George Fein, Christina Franke, Ellen Franklin, Leslie Freeman, Laura Furman, Paul Gimpel, Joan Giummo, Ruth Herman, Esther Katzen, Lee Kirby, Nola Krasko, Carol Libow, George Macduff, Harvey Mayes, Stephanie Noland, Gene Newman, Marice Pappo, Julie Pierce, Adrienne Rich, Ed Rivera, Godfrey Rubins, David Singer, Mark Stern, Jane Tillsworth, Marcia Yutman, and especially Toni Cade and Tony Penale. I also want to extend my gratitude to the library of the School of Oriental and African Studies, London University; the New York Public Library, The Schomburg Collection; the library of the New York Urban Coalition; and Mrs. A'Lelia R. Nelson of the library of The City College of New York, C.U.N.Y.

A textbook like this, of course, is never complete. I have covered areas of writing that I felt were most in need of proper lessons and exercises. But you, as students and teachers, are the final authorities on what else needs to be included, what has been unclear, what has not worked as a lesson, what exercises have been confusing, etc. I welcome your comments and suggestions.

Janet R. Mayes
New York City

Contents

Preface	ix
Charts	xvii
How to Use *Writing and Rewriting*	1

SECTION ONE: The Whole Sentence — 5

1 The Whole Thought — 7
Exercises — 13

2 Using Fragments—Attach Them to Whole Thoughts — 17

A. "Because I Want to" Is a Fragment — 17
   Exercises: Editing for Fragments 23
B. "The Man Who Came to Dinner" Is a Fragment — 29
   Exercises: Editing for "The Man Who" Fragments 33
C. Other Fragments That Rename — 37
   Exercises: Editing for Fragments That Rename 41
D. "Breaking Through the Sound Barrier" Is a Fragment — 49
   Exercises: Editing for "Breaking Through" Fragments 53
E. Supplementary: Another Use of the "Breaking Through" Fragment — 57
   Exercises: Editing for "The Jet Breaking Through" Fragments 61
   Adding the "Breaking Through" and "The Jet Breaking Through" Fragments 63
F. "To Offer a Ride" Is a Fragment, "To Be a Man" Is a Fragment — 65
   Exercises: Editing for the "To Offer a Ride" Fragments 67
G. "Afraid of His Shadow" Is a Fragment — 70
   Exercises: Editing for the "Afraid of His Shadow" Fragments 73
H. "Because of You" Is a Fragment; Any Word Group Without a Noun-Verb Pair Is a Fragment — 75
   Exercises: Editing for the "Because of You" Fragments 79
   Cumulative Editing for All Fragments in Chapter 2 85

xiv Contents

3 Comma-splice and Run-on Sentences 91

- A. Basic Definitions 91
  Exercises: Editing for Comma-splices and Run-ons: Using the Connecting Words   95
  Editing for Comma-splices and Run-ons: Using All Methods   99
- B. Other Approaches to Comma-splices and Run-ons 103
  Exercises: Editing for Comma-splices, Run-ons, and Fragments. Read out Loud   107
- C. Yes, You Can Start a Sentence with "And" 111
- D. "It Is" Can Be a Noun-Verb Pair; "Which Is" Introduces a Fragment; The Many Uses of "That Is" 111
  Exercises: Editing for Comma-splices and Run-ons   115
- E. "However" and "Therefore": The Logical Words 119
- F. Summary of Punctuation to Attach Two Whole Thoughts to Each Other 122
  Exercises: Editing for Comma-splices, Run-ons, and Fragments   125
- G. Choppy Sentences Can Result from Being Too Careful 129
- H. Editing for Comma-splices and Run-ons Can Lead to Fragments 129
  Cumulative Editing for Comma-splices, Run-ons, and Fragments   131

SECTION TWO: The Ends of Words 139

4 Spelling the Verb 141

- A. Definition of a Verb 141
- B. When Does the S Go at the End of a Verb? (Noun-Verb Pair Agreement) 141
  Exercises   149
- C. When Does "ed" Go at the End of a Verb? 155
  Exercises   159
- D. Verbs and "Helping Verbs": Verb Group 1 167
  Exercises: 175
  Exercises: Editing for Verb Group 1   177
- E. Verb Group 2: The Verb Ending in "ing" 181
  Exercises   189
  Exercises: Editing for Verb Group 2   191
- F. "Lay" and "Lie" As Verbs; "Supposed to" and "Used to"; "Would Have," "Could Have," and "Should Have" 195
  Exercises: Editing   197
- G. Complications of Noun-Verb Pair Agreement 199
- H. "There Is" or "There Are"? "Here Is" or "Here Are"? 200
  Exercises: Editing for Noun-Verb Agreement   203
- I. Two Words in One: Contractions—Where to Put the Apostrophe 207
  (For exercises in editing for contractions, see 5E)
- J. Verbs, and How They Express Time 209
  Exercises   213

5 Other Uses of **S** — 215

- A. The Noun and Pronoun: Definitions — 215
  Exercises 219
- B. The Difference Between S and 'S — 221
- C. Plural Nouns — 223
  Exercises: Editing for Plural Nouns 227
  Exercises: Editing for Plural Nouns and Words That Tell You a Noun Is Coming 229
- D. Ownership (and the Difference Between "Their," "They're," and "There" and Between "Your" and "You're") — 231
  Exercises: Editing for Ownership Nouns and Pronouns 235
- E. Two Words in One (Contractions): The Difference Between "Its" and "It's"; The Difference Between "Whose" and "Who's" — 237
  Exercises: Editing for Contractions 239
  Cumulative Editing for Chapter 5 245

SECTION THREE: When Ideas Become Complicated — 249

6 Special Pronoun Traps — 251

- A. The Pronoun with the Double Meaning — 251
- B. The Pronoun with No Meaning: Make Sure Each Pronoun Really Renames Something — 252
- C. Is the Pronoun Singular or Plural? Is the Pronoun "Him" or "You"? (Pronoun Reference) — 252
  Exercises: Editing for Pronoun Reference 255
- D. "Which Is" or "Which Are"? "Who Is" or "Who Are"? — 259
  Exercises: Editing for Verbs after "Who," "Which," or "That" 261

7 What the Word "Awkward" Usually Means — 265

- A. Equal or Balanced Ideas (Parallel Construction) — 265
  Exercises: Editing for Balanced Ideas 273
- B. When Does a Question Not Have a Question Mark After It? — 279
- C. What Comes After the Words: "He Said That . . ."? Other Indirect Statements — 281
  Exercises: Editing for Indirect Questions and Statements 285
  Exercises: Add Indirect Questions and Statements 289
  Exercises for Writing Dialogue 293
- D. Other Problems with Word Order — 295
- E. When You Leave Words Out — 299

8 Have Faith in the Paragraph as a Unit of Thought. Turning a Paragraph into an Essay. — 301

A.	Definition of a Paragraph	301
B.	A Paragraph Is Usually a <u>Group</u> of Sentences	301
C.	Two Major Types of Paragraphs	302
D.	Paragraphs That Come <u>Within</u> a Whole Essay	302
E.	The Opening or Introduction Paragraph of an Essay	307

Exercises   315

APPENDIX A: Punctuation   317

APPENDIX B: Some Dictionary Guidelines   325

APPENDIX C: Bibliographic "Answer" Section   331

Final Cumulative Editing   389
Glossary-Index of Terms   395

Charts

CHAPTER 1	**The Whole Thought**	
1	Four Types of Whole Thoughts	9
CHAPTER 2	**Using Fragments**	
2	Words That Commonly Make Fragments	19
3	Punctuation when Attaching Fragments to Whole Thoughts	22
4	The Pattern of "The Man <u>Who</u>" Fragment	29
5	Punctuation for "The Man <u>Who</u>" Fragment	31
6	The Pattern of the Fragment That Renames	37
7	Punctuation for the Fragment That Renames	39
8	Punctuation for the "<u>Breaking</u> Through" Fragment	51
9	Punctuation for "The Jet <u>Breaking</u> Through" Fragment	60
10	The Pattern of the "<u>To Offer</u> a Ride" Fragment	65
11	Punctuation for the "<u>To Offer</u> a Ride" Fragment	66
12	Punctuation for the "<u>Afraid</u> of His Shadow" Fragment	72
13	Signal Words for the "<u>Because of</u> You" Fragment	76
14	Punctuation for the "<u>Because of</u> You" Fragment	77
CHAPTER 3	**Comma-splice and Run-on Sentences**	
15	Punctuation Between Two Whole Thoughts	93
16	The Difference Between "Which Is" and "It Is"	112
17	The Many Uses of "That"	114
18	List of Logical Words	121
19	Summary of Punctuation to Attach Two Whole Thoughts to Each Other	127
CHAPTER 4	**Spelling the Verb**	
20	Noun-Verb Pair Agreement	144
21	Noun-Verb Pair Agreement for Those Who Know Some Spanish	147
22	Summary of Noun-Verb Pair Agreement	148
23	Helping Verbs for Verb Group 1	168
24	Summary of Simple Past Time and Verb Group 1	170
25	Some Important Verbs in Present, Past, and Verb Group 1	171
26	Helping Verbs for Verb Group 2	182
27	Summary for Verbs and Verb Groups	183

28	Final List of Important Verbs	184
29	Spelling of "Lay" and "Lie"	195
30	Pronoun-Verb Pair Contractions	207
31	Contractions for Verbs Combined with "Not"	209

CHAPTER 5 Other Uses of **S**

32	Common Pronouns	217
33	Words That Precede Plural Nouns	225
34	Summary of Ownership	232
35	Summary Chart of S, 'S, and S'	242

CHAPTER 7 What the Word "Awkward" Usually Means

36	Words That Introduce Indirect Questions	280
37	Words That Introduce Indirect Statements	282

How to Use Writing and Rewriting

A. Starting to write

Each author has his own method of writing, and you, the student, should work out the one that makes you feel most comfortable. But perhaps one of the best ways to begin—especially when you feel you have to say things "just right"—is to write down all the ideas flowing from your mind, without stopping or worrying about saying them "properly." After you have finished the first copy of your work, put it away for a while (if you have left yourself enough time!) and then go back to it for rewriting and editing. First make sure your reader will really understand your ideas. Have you left anything out? Assume that your reader knows almost nothing about your topic and that you must teach him. Many college instructors prefer this approach anyway. Usually pieces that are written for outside college express new ideas to an audience, so especially if you are planning to do such writing, you need to explain things carefully—depending upon how much you think your audience already knows.

After you have done all this, edit for the college writing conventions covered in the book—if you feel editing is necessary. Finally, it is extremely useful to have a friend look over your paper before you hand it in. Exchange papers with each other and edit them. This gives each of you more editing practice, and your discussions and questions should provide you both with new ideas and will indicate places in your papers where the ideas fall apart. It is sometimes difficult to avoid feelings of competition and self-defense when working on papers with a friend, but there is also usually a lot you can learn from each other.

B. How to use the chapters

Most chapters are self-sufficient. You don't need to go through the book chapter by chapter. If you are having difficulty with spelling the ending of a verb (a common problem for those who did not have a good writing education before college), you can turn to the verb chapter and find the particular section that pertains to your need. Study the lesson. Very often you will be asked to

2   Writing and Rewriting

memorize a list of words or a type of spelling. Get a friend to test you on these. Once the lists are in your head, you are in control any time you need to fall back on them. For example, in the chapter on fragments, it is suggested that you religiously memorize a list of words that most often tell you a fragment is going to follow. Once you know this list, you can skim your own papers for these words and check to see if you have written a fragment.

Some chapters depend upon lessons in earlier sections, but you will be told what to review before studying them.

C. How to use the exercises

After you have studied the lesson, go on to the exercises. Most often the exercises ask you to read the sentences and paragraphs and change them into college writing. For example, after reading about how to find fragments, you can practice finding them in the exercises on fragments. Finally, you can use the same methods when you edit your essays for fragments. Most lessons in the book are followed by a group of exercises that pertains only to that lesson. You need not look for anything other than what the lesson covers when you edit these.

Each exercise sentence and paragraph is taken from a novel, essay, or short story: James Baldwin's *Another Country*, for instance. However, we have altered the excerpt slightly so that you can practice finding the alteration and restoring the excerpt to its original condition by asking yourself how the author might have written the passage originally.

D. How to use the Bibliographic "Answer" Section

In order to find the answer, the original passage, you must look in the Bibliographic "Answer" Section given as Appendix C in the back of the book. After each exercise selection, you will find a number in parentheses. That number refers to a name of an author. Let's say that you find a number (10e) at the end of an exercise passage:

   In the fall of last year. My plane hovered over the rust-red earth of Georgia. (10e)

First you would put the excerpt back into college writing.

   In the fall of last year, my plane hovered over the rust-red earth of Georgia. (10e)

Then you look for number (10e) in the "Answer" Section. Next to number (10e) you will find the author, James Baldwin, and the passage of James Baldwin that is altered in the exercises: *Nobody Knows My Name: More Notes of a Native Son*. There you will find the original version, the "answer" to the editing problem in that exercise sentence. Look on page 339 to see how this particular answer appears.

Most excerpts are in context in the "Answer" Section. Our purpose is twofold: 1) you will find the answer to the exercise, and 2) you will have to read a bit of Baldwin to find the answer. Because it is our expressed intention to encourage further reading and study of the material sampled in these excerpts, each selection includes a complete bibliographic reference. The authors are listed in alphabetical order, and labels like "Afro-American" or "Puerto Rican" or "American Indian" are included in case you are concentrating on a particular type of literature.

E. If you are using the book for a college course

There are several effective ways to use this book. One method is to write a few papers—for yourself, not for the instructor—without watching too carefully for all the so-called college writing mistakes. Then you can find out what you need to study. Have a friend who knows college writing or a tutor look it over. Then you can work on those chapters that pertain to your own needs. Sometimes an instructor will be willing to help you in this extra project. If your reader says that you write too many fragments, then you can spend time on that chapter. If you are using the book as your own private supplement to a course, you may find that your instructor has other labels for the writing "faults." For example, he may put the letters C.S. on your papers. Look up C.S. in the index of terms, and you will find that it means "comma splice" and that it is covered in Chapter 3.

F. If you are learning college writing on your own

The chapters are arranged in the order that makes the most sense for people studying on their own. However, just going through the book and doing the exercises is not enough. You must do a lot of reading and writing. It is usually most profitable to work with a friend or two, getting together regularly and disciplining each other. Decide what you are going to read (perhaps using the bibliography in the back as a guide) and discuss the work together at weekly meetings. Draw up a list of some topics that interest you and write papers for each other to look at and evaluate. Being a teacher is one of the best ways to learn, and writing for your friends is one of the most challenging tasks you could undertake; for your friends are usually much harsher critics than instructors are. Ideally, getting together with friends in a study group plus taking a course in college writing can be the best combination, for there is a danger in depending too much on just one approach to learning.

G. Editing your own essays

After you are through composing your essay and checking it for content, you should devote several editing sessions to it in order to check it for those particular areas of writing you are working on. Use the methods suggested in the lessons and exercises. For example, if you tend to write fragments, you should devote one editing session just to fragments. If you are also studying noun-verb pair agreement, a separate editing session should be devoted just to that. After a while, when you have a clear idea of those aspects of writing that give you the most trouble, you might have four or five separate editing processes, each one devoted to a different aspect.

Even if it has not been stressed in a lesson, it is always useful to read your essay out loud to see if it is written the way you want it to sound. For example, you might be pronouncing the letter "s" at the end of a plural noun or a singular verb, but you may be forgetting to put it in. Finally, it is helpful to edit backwards, by reading one sentence at a time starting at the end of the essay. This way you can look for fragments, run-ons, etc., without being distracted by the style or ideas.

SECTION ONE

The Whole Sentence

Although this section is devoted to the individual sentence, you are strongly urged not to write one sentence at a time. If you stop to edit each sentence as you compose your thoughts, you are bound to lose your flow of ideas, the logic behind your argument. <u>Write first; edit later</u>.

1 The Whole Thought

The best way to study college writing is to examine what fine authors do. Study the following sentence by Richard Wright.

> Even before the front door was opened, he heard the faint roar of voices.
> (Richard Wright, *Native Son*) (140)[1]

Now look at the two word groups.

(a) Even before the front door was opened
(b) he heard the faint roar of voices

The first word group tells you that he did <u>something</u> before the door was opened, but it leaves you wondering. What did he do first? The words "even before" make you want to know more. So word group (a) is not a whole thought. The second word group tells you more: it completes the thought by telling you that "<u>he heard</u>" something before the door opened. The two word groups together make up one finished sentence.

Note, however, that if you read the second word group alone, it does NOT leave you wondering. It seems to be whole or finished.

> He heard the faint roar of voices.

The word group could be read alone as a finished sentence with a capital letter at the beginning and a period at the end.[2] But what would happen if you put the words "even before" before the <u>second</u> word group? All of a sudden it also does not sound whole or finished any more.

> <u>Even before</u> he heard the faint roar of voices,

Likewise, if you took away the words "even before" from the <u>first</u> word group, it would now sound completed.

> The front door was opened.

Thus the words "even before" can make a whole thought into an unfinished thought, or a FRAGMENT.

---

[1] Numbers refer to entries in Bibliographic "Answer" Section.
[2] A sentence has at <u>least</u> one whole thought. See page 10.

7

8   *The Whole Sentence*

A. There are certain words like "even before" which make whole thoughts into fragments

See page 10 and Chapter 2.

B. A whole thought has two parts

DO-ER[3]	WORD EXPRESSING WHAT HE IS DOING
(noun or pronoun)	*(verb)*
He	heard
John	ran

C. Another kind of whole thought has three parts

DO-ER	WORD EXPRESSING THAT HE IS OR FEELS (verb)	WORD EXPRESSING WHAT OR HOW HE IS OR FEELS
(noun or pronoun)		
He	is	happy
John	feels	sad

D. The four types of whole thoughts

In fact, there are four kinds of whole thoughts in college writing. It is not necessary to know the technicalities of what goes into a whole thought, but you should have a general idea of what is meant by one. Keep in mind that a whole thought can also be a sentence. Just put a capital letter at the beginning and a period at the end of the whole thought:

He ran.
John feels sad.

Study Chart 1, page 9.

E. Noun-verb pairs (or pronoun-verb pairs)[4]

For convenience, the book will occasionally refer to noun-verb pairs (or pronoun-verb pairs). The first column in Chart 1 is the noun; the second column is the verb. Together they make up a noun-verb pair. There are other uses of the noun. Nouns can be found outside the noun-verb pair. See pages 215 and 296.

TYPE OF WHOLE THOUGHT	NOUN (DO-ER)	VERB (WHAT HE DOES OR IS OR FEELS)
1	A crowd	gathered
	They	are studying[5]
2	John	chose[6]
3	His friend	was punched
4	They	were[6]

[3] Some textbooks would call the "do-er" the "subject."

[4] Or, if you wish, we can call these "subject-verb pairs."

[5] Note that you cannot leave the "are" off "are studying." You cannot say: "They studying." According to college writing conventions, "studying" is not a true verb: all verbs ending in "ing" need a helping verb like "are" before they are considered true verbs. See page 18. Also note that we could call this one a "pronoun-verb pair." See pages 111-113.

[6] While types 1 and 3 can be whole sentences with just a noun and a verb, types 2 and 4 need another word or two before they can be sentences. See page 9.

CHART 1. Four Types of Whole Thoughts

Type 1

Do-er*	What He Does
He	ran.
Gus	sat.
John	smiled.
Debra	reads.
He	listens.
They	are studying.

Type 2

Do-er*	What He Does	What He Does It to
He	grabbed	the pen.
Gus	punched	his friend.
John	wrote	the speech.
They	chose	a leader.
She	parks	the car.
He	heard	the roar.

Type 3 Another Form of 2 (backwards)

What He Does It to*	What He Does	Do-er (not needed)
The pen	was grabbed	(by him).
His friend	was punched	(by Gus).
The speech	was written	(by John).
A leader	was chosen	(by them).
The car	is parked	(by her).
The roar	was heard	(by him).
The door	was opened	(by the guards).

Type 4

Do-er*	Is or Feels	How or What He Is or Feels (or Where He Is)
He	was	happy.
Gus	is	a student.
He	feels	fine.
Life	can be	weird.
Debra	will be	the speaker.
They	were	in the room.
The room	appears	cheerful.

*Some textbooks would call this a "subject."

F. Sentences

A sentence usually has at least ONE WHOLE THOUGHT.

A crowd gathered.

However, if all sentences were short, reading them would be boring, so authors often add together two or more whole thoughts to make one sentence:

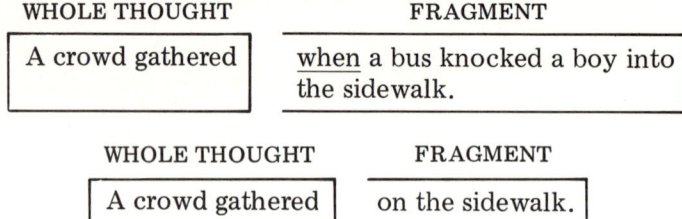

(35)

Or they may add one or more fragments to one whole thought to make one sentence:

WHOLE THOUGHT	FRAGMENT
A crowd gathered	when a bus knocked a boy into the sidewalk.

WHOLE THOUGHT	FRAGMENT
A crowd gathered	on the sidewalk.

NOTE THAT EVERY SENTENCE IN COLLEGE WRITING MUST HAVE AT LEAST ONE WHOLE THOUGHT.

G. Fragments

A whole thought must have a noun-verb pair. "On the sidewalk" is not a whole thought because there is no do-er and no word expressing what he is doing. In other words, there is no noun-verb pair in the words "on the sidewalk." Fragments like this one must be added on to a whole thought in college writing:

WHOLE THOUGHT	FRAGMENT
A crowd gathered	on the sidewalk.

In addition, if you put a word like "when" in front of any one of the whole thoughts outlined above, it automatically becomes a fragment: "<u>When</u> a bus knocked a boy into the sidewalk" is a fragment. It too must be added onto a whole thought. It cannot stand alone because EVERY SENTENCE IN COLLEGE WRITING MUST HAVE <u>AT</u> <u>LEAST</u> ONE WHOLE THOUGHT.[7] See Chapter 2.

WHOLE THOUGHT	FRAGMENT
A crowd gathered	when a bus knocked a boy into the sidewalk.

---

[7]In a <u>command</u>, the sentence does not usually have the <u>noun</u> of the <u>noun-verb pair</u>. "<u>Take</u> me to your leader!" has the verb "take." The noun is not there, but we can assume it is the person being spoken to.

H. Comma—splices and run-ons

College writing has developed certain "rules" for adding two whole thoughts together. For example, you can put a COMMA PLUS THE WORD "AND" between the two whole thoughts:

WHOLE THOUGHT		WHOLE THOUGHT
A bus had knocked a boy into the sidewalk	**,** and	a crowd gathered.

But if you leave the word "and" out, you have a COMMA-SPLICE, which is rarely acceptable in college writing.

COMMA-SPLICE

A bus had knocked a boy into the sidewalk, a crowd gathered.

When there is <u>no punctuation at all</u> between two whole thoughts and no word like "and" to join them together, you have a RUN-ON, also rarely acceptable in college writing.

RUN-ON

A bus had knocked a boy into the sidewalk a crowd gathered.

See Chapter 3.

I. How authors use the four types of whole thoughts

Type 1—A crowd gathered.

Type 2—John wrote a speech.

Although most styles of writing have all four types of whole thoughts, certain topics lend themselves to particular types. For example, in the following passages by Ralph Ellison and Roa Augusto Bastos, note that Types 1 and 2 are most frequently used. The underlined whole thoughts are Types 1 and 2.

> <u>I stretched</u> out beneath the covers, hearing the springs groan beneath me. The room was cold. <u>I listened</u> to the night sounds of the house. <u>The clock ticked</u> with empty urgency as though trying to catch up with time. In the street <u>a siren howled</u>.
>
> (Ralph Ellison, *Invisible Man*) (43)

> Suddenly the earth seemed to give way a bit. <u>He clawed</u> in the emptiness. Like a stone, <u>he remained</u> behind, strangling on the air. <u>He tried</u> to advance, but now his <u>legs formed</u> an irremediable <u>part</u> of the block that had slid down on them. <u>He</u> no longer even <u>felt</u> them. <u>He felt</u> only the <u>asphyxia</u>. <u>He was drowning</u> in a solid, dark river. <u>He stopped moving</u>, <u>stopped the</u> useless <u>struggle</u>. <u>The torment</u> slowly <u>changed</u> into an inexplicable delight.
>
> (Roa Augusto Bastos, "The Excavation") (13)

Both passages are full of activity. People, a clock, a siren, etc. are all involved in DOING things.

Type 3—The speech was written (by John).

Sometimes an author writes about something that happened to him, an important character, or a thing. But now he may use a lot of whole thoughts that are in Type 3. He generally doesn't plan it that way; it just happens. Note how often the authors use Type 3 in these next passages. Observe how the do-er is not always named. Type 3 allows you to describe what happens without pointing out who is doing the action. Type 3 whole thoughts are underlined.

> For the last three hundred years <u>Africa and its people have been viewed</u> mainly through European eyes and for European reasons. <u>The entire history of Africa will have to be</u> literally <u>rewritten</u>, challenging and reversing the European concept.
> (John Henrik Clarke, "Reclaiming the Lost African Heritage") (31)

> <u>Our continent has been carved up</u> [by the great powers], <u>alien governments have been forced</u> upon the African people [by military conquest and by economic domination], <u>strivings of nationhood and national dignity have been beaten down</u> [by force], <u>traditional economies and ancient customs have been disrupted</u>, and <u>human skills and energy have been harnessed</u> for the advantage of our conquerors.
> (Albert Luthuli, "The Chief") (81)

(Brackets indicate that the do-er is <u>grammatically</u> not needed. See Chart 1.)

Type 4—He was happy.

Gus was a student.

Now notice how whole thoughts in Type 4 fill the next passages, both of which paint a picture of a person with words. However, if each author had merely described what the person looked like, the person might seem dead and uninteresting. The authors also use the other three types of whole thoughts in their sentences in order to make the person come alive. Not only must the reader see what the person looks like, he must also see what he does, how he moves and speaks, what others think of him, and so on. Type 4 thoughts are underlined.

> <u>He was</u>, I think, <u>very handsome</u>. I gather this from photographs and from my own memories of him, dressed in his Sunday best and on his way to preach a sermon somewhere, when I was little. Handsome, proud, and ingrown, "like a toe-nail," somebody said. But <u>he looked</u> to me, as I grew older, <u>like pictures</u> I had seen of African tribal chieftains: <u>he really should have been naked</u>, with war-paint on and barbaric mementos, standing among spears. <u>He could be chilling</u> in the pulpit <u>and indescribably cruel</u> in his personal life and <u>he was certainly the most bitter man</u> I have ever met; yet it must be said that there was something else in him, buried in him, which lent him his tremendous power and, even, a rather crushing charm. It had something to do with his blackness, I think—<u>he was very black</u>—with his blackness and his beauty, and with the fact that he knew that he was black but did not know that he was beautiful.
> (James Baldwin, *Notes of a Native Son*, Boston: Beacon Press, 1955)

> Esther's hair falls in soft curls about her high-cheekboned chalk-white face. <u>Esther's hair would be beautiful</u> if there were more gloss to it. . . . <u>Her cheeks are too flat and dead</u> for a girl of nine. <u>Esther looks like a little white child</u>, starched, frilled as she walks slowly from her home towards her father's grocery store.
> (Jean Toomer, *Cane*) (127)

Exercises for Chapter 1

1. Write very simple whole thoughts that follow Type 1 on page 9.

WHOLE THOUGHT—TYPE 1

	DO-ER *(noun)*	WHAT HE DOES *(verb)*
a.	William	laughed.
b.	Jean	is eating.
1.	_____	_____
2.	_____	_____
3.	_____	_____
4.	_____	_____
5.	_____	_____
6.	_____	_____
7.	_____	_____
8.	_____	_____
9.	_____	_____
10.	_____	_____

2. Write very simple whole thoughts that follow Type 2 on page 9.

WHOLE THOUGHT—TYPE 2

	DO-ER *(noun)*	WHAT HE DOES *(verb)*	WHAT HE DOES IT TO
a.	William	drove	a truck.
b.	Jean	is eating	the pie.
1.	_____	_____	_____
2.	_____	_____	_____
3.	_____	_____	_____
4.	_____	_____	_____
5.	_____	_____	_____

14 *The Whole Sentence*

6. _____ _____ _____

7. _____ _____ _____

8. _____ _____ _____

9. _____ _____ _____

10. _____ _____ _____

3. Write very simple whole thoughts that follow Type 3 on page 9.

WHOLE THOUGHT—TYPE 3

	WHAT THE DO-ER DOES IT TO *(noun)*	WHAT HE DOES *(verb)*	(DO-ER)
a.	A leader	is chosen	(by a vote).
b.	The speech	was written	(by Jean).
1.	_____	_____	(_____)
2.	_____	_____	(_____)
3.	_____	_____	(_____)
4.	_____	_____	(_____)
5.	_____	_____	(_____)
6.	_____	_____	(_____)
7.	_____	_____	(_____)
8.	_____	_____	(_____)
9.	_____	_____	(_____)
10.	_____	_____	(_____)

4. Write very simple whole thoughts that follow Type 4 on page 9.

WHOLE THOUGHT—TYPE 4

	DO-ER *(noun)*	IS OR FEELS *(verb)*	WHAT HE IS OR FEELS (OR WHERE HE IS)
a.	Gus	is	a student.
b.	Pat	will be	here.

1. _____ _____ _____
2. _____ _____ _____
3. _____ _____ _____
4. _____ _____ _____
5. _____ _____ _____
6. _____ _____ _____
7. _____ _____ _____
8. _____ _____ _____
9. _____ _____ _____
10. _____ _____ _____

5. Topics to write about

In these short writing assignments, use any style of writing you feel most comfortable with. You will have many opportunities throughout your college career to practice writing the more formal types of essays in college writing, but for the moment the task is to get used to expressing yourself in the most creative and relaxed manner possible. If you want to do college writing, you have the rest of this text to consult for guides on how to do it, but even in the most formal college writing, it is best to write freely first WITHOUT WONDERING IF YOU ARE SAYING IT THE WAY THE PROFESSOR WANTS IT SAID. Then AFTERWARD you can—if you choose to—edit your work, changing spelling, punctuation, and so on, into college writing. But, as much as possible, try not to cut off your creativity.

MOST IMPORTANT OF ALL: Whenever you write you are automatically an author, and there is no right or wrong way to be an author. Unfortunately, certain types of writing are considered "proper" for college essays, and when you need to write that kind of essay, then the editing guidelines provided by this text should be helpful.

1. Write a very active description of an event in one or two paragraphs. Forget completely about "correctness" and college writing. Just let yourself go. Most authors describe events that are close to them, events from their own experiences, either from real life or from dreams and day dreams. AFTER you have finished writing, check to see if you really did end up writing in whole thoughts, Types 1 and 2, but don't be concerned if you did not. Simply get a feel for the various types of whole thoughts by trying to decide which ones occur most frequently in your description of an event. See the models on page 11 for ideas, but don't feel you have to follow them.

2. Write a description of an event that happened to you in which people did things TO you. For example, if you are describing your draft physical, you might

say something like: "<u>I was pushed</u> from line to line and <u>I was asked</u> hundreds of stupid questions." Again, do not be concerned about writing a "perfect" college essay. Do not even worry about whether or not you are writing in Type 3. After you have finished, however, see what types of whole thoughts seem to appear most frequently. See the models on page 12 for ideas, but don't feel you have to follow them.

3. Write a description of a place that you know very well. For example, look around you and try to describe where you are. After you have written the description, decide how often you used whole thoughts in Type 4.

4. Write a description of a real person. Sit down, for example, in a public place and paint a person in words, as an artist would paint a portrait on a canvas. Include a bit of movement so that the person you describe becomes alive. What types of whole thoughts did you use? See the models on page 12 for ideas, but don't feel you have to follow them.

5. Let yourself go and write a short narration or short story that combines all the types of whole thoughts and kinds of writing you have been practicing in the earlier essays. Use descriptions of events, places, and people in whatever way appeals most to you. You are your own boss when you write creatively, so do it freely. If you want to include dialogue, study the example on pages 322-323. It is sometimes helpful to get inspiration from someone else's writing. For suggestions of short stories to read, check the Bibliographic "Answer" Section that starts on page 331.

2 Using Fragments—
Attach Them to Whole Thoughts

Note: Review Chapter 1 before going on.

A. "<u>Because</u> I want to" is a fragment

The fragment is a very useful group of words and the basic ingredient for expressing complex ideas. But college writing has developed particular ways of using fragments. So, if you want to follow the "rules" of college writing, you must be able to recognize fragments in your own work.

First, let us not kid ourselves. The best of writers violate all the rules of college writing in their use of fragments. The most renowned college scholars constantly do all the things this chapter is going to show you how NOT to do. Unfortunately, most of you are probably not renowned authors yet, so you may want to know when using a fragment "incorrectly" will get you into trouble—because an instructor with a red pen in his hand may assume that you "misused" the fragment out of ignorance. You might need to show him that you know all his "rules" before you try breaking a few.

People tend to speak in fragments, not only in everyday conversation, but also in formal college speeches. For example, someone from the audience might ask a speaker a question:

Why must we learn college writing?

And the speaker might answer the question with a fragment starting with the word "because":

<u>Because</u> it gives you more ways of making a living to choose from.

Or the speaker might pause between two ideas in order to create a certain effect, to emphasize something. He might also pause and then add an afterthought:

The group decided to present street plays. Because street plays are political statements.

The speaker wanted a long pause between "plays" and "because," so when he wrote his words down, he inserted a period. However, in college writing the second "sentence" is not a sentence at all, but a FRAGMENT. Try reading the second word group alone to see how it leaves you wanting more information.

Because street plays are political statements.

It provides a <u>reason</u> for the first sentence, and it cannot remain unattached to it.

17

If the writer wanted a long pause before the word "because," he could have used a <u>dash</u> instead of a period between the two word groups:

> The group decided to present street plays—because street plays are political statements.

A shorter pause between the whole thought and the fragment would call for a <u>comma</u>:

> The group decided to present street plays, because street plays are political statements.

And if he wanted no pause at all, he could have left out all punctuation between the two word groups:

> The group decided to present street plays because street plays are political statements.

A fragment must be attached to a whole thought

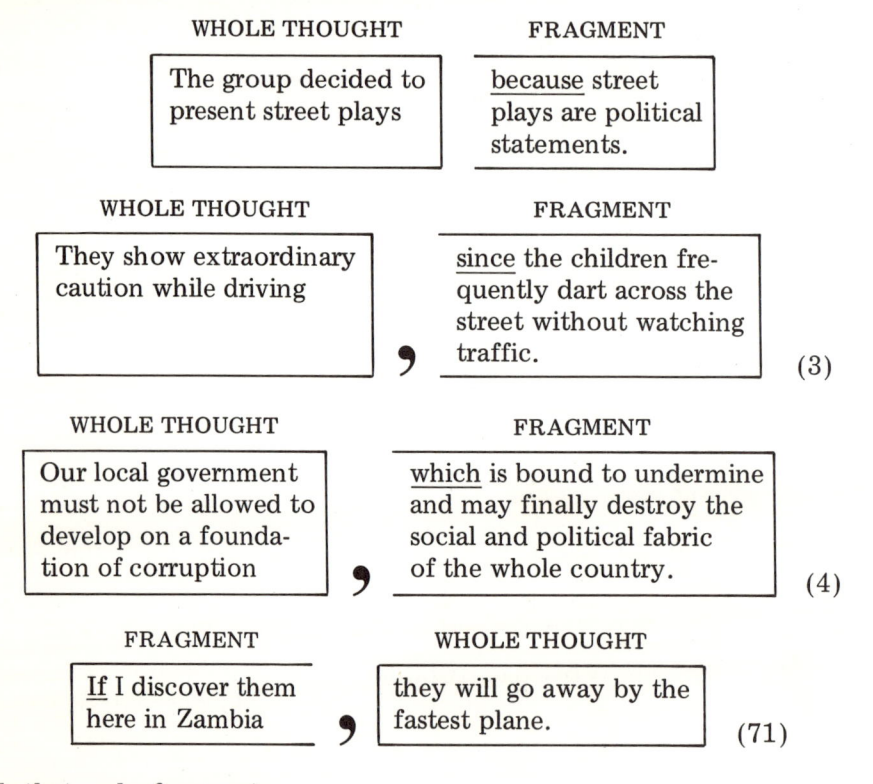

WHOLE THOUGHT		FRAGMENT	
The group decided to present street plays		<u>because</u> street plays are political statements.	
WHOLE THOUGHT		FRAGMENT	
They show extraordinary caution while driving	**,**	<u>since</u> the children frequently dart across the street without watching traffic.	(3)
WHOLE THOUGHT		FRAGMENT	
Our local government must not be allowed to develop on a foundation of corruption	**,**	<u>which</u> is bound to undermine and may finally destroy the social and political fabric of the whole country.	(4)
FRAGMENT		WHOLE THOUGHT	
<u>If</u> I discover them here in Zambia	**,**	they will go away by the fastest plane.	(71)

Words that make fragments

In short, there are certain words, words like "because," "since," "which," and "if," which can turn any group of words into a fragment. As we have just seen, a fragment can usually be attached to the preceding whole thought with the appropriate punctuation. What follows is a list of words that can make a group of words into a fragment. They are organized according to the ideas they convey and should be RELIGIOUSLY COMMITTED TO MEMORY, especially if you tend to write fragments in your essays. ONLY after you have mastered this list—get someone to test you by giving you a quiz—should you attempt the editing exercises.

The reason for memorizing this list is that you can then quickly find the words that make fragments in your own writing. Also, they are easily confused with a similar list of words in Chapter 3, mainly because college writing is not always very logical with its rules. If you really memorize this list rather than hoping to find logical differences between this list and the list in Chapter 3, you will not confuse the two lists.

CHART 2. Words that Commonly Make Fragments

Function in the Finished Sentence	Tells When	Gives a Reason	Sets Up a Condition	Although	Makes a Comparison
	before	because*	if	although	as
	after	since*	unless	though	just as
	until	so that		even though	as if
	since	in order that		even if	as though
	when			whereas†††	
	whenever				
	while				
	even before				
	even after				
	even when				
	even while				

The W Words and "That"

who†	whom†**	whose†	while
which†			whoever
when†			whichever
where†			whenever
what†			wherever
why†			whatever
whether			
			that††

*Use "because" and "since," not "being that."
†The "daggered" W words also can be used to ask questions. Questions are not fragments. Also avoid putting the words "of," "on," "in," "to," and so on before these words whenever possible.
**Avoid "whom" when possible.
††"That" has lots of uses. See p. 114. Sometimes the word "that" can be left out. See p. 21.
†††When "whereas" means "although," it introduces a fragment.

20   *The Whole Sentence*

Any whole thought can be made into a fragment by adding a word from Chart 2. For example, take the whole thought Type 2 on page 9:

WHOLE THOUGHT

He wrote the speech.

Now add a word from Chart 2:

FRAGMENT

Because he wrote the speech.

But once you have a fragment, it must be attached to a whole thought:

WHOLE THOUGHT	FRAGMENT
They interviewed John	because he wrote the speech.

In the following illustrations, these important points should be noticed:
1. Each underlined word group is a fragment.
2. EACH FRAGMENT IS ATTACHED TO A WHOLE THOUGHT.
3. Each whole thought can be a sentence by itself, but each fragment cannot be a sentence by itself.
4. Fragments are attached BEFORE OR AFTER the whole thought.
5. Each fragment is attached to a whole thought with the punctuation outlined on page 9.
6. If you pause slightly or if your voice goes up between the fragment and the whole thought, a comma is probably needed. Read the sentences out loud and see if your voice pauses or if it goes up when a comma appears.
7. NO PERIOD OR SEMICOLON[1] appears between the fragment and the whole thought.
8. The underlined fragment is contributing to the idea in the whole thought.

TELLS WHEN

When I was at work, up in the Roseland men's room, I just couldn't keep still.
(Malcolm X, *The Autobiography of Malcolm X*) (83)

GIVES A REASON

I simply wondered about the dead because their days had ended and I did not know how I would get through mine.
(James Baldwin, *Giovanni's Room*) (9)

SETS UP A CONDITION

I would be convicted even with a fair trial, unless the real murderer were discovered beforehand.
(Charles W. Chesnutt, "The Sheriff's Children") (28)

---

[1] Special exceptions are found on page 321.

"ALTHOUGH"

> Although the unemployment rate of black males is disproportionately higher than that of white males, only a very small minority of black females with both parents present are dependent on the mother for their maintenance.
> (Robert Staples, "The Myth of the Black Matriarchy") (119)

MAKES A COMPARISON

> The plane flew on, as though I had simply blown my breath after it.
> (Ralph Ellison, "Flying Home") (42)

THE W WORDS

> And I look at my body, which is under sentence of death.
> (James Baldwin, *Giovanni's Room*) (9)

"THAT"

> One psychologist, Jensen, just out and out states that it is a genetic thing, that blacks are inferior by birth.
> (Joseph White, "Guidelines for Black Psychologists") (134)

"THAT" LEFT OUT

First the sentence is presented with the word "that" included. Then it is presented as the author wrote it, with the word "that" left out, but still understood as if the "that" were there.

> He said that he was sure that all the other Americans would do the same.

>   removed
> He said he was sure that all the other Americans would do the same.
> (Kurt Vonnegut, Jr., *Slaughterhouse-Five*) (132)

Punctuation when attaching fragments to whole thoughts

When attaching a fragment to a whole thought, use the punctuation in Chart 3 at the place of attachment:

22 *The Whole Sentence*

CHART 3. Punctuation when Attaching Fragments to Whole Thoughts

---

Use a COMMA for short pause or when a fragment comes first.

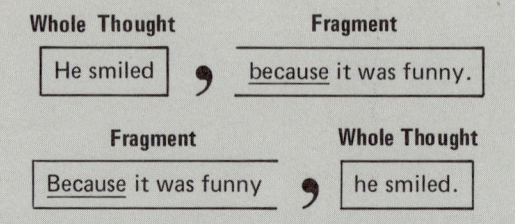

Whole Thought		Fragment
He smiled	**,**	because it was funny.

Fragment		Whole Thought
Because it was funny	**,**	he smiled.

Use a DASH for long pause.

Whole Thought		Fragment
He smiled	**——**	because it was funny.

Use THREE DOTS (. . .) in dialogue or narrative.

Whole Thought		Fragment
He smiled	**. . .**	because it was funny.

Use NO PUNCTUATION when fragment comes last and no pause is needed.

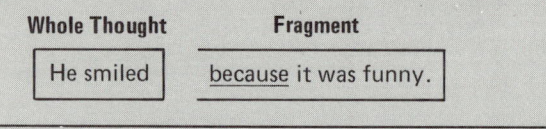

Whole Thought	Fragment
He smiled	because it was funny.

DO <u>NOT</u> USE:

Period

He smiled. Because it was funny.

Colon (:)

He smiled: because it was funny.

Semicolon (;) *

He smiled; because it was funny.

---

*Special exceptions are found on page 321.

2A. Exercises: Editing for Fragments

Look for words that can make fragments in the following excerpts and attach each fragment to the whole thought that it belongs to in order to put the excerpts back into college writing. Make all changes directly in the sentences as if you were editing a paper. If an excerpt does not need to be changed, put a check (√) next to its number. Look only for fragments, using the guidelines given on pages 17-22. Do not edit for anything else. (See page 2 for how to use the "Answer" Section.)

Examples

a. But I could never be a Prince Charming. ᵇBecause I was black. (109)

√b. As soon as Jennie could get on her Sunday shoes and her old black silk dress, they would start. (20)

1. As he made the turning; he saw two men. They were stranger than any men he had seen in all his life. (2)

2. I began to have my doubts and now I realize; that I was given an education which fitted me for nothing in South Africa. (104)

3. When we arrived in Moscow. We went to the hotel Safleski Bazar, and we stayed six days. (1)

4. From the hill where he stood, a path skirted the mountain on his right. He took this walking briskly. (2)

5. But I wanted the merciful distance of father and son; which would have permitted me to love him. (9)

6. We are not a horde of stupid, barbaric things which will fight against a white man. Simply because he is white. (72)

7. As we headed toward the backyard to hide our books. Danny began to explain the great game of hookey. It sounded like lots of fun to me. (22)

8. I'm perfectly aware that I'm in prison. That I'm a Negro. That I've been a rapist. And that I have a Higher Uneducation. (32)

9. Whenever you are badly off. Call me. I can save you in some way, no matter how great the difficulty. If a man does not call me. I will let him go.... (74)

10. His work, after all, is all that will be left when the newspapers are yellowed, all the gossip columnists silenced, and all the cocktail parties over. And when Norman and you and I are dead. (10a)

11. The lot of the evaluative minority will not always be an easy one; just as it has not been an easy one in Western societies. (39)

12. When I saw the house coming at us up the road; I was kind of sad. I looked at Grandma's wrinkled face and liked it. I knew I had fallen in love with that mean old wrinkled lady who, I used to think, had a mouth like a monkey. (22)

13. But sometimes Felipa doesn't feel like eating and then the two little piles are for me. That's why I love Felipa, because I'm always hungry and I never get filled up—never. Not even when I eat up her food. (112)

14. This big spider could travel through the air. Though there was nothing ahead so long as he had his thread behind. It was just like a kite. He could go to a mountain without any trouble. (104)

15. They break into our houses. They dress the way they want to dress. They thumb their noses at us and they smoke marijuana and have drunken parties, and they tell us to drop dead—all because we, their parents, have lied to ourselves and to them! (91)

16. At this time of year, even the taxi drivers cooperate to make it an enjoyable occasion. They show extraordinary caution while driving. Since the children frequently dart across the street without watching traffic. (3)

17. I remember, when we children were on our way to Carlisle School, thinking that we were on our way to meet death at the hands of the white people, the older boys sang brave songs. So that we would all meet death according to the Code of the Lakota—fearlessly. (118)

18. The ghetto moved into the streets from the hovels where they had huddled during the winter. Where they would stay until the Chicago cold forced them to return to their small smelly rooms for another winter. (52)

19. I was told. That Negroes there are not even licensed to become electricians or plumbers. I was also told several times, by white people. That "race relations" there were excellent. I failed to find a single Negro who agreed with this; which is the usual story of "race relations" in this country. (10e)

20. Before arriving in Atlanta I had spent several days in Charlotte, North Carolina. This is a bourgeois town, Presbyterian, pretty—if you like towns—and socially so hermetic; that it contains scarcely a single decent restaurant. (10e)

21. It does not seem to me that nature helps us very much when we need illumination in human affairs. I am certainly convinced; that it is one of the greatest impulses of mankind to arrive at something higher than a natural state. (10d)

22. The body in the mirror forces me to turn and face it. And I look at my body; which is under sentence of death. It is lean, hard, and cold, the incarnation of a mystery. And I do not know what moves in this body. What this body is searching. It is trapped in my mirror; as it is trapped in time and it hurries toward revelation. (9)

23. One afternoon I went with Daddy to the barber shop on Lenox Avenue to pay off a hit from yesterday. Because the barber shop had closed early the night before. When Daddy got the money. Daddy wasn't staying out most of the night playing poker like he used to but coming home early now, and if James Junior hadn't been cooped up down there in that jail, things would've been nice. (89)

24. Nineteen fifty-four, when I was eighteen years old, is held to be a crucial turning point in the history of the Afro-American—for the U.S.A. as a whole. The year segregation was outlawed by the U.S. Supreme Court. It was also a crucial year for me. Because on June 18, 1954, I began serving a sentence in state prison for possession of marijuana. (32)

25. Perhaps, as we say in America; I wanted to find myself. This is an interesting phrase, not current as far as I know in the language of any other people. Which certainly does not mean what it says but betrays a nagging suspicion that something has been misplaced. I think now that if I had had any

intimation that the self I was going to find would turn out to be only the same self from which I had spent so much time in flight, I would have stayed at home. (9)

26. Thereafter they indicate the hut. Where he will sleep and announce to all, "Nyono's child today is a mature young man: he has left off everything of childhood and is as one of yourselves in wisdom." And no one is allowed to call him by the name he had before; even though it be that used as an "avoidance" title among his grown-up relatives. (70)

27. Black people have fought and struggled for an education since the dim days of slavery. When it was a crime for a black man to be taught to read and write. Blacks like Frederick Douglass would hide away in attics studying copybooks and would trick and tease school boys into teaching them to read. It's been a long hard struggle and it won't be over until all black children get the high quality education; that will prepare them for the future. (147)

28. Getting it together for the black church may mean providing public transportation for communities who have none; and who have been unheard and ignored by the power structures in the city.

Getting it together might mean making sure that urban renewal does not mean removal of indigenous people of the black community; and that public housing does not become urban prisons where black people are shuffled as commodities for the conveniences of city planners and profit-mongers. (135)

29. While I was dancing. My boubou, split from top to bottom at each side, would reveal the brightly colored silk handkerchief; which I had knotted round my loins. I was quite aware of this and did nothing to prevent it; in fact I did all I

could to show it off. This was because we each wore a similar handkerchief, more or less colorful, more or less ornate; which we had received from our acknowledged sweetheart. She would make us a present of it for the ceremony, and it was generally taken from her own head. As the handkerchief cannot pass unnoticed. As it is the one personal note that distinguishes the common uniform, and as its design, like its color, makes it easily identified, there is in the wearing of it a kind of public manifestation of a relationship—a purely child-like relationship, it goes without saying. Which the present ceremony may break for ever, or, as the case may be, transform into something less innocent and more lasting. Now if our so-called sweetheart was in the least pretty and consequently desirable; we would swing our hips with great abandon, the better to make our boubou fly from side to side, and thus show off our handkerchief to greater advantage. (76)

B. "The man who came to dinner" is a fragment

Titles of plays are often fragments—like *The Man Who Came to Dinner*. But if this same word group appeared in college writing, IT WOULD HAVE TO BE ATTACHED TO A WHOLE THOUGHT:

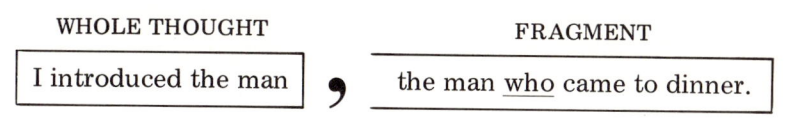

WHOLE THOUGHT		FRAGMENT
I introduced the man	,	the man who came to dinner.

As discussed on page 19, the word group "who came to dinner" is a fragment because of the word "who." If the words "the man" are in front of the fragment, it is still a fragment because of the word "who."

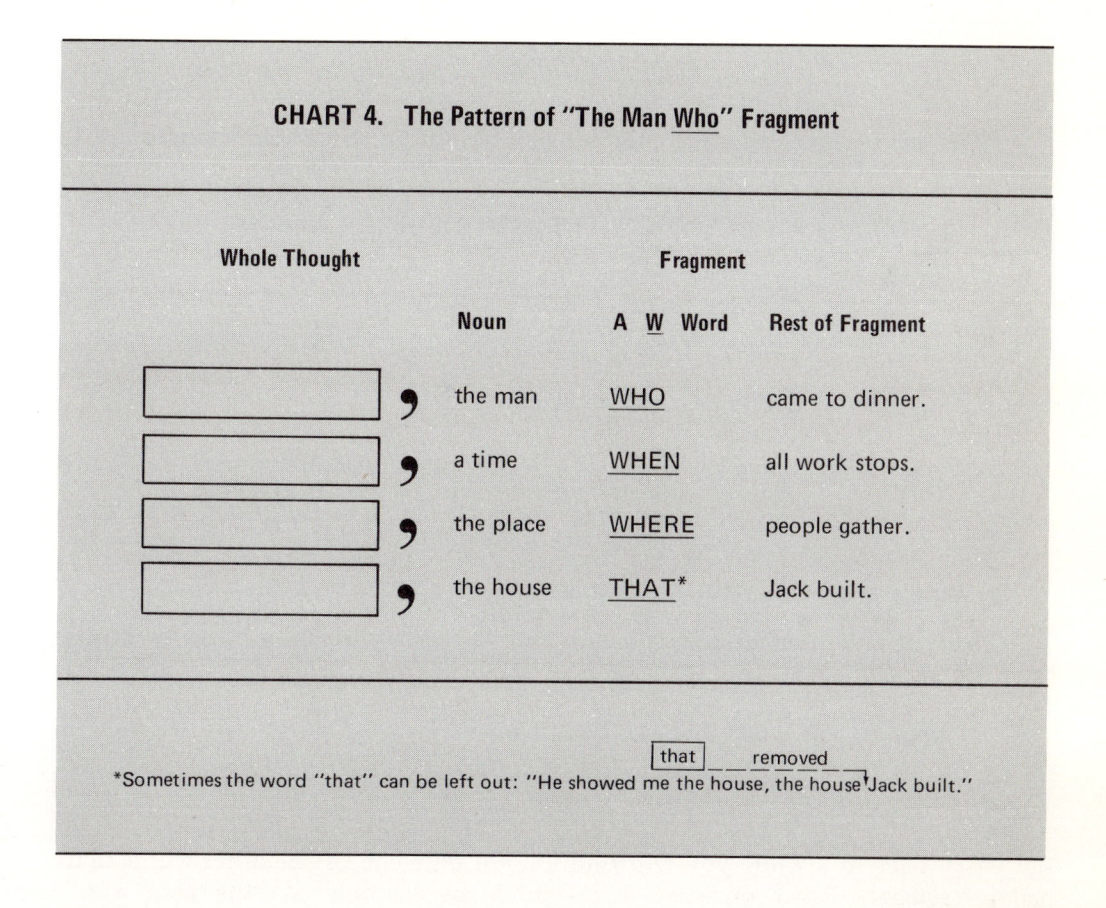

CHART 4. The Pattern of "The Man Who" Fragment

Whole Thought		Fragment		
		Noun	A W Word	Rest of Fragment
	,	the man	WHO	came to dinner.
	,	a time	WHEN	all work stops.
	,	the place	WHERE	people gather.
	,	the house	THAT*	Jack built.

*Sometimes the word "that" can be left out: "He showed me the house, the house [that] Jack built." (that removed)

Examples using "the man who" fragment

When these fragments are attached to whole thoughts, they become one of the most useful word groups in effective writing. Notice that in example [c], below, the word "that" is left out twice.

[a.] Over one thousand slave rebels gathered some six miles from Richmond, capital city of Virginia, <u>the state which was to produce four of the five first American presidents</u>.
                          (C.L.R. James, "The Atlantic Slave Trade and Slavery") (66)

[b.] Historically, it has been true, not in the distant past, but in the recent past, and even today, that white folks don't think in terms of making loans available to black folks for any purpose other than buying Cadillacs, mink coats, and taking vacations—<u>things that will not lead to capital formation</u>.
                          (Dempsey J. Travis, "The 1971 Homestead Act") (128)

[c.] Other things mattered, like walking and talking and drinking and eating, <u>and the way Adele laughed, and the way Norman argued</u>.

        [that] removed   removed   [that]

                          (James Baldwin, "The Black Boy Looks at the White Boy") (10a)

"The man <u>who</u>" fragment may rename a noun in the whole thought

Note that in each case above, the NOUN that begins the fragment word group RENAMES a noun or nouns in the previous whole thought.

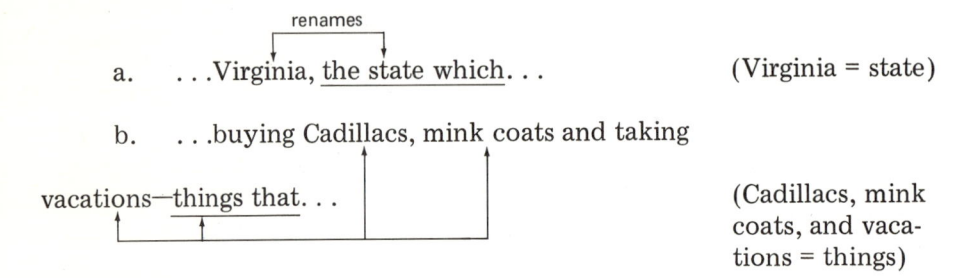

               renames

a.   ...Virginia, the state which...   (Virginia = state)

b.   ...buying Cadillacs, mink coats and taking vacations—things that...   (Cadillacs, mink coats, and vacations = things)

A variation of "the man <u>who</u>" fragment

Most of the time these fragments have a noun plus one of the <u>W</u> words listed on page 19.

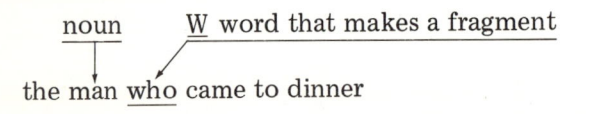

     noun   W word that makes a fragment

the man <u>who</u> came to dinner

But every once in a while you will find a noun plus one of the other words that make fragments listed on page 19. Here is an example of "the man <u>who</u>" fragment. However, this time it is not the word "who" that makes the underlined words into a fragment, but the word "because."

    For any individual, challenging special traditions is a giant step, <u>a giant step because there are no social traditions which do not have corresponding social sanctions</u>....
                      (Shirley Chisholm, "Racism and Anti-Feminism") (30)

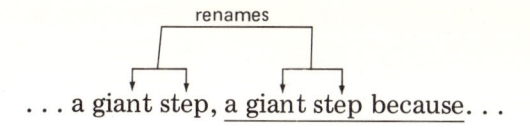

Using Fragments—Attach Them to Whole Thoughts 31

```
          renames
     ┌─────┴─────┐
     ↓  ↓     ↓   ↓
. . . a giant step, a giant step because . . .
```

Punctuation for "the man who" fragment

When attaching "the man who" fragment to a whole thought, use the punctuation in Chart 5 at the place of attachment:

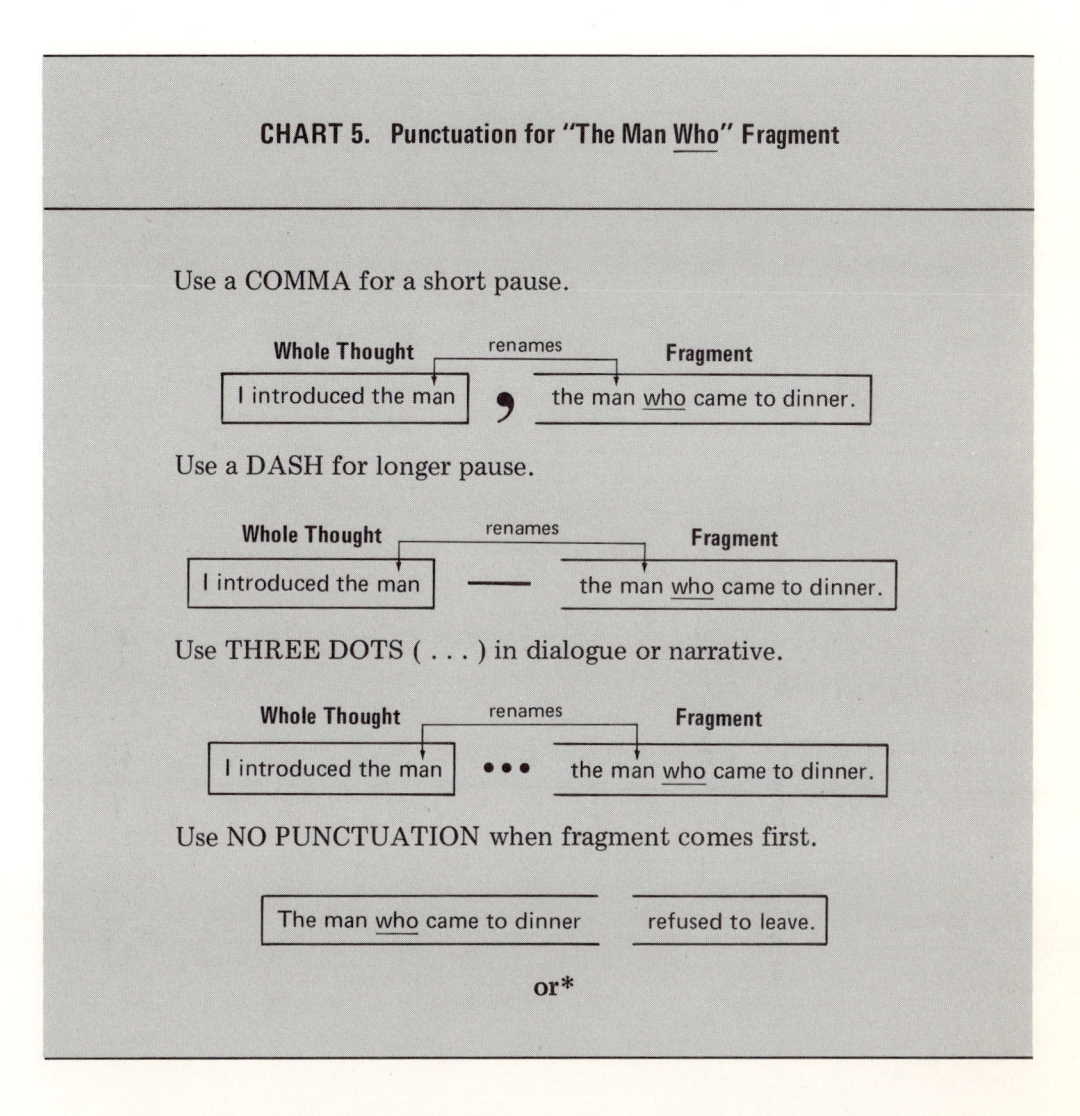

CHART 5. Punctuation for "The Man Who" Fragment

Use a COMMA for a short pause.

Whole Thought	renames	Fragment
I introduced the man	**,**	the man who came to dinner.

Use a DASH for longer pause.

Whole Thought	renames	Fragment
I introduced the man	—	the man who came to dinner.

Use THREE DOTS (. . .) in dialogue or narrative.

Whole Thought	renames	Fragment
I introduced the man	• • •	the man who came to dinner.

Use NO PUNCTUATION when fragment comes first.

| The man who came to dinner | refused to leave. |

or*

---

*When "the man who" fragment comes first, it is easier to understand the sentence if you make "the man" the noun of the noun-verb pair (see Chapter 1). Then "who came to dinner" is a regular fragment as discussed in Part A. In the above sentence, "refused" is the verb of the noun-verb pair.

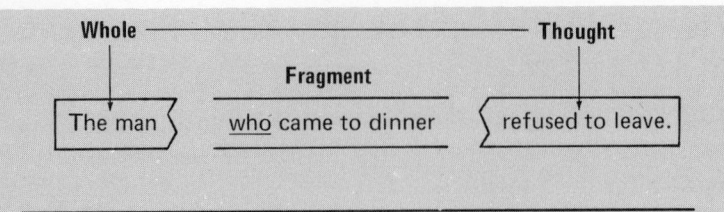

```
         Whole ─────────────────────────── Thought
                         Fragment
        ┌─────────┐ ─────────────────── ┌──────────────┐
        │ The man │   who came to dinner │ refused to leave. │
        └─────────┘                      └──────────────┘
```

DO <u>NOT</u> USE:

Period

I introduced the man_✗ ᵗT̶he man who came to dinner.

Semicolon[†]

I introduced the man_✗; the man who came to dinner.

Comma When the Fragment Comes First

The man who came to dinner_✗ refused to leave.

---

†Special exceptions are found on page 321.

2B. Exercises: Editing for "The Man <u>Who</u>" Fragments

Look for "the man <u>who</u>" fragments in the following excerpts and attach each fragment to the whole thought that it belongs to in order to put the excerpts back into college writing. Make all changes directly in the sentences as if you were editing a paper. If an excerpt does not need to be changed, put a check (√) next to its number. Look only for "the man <u>who</u>" fragments, using the guidelines given on pages 29-32. Do not edit for anything else. (See page 2 for how to use the "Answer" Section.)

Examples

a. They started several new programs. Programs which were failures to begin with.

√ b. Then they built new apartment buildings, buildings that served only families.

1. A massacre followed. The enraged whites shot down innocent Negroes who smiled. And innocent Negroes who did not smile. (16)

2. Other things mattered, like walking and talking and drinking and eating. And the way Adele laughed. And the way Norman argued. (10a)

3. You only have two kinds of men; those who compromise and those who take a stand. And those who take a stand are those who get the respect. (18)

4. I have seen hundreds of objects, signs, and engravings which, when correctly interpreted, represent the solar system as we know it today—representations which were reproduced thousands of years ago. (96)

5. There is no proof for either unless one believes. I wonder how many of you Marxists realize that it is your belief. And not Marx's proof, that has established the truth of materialism. (62)

6. I am charged with inciting people to commit an offense by way of protest against a law. A law which neither I nor any of my people had any say in preparing. (84)

7. This, then, is the importance of black drama. It is hope. Hope that in the world's most powerful country a minority that has made undying contributions can make its greatest contribution and redeem the majority. (91)

8. In the novels written by Negro authors after 1890, there occurs a significant change in subject matter. One that Robert Bone describes as "a shift in theme from attacks upon slavery to attacks upon caste." (60)

9. A major actor in this drama was William Lloyd Garrison; a brilliant young journalist who published the first issue of his famous *Liberator* in 1831. His first editorial sang with indignation. (16)

10. At a time when heart transplant operations are being performed with ever-increasing frequency elsewhere. Large numbers of West African children are still dying of a relatively simple inflammation of the intestine called dysentery. (3)

11. He was soon followed by Phillis Wheatley. A Massachusetts slave, who was given special privileges by the rather unusual Wheatley family and encouraged to write poetry, for which she had a talent rare for that period. Phillis Wheatley's *Poems on Various Subjects, Religious and Moral* was published in 1773. (60)

12. He went out of the hut; he wanted to go to Makuyu to see Kamau, or any other person; a man maybe would understand him. A man to whom he could talk. (99)

13. But now—now—African kings and heroes have come into the world, out of the past; the past that can now be put to the uses of power. And black has become a beautiful color—not because it is loved but because it is feared. (8)

14. Then I could come down from the moon and demand that these fools pay me through the nose for the high value of "my" land. A value which they themselves had created for me while I was enjoying myself on the moon! Such a system is not only foreign to us, it is completely wrong. (105)

15. Poor people are always embarrassed at not having turkey and cranberry sauce for this one day. The same turkey you can't afford in October, the same cranberry sauce they can't afford in May. You try to think that Christmas day is only twenty-four hours long, just like all the days you were satisfied with beans. (53)

16. The theater tomorrow will, therefore, remain much as it is today unless there is a real change in this society. The one hope is that those groups in the ghetto areas—the townships composed of poor whites, Puerto Ricans and Negroes—will create drama as it was intended. As a living instrument that educates, communicates and entertains. An instrument that has a life commitment. (91)

17. We stand for a middle course, for a democratic socialism, which goes so far as to integrate spiritual values; a socialism which ties in with the old ethical current of the French Socialists. Historically and culturally we belong to this current. (115)

18. A judiciary controlled entirely by whites and enforcing laws enacted by a white Parliament in which we have no representation. Laws which in most cases

are passed in the face of unanimous opposition from Africans—cannot be regarded as an impartial tribunal in a political trial where an African stands as an accused. (84)

19. It is singularly the responsibility of the Negro writer to proclaim and celebrate the fact that his people have in their ancestry rulers who expanded kingdoms into empires and built great and magnificent armies. Scholars whose vision of life showed foresight and wisdom. And priests who told of gods that were strong and kind. The American Negro writer should pay particular attention to the Western Sudan (West Africa), his ancestral home. (31)

C. Other fragments that rename

Another effective way of renaming a noun which appears in the whole thought is illustrated by the following sentence:

> Nancy Lee was proud of being American, <u>a Negro American with blood out of Africa a long time ago, too many generations back to count</u>.
> (Langston Hughes, "One Friday Morning") (63)

NOTICE THAT THE UNDERLINED WORD GROUP IS ATTACHED TO THE WHOLE THOUGHT WITH A COMMA. But why must the word group be attached? Why is "a Negro American with blood out of Africa a long time ago, too many generations back to count" a fragment? THERE IS NO NOUN-VERB PAIR IN THESE WORDS, and all whole thoughts must have a noun-verb pair (see page 10).

The pattern of the fragment that renames

Any group of words that RENAMES something in the whole thought that comes before it MAY be a fragment. You cannot use the list on page 19 to find these fragments. All whole thoughts must have a noun-verb pair (see page 10). These fragments that rename are fragments because they do not have a noun-verb pair.

CHART 6. The Pattern of the Fragment That Renames

Whole Thought		Fragment
	Noun	Rest of Fragment (<u>No</u> verb)
▭ ,	a Negro American	with blood out of Africa.
▭ ,	the level	of the nation.
▭ ,	a man	with confidence.

Examples using the fragment that renames

What is beautiful about this kind of fragment is that practically ANYTHING in the whole thought can be RENAMED in the fragment in order to achieve an effect, in order to emphasize it. And then the sentence can continue.

Fanon's account of violence was given justification

at yet a higher level, namely the level of the nation.
                       └──renames──┘

(Dennis Forsythe, "Frantz Fanon: Black Theoretician") (47)

I distinguish between two colonialisms, between a domestic one and an external one.²
                     └──renames──┘

In this early period the slave who ran away was most often

a skilled craftsman, a man with confidence of making his way in the world.
         └──renames──┘

(C.L.R. James, "The Atlantic Slave Trade and Slavery") (66)

At other times the author will rename something in the whole thought using **DIFFERENT WORD OR WORDS MEANING THE SAME THING.**

For persons with black skins, their social lot was obviously intended to be that of

the servant, the slave.
    └──renames──┘

(Phaon Goldman Sundiata, "The White Reaction to the Black Assertion") (123)

It has become a strong emotional need for the white man, expecially the Southern white.
                                                    └──renames──┘

(Thomas Merton, "Conjectures of a Guilty Bystander") (90)

One reason is that many cities have reached the limits of their taxing powers, particularly those with large low-income populations.
          └──renames──┘

(Joyce Ladner and Walter Stafford, "Black Repression in the Cities") (75)

---

[2] Kwame Nkrumah, as quoted in *The Black Scholar*, Vol. I, No. 6, (April, 1970), p. 52.

CHART 7. Punctuation for the Fragment That Renames

Punctuation for attaching a fragment that renames to a whole thought is the same as for "the man <u>who</u>" fragment. See pages 31-32. IN ADDITION: When the fragment that renames comes IN THE MIDDLE OF A WHOLE THOUGHT, there is usually a COMMA BEFORE AND AFTER THE FRAGMENT.

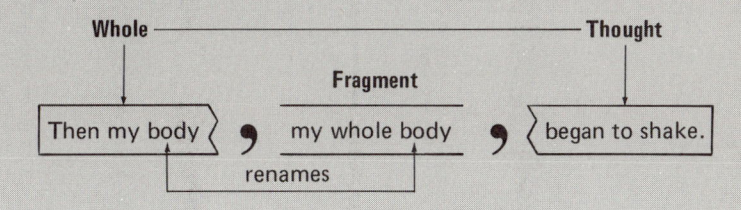

Then my body **,** my whole body **,** began to shake.

(Whole — Thought; Fragment "my whole body" renames "Then my body")

2C. Exercises: Editing for Fragments That Rename

Look for fragments that rename in the following excerpts and attach each fragment to the whole thought that it belongs to in order to put the excerpts back into college writing. Make all changes directly in the sentences as if you were editing a paper. If an excerpt does not need to be changed, put a check (√) next to its number. Look only for fragments that rename, using the guidelines given on pages 37-39. Do not edit for anything else. (See page 2 for how to use the "Answer" Section.)

Examples

a. Richard Wright wrote *Native Son*. A novel with an important message.

√ b. One of his first books was *Black Boy*, a book about his own life.

1. Lewis was the master of his household. The complete master. I never heard him reprimand anyone or issue an order, but his control was absolute. (26)

2. Soldiers moved. Out of the depths of his tired body a prayer rose up in him. A silent prayer. (142)

3. Truly, you must now know that the word Negro in America means something not racial or biological; but something purely social. Something made in the United States. (143)

4. Why is it that no African in the history of this country has ever had the honor of being tried by his own kith and kin; by his own flesh and blood? (84)

5. The children of these disillusioned colored pioneers inherited the total lot of their parents. The disappointments, the anger. To add to their misery, they had little hope of deliverance. (22)

6. Every society is really governed by hidden laws. By unspoken but profound assumptions on the part of the people, and ours is no exception. (10b)

7. Dreams began to dance through her head; plans and ambitions; beauties she would create for herself, her parents and the Negro people—for Nancy Lee possessed a deep and reverent race pride. (63)

8. Landlords, in a society which recognises individual ownership of land, can be, and usually are, in the same class as the loiterers I was talking about; the class of parasites. (104)

9. "Peculiarsome," too, was Frederick Augustus Washington Bailey. A nine-year-old slave in Baltimore, Maryland. Frederick and Abe were two of a kind. (16)

10. There was one more member of the household. Barnaby Conrad, Lewis' secretary. He was an extremely charming and talented young man who had just returned from Spain, where he had been a bullfighter, and was now engaged in writing his first novel. (26)

11. Negro writing in America has a long history. It begins with *A Narrative of Uncommon Sufferings*, by Britton Hamon, published in 1760, and with Jupiter Hammon. A writer of both prose and poetry, whose first work appeared later in the same year. (60)

12. There is no halfway house between fulfillment and extinction; between growth and death. Living is a continuous process of unfolding, whether the subject is the individual or the group. (97)

13. Being a Negro has to do with the American scene. With race hate, rejection, ignorance, segregation, discrimination, slavery, murder, fiery crosses, and fear. (143)

14. The white men stood up, no longer afraid. Again she waited for Silas; waited to see him fight his way out. Waited to hear his call. (142)

15. The foreigner introduced a completely different concept. The concept of land as a marketable commodity. According to this system, a person could claim a piece of land as his own private property whether he intended to use it or not. (105)

16. We walked back home up the highway. Grandma had her arm around my shoulder, and I had my arm around her waist. That was the only time I ever touched Grandma. And the only time I recall wanting her to touch me and liking her touch. (22)

17. When they saw her, they stopped talking, and since then people die from time to time. There are always some being born and some dying at the same time; always some living ones and some dead ones. (124)

18. He wanted to move from the bed, but was afraid he would stumble over something and Mrs. Dalton would hear him. Would know that someone besides Mary was in the room. Frenzy dominated him. (140)

19. During its reign the syndicate noted, too, the rising tide of reaction against the Negro. Other business establishments had noted this, too. Had taken advantage of it and had thus pushed the Negro back toward slavery. (91)

20. We want to live as decent human beings. Free from want. Free from abuse. Free from inhuman treatment by an enemy, because his cities are besieged by the masses, who themselves are seeking a place in the sun. We must unite now, or die later. (126)

21. The greatest change has been in the attitudes of blacks; particularly the so-called black bourgeoisie. Many of them have become more conscious of what's going on—they've been forced to—and are more willing to identify with our people. More race pride is especially apparent among our youth. More co-operation and more militancy. (19)

22. *That* is the real soul-sickness, the spear in the side, the drag by the neck through the mob-angry town. The Grand Inquisition, The embrace of the Maiden, the rip in the belly with the guts spilling out. The trip to the chamber with the deadly gas that ends in the oven so hygienically clean—only it's worse because you continue stupidly to live. But live you must, and you can either make passive love to your sickness or burn it out and go on to the next conflicting phase. (43)

23. Since then time has passed. Time as long as a river that never stops passing. Time as extensive and limitless as the air. Time that is scarcely a second, a brief fluttering of wings, a blow; something that passes, crosses, dampens us inside briefly and then blinds us with a hundred summers together, with a hundred summers weighing on our backs, until it diminishes us to a bit of streaked, reddish earth, only a bit of earth. (114)

24. Within a very short time, the Panthers and similar militant groups among blacks have succeeded in giving black people something even the late Dr. Martin Luther King, for all his abilities and devotion, never succeeded in giving them. A sense of pride in their own race and heritage. (101)

25. In these three boys; in their hopes; in their dreams; in their fears, is the whole story of the crisis which reached a climax in a Civil War and the emancipation of four million slaves with a book value of four billion dollars. (16)

26. In 1829, another book of poems appeared; *The Hope of Liberty*, by George Moses Horton, who was freed late in life, as Phillis Wheatley had been.

In the North during this early period, a number of free Negroes were active as writers and journalists in the anti-slavery cause. Their articles and stories frequently appeared in the abolitionist newspaper *Freedom's Journal*; the first Negro newspaper in the United States, which began publishing in 1818. (60)

27. My father slammed me across the face with his great palm, and in that moment everything flooded back. All the hatred and all the fear, and the depth of a merciless resolve to kill my father rather than allow my father to kill me—and I knew that all those sermons and tears and all that repentance and rejoicing had changed nothing. I wondered if I was expected to be glad that a friend of mine, or anyone, was to be tormented forever in Hell, and I also thought, suddenly, of the Jews in another Christian nation; Germany. (8)

28. How many of our students spend their vacations doing a job which could improve people's lives but for which there is no money; jobs like digging an irrigation channel or a drainage ditch for a village; or demonstrating the construction and explaining the benefits of deep-pit latrines, and so on? A small number have done such work in the National Youth Camps or through school-organized, nation-building schemes, but they are the exception rather than the rule. (105)

29. She tried to turn from him, but his arm held her tightly; she lay still, whimpering. He heard her sigh. A sigh he knew, for he had heard it may times before; but this time he heard in it a sigh deep down beneath the familiar one, a sigh of resignation, a giving up. A surrender of something more than her body. (143)

30. That was a long summer; the summer of 1951. I was waiting for the scholastic record book to come out. In the spring I had won the mile in 4 minutes 28 seconds at the Missouri state meet for Negroes; one of the best high school times of the year, and I could hardly wait to see my name in the book when it came out in the fall. (53)

31. At this stage of our struggle we have a choice before us. Are we still prepared to be half-human beings in our fatherland or are we prepared to be citizens; men and women in a democratic non-racial South Africa? How long shall we be called Bantu, Native, Non-European, Non-White, or black. Kaffir in our fatherland? (72)

32. Perhaps the whole root of our trouble, the human trouble, is that we will sacrifice all the beauty of our lives. Will imprison ourselves in totems, taboos, crosses, blood sacrifices, steeples, mosques, races, armies, flags, nations, in order to deny the fact of death, which is the only fact we have. It seems to me that one ought to rejoice in the fact of death. Ought to decide, indeed, to earn one's death by confronting with passion the conundrum of life. (8)

33. Getting it together may mean educating oneself to and dealing with the issue critical in the 70's for all third world communities and those who dissent. The issue of political prisoners. (135)

34. The purpose of writing is to enforce the sense we have of the future. The purpose of writing is to enforce the sense we have of responsibility. The responsibility of understanding our roles in the shaping of a new world. (120)

35. Then she breathed a long, slow breath, emptying her lungs. She knew now. Silas had killed as many as he could and stayed on to burn. Had stayed without a murmur. She filled her lungs with a quick gasp as the walls fell in; the house was hidden by eager plumes of red. She turned and ran with the baby in her arms. Ran blindly across the fields, crying, "Naw, Gawd!" (142)

D. "Breaking through the sound barrier" is a fragment

Action words such as "breaking," "doing," "studying," and "stopping" often introduce another useful kind of fragment. Look at how Sam Greenlee uses "stopping":

> The squad cars moved slowly through the ghetto, <u>stopping here and there to collect their graft.</u>
>
> (Sam Greenlee, *The Spook Who Sat by the Door*) (52)

NOTICE THAT THE UNDERLINED WORD GROUP IS ATTACHED TO THE WHOLE THOUGHT WITH A COMMA. If it stood alone as a separate sentence, it would not be acceptable in college writing because it is not a whole thought.

FRAGMENT:

stopping here and there to collect their graft.

THERE IS NO NOUN-VERB PAIR IN THIS FRAGMENT, and all whole thoughts must have a noun-verb pair (see page 10).

WHOLE THOUGHT WITH NOUN-VERB PAIR

The <u>squad cars</u> <u>were</u> stopping to collect their graft.
      noun   verb

FRAGMENT

<u>stopping</u> here and there to collect their graft.

The pattern of the "<u>breaking</u> through" fragment

What makes this fragment so useful is that it can introduce a new action into the sentence, with a word like "stopping," and then the sentence can go on to tell more things about this new action.

BUT THIS NEW ACTION IS <u>NOT</u> A TRUE VERB. As discussed on page 181, a verb-like word ending in "ing" needs a HELPING VERB in order for it to be considered a true verb. So a word like "stopping" can give more action to a sentence without your having to put in a new noun-verb pair, without your having to start a new whole thought. Thus you can cram more action ideas into one sentence, and you do not have to start a new sentence. Notice what would happen to Greenlee's sentence if the fragment were not available to him:

> The squad cars moved slowly through the ghetto. <u>They were stopping here and there to collect their graft.</u>

Note how the idea gets broken up. The smooth flow of the sentence is lost. Compare it with the original above.

Examples using the "<u>breaking</u> through" fragment

Using a verb-like word ending in "ing," try adding "<u>breaking</u> through" fragments to the whole thoughts that follow:

WHOLE THOUGHT

He came around in front of me,

ADDED FRAGMENT

_____

_____

_____

WHOLE THOUGHT

I think we had been lying around the beach,

ADDED FRAGMENT

_____

_____

_____

WHOLE THOUGHT

The nausea came back,

ADDED FRAGMENT

_____

_____

_____

Here is how the authors did it:

He came around in front of me, <u>waving the broken bottle in his hand like Humphrey Bogart would do in the movies.</u>

(Dick Gregory, *Nigger*)[3] (53)

I think we had been lying around the beach, <u>swimming a little and watching the near-naked girls pass, whistling at them, and laughing.</u>

(James Baldwin, *Giovanni's Room*) (9)

The nausea came back, <u>making me feel that my belly was about to rise to the roof of my head.</u>

(James Baldwin, *Tell Me How Long the Train's Been Gone*) (11)

Notice that each underlined fragment word group has a verb-like word ending in "ing" which continues the action started in the whole thought. Also notice, for example, that it is obvious who is doing the waving in the first sentence. "He" is doing the action. For more on this aspect, see Dangling Participle in the Index.

---

[3] "Like" is generally acceptable in good writing in place of "as." See *A Dictionary of Contemporary American Usage* by Bergen Evans and Cornelia Evans, Random House, New York, 1957.

CHART 8. Punctuation for the "Breaking Through" Fragment

Punctuation for attaching this fragment to a whole thought is the same as for "the man who" fragment. See pages 31-32. You can also put the "breaking through" fragment BEFORE THE WHOLE THOUGHT.

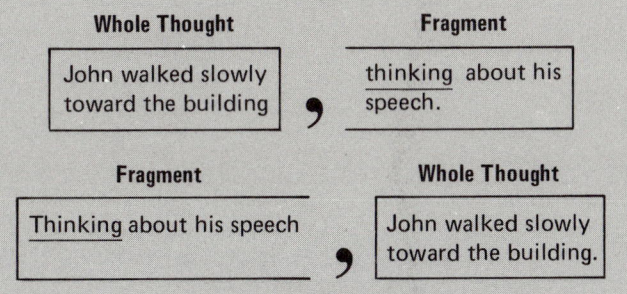

Whole Thought		Fragment
John walked slowly toward the building	**,**	thinking about his speech.

Fragment		Whole Thought
Thinking about his speech	**,**	John walked slowly toward the building.

You can also break up the whole thought and put the fragment next to the noun that's doing the action. Use a comma <u>before</u> and <u>after</u> the fragment. This method is generally not as smooth as the other two.

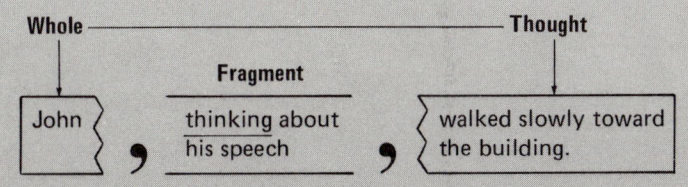

Whole ─────────────────────────── Thought

| John | **,** | Fragment: thinking about his speech | **,** | walked slowly toward the building. |

Sometimes you do not need any commas at all. Let your ear help you.

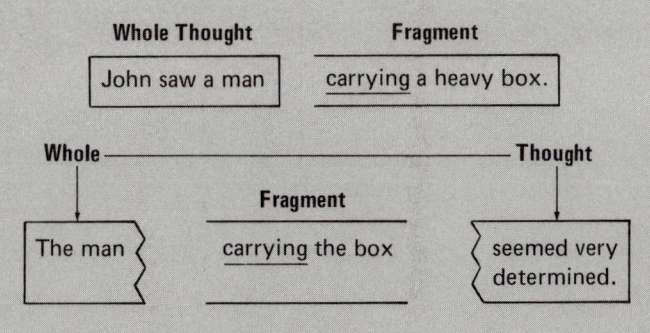

Whole Thought	Fragment
John saw a man	carrying a heavy box.

Whole ─────────────────────────── Thought

| The man | Fragment: carrying the box | seemed very determined. |

2D. Exercises: Editing for "Breaking Through" Fragments

Look for "breaking through" fragments in the following excerpts and attach each fragment to the whole thought that it belongs to in order to put the excerpts back into college writing. Make all changes directly in the sentences as if you were editing a paper. If an excerpt does not need to be changed, put a check (√) next to its number. Look only for "breaking through" fragments, using the guidelines given on pages 49-51. Do not edit for anything else. (See page 2 for how to use the "Answer" Section.)

Examples

a. He looked down the street, shading his eyes with his hands.

√b. He saw the men coming up the block; he braced himself, holding on to the stoop with his bad hand.

1. She saw two white men on all fours creeping past the well. One carried a gun and the other a red tin can. (142)

2. She scrambled up and ran through the dark. Hearing the baby cry. Behind her leather thongs hummed and feet whispered swiftly over the dusty ground. (142)

3. One of the white men was on the ground. The other was in the car. Silas was aiming again. The car started. Running in a cloud of dust. (142)

4. I think we had been lying around the beach. Swimming a little and watching the near-naked girls pass. Whistling at them, and laughing. (9)

5. He went to the drug store and looked inside at the man leaning against a wall. Smoking. (140)

6. This minority stands at a moment in time, poised, with new, vital allies, demanding to be reckoned with. And the world looks on. Waiting. Waiting. (91)

7. But within three months I found myself battling against obstacles to set up an office. Battling to be allowed to accept cases out of Johannesburg, battling to be allowed to make a living. (104)

8. It was a wide, open night. The wind whipped by; seeking in the emptiness of the plain something in which to entangle itself while it swept the starry sky. (38)

9. He sighed; looking about like a sleepwalker. Licking his lips with a dry tongue. Seeing again the vision of Chris's bloody, broken body inert upon the table under the glaring electric bulb. (138)

10. It was a little plane like that at the Fair. Flying no higher than the eaves of our roof. Seeing it come steadily forward I felt the world grow warm with promise. I opened the screen and climbed over it and clung there; waiting. (42)

11. When Todd came to, he saw two faces suspended above him in a sun so hot and blinding that he could not tell if they were black or white. He stirred; feeling a pain that burned as though his whole body had been laid open to the sun which glared into his eyes. (42)

12. And what did the fire say? Now that I knew that I was going to live, at least for awhile, the fire seemed warmer than it ever had before. I sipped my drink; watching that crumbling, shaking, brilliant universe. (11)

13. She moved in the dark toward the door. Struggling with the dress. Jamming it over her head. She heard the thick skin of Silas' feet swish across the wooden planks.

"Ah got mah raw-hide whip n Ahm takin yuh t the barn!"

She ran on tiptoe to the porch and paused; thinking of the baby. (142)

14. The tension of his body, readying itself for the shock of revelation was so great that for a moment he thought he would be torn apart. Panting, sweating, heartsick. Dreading to understand, finally unresisting. He accepted the fact: he lived in an age that was not his own. (85)

15. Quickly he turned and faced the same direction in which it was going; coming behind the elephant, and took his bow. He pierced it in the abdomen and it stood now: looking everywhere without seeing Jumbe and then moving little by little towards a great, upstanding rock. But he moved with it. Coming at the great rock. He climbed hastily up and the elephant never saw him scrambling up to the very top of the rock. "Oho!" and he began to dance and sing a song; testifying to his deliverance. (27)

16. The white man pointed his finger into Silas' face. Then Silas' right arm went up; the whip flashed. The white man turned; bending; flinging his hands to shield his head. Silas' arm rose and fell, rose and fell. She saw the white man crawling in dust; trying to get out of reach. She screamed when she saw the other white man get out of the car and run to Silas. Then all three were on the ground. Rolling in dust, grappling for the whip. (142)

E. Supplementary: Another use of the "breaking through" fragment; "the jet breaking through the sound barrier" is a fragment

This section is supplementary to Part D. If you are still struggling with fragments and run-ons, it is best to leave this lesson alone until you have more control over the basic aspects of college writing; the fragment discussed here may only serve to confuse and complicate the matter.

But if you want another effective fragment word group to give variety to your essays, the following might be fun to try.

Examine one of the most famous passages in James Baldwin's *Another Country*. The fragments covered in this lesson are underlined.

> He saw the train in the tunnel, rushing under water, the motorman gone mad, gone blind, unable to decipher the lights, and the tracks gleaming and snarling senselessly upward forever, the train never stopping and the people screaming at windows and doors and turning on each other with all the accumulated fury of their blasphemed lives, everything gone out of them but murder, breaking limb from limb and splashing in blood, with joy—for the first time, joy, joy, after such a long sentence in chains, leaping out to astound the world, to astound the world again, (7)

To form the fragment, Baldwin started with a whole thought, as usual:

noun verb
He saw the train in the tunnel,

Then he added a "breaking through" fragment covered in Part D, pages 49-51):

WHOLE THOUGHT

He saw the train in the tunnel,

FRAGMENT 1

rushing under water

Then he adds three "breaking through" fragments, but now each fragment starts with a noun that is doing the action:

WHOLE THOUGHT

He saw the train in the tunnel,

FRAGMENT 1

rushing under water,

FRAGMENT 2[4]

the motorman gone mad, gone blind, unable to decipher the lights,

*FRAGMENT 3

       noun
and the tracks gleaming and snarling senselessly upward forever,

*FRAGMENT 4

noun
the train never stopping

---

[4] This fragment is covered in Part G, pages 70-71.

*FRAGMENT 5

and the <u>people</u> screaming at windows and doors and <u>turning</u> on each other with all the accumulated fury of their blasphemed lives,

Finally, after another fragment like Number 2, he ends up with a string of "<u>breaking</u> through" fragments.

Look back at the starred (*) fragments. Notice that Number 3 looks like a whole thought; it looks as if it has a noun-verb pair:

the <u>tracks</u> <u>gleaming</u>

But the word "gleaming" is not a true verb in college writing. Each verb-like word ending in "ing" needs a helping verb in order to be a true verb (see also pages 167-173 and 181-187).

TRUE VERB

helping verb
<u>were</u>   gleaming

WHOLE THOUGHT

noun   true verb
The <u>tracks</u> <u>were gleaming</u>.

FRAGMENT

the <u>tracks</u> <u>gleaming</u>

If Baldwin had written separate sentences—separate whole thoughts—for each new action, the breathless excitement of his description would have been lost. The passage would be choppy, and a different mood would have been created, something like this:

> He saw the train in the tunnel. It was rushing under water. The motorman had gone mad. He had gone blind, unable to decipher the lights. The tracks were gleaming and snarling senselessly upward forever. The train never stopped and the people were screaming at windows and doors and turning on each other with all the accumulated fury of their blasphemed lives. Everything had gone out of them but murder. They were breaking limb from limb and splashing in blood, with joy—for the first time, joy, joy, after such a long sentence in chains. They were leaping out to astound the world, to astound the world again.

Examples using "the <u>jet</u> <u>breaking</u> through" fragment

Try adding your own "the <u>jet</u> <u>breaking</u> through" fragments to the following whole thoughts. Note that a comma usually comes at the point of attachment to the whole thought.

WHOLE THOUGHT

The winos drank their sweet wine beneath the El tracks,

Using Fragments—Attach Them to Whole Thoughts 59

FRAGMENT

_____

_____

_____

WHOLE THOUGHT

The junkies stood and sat in the warm sun,

FRAGMENT(S)

_____

_____

_____

_____

_____

WHOLE THOUGHT

He stood, insolent and dark and leonine,

FRAGMENT(S)

_____

_____

_____

_____

Here is how the authors did it:

The winos drank their sweet wine beneath the El tracks, <u>their hoarse voices rising with laughter as the sweet alcohol filled</u>. . . .
(Sam Greenlee, The Spook Who Sat by the Door) (52)

The junkies stood and sat in the warm sun, <u>their dope-filled blood moving sluggishly in their veins, the ugly world taking on a warm glow</u>, everything soft and pretty prior to their moving through the streets at night looking for loot to support their habits.
(Sam Greenlee, The Spook Who Sat by the Door) (52)

60   *The Whole Sentence*

He stood, insolent and dark and leonine, his elbow leaning on the cash-register, his fingers playing with his chin, looking out at the crowd.

(James Baldwin, *Giovanni's Room*) (9)

Punctuation for "the jet breaking through" fragment

As with other fragments, this fragment can be attached BEFORE or AFTER the whole thought. (See Chart 9.)

CHART 9. Punctuation for "The Jet Breaking Through" Fragment

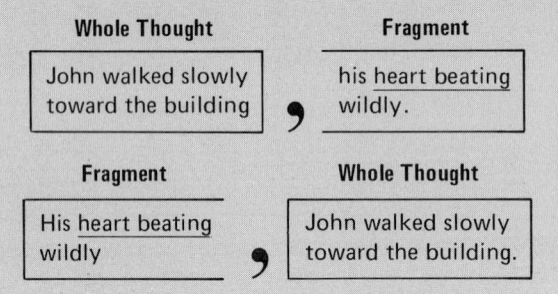

Whole Thought		Fragment
John walked slowly toward the building	**,**	his heart beating wildly.

Fragment		Whole Thought
His heart beating wildly	**,**	John walked slowly toward the building.

Or you can break up the whole thought. This method is not as smooth as the first.

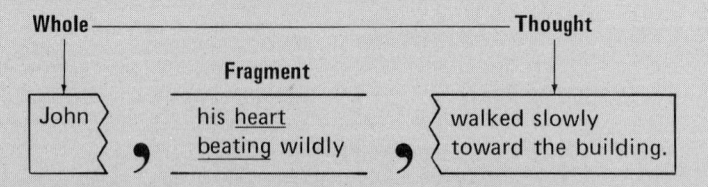

Whole ─────────────────────── Thought

John		Fragment		
John	**,**	his heart beating wildly	**,**	walked slowly toward the building.

Punctuation for attaching "the jet breaking through" fragment to a whole thought is the same as for "the man who" fragment. See pages 31-32.

2E.1. Exercises: Editing for "The Jet Breaking Through" Fragments

Look for "the jet breaking through" fragments in the following excerpts and attach each fragment to the whole thought that it belongs to in order to put the excerpts back into college writing. Make all changes directly in the sentences as if you were editing a paper. If an excerpt does not need to be changed, put a check (√) next to its number. Look only for "the jet breaking through" fragments, using the guidelines given on pages 58-60. Do not edit for anything else. (See page 2 for how to use the "Answer" Section.)

Examples

a. He touched her face with his hand�, his fingers trembling with happiness.

√b. Then he sat down, his face gleaming with satisfaction.

1. She clutched the baby and ran. Lawd! Then she stopped. Her mouth hanging open. (142)

2. She grabbed her dress, got up and stood by the bed; the tips of her fingers touching the wall behind her. A match flared in yellow flame; Silas' face was caught in a circle of light. (142)

3. The white man who had gotten out walked over the ground, going to Silas. They faced each other; the white man standing up and Silas sitting down; like two toy men they faced each other. (142)

4. He stood, insolent and dark and leonine; his elbow leaning on the cash-register. His fingers playing with his chin, looking out at the crowd. It was as though his station were a promontory and we were the sea. Jacques was immediately attracted. (9)

5. I carried my sickness and though for a long time I tried to place it in the outside world, the attempt to write it down shows me that at least half of it lay within me. It came upon me slowly, like that strange disease that affects those black men whom you see turning slowly from black to albino. Their pigment disappearing as under the radiation of some cruel, invisible ray. (43)

2E. 2. Exercises. Adding the "Breaking Through" and "The Jet Breaking Through" Fragments

Add "breaking through" and "the jet breaking through" fragments to the whole thoughts below. Try to be as creative as you can. Let your imagination go. Use the same method you used on pages 50 and 59. Write your sentences on separate paper if necessary.

1. The bus rolled toward the curb, _____

   _____

   _____

   _____

   _____

2. She paused by a stoop, _____

   _____

   _____

   _____

   _____

3. The children's voices echoed across the yard, _____

   _____

   _____

   _____

   _____

4. The soldier moved toward the bunker, _____

   _____

   _____

   _____

   _____

64   *The Whole Sentence*

5. The old man smiled warmly at the child, _____

_____

_____

_____

_____

6. The crowd was angry now, _____

_____

_____

_____

_____

7. He watched the pollution settle on the streets, _____

_____

_____

_____

_____

8. She stood on the empty stage, _____

_____

_____

_____

_____

Write a description of a person using as many "breaking through" and "the jet breaking through" fragments as you can. Do the same for something else that moves, like a car, an animal, or even something like smoke.

F. "To offer a ride" is a fragment
   "To be a man" is a fragment

There is another verb-like word that isn't a verb at all. Any verb that has the word "to" in front of it is no longer a verb, but a verb-like word (also called an "infinitive"). Like the word "breaking" in the "breaking through" fragment, these verb-like words can introduce useful fragments:

WHOLE THOUGHT	FRAGMENT
I went out of my way	to offer a ride to him.

CHART 10. The Pattern of the "To Offer a Ride" Fragment

Whole Thought	Fragment	
	Verb-like Word with "To"	Rest of Fragment
☐	to offer	a ride to the happy boys and girls.
☐ ,	to be	a man in her eyes.
☐ —	to keep	the African in the position of permanent weakness.

Examples using the "to offer a ride" fragment

Is anything being done to help these youngsters?
   (Alfred Acquaye, *Children of West Africa*) (3)

To show that they are caught up in the spirit of the season, many people go out of their way to offer a ride to the happy boys and girls.
   (Alfred Acquaye, *Children of West Africa*) (3)

I wanted her approval, to be a man in her eyes.
The end is always the same—to keep the African in the position of permanent weakness. . . .
   (Jordan E. Ngubane, "An African Explains Apartheid") (97)

66 *The Whole Sentence*

CHART 11. Punctuation for the "To Offer a Ride" Fragment

Punctuation for attaching this fragment to a whole thought is the same as for "the man who" fragment. See pages 31-32.
IN ADDITION:

When the "to offer a ride" fragment comes at the end of the sentence, you often do not need any punctuation. Let your ear guide you.

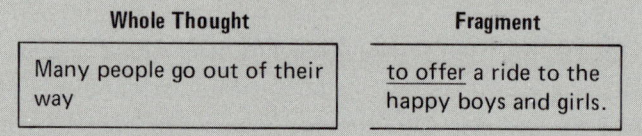

Whole Thought	Fragment
Many people go out of their way	to offer a ride to the happy boys and girls.

When the fragment comes at the beginning of the sentence, you also have to use your ear.

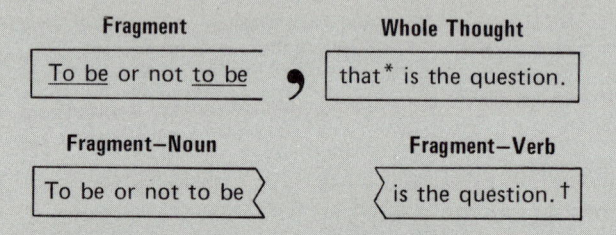

Fragment		Whole Thought
To be or not to be	,	that* is the question.

Fragment—Noun	Fragment—Verb
To be or not to be	is the question.†

When the fragment comes IN THE MIDDLE OF THE SENTENCE, you still have to trust your ear:

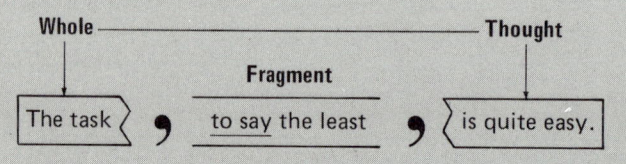

Whole ——————————————— Thought

| The task | , | to say the least | , | is quite easy. |

---

*This use of "that" is different from the "that" discussed in Part A. See page 114 for the various uses of the word "that."
†In this sentence, the fragment is used like a noun in a noun-verb pair (see Chapter 1). The verb in this sentence is "is." The fragment-noun plus the fragment-verb equals a whole sentence.

2F. Exercises: Editing for the "To Offer a Ride" Fragments

Look for "to offer a ride" fragments in the following excerpts and attach each fragment to the whole thought that it belongs to in order to put the excerpts back into college writing. Make all changes directly in the sentences as if you were editing a paper. If an excerpt does not need to be changed, put a check (√) next to its number. Look only for the "to offer a ride" fragments, using the guidelines given on pages 65-66. Do not edit for anything else. (See page 2 for how to use the "Answer" Section).

Examples

a. I wanted to be happy. To be creative and carefree.

√b. There is a lot to be done.

1. I suppose this was why I asked her to marry me. To give myself something to be moored to. (9)

2. Getting it together may mean working with welfare recipients. To help them move beyond the point of mere survival. (135)

3. To show that they are caught up in the spirit of the season, many people go out of their way. To offer a ride to the happy boys and girls. (3)

4. It is up to the American writer. To find out what these laws and assumptions are. In a society much given to smashing taboos without thereby managing to be liberated from them, it will be no easy matter. (10b)

5. Foundations have made it clear that all kinds of groups can get money except those in Negro areas. Therefore, the Negro artist and the Negro masses will have to reckon with this. To strike out for themselves. (91)

6. To meet the demand for better hospital care. Mobile medical teams have been organized by most of the West African nations, supported by funds and

supplies furnished through the United Nations and its various health and educational branches. (3)

7. In particular they held that if any youth of rude and impertinent ways were to marry, he would cause deep shame to his community. There was no inducement. To arrange marriage for such a one since he would surely bring disgrace on the family from which he came. (29)

8. Back then the going thing was what the white man had told them. To turn the other cheek and appeal to the conscience of the white oppressor. I knew that you couldn't do that; you can't appeal to the conscience of a beast, when you're dealing with savages and brutes and tyrants. (19)

9. Once upon a time, Stokely Carmichael believed in an ultimate humanism. But the layers of hatred and injustice in this country deterred him from its pursuit. He left the country. Perhaps to try and find it in Africa. Or perhaps simply to breathe awhile. The generation behind him has to struggle with that same problem. (64)

10. Because we were locked up in our cells before darkness fell, I used to lie awake at night racked by painful craving to take a leisurely stroll under the stars, or to go to the beach; to drive a car on a freeway. To grow a beard. Or to make love to a woman. (32)

11. The Black child should master standard English. Not simply to understand Shakespeare and the classics, but also to be able to understand how he is being and has been manipulated by language. The Louisiana State Voter Applica-

tion is a better argument for his learning standard English than *Macbeth*. But he should also know his own language first. (24)

12. Gas chambers, pogroms, and possibly concentration camps are the handiest instruments by which a majority seeks to liquidate a minority. The few, however, cannot use these instruments against the many unless they want to release forces among the many that might in the end destroy the few. Survival is too precious to the Afrikaner nationalist; to be risked in adventures that might endanger his own existence. As a result, he uses quite a number of techniques. To frustrate life's purpose for the African. The end is always the same. To keep the African in the position of permanent weakness. In order to preserve the Boer's pattern of justice. To transform him into a pliable tool in the hands of the Afrikaner nationalists. In this chapter, we shall pick only a few techniques at random; to show different aspects of the pattern of "just" laws. (97)

G. "Afraid of his shadow" is a fragment

Not only can verb-like words introduce fragments, but so can descriptive words such as "afraid" or "unaware." Take the following, for example.

> White men, <u>unaware of him</u>, continue squirting tobacco juice in his direction.
> (Jean Toomer, *Cane*) (127)

The underlined word group is a fragment introduced by the descriptive word "unaware." Note that the descriptive word describes something in the whole thought. "Unaware" describes "white men." They are <u>unaware white men</u>.

Sometimes the descriptive word looks like a verb. But in the following sentence, "starched" and "frilled" are not being used as verbs. They are being used to describe Esther. She is a <u>starched and frilled person</u>.

> Esther looks like a little white child, <u>starched, frilled</u>, as she walks slowly from her home towards her father's grocery store.
> (Jean Toomer, *Cane*) (127)

If a descriptive word looks like a verb, the spelling of that descriptive word is the same as the spelling of the main verb for Verb Group 1 (see Chart 25). For editing exercises on spelling the descriptive word that looks like a verb, see pages 177-180 at the end of Chapter 4, Part D.

Examples using the "<u>afraid</u> of his shadow" fragment

> To meet the demand for better hospital care, mobile medical teams have been organized by most of the West African nations, <u>supported by funds and supplies furnished through the United Nations and its various health and educational branches</u>.
> (Alfred Acquaye, *Children of West Africa*) (3)

> <u>Held in bondage, stripped of his culture, denied family life for centuries, made to labor for others</u>, the Negro tried to learn to live the life of the New World in an atmosphere of rejection and hate.
> (Richard Wright, *White Man, Listen!*) (143)

> Around him he would have seen weather-beaten houses <u>innocent of paint</u>, <u>the shingled roofs in many instances covered with a rich growth of moss</u>.
> (Charles V. Chesnutt, "The Sheriff's Children") (28)

Notice that this last fragment begins with a noun, like "<u>the jet breaking through</u>" fragment. Now the noun "roofs" goes before the descriptive word "covered." They are <u>covered roofs</u>. This is not a whole thought because the helping verb "were" is missing.

WHOLE THOUGHT

The shingled <u>roofs</u> (noun) in many instances <u>were</u> <u>covered</u> (true verb) with a rich growth of moss.

FRAGMENT

the shingled <u>roofs</u> (noun) in many instances <u>covered</u> with a rich growth of moss.

72   *The Whole Sentence*

See other examples in Part E, page 57.

CHART 12.   Punctuation of the "Afraid of His Shadow" Fragment

Like several other fragments, this fragment can come BEFORE or AFTER the whole thought, or you can break up the whole thought and put the fragment next to the noun that is being described (though this is not as smooth as the other ways).

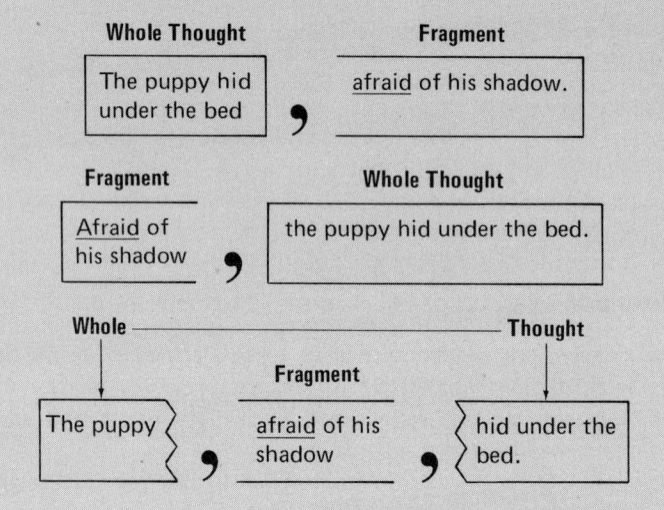

Whole Thought		Fragment
The puppy hid under the bed	**,**	afraid of his shadow.

Fragment		Whole Thought
Afraid of his shadow	**,**	the puppy hid under the bed.

Whole ──────────────── Thought

| The puppy | **,** | Fragment
afraid of his shadow | **,** | hid under the bed. |

Punctuation for attaching the "afraid of his shadow" fragment to a whole thought is the same as for the fragments covered in Part A. See page 22.

2G. Exercises: Editing for the "Afraid of His Shadow" Fragments

Look for the "afraid of his shadow" fragments in the following excerpts and attach each fragment to the whole thought that it belongs to in order to put the excerpts back into college writing. Make all changes directly in the sentences as if you were editing a paper. If an excerpt does not need to be changed, put a check (√) next to its number. Look only for the "afraid of his shadow" fragments, using the guidelines given on pages 70-71. Do not edit for anything else. (See page 2 for how to use the "Answer" Section.)

Examples
   a. I continued to talk, confused by the expression on his face.

√b. The children, happy and playful, came racing through the park.

   1. Karintha is a woman. Men do not know that the soul of her was a growing thing. Ripened too soon. (127)

   2. Crises breed big men. They come forth like diamonds. Perfected by the pressures they have been subjected to. (16)

   3. Stretched on a bed of pain. I spent two weeks of misery. Later, when I left the hospital, I had grown skinny, but I was cured, completely cured, of my illness. (77)

   4. How strange, then, it is that a man of Africa should be here to receive an award given for service to the cause of peace and brotherhood between men. (81)

   5. These boys and girls were will-less. Their speech flat. Their gestures vague. Their personalities devoid of anger, hope, laughter, enthusiasm, passion or despair. (137)

   6. A little later it lodged in the mud of a shallow place. One wheel of the crushed and upturned little Ford became visible above the rushing water. (20)

7. Around him he would have seen weather-beaten houses, innocent of paint; the shingled roofs in many instances covered with a rich growth of moss. (28)

8. The weight of Harlem and my whiteness and strangeness hung in the air as I droned on; lost in my righteous monologue. The uproar turned into sullen silence. (73)

9. Mary's body surged upward and he pushed downward upon the pillow with all of his weight; determined that she must not move or make any sound that would betray him. (140)

10. All 250 had been found "suspect". Accused of being "activists", hunted like wild animals, persecuted by the PIDE, the famous secret police. They bolted and took refuge in other countries in Europe. (86)

H. "Because of you" is a fragment; any word group without a noun-verb pair is a fragment

The preceding parts of this chapter have outlined the most common kinds of fragments. Parts A and B showed how any whole thought, any word group with a noun-verb pair, can be turned into a fragment just by adding a word like "because" or "who." Parts C, D, E, F and G showed various ways of introducing other fragments which do not have the noun-verb pair in them.

This last group of fragments also does not have a noun-verb pair, but the fragment can be recognized because it usually starts with words like "because of," "except," "like," or "with."

> The Russians set fire to it themselves on purpose, because of the French. . . .
> (Salim Bin Abakari, "A Journey to Russia and Siberia in 1896") (1)

> As the sun was setting we started up the boardwalk towards his house, with our wet bathing trunks on under our trousers.
> (James Baldwin, *Giovanni's Room*) (9)

> Nothing in this block ever changes, except the seasons.
> (Jim Haskins, *Diary of a Harlem Schoolteacher*) (58)

Like all the other fragments, the "because of you" fragment MUST ALSO BE ATTACHED TO A WHOLE THOUGHT.

Signal words for the "because of you" fragment

Every writer has his own favorite words that he usually uses to introduce a fragment. Much overused is the word "like," but if you are using that word, you must be alert to attach its fragment to a whole thought.

The chart that follows lists the words most commonly used to introduce these fragments. Check to see which words you use frequently, and if you know that you tend to separate fragments from the whole thoughts they are "supposed to be" attached to, then you should look for these words in your own essays. A word such as "except" or "not like" can sometimes be a signal to you that the whole word group is a fragment. Check it out. Does the word group have a noun-verb pair? Is it attached to a whole thought?

CHART 13. Signal Words for the "<u>Because of You</u>" Fragment

after	during	like	through
as	except	not like	until
because of	excepting	of	with
before	from	regarding	without
between	in	since	with the
by	just as	till	exception of

This list is far from complete. Do not memorize it; just circle those words that you seem to use a lot and be aware of them in your essays so you can find your own fragments when you edit. ADD to this list any word that introduces your favorite fragment.

CHART 14. Punctuation for the "Because of You" Fragment

Punctuation for attaching this fragment to a whole thought is the same as for "the man who" fragment. See pages 31-32.

IN ADDITION:

When the fragment comes IN THE MIDDLE OF THE SENTENCE, you have to trust your ear.

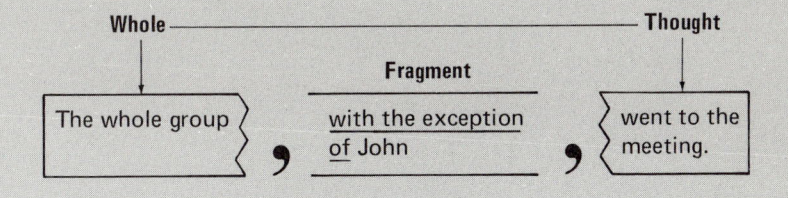

Whole ─────────────────────────── Thought
                    Fragment

| The whole group | , | with the exception of John | , | went to the meeting. |

2H. Exercises: Editing for the "Because of You" Fragment

Look for the "because of you" fragments and any fragment that does not have a noun-verb pair in the following excerpts and attach each fragment to the whole thought that it belongs to in order to put the excerpts back into college writing. Make all changes directly in the sentences as if you were editing a paper. If an excerpt does not need to be changed, put a check (√) next to its number. Look only for the "because of you" fragments, and those that do not have a noun-verb pair, using the guidelines given on pages 75-77. Do not edit for anything else. (See page 2 for how to use the "Answer" Section.)

Examples

a. The game was called off, because of rain.

b. They wandered around the city, and looked for an open bookstore.

1. Her knees gave. Fear oozed from her throat. To her stomach. (142)

2. In the fall of last year. My plane hovered over the rust-red earth of Georgia. (10c)

3. She saw Silas point the whip to the smashed graphophone. The white man looked down. And took a quick step backward. (142)

4. Years ago, we used to say, "Yes, I'm black, goddammit, and I'm beautiful!" In defiance. Into the void. (8)

5. Boys and girls in remote areas learned about hunting, crafts and farming. But little else. (3)

6. I did not want to think so. I did not want to think that my life would be like his, or that my mind would ever grow so pale; so without hard places and sharp, sheer drops. (9)

7. How to be natural does not seem to me to be a problem. Quite the contrary. The great problem is how to be—in the best sense of that kaleidoscopic word. A man. (10d)

8. She shrank as something whined through the air. A red streak of pain cut across the small of her back and burned its way into her body. Deeply. (142)

9. The two old black folks, sitting quietly side by side. Showed no excitement. In another instant the car hit the water and dropped immediately out of sight. (20)

10. Even before waking; I heard the rain falling. At first I thought it must be six-fifteen in the morning and I should be going; to the office. (15)

11. Reuben started to say something, but Harriet clapped her hand over his mouth; and pushed him. Through the door.

"Do like he says, Reuben," she pleaded. "Don't say no more. It'd only make it worse. Just go now." (95)

12. There was nothing subdued about Grandmother. She blurted out exactly what she thought. And was afraid of no one. She never called anyone "Marse." She had the Smith pride and refused to regard herself as a slave. (95)

13. She tried to be as pleasant with him as with others, but it was difficult. For she was all beauty, all daintiness, all tiny vanilla. With blue eyes and fluffy sun-hair. One afternoon she saw him in the hall looking very bleak against the wall. (21)

14. I could take a few square miles of land, call them "mine." And then go off to the moon. All I had to do to gain living from "my" land was to charge a rent; to the people who wanted to use it. (105)

15. An early folk tradition based mainly upon Southern rural material has been richly exploited by several generations of Negro writers. As in the dialect stories and poems of Daniel Webster Davis, Paul Lawrence Dunbar, and others. The best and most sophisticated writer in this genre was James Weldon Johnson, as he shows in "God's Trombones" (1927). (60)

16. He caught one of the man's legs; and dragged the body into the middle of the road. Then he turned and came slowly back to the house. She ran, holding the baby. And fell at his feet. (142)

17. "There's nobody here but us," she said. Her fingers unbuttoned the first button on his shirt; the second. Her fingers crept in on his chest, playing with the little hairs there.

"There's nobody here but us," she said, and she ran her fingers inside his shirt. Over his shoulders and the back of his neck. (93)

18. In due time the beer is brought to the "talking-place" (where men always hold meetings and where visitors and travelers in a strange village always report their presence); and is poured out for the lad's uncles and other relatives that might be with them on this mission. (29)

19. She watched from the hill-slope; the back steps blazed. The white men fired a steady stream of bullets. Black smoke spiraled upward in the sunshine.

Shots came. From the house. The white men crouched out of sight; behind their cars. (142)

20. But when their more acceptable friends came, were around, they turned their handsome backs on him. He hated himself for responding gratefully to their later "Hi, Linc!" Hated himself for his feeling of well-being when with them, despite—everything. (21)

21. In the weird green light. Frantic people in defiant garb created the illusion of a costume ball. But the workers had come as workers, proudly. The Negroes as Negroes, apologetically. The Jews as Jews, defiantly. Only the two Mexican girls had come in costume—they had come as Castilian Spanish. (62)

22. Brown, who was active in the abolitionist movement, was a serious writer, and after the Civil War he produced several ambitious historical and narrative works which achieved a rather large circulation. At the time. He was the first American Negro who devoted his life to literature. And the first to earn his living as a writer. (21)

23. Meals were served on time. Eight o'clock for breakfast, one o'clock for lunch, and seven o'clock for dinner. And were announced by a large gong near the head of the stairs in the living room. I was warned by Barney that everyone was expected to be on time. The household followed Lewis' routine; people fitted into his mold. He was a stubborn man, set in his ways; while living in his home one conformed; to his pattern of life. (26)

24. Alma was the maid, and Wilson, her husband; the gardener-handyman. They had one small child. Alma was a light-colored, plump, and attractive creole

from Louisiana; in her late twenties or early thirties. She seemed to dominate the quiet, easygoing Wilson. She outwardly accepted her position. Kept her place. Did her work, and demanded and received respect. (26)

25. Going to New York was good-bye to the cotton fields. Good-bye to "Massa Charlie." Good-bye to the chain gang, and, most of all, good-bye to those sunup-to-sundown working hours. One no longer had to wait to get to heaven to lay his burden down; burdens could be laid down in New York. (22)

26. But I have a suspicion that, because of these aspects of my character, "free-normal-educated" people rather expect me to be more reserved. Penitent. Remorseful. And not too quick to shoot off my mouth on certain subjects. But I let them down, disappoint them. Make them gape at me in a sort of stupor, as if they're thinking: "You've got your nerve! Don't you realize that you owe a debt to society?" (32)

27. African and Afro-American intellectuals sometimes unconsciously forget, and always find it painful to consciously accept, the disconcerting fact that many African societies and the cultures that they embody are often viewed with contempt. And sometimes with fascinated horror. By the peoples of the Western world. Including the black masses of the United States. (39)

Cumulative Editing for All Fragments in Chapter 2

Look for all the types of fragments covered in this chapter in the following excerpts and attach each fragment to the whole thought that it belongs to in order to put the excerpts back into college writing. Make all changes directly in the sentences as if you were editing a paper. If an excerpt does not need to be changed, put a check (√) next to its number. Look only for fragments, using the guidelines given on pages 17-77. Do not edit for anything else. (See page 2 for how to use the "Answer" Section.)

Example
She lifted the baby and stood. Waiting for him to speak. to tell her something to change all this. (142)

1. I have always led a fighting life. In a struggle which has always had in view the ultimate independence of my people. My struggle has caused me to be called many things. Criminal—a wild man—a black mamba—an agitator. Once I was even called a diplomat. (71)

2. And this was one thing they could not hang on the nigger, he thought with sharp disdain. The nigger loved his watermelon, even though the white folks ate most of them. And the nigger loved his chicken—what little the white folks left. But everybody got drunk—nigger, white man, gentile, Jew. (62)

3. At the same time we would keep our ears open. To catch anything that might be said about us. About our sweetheart and about our good fortune; but our ears caught very little, for the music was deafening; and there was extraordinary animation in the tightly packed crowds all around the square. (76)

4. It was at this juncture that he had to make use of other resources; whether African, subcultural, or hermetic. And it was this boundary, this no man's land; that provided the logic and beauty of his music. (68)

5. So, when the day of the ceremonies has come; all assemble at the village and begin song and dance. While the beer is being drunk. The parents of the young lad prepare his food; and give him a fowl, that he may eat at his going out from the village. In the morning, at dawn, they cut the lad's hair, give him food, and when this is finished those who are in the dance take some of the drums to the bush and all follow. Following, in a crowd, the young lad. (78)

6. The critics had jumped on him with both their left feet when he published *The Deer Park*. Which I still had not read—and this created a kind of bond; or strengthened the bond already existing between us. About a year and several overflowing wastebaskets later, I, too, returned to America. Not vastly improved by having been out of it, but not knowing where else to go; and one day, while I was sitting dully in my house. Norman called me from Connecticut. (10a)

7. We heard nothing but bragging and boasting. And already, after this very short time, we had become accustomed to his flow of words. To his way of turning his material wealth into a celebration. Wealth acquired honestly or dishonestly (a diamond trafficker is hardly likely to be honest). Our laughter awakened Marie. Who soon joined the swarm of my sisters and "little sisters" in the kitchen. (77)

8. The sense in which "revolutionary" is understood is; that a revolutionary is against the established order, regime; or culture. The bourgeoisie calls him a revolutionary because he threatens the established way of life. Things as they are. They can not accept change; though change is inevitable. The revolutionary

understands change. Change is what it is all about. He is not a revolutionary to his people; to his compatriots. To his comrades. (120)

9. It was the vision of a people who could trust one another. Who would sit side by side. Singing the song of love which harmonized with music from the birds, and all their hearts would beat to the rhythm of the throbbing river. The children would play there; jumping from rock on to rock, splashing the water which reached fathers and mothers sitting in the shade around, talking; watching. Birds sang as they hovered from tree to tree; while farther out in the forest beasts of the land circled around. . . . In the midst of this Nyambura would stand. (99)

10. One day the inevitable occurred. As if they had agreed beforehand; six common ants—apparently of the most ordinary sort—arrived at the anthill. Each with a strange object which was passed off, amid general anticipation, as a prodigious milligram. Naturally, they did not obtain the honors they had hoped for, but they were excused that same day from all further service. And were granted pensions. (5)

11. Miss Cynthie hardly noted that she had been left; so absorbed was she in the spectacle. To her, the theater had always been the antithesis of the church. As the one was the refuge of righteousness, so the other was the stronghold of transgression. But this first scene awakened memories. Captured and held her attention by offering a blend of truth and novelty. Having thus baited her interest; the show now proceeded to play it; like the trout through swift-flowing waters of wickedness. Resist as it might. Her mind was caught and drawn into the impious subsequences. (46)

12. The shack blazed, flanked on all sides by whirling smoke filled with flying sparks. She heard the distant hiss of flames. White men were crawling on their stomachs. Now and then they stopped. Aimed. And fired into the bulging smoke. She looked with a tense numbness; she looked, waiting for Silas to scream. Or run out. But the house crackled and blazed; spouting yellow plumes to the blue sky. The white men shot again, sending a hail of bullets into the furious pillars of smoke. And still she could not see Silas running out. Or hear his voice calling. Then she jumped, standing. There was a loud crash; the roof caved in. A black chimney loomed amid crumbling wood. Flames roared and black smoke billowed; hiding the house. (142)

13. A quarter of a century was to elapse between the time when I saw my father sitting with the strange woman and the time when I was to see him again. Standing alone upon the red clay of a Mississippi plantation. A sharecropper, clad in ragged overalls. Holding a muddy hoe in his gnarled, veined hands. A quarter of a century during which my mind and consciousness had become so greatly and violently altered that when I tried to talk to him I realized that, though ties of blood made us kin, though I could see a shadow of my face in his face, thought there was an echo of my voice in his voice, we were forever strangers. Speaking a different language. Living on vastly distant planes of reality. (137)

14. There have been actual cases where bitter conflicts existed between the villagers backing their traditional rulers on the one side and the young councilors with a hardly appreciable number of outside supporters on the other. The conflict sometimes reached a stage where the councilors were ostracized by the whole community. Or punished with village fines and "excommunication." Which in one case meant the extremely serious step in African custom of refusal by the village to join in burying dead relatives of the councilors. For their lawful performance of council duties. In some cases it was necessary for Government administrative officers. To intervene in the interests of law and order. (4)

3 Comma-splice and Run-on Sentences

Note: Review Chapter 1 before going on.

A. Basic definitions

Definition of a comma-splice (C.S.)

In college writing the following sentence, an example of a comma-splice, is generally not acceptable in college essays:

> The Hawks were smug and self-righteous, the Doves were evasive of the real question.

The sentence is called a comma-splice because only <u>a comma</u> separates two whole thoughts instead of a period or semicolon, which would be "proper" in formal college writing. If a college student were to write the sentence, he would probably find a red "C.S." for comma-splice in the margin. But Norman Mailer, the author of the words, is a prominent American writer, and the sentence appears in *Armies of the Night*, (82) which won the National Book Award in 1969—comma-splices and all. If he had used the "acceptable" punctuation, his sentence would have looked like this:

> The Hawks were smug and self-righteous; the Doves were evasive of the real question.

Definition of a run-on (R.O.)

If Mailer had left out the comma altogether, the sentence would have looked like this:

> The Hawks were smug and self-righteous the Doves were evasive of the real question.

This is considered a run-on (R.O.) in formal writing.

Of course, like the fragment, the terms "comma-splice" and "run-on" are words pertaining to college writing. In writing outside of college, authors often do not bother about them. It is not wrong to put a comma between two whole thoughts or to leave out the comma all together. It is just not formal enough for most college essays.

91

Here is a comma-splice:

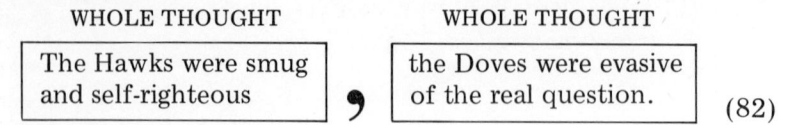

WHOLE THOUGHT		WHOLE THOUGHT	
The Hawks were smug and self-righteous	**,**	the Doves were evasive of the real question.	(82)

This is a run-on:

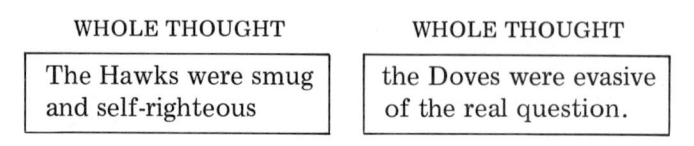

WHOLE THOUGHT	WHOLE THOUGHT
The Hawks were smug and self-righteous	the Doves were evasive of the real question.

This is the sentence in college writing:

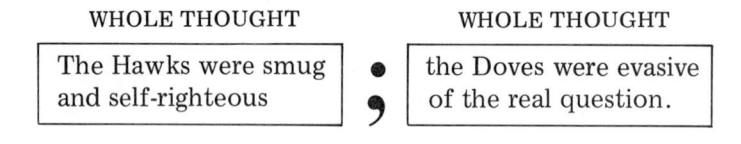

WHOLE THOUGHT		WHOLE THOUGHT
The Hawks were smug and self-righteous	**;**	the Doves were evasive of the real question.

Recognizing the comma-splice and run-on

The best way to find comma-splices or run-ons in your own writing—when you are handing it in to a professor who cares about such things—is to forget about them while you write. When you reread for editing, check your commas according to the guidelines that follow. Replacing a comma with another punctuation mark will not usually change the way your paper sounds—so your writing style will very rarely be altered. Nor will the meaning of your thoughts usually change. These are important considerations.

In order to recognize a C.S. or R.O., you must know—in a general way—what a whole thought is. Review pages 5-12 on whole thoughts before going on.

When two whole thoughts are attached together, some connecting device is needed between them, and a comma is NEVER strong enough to separate the two thoughts from each other in college writing. So the following is a C.S.:

> The huge plantation fields had many slaves, they sang together.

The first whole thought is:

> The huge plantation fields had many slaves.

The second one is:

> They sang together.

Note that each group of words can stand alone. Neither one turns into a fragment when it appears as a complete sentence. (See Chapter 1.) But when both whole thoughts are attached to make one sentence, college writing demands specific punctuation and connecting words, NOT A COMMA ALONE.

WHOLE THOUGHT		WHOLE THOUGHT	
The huge plantation fields had many slaves	, AND	they sang together.	(68)

Punctuation between two whole thoughts

There are many ways to attach two whole thoughts to each other, according to what your ear and ideas dictate.

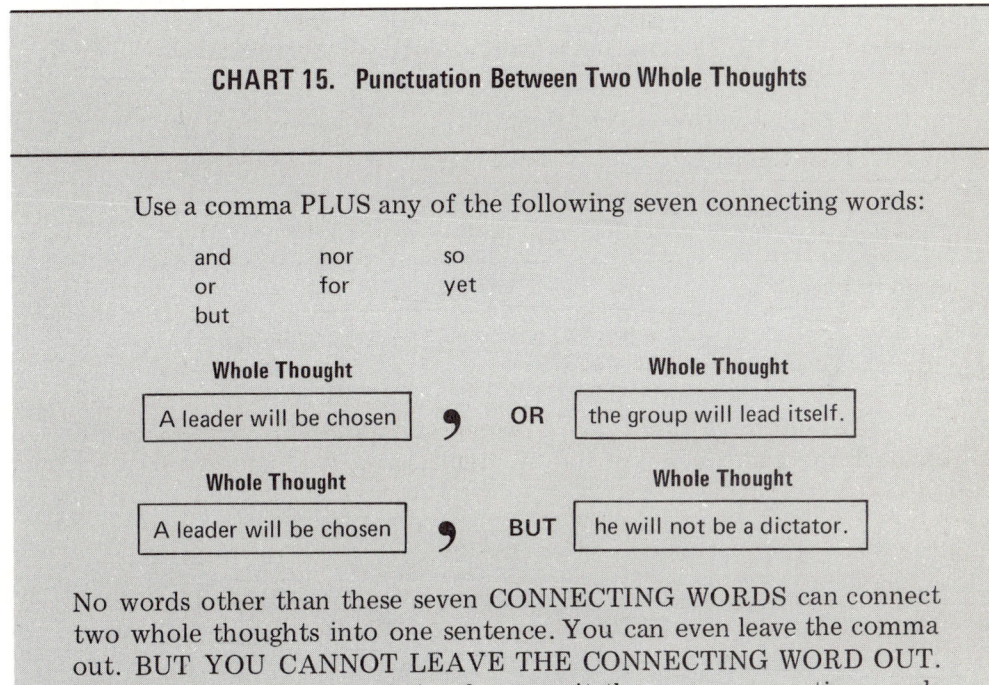

CHART 15. Punctuation Between Two Whole Thoughts

Use a comma PLUS any of the following seven connecting words:

and	nor	so
or	for	yet
but		

Whole Thought		Whole Thought
A leader will be chosen	, OR	the group will lead itself.

Whole Thought		Whole Thought
A leader will be chosen	, BUT	he will not be a dictator.

No words other than these seven CONNECTING WORDS can connect two whole thoughts into one sentence. You can even leave the comma out. BUT YOU CANNOT LEAVE THE CONNECTING WORD OUT. Therefore, you should religiously commit the seven connecting words to memory. Have a friend or your instructor quiz you on them before you go on to the editing exercises.

You could also make one whole thought into a fragment by using the list of words that make fragments on page 19. For example:

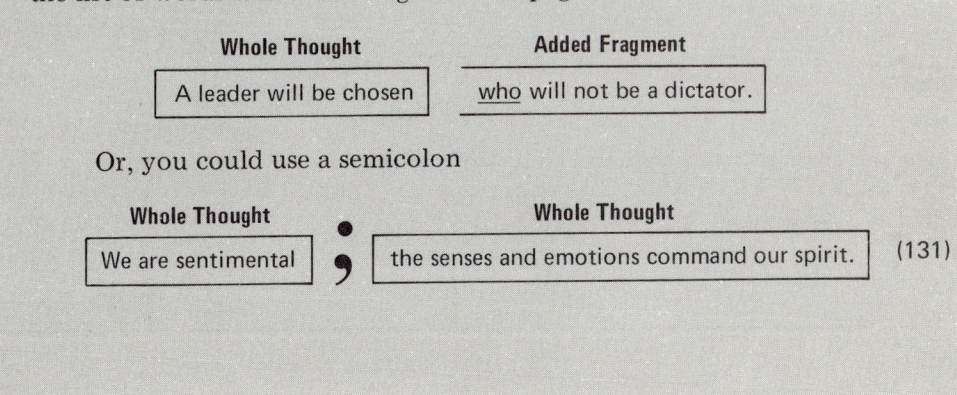

Whole Thought	Added Fragment
A leader will be chosen	who will not be a dictator.

Or, you could use a semicolon

Whole Thought		Whole Thought	
We are sentimental	;	the senses and emotions command our spirit.	(131)

Or, you could use a period and a capital letter

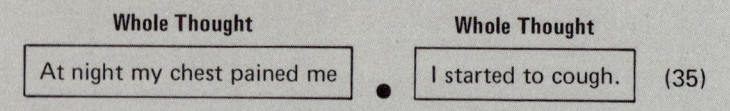

Whole Thought: At night my chest pained me **.** **Whole Thought**: I started to cough. (35)

Or, when you are connecting three or more whole thoughts together you can use:

1. Just a comma between <u>the first two</u>.

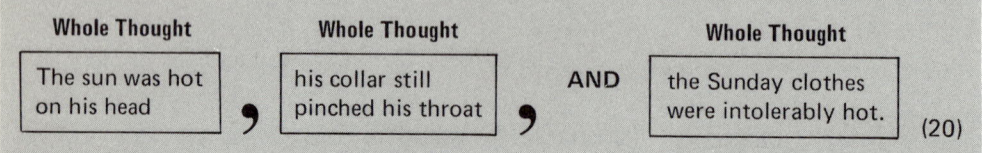

Whole Thought: The sun was hot on his head **,** **Whole Thought**: his collar still pinched his throat **,** AND **Whole Thought**: the Sunday clothes were intolerably hot. (20)

2. Dashes between all of them.

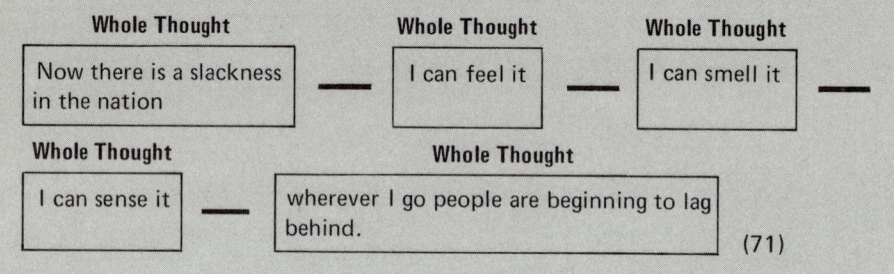

Whole Thought: Now there is a slackness in the nation — **Whole Thought**: I can feel it — **Whole Thought**: I can smell it —

Whole Thought: I can sense it — **Whole Thought**: wherever I go people are beginning to lag behind. (71)

Or, you can break up a whole thought with another whole thought.

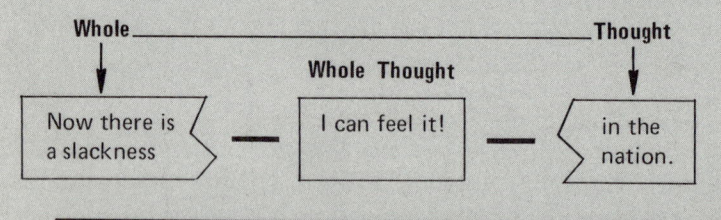

Whole ——————————————————————— Thought

Now there is a slackness — **Whole Thought**: I can feel it! — in the nation.

DO <u>NOT</u> USE:

Just a Comma (,).

At night my chest pained me,^and I started to cough.

No Punctuation If There Is Also No Connecting Word.

At night my chest pained me^and I started to cough.

At night my chest pained me^,and I started to cough.

3A. 1. Exercises: Editing for Comma-splices and Run-ons Using the Connecting Words

Look for comma-splices and run-ons in the following excerpts and change the punctuation to a comma PLUS any one of the seven connecting words listed on page 93 in order to put the excerpts back into college writing. Make all changes directly in the sentences as if you were editing a paper. If an excerpt does not need to be changed, put a check (√) next to its number. Look only for comma-splices and run-ons, using the guidelines given on pages 91-93. Do not edit for anything else. (See page 2 for how to use the "Answer" Section.)

Example:
Now we will open your ears, and also your throat, for there is something that has been choking you, *and* we will also give you the water that shall wash down all the troubles in your throat. (55)

1. Her answer was not strong enough to reach him presently, *and* the old woman came to the door, feeling her way with a stick. (20)

2. We do not trust educated people and rarely, alas, produce them, we do not trust the independence of mind which alone makes a genuine education possible. (10e)

3. Now I keep quiet. I go to bed on my sacks, as soon as I feel a cockroach walking along my neck with its scratchy feet I give it a slap with my hand and squash it. (112)

4. I believe that armed struggle is the only solution for people who are fighting for freedom, I act according to his belief. (41)

5. The other side of the avenue—for progress takes time—has not been rehabilitated yet and it looks exactly as it looked in the days when we sat with our noses pressed against the windowpane, longing to be allowed to go "across the street." (10c)

6. In the immediate neighborhood there were many schoolchildren who, in the afternoons, would stop and play en route to their homes; they would leave their books upon the sidewalk, I would thumb through the pages and question them about the baffling black print. (137)

7. We didn't have any money at all, that was the truth. When we got our relief check each month all we did was take it across the street to Mr. Burnett, the West Indian grocer, and pay him what we owed. This left us with nothing, the next day we started buying on credit again. (89)

8. We had been together many times, always the shadow of Tunilo kept us apart. We felt that his blistered hands came between us and carried Natalia away so that she would keep on nursing him, we knew that it would always be like that as long as she lived. (113)

9. Norman came on to America, I went to Corsica. We wrote each other a few times. I confided to Norman that I was very apprehensive about the reception of *Giovanni's Room* he was good enough to write some very encouraging things about it when it came out. (10a)

10. One can never really see into the heart, the mind, the soul of another. Norman is my very good friend, perhaps I do not really understand him at all, and perhaps everything I have tried to suggest in the foregoing is false. I do not think so, it may be. One thing, however, I am certain is *not* false, and that is simply the fact of his being a writer, and the incalculable potential he as a writer contains. (10a)

11. It is a terrible thing to say I am afraid that for a very long time the troubles of white people failed to impress me as being real trouble. They put me in mind of children crying because the breast has been taken away. Time and love have modified my tough-boy lack of charity, the attitude sketched above was my first attitude I am sure that there is a great deal of it left. (10a)

12. You are dependent, very dependent, upon my proddings, my ideas, my dreams, at first I am glad that you need me so. I eagerly and happily feed you from the plate of motivation knowing that it is difficult for you to help yourself, then at times you cause my arms to grow weary as I work harder straining myself in order to build you up. (121)

13. He came around in front of me, waving the broken bottle in his hand like Humphrey Bogart would do in the movies. There were others in back of him, grinning. He shoved the broken bottle at me, I put my hand in front of my face. I didn't feel anything, they started yelling. The soda jerk came flying over the counter like Alan Ladd, he and Humphrey Bogart threw me out. (53)

14. The Supreme Court decision was only one month old when I entered prison I do not believe that I had even the vaguest idea of its importance or historical significance. But later, the acrimonious controversy ignited by the end of the separate-but-equal doctrine was to have a profound effect on me. This controversy awakened me to my position in America I began to form a concept of what it meant to be black in white America. (32)

3A. 2. Exercises: Editing for Comma-splices and Run-ons Using All Methods

Look for comma-splices and run-ons in the following excerpts, changing the punctuation and adding connecting words when necessary in any of the ways covered in Part A in order to put the excerpts back into college writing. Make all changes directly in the sentences as if you were editing a paper. If an excerpt does not need to be changed, put a check (√) next to its number. Look only for comma-splices and run-ons using the guidelines given on pages 91-94. Do not edit for anything else. (See page 2 for how to use the "Answer" Section.)

Example:
After tramping the streets and pounding on doors to collect premiums, I was dry, strained, too tired to read or write. I hungered for relief,^and as a salesman in insurance to many young black girls, I found it. (139)

1. The Negro writer had no choice in his subject matter; he could not select his experiences. (143)

2. And yet—one would prefer, after all, not to be locked out one would prefer, merely, that the key unlocked a less stunningly unusual door. (11)

3. Come, then comrades, it would be as well to decide at once to change our ways, we must shake off the heavy darkness in which we were plunged, and leave it behind. (45)

4. Yet they were white men. They never talked of color; they never talked down to Africans; and they could work closely, joke, and laugh with their black colleagues who came from different tribes. Njoroge at times wished the whole country was like this. (100)

5. I wanted to be many things, I wanted to be a basketball player. I wanted to be an actor, I wanted to be a writer. I wanted to be a physical education instructor, I became a dope addict. (133)

6. This contribution is not in any way unique I did not initiate the struggle to extend the area of human freedom in South Africa, other African patriots—devoted men—did so before me. (81)

7. Finer residential areas of private homes have not been zoned or established, well-recognized and accepted communities of upper class Nigerians have yet to come into being. (117)

8. If this piece of land was in an urban area I had no need to develop it at all, I could leave it to the fools who were prepared to develop all the other pieces of land surrounding "my" piece, and in doing so automatically to raise the market value of mine. (105)

9. For all his role as commander, Che was often off in a corner either writing or reading. The guerrillas were wordy, too, the Bustos testimony, after his arrest, described his visit with Che, in a total of 20,000 words. (41)

10. There was always a possible limitation to any dilution or excession of cultural or spiritual references, the Negro could not ever become white and that was his strength, at some point, always, he could not participate in the dominant tenor of the white man's culture. (68)

11. In the sky, flying quite low and about a hundred yards off was a plane! It came so slowly that it seemed barely to move, my mouth hung wide, my bread and butter fell into the dirt I wanted to jump up and down and cheer. (42)

12. Here and there he would have met a razor-backed hog lazily rooting his way along the principal thoroughfare, more than once he would probably have

had to disturb the slumbers of some yellow dog, dozing away the hours in the ardent sunshine, and reluctantly yielding up his place in the middle of the dusty road. (28)

13. My life, that desperately treacherous labyrinth, seemed for a moment to be opening out behind me a light seemed to fall where there had been no light before. I began to see myself in others, I began for a moment to apprehend how Christopher must sometimes have felt. Everyone wishes to be loved, in the event, nearly no one can bear it. (11)

B. Other approaches to comma-splices and run-ons

If you have no trouble recognizing when one whole thought ends and the second one begins, the above punctuation outlined in Part A is all you need to know. SKIP TO Part C. If, however, you feel shaky recognizing where the "break" comes, the following suggestions might be helpful.

Edit "out loud"

After you have written your essay, read it out loud and listen for your voice to go down in pitch or for when you take a deep breath. Chances are you will do so between two whole thoughts. Read the following out loud.

> The Lords' ministers and cadres and active sympathizers go out together to distribute leaflets or move through the tenements with the tuberculin tests their leaders are available to anyone.

If you hear your voice low in pitch after "tests," your particular manner of speaking allows you to hear the separation between whole thoughts in college writing. Note that the above sentence is a run-on because there is nothing at all separating the two whole thoughts. The sentence as Yglesias wrote it has a semicolon separating the two whole thoughts:

> The Lords' ministers and cadres and active sympathizers go out together to distribute leaflets or move through the tenements with the tuberculin tests; their leaders are available to anyone.
> (Jose Yglesias, "Right On with the Young Lords") (144)

Of course, the author could have used any one of the punctuation methods listed on pages 93-94.

However, some accents do not include this pitch change. Listen to your voice to see if there is some change in sound at the "break" that would indicate to you that you have just read one whole thought and are about to read another one. Use that sound as your guide.

Look for noun-verb pairs

Note: Review Chapter 1 before going on.

Unfortunately, reading out loud is not foolproof. Another method that some students have found helpful is to look for noun-verb pairs in a sentence. This method takes a long time at first, but once you have practiced for a while, you will perform the task almost automatically. Even if you do not have a taste for grammar, try this method out for a while; you can always choose to forget about it if it is not helping you.

As outlined on page 8, all whole thoughts have a noun-verb pair:

WHOLE THOUGHT TYPE	NOUN	VERB	
1.	John	smiled.	
2.	John	wrote	a speech.
3.	The speech	was written	(by John).
4.	John	is	a student.

104 *The Whole Sentence*

What is the noun-verb pair in the following sentence?

The Lords also demand "freedom for all political prisoners."

NOUN	VERB
The Lords	demand

Certain words belong naturally to the noun-verb pair.

The word "also" belongs to the noun-verb pair. The word says that they have also demanded other things. The words "freedom for all political prisoners" belongs to the noun-verb pair because the words tell WHAT the Lords demand. The Lords demand "freedom for all political prisoners."

The whole word group is a whole thought because:
1. It has a noun-verb pair.
2. There are no words like "because" or "who" to make it into a fragment. (See page 10 and Chapter 2.)

WHOLE THOUGHT

The Lords also demand "freedom for all political prisoners."

FRAGMENT

<u>Because</u> the Lords also demand "freedom for all political prisoners."

Now, if the sentence continues, look for another noun-verb pair.

The Lords also demand "freedom for all political prisoners" they oppose "capitalists and alliances with traitors" and the "american military."[1]

What is the second noun-verb pair?

NOUN	VERB
they	oppose

What words belong naturally to the second noun-verb pair? "Capitalists and alliances with traitors" and the "american military" all belong to the noun-verb pair because they tell WHAT the Lords oppose. Does this noun-verb pair have a word like "because" or "who" to make it into a fragment?

WHOLE THOUGHT

They oppose "capitalists and alliances with traitors" and the "american military."

FRAGMENT

<u>Because</u> they oppose "capitalists and alliances with traitors" and the "american military."

Use punctuation outlined on pages 93-94 for attaching the two whole thoughts together.

---

[1] While the first letter of a name of a nationality usually is capitalized, the word "american" appears with a small "a" in the writings of the Young Lords because they mean a small "a."

In the original article by Yglesias, there is a semicolon between the two whole thoughts.

> The Lords also demand "freedom for all political prisoners"; they oppose "capitalists and alliances with traitors" and the "american military."
>
> (Jose Yglesias, "Right On With the Young Lords") (144)

He put the semicolon at the end of the words belonging to the first noun-verb pair and at the beginning of the words belonging to the second noun-verb pair.

Sometimes the second whole thought starts with a noun-verb pair.

RUN-ON

The models must be non-white our models must be consistent with a black style, our natural aesthetic styles, and our moral and spiritual styles.

EDITED

The models must be non-white. Our $\underline{\text{models}}$ $\underline{\text{must be}}$ consistent with a black style,
(noun) (verb)

our natural aesthetic styles, and our moral and spiritual styles.

(James Stewart, "The Development of the Black Revolutionary Artist") (120)

COMMA-SPLICE

He is instead, a brother, he is a son.

EDITED

He is instead, a brother. $\underline{\text{He}}$ $\underline{\text{is}}$ a son.
(noun verb)

(James Stewart, "The Development of the Black Revolutionary Artist") (120)

COMMA-SPLICE

I grabbed my face with both hands and squeezed hard, pushing it all out of shape, I pulled my lips out and my face down.

EDITED

I grabbed my face with both hands and squeezed hard, pushing it all out of shape;

(noun verb)
$\underline{\text{I}}$ $\underline{\text{pulled}}$ my lips out and my face down.

(Piri Thomas, *Down These Mean Streets*) (125)

Often, however, the noun-verb pair has several words before it:

COMMA-SPLICE

He felt his poverty, without a cent, without a home, without land, tools or savings, he had entered into competition with rich, landed, skilled neighbors.

But now you have to decide which words go with which noun-verb pair.

EDITED

He felt his poverty; without a cent, without a home, without land, tools or savings,
he had entered into competition with rich, landed, skilled neighbors.

(noun: he, verb: had entered)

(W. E. B. Dubois, *The Souls of Black Folk*) (40)

WHOLE THOUGHT	WHOLE THOUGHT
He felt his poverty	without a cent, without a home, without land, tools or savings, he had entered into competition with rich, landed, skilled neighbors.

separator: **.** or **,**   (40)

RUN-ON

The car was now purring through the paved streets of town for a moment, he was three blocks from his father's undertaking establishment!

EDITED

The car was now purring through the paved streets of town, and, for a moment, he was three blocks from his father's undertaking establishment!

(noun: he, verb: was)

(Richard Wright, *The Long Dream*) (138)

WHOLE THOUGHT		WHOLE THOUGHT
The car was now purring through the paved streets of town	AND **,**	, for a moment, he was three blocks from his father's undertaking establishment!

(138)

IF YOU DO NOT HAVE PATIENCE FOR GRAMMAR, the method just outlined might not be for you. Try it for a while, and if it does not work, use the other methods. Many fine writers do not know the first thing about grammar.

3B. Exercises: Editing for Comma-splices, Run-ons, and Fragments. Read Out Loud

Read the following excerpts out loud in order to determine where to put the punctuation for comma-splices, run-ons, and fragments. Put the excerpts back into college writing by making all changes directly in the sentences as if you were editing a paper. If an excerpt does not need to be changed, put a check (√) next to its number. Look only for comma-splices, run-ons, and fragments, using the guidelines given on pages 103-106. Do not edit for anything else. (See page 2 for how to use the "Answer" Section.)

Example
We had been together many times, always the shadow of Tunilo kept us apart. (113)

[edit mark: ";but" inserted replacing the comma]

1. There is a difference, though, between Norman and myself in that I think he still imagines that he has something to save, whereas I have never had anything to lose. Or, perhaps, I ought to put it another way, the thing that most white people imagine that they can salvage from the storm of life is really, in sum, their innocence, it was this commodity precisely which I had to get rid of at once, literally, on pain of death. (10a)

2. This speech gave tone and direction to the rest of the conversation. Whether the fear of losing the round-shouldered farmer operated to bring about the result or not is immaterial to this narrative; but, at all events, the crowd decided to lynch the Negro they agreed that this was the least that could be done to avenge the death of their murdered friend, and that it was a becoming way in which to honor his memory they had some vague notions of the majesty of the law and the rights of the citizen, in the passion of the moment these sunk into oblivion, a white man had been killed by a Negro. (28)

3. The Master swept the ground and made the plot smooth. The turkey went to the middle of the plot and shook himself, white corn came down. His

master swept another little plot clear. The turkey went to the middle of this and shook himself, yellow corn came down. A third place was cleared in the same manner. The turkey went to the center of it and shook again, this time blue corn fell. The fourth time that a plot was cleared and the turkey shook himself, corn of different colors, blue, white, and red mixed fell Tobacco fell also. (106)

4. His conduct in public is controlled to fit the occasion. At social affairs, such as cocktails or dinner parties, he is urbane, smiling, talkative (but not too much so), he carries conversation well and listens, or pretends to, when other persons of importance are speaking. He cultivates foreign contacts at interracial or international affairs, he is not obvious about it. (117)

5. "I will be as harsh as truth, and as uncompromising as justice. On this subject [slavery] I do not wish to think, to speak, or write, with moderation. No! No! Tell a man whose house is on fire to give a moderate alarm, tell him to moderately rescue his wife from the hands of the ravisher, tell the mother to gradually extricate her babe from the fire into which it has fallen, urge me not to use moderation in a cause like the present! I am in earnest, I will not equivocate, I will not excuse, I will not retreat a single inch, I WILL BE HEARD." (16)

6. Our popular music has the sensual monotony of all tropical music and it sounds similar, in the plenas, to Puerto Rican everyday speech. We are sentimental, the senses and the emotions command our spirit. Our hospitality sometimes reaches indiscretion. Having learned empirically though the ages, we lean toward the fatalistic. Our nervous and sensitive temperament makes us undecided and mistrustful, we display a free and bantering mirth which is contradicted by the mute nostalgia in our eyes. We ripen early, as tropical fruits do, and soon turn

lifeless, as does the orgy of colors in our twilight. In love and face to face with death we keep acting like Spaniards, we go through everyday life with the Negro's tenderness and the parsimony of the Castilian. (131)

C. Yes, you can start a sentence with "and"

Note the following sentences. All are acceptable in college writing. But they begin with words that some people consider "illegal" as sentence starters. As in the previous sentence, you CAN start a sentence with "but." You can also start one with "and," "when," "if," or ANY OTHER WORD YOU WANT.

> And I walk up and down, up and down, glad to be alone.
> (James Baldwin, "This Morning, This Evening, So Soon") (12)

> [2] When I came back, Harriet thought that the change in me was due to my grief—I was very silent, very thin. But it had not been my mother's death that accounted for the change.
> (James Baldwin, "This Morning, This Evening, So Soon") (12)

> [2] If we learned anything from having a black man in charge of this country's major urban bureaucracy, it was that patterns are not easily altered in urban areas.
> (Joyce Ladner and Walter W. Stafford, "Black Repression in the Cities") (75)

D. "It is" can be a noun-verb pair
"Which is" introduces a fragment
The many uses of "that is"

As has been stressed on page 19, "which" and "who" are words that can make fragments. However, "it" and "he" are NOT words that can make fragments: they are NOT included in the list on page 19. Therefore the following is a fragment:

> Which is not to be believed.

And the following is a whole thought:

> It is not to be believed.

Pronouns in the noun-verb pairs (pronoun-verb pairs)

In short, the following pronouns act the same way a noun does in a noun-verb pair.

ONE PERSON OR THING	MORE THAN ONE PERSON OR THING
I	we
you	you
he, she, it	they
this, that	

Also, the following words are ALREADY PRONOUN-VERB PAIRS because the verb is attached to the pronoun:

ONE PERSON OR THING	MORE THAN ONE PERSON OR THING
I'm (I am)	we're (we are)
you're (you are)	you're (you are)
he's, she's, it's, that's (he is, she is, it is, that is)	they're (they are)[3]

---
[2] Make sure, however, that when a fragment begins a sentence, a whole thought ends it.
[3] Confusions between "They're," "Their," and "There" are covered on page 19.

So all of the following sentences are whole thoughts:

<pre>
pn   v
He is a good friend

pn-v
He's a good friend.

pn   v
It is warm down there.

pn-v
It's warm down there.

pn   v
That is a lie.

pn-v
That's a lie.

pn   v
They are voting now.

pn-v
They're voting now.
</pre>

CHART 16. The Difference Between "Which Is" and "It Is"

Whole Thought	Fragment		Whole Thought	Whole Thought
a. He will have new standards	, which will help him.		He has a new standard •	It is a good one.

(or)

It's a good one.

Whole Thought Plus a Fragment

Rather, the man is himself in sore need of new standards, <u>which will release him from his confusion and place him once again in fruitful communion with the depths of his own being.</u>
(James Baldwin, *The Fire Next Time*) (8)

Two Whole Thoughts

Individuality is not nourished in prison, neither by the officials nor by the convicts. It is a deep hole out of which to climb.
(Eldridge Cleaver, *Soul on Ice*) (32)

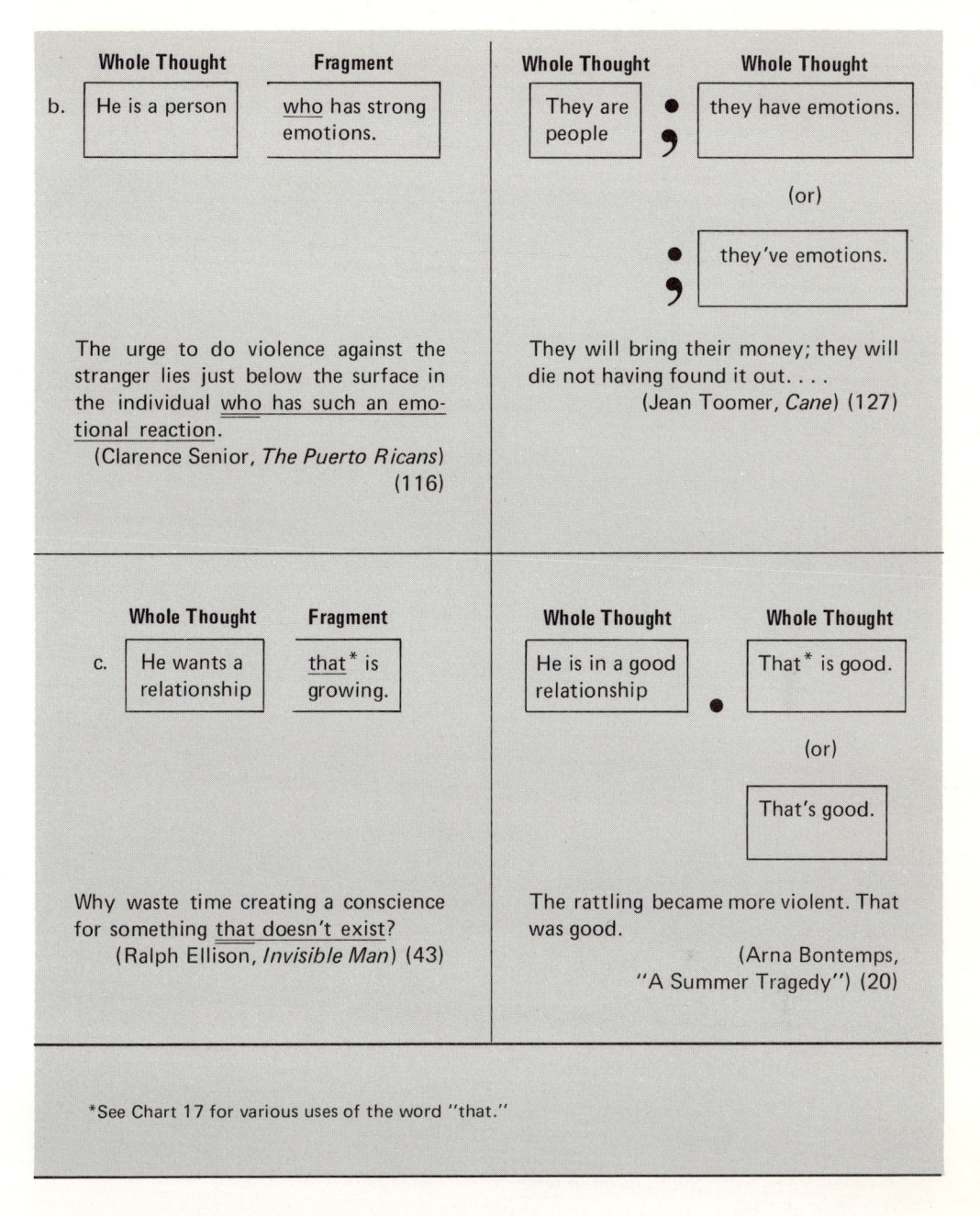

Comma-splice and Run-on Sentences 113

b.

Whole Thought	Fragment
He is a person	<u>who</u> has strong emotions.

Whole Thought		Whole Thought
They are people	● **,**	they have emotions.

(or)

● **,**	they've emotions.

The urge to do violence against the stranger lies just below the surface in the individual <u>who has such an emotional reaction</u>.
(Clarence Senior, *The Puerto Ricans*) (116)

They will bring their money; they will die not having found it out. . . .
(Jean Toomer, *Cane*) (127)

c.

Whole Thought	Fragment
He wants a relationship	<u>that* is growing.</u>

Whole Thought		Whole Thought
He is in a good relationship	●	That* is good.

(or)

That's good.

Why waste time creating a conscience for something <u>that doesn't exist</u>?
(Ralph Ellison, *Invisible Man*) (43)

The rattling became more violent. That was good.
(Arna Bontemps, "A Summer Tragedy") (20)

*See Chart 17 for various uses of the word "that."

"That" is a special word with many uses

Study the following sentences and how they use the word "that."
The "that" in sentence (a) introduces a whole thought.
The "that" in sentences (b) and (c) is INSIDE a whole thought.
The "that" in sentences (d), (e), and (f) introduces fragments. It is easiest to see the various uses of "that" in action rather than to try and find a "foolproof rule." (The "that" fragments are underlined.)

CHART 17. The Many Uses of "That"

a. [Whole Thought: People love] • [Whole Thought: THAT is good.]

The rattling became more violent. THAT was good.
(Arna Bontemps, "A Summer Tragedy") (20)

b. [Whole Thought: I love THAT book.]

But the silence of the evening, as I wandered home, had nothing to do with THAT storm. . . .
(James Baldwin, *Giovanni's Room*) (9)

c. [Whole Thought: I did not know THAT.]

Nothing ever turns out as one has planned. How many times have you heard THAT said?
(Chester Himes, "Excursion in Paradox") (61)

d. [Whole Thought: I saw the house] [Fragment: THAT Jack built.]

This was the building THAT I loved more than anyplace else in the world.
(Claude Brown, *Manchild in the Promised Land*) (22)

e. [Whole Thought: This country is a place] , [Fragment: THAT is not really free.]

It reminds me that I am voteless because there is a Parliament in this country THAT is vote-controlled.
(Nelson Mandela, "An Outlaw") (84)

f. [Whole Thought: I know] [Fragment: THAT we will win.]

It seems to me THAT one ought to rejoice in the fact of death. . . .
(James Baldwin, *The Fire Next Time*) (8)

3C, D. Exercises: Editing for Comma-splices and Run-ons

Look for comma-splices and run-ons in the following excerpts, changing the punctuation and adding connecting words when necessary in order to put the excerpts back into college writing. Make all changes directly in the sentences as if you were editing a paper. If an excerpt does not need to be changed, put a check (√) next to its number. Look only for comma-splices and run-ons, using the guidelines given on pages 111-114. Do not edit for anything else. (See page 2 for how to use the "Answer" Section.)

Example
The government should act, it must deal firmly with anyone who is found exploiting racial, tribal or religious differences. (98)

1. And the old city of Moscow was burned down. The Russians set fire to it themselves on purpose, because of the French when they went to fight there. (1)

2. But I don't light the torch, I'm not going to let my sins catch me off guard with my torch lit looking for cockroaches under my blanket, cockroaches pop like firecrackers when you mash them. (112)

3. Everyone desires love but also finds it impossible to believe that he deserves it. (11)

4. To get food we must work hard, too. Now, there is a slackness in the nation I can feel it I can smell it I can sense it wherever I go people are beginning to lag behind, this is the wrong spirit. (71)

5. Then they took the title unjustly, I'm supposed to be selling shoe strings and walking around somewhere broke, I surprised them, I'm doing better. (18)

6. Gudatrigakwitl thought: "When something is alive like a plant, it will not die, it will come up again from the roots and grow again and again. So it will be with men, and animals, and everything alive. . . ." (74)

7. After all, experience is development; and development is destruction. The great Indian thinkers had this figured out centuries ago, that is why, in the Hindu religion, the god Siva appears—Siva, the god of destruction. (120)

8. And these nights were being acted out under a foreign sky, with no one to watch, no penalties attached, it was this last fact which was our undoing, for nothing is more unbearable, once one has it, than freedom. (9)

9. This was the building that I loved more than anyplace else in the world. The thought that I would never see this building again scared the hell out of me. (22)

10. When the first slaves were brought to this country, there was no idea at all of converting them. Africans were thought of as beasts, there was certainly no idea held among the whites that, somehow, these beasts would benefit by exposure to the Christian God. (68)

11. The Negro theater artist is, therefore, going to have to reckon with the fact that he can get a job in the theater if there is one to be gotten, there are fewer and fewer shows being produced. The Broadway theater has become not only a middle-class one. (91)

12. They may love or hate or admire or fear or envy this country they see it, in any case, from another point of view, this forces the writer to reconsider many

things he had always taken for granted, This reassessment, which can be very painful, is also very valuable. (10b)

13. I knew I had been working too hard, I had been warned. But I have always worked too hard, I came offstage at the end of the second act. I felt hot and I was having trouble catching my breath. But I knew that I was tired, I went to my dressing room and poured myself a drink and put my feet up, then I felt better. (11)

14. Nothing ever goes right, nothing ever turns out as one has planned. How many times have you heard that said? How many times have you said it? And yet, it is never an expression of cynicism, defeatism or nihilism, it is always a confession of faith. (61)

15. Then one day a strange thing happened, it was spring and for some reason I had been hot and irritable all morning, it was a beautiful spring. I could feel it as I played barefoot in the backyard. Blossoms hung from the thorny black locust trees like clusters of fragrant white grapes, butterflies flickered in the sunlight above the short new dew-wet grass. (42)

16. And as for the dirt of their carriages, as many as twenty or thirty loads can be brought into the passenger compartment, but in Europe this is not allowed, for there is a luggage van as well as a passenger compartment, in Russia they take on loads at every place and they spit in the compartment, it is very dirty, so much so that one cannot eat when traveling with them. (1)

E. "However" and "therefore": the logical words

"However" and the semicolon are not married to each other!

It is commonly assumed that one must always put a semicolon before "however" or "therefore." Sometimes writers do this to separate two whole thoughts.

a. The government pours lots of money into medical plans; however, people still cannot afford proper services.

b. We only live a short amount of time; therefore, we should try to get as much out of each day as we can.

But words like "however" and "therefore" often do not come at the place for attaching two whole thoughts. They can appear ANYWHERE in the sentence.

a. I do not think so, but it may be. One thing, <u>however</u>, I am certain is *not* false, and that is simply the fact of his being a writer, and the incalculable potential he as a writer contains.
(James Baldwin, "The Black Boy Looks at the White Boy") (10a)

b. There was conflict, <u>however</u>, in the minds of some revolutionary African leaders who wished not to discard the glories of their people's troubled past yet longed to move ahead into a new generation of black men on the rise.
(Nathan Hare, "Algiers 1969") (57)

A semicolon can separate whole thoughts from each other.

"However" and "therefore" can appear ANYWHERE in a sentence (as above) or not at all.

The worker must work for the glory of his handiwork, not simply for pay; the thinker must think for truth, not for fame.
(W. E. B. Dubois, *The Souls of Black Folk*) (40)

Usually, these words are followed by a comma; often, when they come in the middle of a whole thought, they are surrounded by a comma on each side. You must use your ear to tell when "however" or "therefore" should be surrounded by two commas.

How to use and not use the logical words

The logical words are not connecting words. They do <u>not</u> connect two whole thoughts. They can connect <u>ideas</u>, but they cannot be used to <u>attach</u> ideas together as the seven connecting words can (see page 93). "However" and "therefore" belong to a list of words (Chart 18) that are often mistaken for words that can connect two whole thoughts, words like "and" and "but" (which are listed on page 93). There is no practical reason why "and" can connect two whole thoughts and "therefore" cannot. As has been stressed before, the "rules of college writing" do not always make sense.

COMMA-SPLICE

I had begun to sweat, however, I was very cold.

EDITED

I had begun to sweat; however, I was very cold.

or

I had begun to sweat and I was very cold.
(James Baldwin, *Tell Me How Long The Train's Been Gone*) (11)

The logical words are NOT words that can make whole thoughts into fragments.

"However" and "therefore" do not introduce fragments. Therefore, you do not attach a group of words introduced by "therefore" to a whole thought in the way you would a fragment. (See page 22.)

In short, the logical words are in a category all by themselves and must be treated differently from the other kinds of words covered in Chapters 2 and 3.

The logical words are very useful in carrying on an argument or in describing a sequence of events in a logical order. They are also helpful in linking large units of thoughts (such as paragraphs) to each other so that your entire essay hangs together. (See page 22.)

As the following sentences illustrate, the words can come anywhere in a sentence, but they most often come first. They have nothing whatsoever to do with the punctuation when attaching two whole thoughts to each other; they can be left out and the sentence and punctuation will not become "faulty." However, authors include them in their sentences to provide smoother transitions from one idea to the next.

> It provides for smaller classroom situations and two teachers instead of one to deal with these problems. <u>However</u>, the overwhelming number of problems facing the black children are those inherent in their blackness, or those directly related to their blackness.
>
> (Jim Haskins, *Diary of a Harlem Schoolteacher*) (58)

His streets are the last to be swept. His building codes are the last to be enforced. His police protection is perfunctory. <u>In short</u>, living in a ghetto makes it brutally plain how little the rest of society values the black man.

(Richard G. Hatcher, "The Black City Crisis") (59)

CHART 18. The List of Logical Words

The logical words are listed according to their meanings, so that you can use them in your essays.

Function in Sentence	Shows Result	Shows Contrast	Makes an Addition	
	accordingly	however*	also	first
	consequently	in contrast	furthermore	second, etc.
	hence	nevertheless	in addition	secondly, etc.
	therefore	on the other hand	likewise	lastly
	thus	still	moreover	finally
				next

Function in Sentence	Shows Similarity	Gives a Time Sequence	Gives an Illustration or Elaboration
	likewise	afterward	for example
	similarly	later	for instance
		meanwhile	indeed
		next	in fact
		soon	in other words
		then	similarly

Function in Sentence	Introduces a Summary
	in brief
	in short
	in sum
	to summarize

*"However" can also be used as a word that introduces a fragment, and the two uses are often confusing. When "however" introduces a fragment, it acts like a descriptive word meaning "no matter how." Notice the following sentence: "However ruined the car may look, it still runs." Here the word "however" describes "ruined." It really says, "No matter how ruined...." Watch that you do not treat this kind of "however" the same way as you treat the "however" that acts like a logical word. If you put a period between "look" and "it" in the above sentence, you will have a fragment because of this special use of the word "however."

Finally, in editing your essay for comma-splices and run-ons be careful to notice the logical words. Nine times out of ten, a logical word DOES introduce a new whole thought. Check out the sentence to see if it is a whole thought, and punctuate accordingly.

122 *The Whole Sentence*

F. Summary of punctuation to attach two whole thoughts to each other

---

CHART 19. Summary of Punctuation to Attach Two Whole Thoughts to Each Other

---

1. Use a comma <u>plus</u> a connecting word.

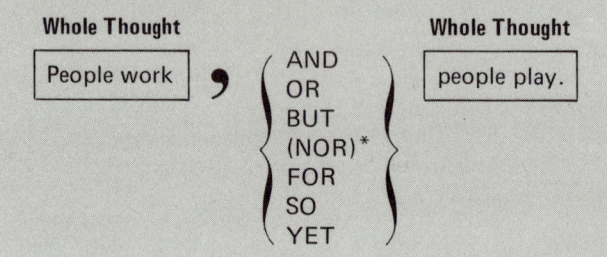

   Whole Thought | Whole Thought
   [People work] , { AND / OR / BUT / (NOR)* / FOR / SO / YET } [people play.]

2. Use a connecting word without the comma.

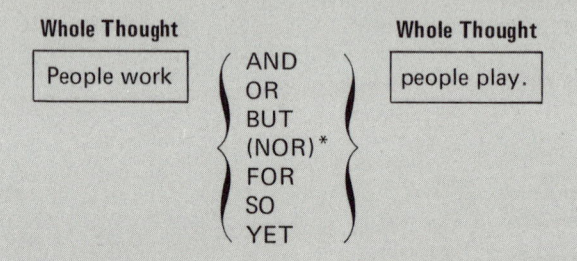

   Whole Thought | Whole Thought
   [People work] { AND / OR / BUT / (NOR)* / FOR / SO / YET } [people play.]

3. Use a semicolon (;).

   Whole Thought | Whole Thought
   [People work] ; [people play.]

4. Use a semicolon <u>plus</u> a logical word.

   Whole Thought | Whole Thought
   [People work] ; [<u>however</u>, people also play.]

   Whole Thought | Whole Thought
   [People work] ; [people also play, <u>however</u>.]

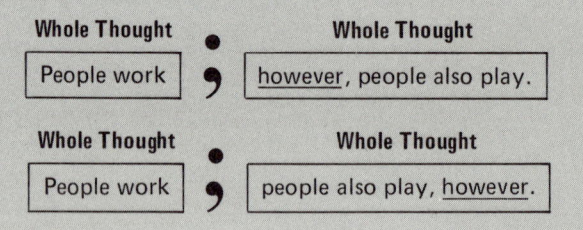

*"Nor" is often used with an extra verb: "Charles hardly laughs now, nor <u>does</u> he sing."

5. Use a period and a capital letter.

        Whole Thought   **Whole Thought**

        | People work | ● | People play. |

DO NOT USE:

Two Whole Thoughts Without Punctuation Between Them

    People work_∧[;] people play.

Merely a Comma Between Two Whole Thoughts

    People work,_∧^{and} people play.

Merely a Logical Word Between Two Whole Thoughts

    People work_∧[;] however, they also play.

Merely a Comma Plus a Logical Word Between Two Whole Thoughts

    People work,_∧[;] however, they also play.

3E, F. Exercises: Editing for Comma-splices, Run-ons, and Fragments

Look for comma-splices, run-ons, and fragments in the following excerpts and change the punctuation, watching especially for the various uses of the logical words, in order to put the excerpts back into college writing. Make all changes directly in the sentences as if you were editing a paper. If an excerpts does not need to be changed, put a check (√) next to its number. Look only for comma-splices, run-ons, and fragments using the guidelines given on pages 17-123. Do not edit for anything else. (See page 2 for how to use the "Answer" Section.)

1. Waiyaki was often surprised at his father, who in some ways seemed to defy age. His voice; however, thin and tremulous, betrayed him. (99)

2. The dance finished and she went to someone else, then Mollie took Lee for a dance and they did her special crawl. Between laughs she said: "Everybody is for you, dear." (62)

3. Before the soreness of the cotton fields had left Mama's back, her knees were getting sore from scrubbing "Goldberg's" floor, nevertheless, she was better off; she had gone from the fire into the frying pan. (22)

4. This respectable ghetto does not even have the advantages of the disreputable one—friends, neighbors, a familiar church, and friendly tradesmen; and it is not; moreover, in the nature of any ghetto to remain respectable long. (10c)

5. The guerrilla fighter, as we have said, is a soldier who carries his house on his back like a snail, therefore, he must arrange his knapsack in such a way that the smallest quantity of utensils will render the greatest possible service. (54)

6. In the Federation of Mali; however, the important thing is that there is

no leader-state, but complete solidarity among the member states, in other words, the only leadership belongs to the Federation, to the general interest. (115)

7. Every republic in Black Africa can take its independence whenever it deems the moment opportune, nevertheless, the sequels of colonialism remain and we must absorb and transcend them. As for our West African civilization; however, charred it may be by the fire of conquest, it is now becoming verdant once again in the springtime of a new era, even before the first shower of Independence. (115)

8. However great the private disasters to which love may lead, love itself is strikingly and mysteriously impersonal, it is a reality which is not altered by anything one does, therefore, one does many things, turns the key in the lock over and over again, hoping to be locked out. (11)

9. The Obong of Calabar; however, though popularly crowned with pomp and splendor a few years ago, does not appear to have any special recognition in his person or office. There is no objection; however, to his being elected by other traditional leaders. (4)

10. I will tell your Worship why: the real purpose of this rigid color bar is to ensure that the justice dispensed by the Courts should conform to the policy of the country; however much that policy might be in conflict with the norms of justice accepted in judiciaries throughout the civilized world. (84)

11. Art can not apologize out of existence the philosophical ethical position of the artist, after all, the artist is a man in society, and his social attitudes are just as relevant to his art as his aesthetic position, however, the white Western

aesthetics is predicated on the idea of separating one from the other—a man's art from his actions. It is this duality that is the most distinguishable feature of Western values. (120)

12. In South Africa complaints are neither freely heard nor deeply considered, let alone speedily reformed, there is nothing to persuade us that Dr. Verwoerd's government is going to change in the near future, however, since it is obvious that this mad and savage traffic in slave labor has to be stopped, and since it is palpably obvious how white power works in the world today, it takes a superhuman exercise of will not to work and hope for a world where power is in the hands of black people. (102)

13. At first there were no trees nor rivers and no people on the earth. Nothing except ground was visible. There was no ocean, then Gudatrigakwitl was sorry that it was so. He thought, "How is it that there are no animals?" He looked, but he saw nothing, then he deliberated. He thought, "I will try. Somebody will live on the earth. But what will he use?" then he decided to make a boat for him. He made things by joining his hands and spreading them. He used no tools. In this way he made people. The first man was *wat*, the abalone. The first people were not right, they all died. Gudatrigakwitl thought that they were bad. He wanted good people who would have children. At first he wanted every man to have ten lives. When he was an old man he was to become a boy again, afterwards Gudatrigakwilt found that he could not do this. He gave the people all the game, the fish, and the trees....

Gudatrigakwitl used no sand or earth or sticks to make the people, he merely thought and they existed. (74)

G. Choppy sentences can result from being too careful

Sometimes students tend to get too careful about fragments and run-ons and end up writing a string of small "safe" sentences. This attitude can ruin your style. To prevent your readers from getting bored and to convince your readers of the truth of your ideas, your essay needs variety: a mixture of long and small sentences. A string of small sentences tends to make your work sound like a first grade reader, and your essay usually sounds more together when it doesn't have a lot of breaks. It needs sentences with more than one whole thought; it needs sentences attached to fragments; it also needs several small sentences, each with a short and forceful punch.

Note the following paragraph, beautiful but choppy:

> Monsona Quintana is an emaciated country woman. She lives in my land. She has given birth seventeen times. Her belly is stretched. Her husband can no longer tell when she is pregnant. Childbearing has devoured the youth of this country girl. She once had the color of camádula seeds. She once had breasts of a sleepy turtledove.

Here is how Emilio Belaval, the author of the paragraph, has combined his ideas to make smooth, varied, and vivid prose.

> Monsona Quintana is an emaciated country woman of my land who has given birth seventeen times; her belly is so stretched that her husband can no longer tell when she is pregnant. Childbearing has devoured the youth of this country girl who once had the color of camádula seeds and breasts of a sleepy turtledove.
> (Emilio Belaval, "El Niño Morando de Monsona Quintana") (14)

H. Editing for comma-splices and run-ons can lead to fragments

Sometimes students worry so much about comma-splices and run-ons that they put semicolons and periods all over the place and find themselves with a bunch of fragments. If this is happening to you, don't worry—you are not alone. Practice looking for comma-splices and run-ons during your first editing and then look for fragments when you edit again. With practice, the two kinds of "problems" become easier to spot. The main point to remember is that you should always write freely without worrying about any rules. Put your work into college writing using several careful editing sessions—AFTER YOU HAVE RUN OUT OF THINGS TO SAY.

For practice, what would you do with the following sentence?

> Nobody but us is going to worry about our people and whether they live or die—especially not people who live a million miles away and go home to clean, lily-white communities where they don't know what it is to sit hours in hot, dirty rooms waiting to be treated.
> (Young Lords Party, Health Ministry, "Lincoln Hospital Must Serve the People!") (145)

If you changed anything in this sentence, if you put different punctuation marks between "die" and "especially," between "communities" and "where" and between "rooms" and "waiting," then you are forgetting what you know about fragments. The sentence needs no changes in punctuation.

WHOLE THOUGHT

Nobody but us is going to worry about our people

ADDED FRAGMENT

(See page 19)

and <u>whether</u> they live or die—

ADDED FRAGMENT

("the man <u>who</u>" fragment, see page 29)

especially not <u>people who</u> live a million miles away and go home to clean, lily-white communities

ADDED FRAGMENT

(See page 19)

<u>where</u> they don't know

ADDED FRAGMENT

(See page 19)

<u>what</u> it is to sit hours in hot, dirty rooms

ADDED FRAGMENT

("<u>Breaking</u> through" fragment, see page 49)

<u>waiting</u> to be treated.

Cumulative Editing for Comma-splices, Run-ons, and Fragments in Chapter 3

Look for comma-splices, run-ons, and fragments in the following excerpts and change punctuation (watch out that you do not end up with fragments!) in order to put the excerpts back into college writing. Make all changes directly in the sentences as if you were editing a paper. If an excerpt does not need to be changed, put a check (√) next to its number. Look only for comma-splices, run-ons, and fragments, using the guidelines given on pages 17-130. Do not edit for anything else. (See page 2 for how to use the "Answer" Section.)

1. I had to curb my habit of cursing: but not before I had shocked more than half of them and had embarrassed Aunt Addie to helplessness. (137)

2. Life is tragic simply because the earth turns and the sun inexorably rises and sets, and one day, for each of us, the sun will go down for the last, last time. (8)

3. For this reason it is the responsibility of the mother and father, and even more the responsibility of the maternal uncle; to supervise the life of the young man so that he may be a lover of work with his hands while he has not departed to the village of another group. In marriage. (29)

4. Early in September, after having Paris largely to themselves during August; the tourists went home. The new Negro expatriates cast about with increasing desperation. Summer was over and so was the first flush of Paris, they had to be set for winter; somewhere; somehow. (136)

5. He felt the weight of his ignorance. Not simply of letters, but of life, of business, of the humanities, the accumulated sloth and shirking and awkwardness of decades and centuries shackled his hands and feet. (40)

6. But Miss Dietrich had not said make it like any other spring-people-breeze ever seen before. She let it remain Nancy Lee's own, that is how the old Negro woman happened to be there looking at the flag, in her mind the flag, the spring and the woman formed a kind of triangle holding a dream Nancy Lee wanted to express. (63)

7. The economic panic brought on by the 1929 Crash also caused cultural panic among the white intellectuals, from the point of view of their own class and creative status, they saw in these events the beginning of the terrible disintegration of Western civilization. Where was American culture going as a result of all this? (33)

8. It worked as I had planned. When I broke the news of my leaving two days before I left—I was afraid to tell it sooner for fear that I would create hostility on the part of the whites with whom I worked—the boss leaned back in his swivel chair and gave me the longest and most considerate look he had ever given me. (137)

9. When the Negro masses acquired the right to vote in northern cities. They continued for a while to give their support to the Republican Party. Chiefly on sentimental grounds. Though there were some good reasons for their sentimental attachment to the Republican Party. The Republican Party was the party of Lincoln, it was the party which had given them their freedom. (49)

10. Jim and Cora went together for four months. And they had an awful time of it. But they were unhappy apart. Yet when they were together their eyes were always accusing each other. Sometimes they seemed to enjoy hurting each other. Jim wouldn't call her up; and he'd be miserable. She wouldn't write to him

or would stand him up on a date for Chuck Nelson or Fred Schultz, then she'd be miserable. Something held them apart. And something pulled them together. (93)

11. Instead of going to school, we would go all over the city stealing, sneak into a movie, or go up on a roof and throw bottles down into the street. Danny suggested that we start the day off by waiting for Mr. Gordon to put out his vegetables, we could steal some sweet potatoes and cook them in the backyard. I was sorry I hadn't started school sooner; because hookey sure was a lot of fun. (22)

12. It is certainly sad; that the awakening of one's senses should lead to such a merciless judgment of oneself—to say nothing of the effort to arrive at any other—but it is also inevitable that a literal attempt to mortify the flesh should be made among black people. Like those with whom I grew up. (8)

13. So, they came, from all parts of the South. Like all the black chillun o' God following the sound of Gabriel's horn on that long-overdue Judgment Day. The Georgians came as soon as they were able to pick train fare off the peach trees, they came from South Carolina where the cotton stalks were bare. The North Carolinians came with tobacco tar beneath their fingernails. (22)

14. Black culture implies, indeed engenders, for the black artist another order. Another way of looking at things. It is apparent in the music of Giuseppe Logan, for example; that the references are not white or European. But it is jazz and it is firmly rooted in the experiences of black individuals in this country, these references are found also in the work of John Coltrane. Ornette Coleman. Grachan Moncur and Milford Graves. (120)

15. Reluctantly, one comes to the conclusion that white people as a group, after all it is white people as a group who matter. Are prepared to respect the rights of black people only when they have the same power that white people have. And, further, when they are able to exercise it as dangerously as white people do. My natural inclinations resist this kind of conclusion, all the facts available repeatedly and inexorably bring me to this conclusion. (102)

16. He understands that he cannot possibly exist in the future. Or even in the present. For instance with the idea of art, what is done now, in the present, or with presage of some stronger future is always treated shabbily by mainstream white society. For one reason because it makes reference to living humanity, which is always threatening to what is "established." The white man worships the artifact, his museums are full of dead things, artifacts; which at best, can only make reference to life. (67)

17. We have not destroyed anything, nor will we allow ourselves or our people to be destroyed. It has been said that "the urge to destroy is really a creative urge." Well, we are not the "useful idiot" type, nor do we suffer from "Icarus Complexes." We are firm in our resolve that we are innocent of any wrong doing and that our pleas should not go unanswered by the masses. Peace! power through unity! (126)

18. Granny Judith said that in Africa they had very few pretty things, and that they had no red colors in cloth, in fact, they had no cloth at all. Some strangers with pale faces come one day and dropped a small piece of red flannel down on the ground. All the black folks grabbed for it, then a larger piece was dropped a little further on, and on until the river was reached, then a large piece was dropped in the river and on the other side. . . . Finally, when the ship was reached, they dropped large pieces on the plank and up into the ship till they got as many blacks on board as they wanted, then the gate was chained up and they could not get back. (78)

19. I was very familiar with the Eldridge who came to prison, that Eldridge no longer exists. And the one I am now is in some ways a stranger to me. You may find this difficult to understand but it is very easy for one in prison to lose his sense of self. And if he has been undergoing all kinds of extreme, involved, and unregulated changes; then he ends up not knowing who he is. Take the point of being attractive to women, you can easily see how a man can lose his arrogance or certainty on that point while in prison! When he's in the free world, he gets constant feedback on how he looks from the number of female heads he turns when he walks down the street. In prison he gets only hatestares. And sour frowns. (32)

20. Back then the going thing was what the white man had told them: to turn the other cheek and appeal to the conscience of the white oppressor. I knew that you couldn't do that, you can't appeal to the conscience of a beast, when you're dealing with savages and brutes and tyrants. So this is one major thing that I see. And it is a change that has influenced the black bourgeoisie and the power structure; though the power structure lately has become even more repressive. But in some ways the fact; that the black man was no longer passive and would fight caused the power structure to give more attention to the black man. (19)

21. If they take much longer to come out; I may go to sleep and then there won't be any way to kill them and Godmother won't be able to sleep at all if she hears them singing she'll get very angry. And then she'll ask one of those string of saints she has in her room to send the devils after me; to take me off to eternal damnation; right now. Without even passing through Purgatory, and then I won't be able to see my papa or mamma. Because that's where they are, I just better keep on talking—What I would really like to do is take a few swallows of Felipa's milk; that good milk as sweet as honey that comes from under the hibiscus flowers— (112)

22. It is one of the facts of life that there are two sexes; which fact has given the world most of its beauty, cost it not a little of its anguish, and contains the hope and glory of the world. And it is with this fact, which might better perhaps be called a mystery, that every human being born must find some way to live. For, no matter what demons drive them, men cannot live without women and women cannot live without men. And this is what is most clearly conveyed in the agony of Gide's last journal, however little he was able to understand it, or, more important perhaps, take upon himself the responsibility for it, Madeleine kept open for him a kind of door of hope. Of possibility. The possibility of entering into communion with another sex. This door, which is the door to life and air and freedom from the tyranny of one's own personality, *must* be kept open, none feel this more keenly than those on whom the door is perpetually threatening or has already seemed to close. (10d)

23. Later that day I rummaged through drawers and found Granny's address, I wrote to her. Pleading with her to come and help us. The neighbors nursed my mother day and night. Fed us and washed our clothes. I went through the days with a stunned consciousness. Unable to believe what had happened. Sup-

pose Granny did not come? I tried not to think of it, she had to come. The utter loneliness was now terrifying, I had been suddenly thrown emotionally upon my own. Within an hour the half-friendly world that I had known had turned cold and hostile, I was too frightened to weep. I was glad that my mother was not dead, but there was the fact that she would be sick for a long, long time. Perhaps for the balance of her life. I became morose. Though I was a child, I could no longer feel as a child. Could no longer react as a child. The desire for play was gone and I brooded. Wondering if Granny would come and help us. I tried not to think of a tomorrow that was neither real nor wanted, for all tomorrows held questions that I could not answer. (137)

SECTION TWO

The Ends of Words

Section One focuses on the large group of words; Section Two focuses on the individual word. And again you are strongly urged not to look at each individual word as you write. After you have written several essays, you will have a fairly good idea what kinds of things you need to look for in your own essays when editing. So, for example, if you know that you tend to confuse the various uses of **S**, one of your editing sessions should be devoted to checking the ends of words to see if you need **S** or **'S**. After a while, such painful editing will not be necessary because you will automatically begin to put the "appropriate" **S** in as you write. Then the only time you will really have to watch out for verb endings and various uses of the **S** will probably be when you are extremely nervous or tired—times when all the old "habits" tend to come back (i.e., at three in the morning when a paper is due the next day, or during an important examination). Then a very careful editing session in which you look for those things you know you have trouble with will be useful.

Above all, be aware that spelling something "right" in college writing IS NEVER as important as getting across your ideas so that others will understand you and learn from you. However, it is important to know the little "rules" of spelling in college-writing so that you have the power, the choice, to implement these skills when necessary.

Finally, before actually studying any of these chapters, it might be useful to check and see if you do indeed pronounce the ends of words but forget to include the sounds when you spell the words out. If you tend to do this, your voice might be your safest guide: make sure your writing includes all the sounds you say when you read out loud.

4 Spelling the Verb

A. Definition of a verb

The verb is one of the more difficult kinds of words in the English language mainly because its various spellings are important in telling the reader subtle shades of meaning—i.e., when an action happened and whether it took a long or short time to happen.

A verb is a word that expresses action

John wrote a speech.

A verb may express existence—the fact that someone or something is or feels

John is a student.
John feels good.

The spelling of the verb itself tells you whether the action happened in the past, present, or future

John wrote a speech. PAST—BEFORE RIGHT NOW
John writes a speech. PRESENT—RIGHT NOW
John will write a speech. FUTURE—AFTER RIGHT NOW

The spelling of the verb sometimes changes according to who is doing the action or who is feeling

Part B of this chapter covers this topic.

B. When does the S go at the end of a verb? (Noun-verb pair agreement)

In most languages the spelling of the verb changes depending upon the noun-verb or pronoun-verb pair (see page 8). Take classical Latin, for example. Note how the spelling changes for the verb "love" in the PRESENT TIME.

142 *The Ends of Words*

ONE PERSON (SINGULAR)   MORE THAN ONE PERSON (PLURAL)

1. I love   =   am<u>o</u>   4. We love   =   am<u>amus</u>
2. You love   =   am<u>as</u>   5. You love   =   am<u>atis</u>
   He
3. She loves   =   am<u>at</u>   6. They love =   am<u>ant</u>
   It

Here is the verb "speak" in Spanish.

1. I speak   =   habl<u>o</u>   4. We speak   =   habl<u>amos</u>
2. You speak   =   habl<u>as</u>   5. You speak =   habl<u>ais</u>
   He
3. She speaks =   habl<u>a</u>   6. They speak =   habl<u>an</u>
   It

Here is the verb "hear" (as in "I <u>hear</u> music") in Middle English (the language spoken in England between, roughly, 1100 and 1400 A.D.).

1. I hear   =   hèr(e)   4. We hear   =   here<u>s</u>
2. You hear   =   here<u>s</u>   5. You hear   =   here<u>s</u>
   He
3. She   =   here<u>s</u>   6. They hear =   here<u>s</u>
   It

And here is the same verb in modern English. Note that the spelling of the modern English verb "hear" has the letter <u>s</u> at the end of it in only <u>one</u> place. Compare it to Middle English. In Middle English, the letter <u>s</u> is at the end of numbers 2, 3, 4, 5, and 6. In modern English the letter <u>s</u> is at the end of number 3 ONLY.

1. I hear   4. We hear
2. You hear   5. You hear
   He
3. She hear<u>s</u>   6. They hear
   It

WHAT MUST BE RELIGIOUSLY REMEMBERED IS THAT IN <u>PRESENT TIME</u> (RIGHT NOW) THE VERB WITH "he, she, it" ALWAYS ENDS IN <u>S</u> (except for "he may" and "he can").

Note the present form of the verb "eat."

ONE PERSON (SINGULAR)   MORE THAN ONE PERSON (PLURAL)

1. I eat   4. We eat
2. You eat   5. You eat
   He
3. She eat<u>s</u>   6. They eat
   It

Here is the present form of the verb "live".

1. I live
2. You live
3. He
   She lives
   It
4. We live
5. You live
6. They live

In Spanish, when "he," "she," or "it" is doing the action the ending of the present-time verb is usually "a" or "e."

he, she, it, speaks = habla   he, she, it comes = viene
he, she, it lives = vive

But in English, when "he," "she," or "it" is doing the action, the present-time verb ends in **s**.

One person equals "he" or "she"
One thing equals "it"

a. She lives here.

Helen lives here.

b. He lives here.

John lives here.

c. It burns quickly.

The fire burns quickly.

CHART 20. Noun-Verb Pair Agreement*

	Singular Noun-Verb Pair	Plural Noun-Verb Pair

Present Time— Right Now	1. I live
	2. You live
	3. He
	   She
	   It
	   This
	   That
	   Helen
	   The cat
	   Lives
		4. We live
		5. You live
		6. They
		   These
		   Those
		   Helen
		      and Jim
		   The cats
		   Live

*You are not "cheating" if you copy this chart and paste it in your notebook, on your wall, on the palm of your hand, and by the stove. When medical students memorize parts of the body, they even put a chart in the shower stall so they can study it while they wash.

Another way to remember when to put <u>S</u> at the end of a verb

            He'<u>s</u> great!   =   He <u>is</u> great!
            She'<u>s</u> happy! =   She <u>is</u> happy!
            It'<u>s</u> a bird!   =   It <u>is</u> a bird!

Just like in "he's," "she's," and "it's," the letter s goes with the verbs belonging to "he," "she," and "it" and with the verbs belonging to all nouns that can be changed to "he," "she," and "it."

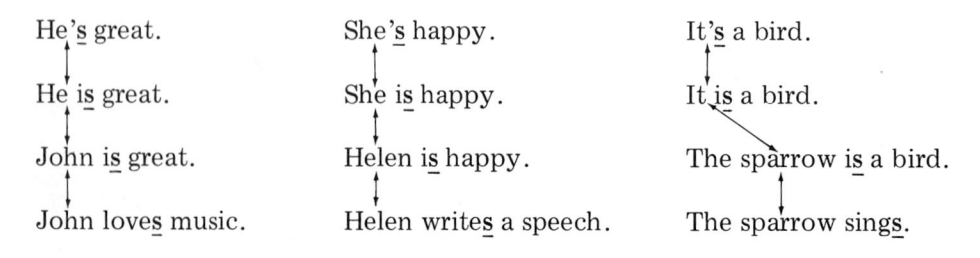

He'<u>s</u> great.   She'<u>s</u> happy.   It'<u>s</u> a bird.

He <u>is</u> great.   She <u>is</u> happy.   It <u>is</u> a bird.

John <u>is</u> great.   Helen <u>is</u> happy.   The sparrow <u>is</u> a bird.

John love<u>s</u> music.   Helen write<u>s</u> a speech.   The sparrow sing<u>s</u>.

Spelling the Verb 145

Notice that the letter s appears in

>
> he's
> she's
> it's

The letter s does NOT appear in the other noun-verb pair combinations outlined in Chart 20:

>
> I'm
> you're
> they're

SINGULAR | PLURAL

1. I'm over here
2. You're over here
3. He's over here
   She's over here
   It's over here

4. We're over here
5. You're over here
6. They're over here

Summary:
a. No s at the end of the verb in the noun-verb pairs numbered 1, 2, 4, 5, 6:

<u>1</u>

I'm over here.
↑
↓
I am over here.
↑
↓
I sing.

<u>2 & 5</u>

You're over here.
↑
↓
You are over here.
↑
↓
You sing.

<u>4</u>

We're over here.
↑
↓
We are over here.
↑
↓
We sing.

<u>6</u>

They're over here.
↑
↓
They are over here.

Many people are over here.

John and Helen are over here.
↑
↓
John and Helen sing.

b. The letter s goes at the end of the verb in the noun-verb pair numbered 3:

He's over here.
↑
↓
He is over here.
↑
↓
John is over here.
↑
↓
John sings.

She's over here.
↕
She is over here.
↕
Helen is over here.
↕
Helen sings.

It's over here.
↕
It is over here.
↘
The bird is over here.
↕
The bird sings.

Spelling the Verb   147

**CHART 21. Noun-Verb Pair Agreement for Those Who Know Some Spanish
Time: Present, Right Now**

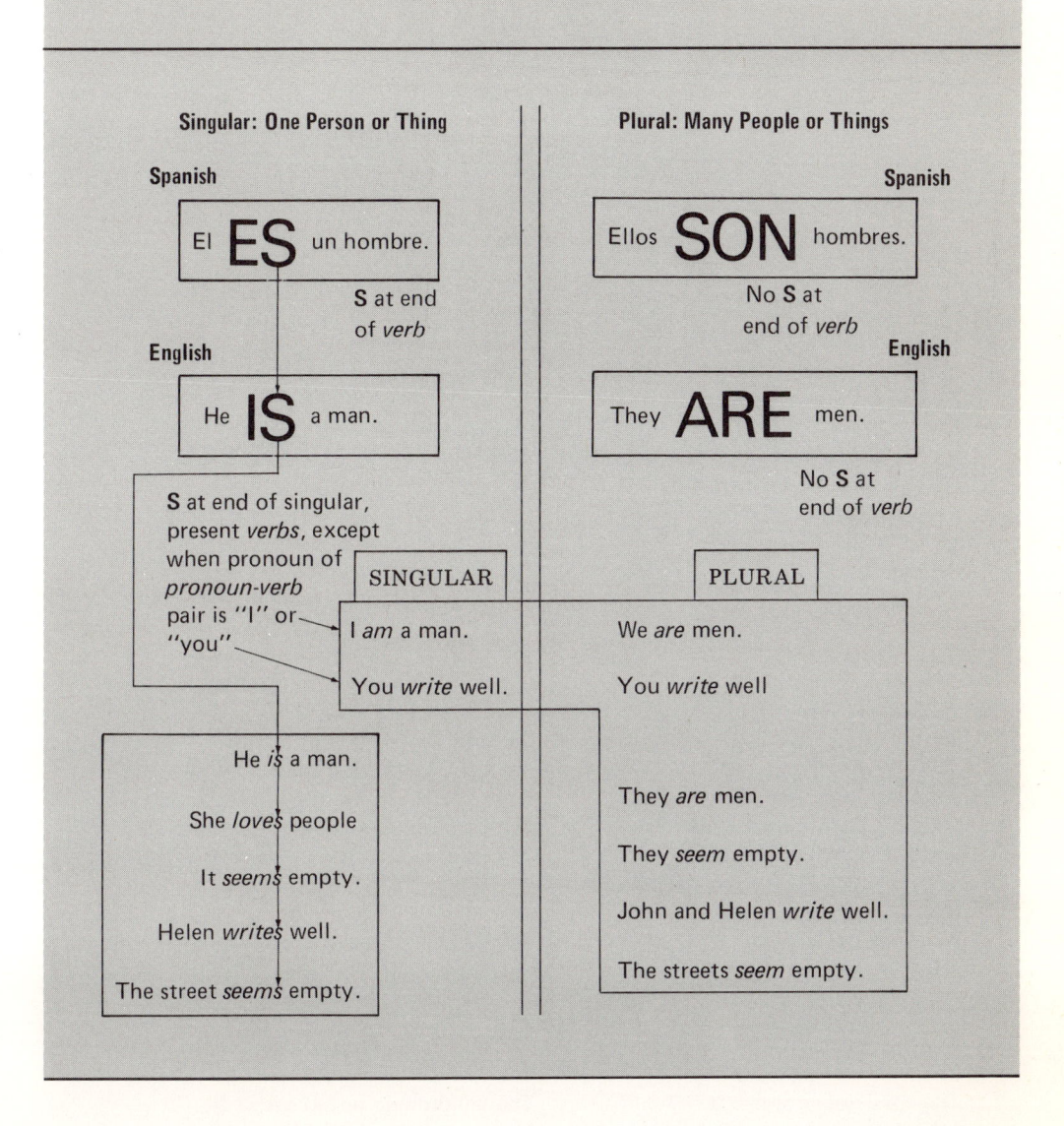

Singular: One Person or Thing

Spanish

El **ES** un hombre.

S at end of *verb*

English

He **IS** a man.

S at end of singular, present *verbs*, except when pronoun of *pronoun-verb* pair is "I" or "you"

SINGULAR

I *am* a man.

You *write* well.

He *is* a man.

She *loves* people

It *seems* empty.

Helen *writes* well.

The street *seems* empty.

Plural: Many People or Things

Spanish

Ellos **SON** hombres.

No S at end of *verb*

English

They **ARE** men.

No S at end of *verb*

PLURAL

We *are* men.

You *write* well

They *are* men.

They *seem* empty.

John and Helen *write* well.

The streets *seem* empty.

CHART 22. Summary of Noun-Verb Agreement
(for complications of agreement, see page 99)

Present Time (Right Now)

Singular	**Plural**
(He, She, It)	(We, You, They)

He make<u>s</u> furniture.	They make furniture.
He doe<u>s</u> it well.	They do it well.
He doe<u>s</u> not like it.	They do not like it.
He doe<u>s</u>n't like it.	They don't like it.
He ha<u>s</u> found the card.	They have found the card.
He ha<u>s</u> not found the card.	They have not found the card.
He ha<u>s</u>n't found the card.	They haven't found the card.

Substitution of a Name   **Substitution of Names**

(One person)   (Many people)

John make<u>s</u> furniture.	John and Helen make furniture.
John doe<u>s</u> it well.	John and Helen do it well.
John doe<u>s</u> not like it.	John and Helen do not like it.
John doe<u>s</u>n't like it.	John and Helen don't like it.
John ha<u>s</u> found the card.	John and Helen have found the card.
John ha<u>s</u> not found the card.	John and Helen have not found the card.
John ha<u>s</u>n't found the card.	John and Helen haven't found the card.

Substitution of a Person   **Substitution of Persons**

(One person)   (Many people)

The man make<u>s</u> furniture.	The men make furniture.
The woman doe<u>s</u> it well.	The women do it well.
The child doe<u>s</u> not like it.	The children do not like it.

       etc.   *etc.*

4B. 1. Exercises

Change all underlined verbs to present time. For the original versions of the excerpts, see the Bibliographic "Answer" Section, page 331.

Example
At home, the mother <u>remain</u>ed alone. (70)
(with an "s" marked above "remained")

1. Men <u>loved</u> war because it <u>allowed</u> them to look serious. (48)

2. The University of Science and Technology in Kumasi <u>was</u> where the pupils <u>specialized</u> in scientific subjects and research. (3)

3. She <u>was</u> about to turn in Broad from Maple Street. White and black men loafing on the corner <u>held</u> no interest for her. Then a strange thing <u>happened</u>. A clean-muscled, magnificent, black-skinned Negro, whom she had heard her father mention as King Barlo, suddenly <u>dropped</u> to his knees on a spot called the Spittoon. (127)

4. Wealth <u>sprang</u> from the diversities of countries and persons, from the fact that they <u>complemented</u> each other. We shall always remember a truth expressed by Father Teilhard de Chardin: Races <u>were</u> not equal but complementary, which <u>was</u> a superior form of equality. (115)

5. The saffron fluid <u>splashed</u> on his face. His smooth black face <u>began</u> to glisten and to shine. Soon, people <u>noticed</u> him, and <u>gathered</u> round. His eyes <u>were</u> rapturous upon the heavens. Lips and nostrils <u>quivered</u>. Barlo <u>was</u> in a religious trance. Town folks <u>knew</u> it. (127)

6. Jerky, aflutter, she <u>closed</u> the store and <u>started</u> home. Folks lazing on store window-sills <u>wondered</u> what on earth <u>could</u> be the matter with Jim Crane's

gal, as she passed them. "Come to remember, she always was a little off, a little crazy, I reckon." Esther sought her own room, and locked the door. Her mind was a pink mesh-bag filled with baby toes. (127)

7. This issue of life-style differences was crucial in education. Consider the traditional lesson of "A Good Diet Consists of the Daily Basic Seven." The white teacher, in speaking of leafy green vegetables, never seemed to have heard of collard greens or turnip greens. When she listed the other basic foods, she overlooked beans and rice and other dishes characteristic of the children's homes. The children began to suspect that something was wrong with their mothers' notion of diet. There was nothing wrong at home, necessarily. But something was wrong at school; the white teacher was talking about a white diet only. (24)

8. The black man was a born poet and some of the hymns the Bantu had composed, both in words and tune, were far more suitable than those imported from Europe. When a black man prayed, he wanted to gesticulate and pray at the top of his voice; he wanted to weep before God, or laugh aloud if the occasion was one of happiness. This nature of the Bantu had enabled him to survive pressures that had driven scores of nations to rebellion and war. (96)

9. The boy explored further. He was not surprised to find a large hole yawning blackly at him on the side of the depression. Well did he know what it was—a goldmine. He had stumbled across one of the numerous mines operated by the Ma-Hi, with Bantu and Bushman slave labor, more than two thousand years ago. The strange round stones, he now realized, were grindstones, which were used to crush the rocks in which the sun metal was contained as fine dust and tiny grains. These, he remembered being told, were washed from the crushed rocks

with water, and then melted and poured into molds in the shapes of little crosses and discs. (96)

10. Listen to Sojourner Truth. She stood on an Indiana platform, braving the taunts of proslavery Northerners. A local doctor rose and said there was some doubt about the sex of the speaker. He asked Sojourner to submit to an inspection by local ladies. The meeting went up in an uproar; there were shouts, screams, coarse laughs. Sojourner looked out into the audience and shouted: "My breasts have suckled many a white babe, even when they should have been suckling my own." She stabbed a bony finger. "Some of those white babes are now grown men, and even though they have suckled my Negro breasts, they are in my opinion far more manly than any of you appear to be." Suddenly, without warning, she ripped open the front of her dress. "I will show my breasts," she said, "to the entire congregation. It's not my shame but yours. Here then, see for yourself." Her eyes locked on the face of the doubting doctor and she said quietly, "Do you wish also to suck?" (16)

11. As another mode of securing a wife, capture or kidnaping was not unknown among the Chewa people. The usual procedure was to waylay the intended bride, along the footpath that led from the village to the stream, well, or garden. The prospective bridegroom always asked one or more of his friends to assist him with the capture. The party hid somewhere along the footpath. In this, the conspirators were aided by a rich and benevolent Nyasaland nature, which erected from the ground a thick shroud of grass to interlace with an equally thick canopy of tree leaves overhead. As the intended victim approached, or came past the spot where they were hiding, the men broke cover and, seizing their prey by the arms and legs, carried her away between them on their shoulders. (146)

12. Of the earth's inhabitants, 50 per cent did not get the minimum of calories physiologically necessary; 25 per cent lacked proteins; 75 per cent were undernourished. In the first group of privileged countries, the mortality rate was 10 per cent and the life expectancy from sixty to seventy years. In the second group, comprising Latin America and a few African and Asian countries, the mortality rate was between 10 and 20 per cent, the life expectancy from forty to sixty years. And finally, in the third group, which included the greater part of Africa and Asia, the mortality rates varied between 25 and 30 per cent with a life expectancy of thirty to thirty-five years—the life expectancy in European countries at the beginning of the nineteenth century. Thus "the geography of hunger was also the geography of death". One was amazed that in this century, when men talked so much about social justice and boasted so lyrically about the progress of universal solidarity, one sixth of the global population, composed primarily of white people, possessed 80 per cent of the total income. This fact alone was eloquent enough and excused us, we think, from multiplying the statistical comparisons that abounded in this area and that stressed the great disparity in the living standards of men on our planet, at the very moment when, paradoxically, science was rushing out to conquer other planets. How had humanity reached such a degree of imbalance? (37)

4B. 2. Exercises

1. Keep a journal for a week or so in which you record all the important events of your day. Write the events in present time so that you have practice putting the <u>s</u> at the end of singular verbs except when the noun of the noun-verb pair is "I" or "you," and except when the verb is "can" or "may."

2. Choose a short story that you like very much and change it into present time. There is no need to rewrite the whole story; merely pencil the present form of the verb right in the text.

3. Write your own short story in present time. Use descriptions of places and people. Describe events, using lots of active words, descriptive words, and dialogue. Review Chapter 1 and the Appendix Section on dialogue if you run into trouble. <u>Make sure that you stay in present time.</u> It is usually wise to write about your own experiences or about events you know quite well.

C. When does "ed" go at the end of a verb?
(For various uses of the verbs in terms of time, see Chapter 8.)

The reason why so many people are confused by English verb endings is simple: Americans often do not pronounce the ends of words very clearly, and some accents tend to lose the sound of word endings altogether. Because a person coming to the United States will usually learn spoken English before he ever really writes English on paper, he is probably not going to HEAR the unpronounced word endings. For example, compare the spelling of the following words with the way they are generally pronounced:

WRITTEN WORDS	PRONOUNCED WORDS
Looking	Lookin_
Hardware store	Har_ware sto_
Grandmother	Gran_mother
And	An_
Ghost	Ghos_
I finished the job.	I finish_ the jo_
He's supposed to do it.	He's suppose_ ta do it.

Because most people spell a word the way they hear it, there should be no mystery about why spelling verb endings becomes a "problem" in writing. However, if this is one of your areas of difficulty, a small amount of strict memorizing and a lot of steady work can make editing for verb endings a fairly easy task; and with patient practice, the task of remembering when to add the "ed" becomes automatic. DO NOT GIVE UP. THIS PROCESS MAY TAKE A LONG TIME. AFTER WRITING YOUR ESSAY, DEVOTE ONE OR MORE EDITING SESSIONS JUST TO VERB ENDINGS.

Guides for forming the simple past time of regular verbs

Memorize the types of spelling methods.
The usual way is to ADD "ED" to the PRESENT FORM OF THE VERB.

PRESENT (NOW)	SIMPLE PAST (BEFORE NOW)
call	callED
drown	drownED
help	helpED
mail	mailED
resist	resistED
sneak	sneakED

If the "E" is already in the PRESENT form, just add "D."

| like | likeD |
| smile | smileD |

If the PRESENT form ends in "Y," change "Y" to "IED."

carry	carrIED
cry	crIED
marry	marrIED
study	studIED

156 *The Ends of Words*

EXCEPTIONS. There are always exceptions!

stay	stayED
play	playED
pay	paID

A few verbs DOUBLE THE FINAL LETTER before adding "ED." You should memorize these.

plan	plaNNED
fit	fiTTED (or fit)
allot	alloTTED
mop	moPPED
wrap	wraPPED

THE MOST IMPORTANT THING TO REMEMBER IS THAT YOU START WITH THE PRESENT FORM OF THE VERB AND CHANGE THAT FORM TO THE SIMPLE PAST FORM.

Guides for forming the simple past time of irregular verbs

There is a whole set of verbs that have no special "rules" for forming the past. These are best memorized according to the categories below. Add your own verbs to the categories as they come up in your writing.

Usually ONE VOWEL (a,e,i,o,u) in the present form of the verb changes to ANOTHER VOWEL in the past form.

PRESENT (NOW)	SIMPLE PAST (BEFORE NOW)
sIt	sAt
rIng	rAng
wrIte	wrOte
cOme	cAme
thrOw	thrEw

Other verbs change TWO VOWELS in the present form to ONE VOWEL in the simple past form.

frEEze	frOze
chOOse	chOse
mEEt	mEt

Some verbs CHANGE COMPLETELY from present to simple past forms. These, especially, need to be memorized.

eat	ate
speak	spoke
see	saw
do	did
go	went
bring	brought
teach	taught
build	built
lie[1]	lay
lay[1]	laid

[1] "lie" and "lay" are discussed on page 195.

Finally, some verbs HAVE THE SAME SPELLING for present and simple past forms.

burst	burst
fit	fit (or fitted)
hit	hit

An excerpt in present and past time

What follows is an excerpt by Ann Petry which has been changed to the present time. Then the excerpt appears in the original simple past time. Verbs are underlined.

PRESENT TIME (RIGHT NOW)

The woman slaps the man across the face. The sound is like a pistol shot, and for an instant William feels his jaw relax. It seems to him that the block grows quiet and waits. He waits with it. The man grabs his belt and lashes out at the woman. He watches the belt rise and fall against her brown skin. The woman screams with the regularity of clockwork. The street comes alive again. There is the sound of voices, the rattle of dishes. A baby whines. The woman's voice becomes a murmur of pain in the background.

PAST TIME (BEFORE NOW)

The woman slapped the man across the face. The sound was like a pistol shot, and for an instant William felt his jaw relax. It seemed to him that the block grew quiet and waited. He waited with it. The man grabbed his belt and lashed out at the woman. He watched the belt rise and fall against her brown skin. The woman screamed with the regularity of clockwork. The street came alive again. There was the sound of voices, the rattle of dishes. A baby whined. The woman's voice became a murmur of pain in the background.

(Ann Petry, "In Darkness and Confusion") (108)

4C. 1. Exercises

Change all underlined verbs to the simple past form. For the original versions of the excerpts, see the Bibliographic "Answer" Section, page 331.

Example
Now his muscles and everything about his body seem*ed* to vibrate with tautness. (99)

1. He <u>feels</u> Mary trying to rise and quickly he <u>pushes</u> her head back to the pillow. (140)

2. When I <u>leave</u> Fort Hare I quickly <u>discover</u> an engineering degree <u>is</u> not going to help me get work. (104)

3. Until recently, the only education most West African village children <u>receive</u> <u>is</u> in a bush camp close to home. (3)

4. Suddenly the earth <u>seems</u> to give way a bit. He <u>claws</u> in the emptiness. Like a stone, he <u>remains</u> behind, strangling on the air. (13)

5. He <u>sees</u> a little girl pick her way through the snow and stop at a corner newsstand; a man <u>hurries</u> out of a drug store and <u>sells</u> the girl a paper. <u>Can</u> he snatch a paper while the man <u>is</u> inside? (127)

6. Henry "Box" <u>escapes</u> from slavery in a box lined with baize. A friend <u>locks</u> him in the box and <u>ships</u> it from Richmond to Philadelphia. Brown <u>steps</u> from the box and <u>sings</u>: "I waited patiently for the Lord, and he heard my prayer." (16)

7. My bitterest moment <u>comes</u> when I <u>go</u> to the Bar Council buildings to be introduced to my colleagues. One advocate, who has since stood as a National-

ist candidate for Parliament, <u>looks</u> at my outstretched hand and <u>says</u>: "No money today ... out".

Today I am bitter and disappointed. (104)

8. After I <u>am refused</u> permission under the Group Areas Act to have an office in the Bar Council building in the center of Johannesburg, members of the Council <u>do appeal</u> to the Prime Minister, but nothing ever <u>comes</u> of it.

I <u>set</u> up an office in down-town Johannesburg and <u>accept</u> the fact that I <u>will have</u> a double struggle to get clients in that area of town. (104)

9. When the amount <u>falls</u> off, then the Capita <u>is</u> himself made to feel some of those physical pains which he <u>has</u> inflicted upon others. Often the white agent far <u>exceeds</u> in cruelty the barbarian who <u>carries</u> out his commissions. Often, too, the white man <u>pushes</u> the black aside, and <u>acts</u> himself as torturer and executioner. (103)

10. Jeff <u>adjusts</u> the crank and <u>puts</u> his weight upon it. The engine <u>comes</u> to life with a sputter and bang that <u>rattles</u> the old car from radiator to tail light. Jeff <u>hops</u> into the seat and <u>puts</u> his foot on the accelerator. The sputtering and banging <u>increases</u>. The rattling <u>becomes</u> more violent. That <u>is</u> good. It <u>is</u> good banging, good sputtering and rattling, and it <u>means</u> that the aged car <u>is</u> still in running condition. She <u>can</u> be depended on for this trip. (20)

11. He <u>holds</u> his hand over her mouth and his head cocked at an angle that <u>enables</u> him to see Mary and Mrs. Dalton by merely shifting his eyes. Mary <u>mumbles</u> and <u>tries</u> to rise again. Frantically, he <u>catches</u> a corner of the pillow and <u>brings</u> it to her lips. He <u>has</u> to stop her from mumbling, or he <u>will</u> be caught. Mrs.

Dalton is moving slowly toward him and he grows tight and full, as though about to explode. Mary's fingernails tear at his hands and he catches the pillow and covers her entire face with it, firmly. (140)

12. And the little things that in the day appear ordinary now seem to be changed into an unearthliness that is both alluring and frightening. Waiyaki listens for voices on the ridge but he can only hear silence. As he moves across the ridge, through small bushes and trees, the silence and the moon's glare seem to have combined into one mighty force that breathes and has life. (99)

13. He goes to the drug store and looks inside at the man leaning against a wall, smoking. Yes. Like this! He reaches out and grabs a paper and in the act of grabbing it he turns and looks at the man who is looking at him, a cigarette slanting whitely across his black chin. Even before he moves from his tracks, he runs; he feels his legs turn, start, then slip in snow. Goddamn! The white world tilts at a sharp angle and the icy wind shoots past his face. He falls flat and the crumbs of snow eat coldly at his fingers. He gets up, on one knee, then on both; when he is on his feet he turns toward the drug store, still clutching the paper, amazed and angry with himself for having been so clumsy. The drug-store door opens. He runs. (140)

14. I will catch the plane as it comes over and swing down fast and run into the house before anyone can see me. Then no one can come to claim the plane. It drones nearer. Then when it hangs like a silver cross in the blue directly above me I stretch out my hand and grab. It is like sticking my finger through a soap bubble. The plane flies on, as though I have simply blown my breath after it. I grab again, frantically, trying to catch the tail. My fingers clutch the air and

disappointment surges tight and hard in my throat. Giving one last desperate grasp, I strain forward. My fingers rip against the screen. I am falling. The ground bursts hard against me. I drum the earth with my heels and when my breath returns, I lie there bawling. (42)

15. Imagine the nightmare which lies upon each village while this barbarian squats in the midst of it. Day or night they can never get away from him. He calls for palm wine. He calls for women. He beats them, mutilates them, and shoots them down at his pleasure. He enforces public incest in order to amuse himself by the sight. Sometimes they pluck up spirit and kill him. The Belgian Commission records that 142 Capitas have been killed in seven months in a single district. Then comes the punitive expedition, and the destruction of the whole community. The more terror the Capita inspires, the more useful he is, the more eagerly the villagers obey him, and the more rubber yields its commission to the agent. (103)

16. If not employed, that is to say, by Europeans, you have to quit, return to the Reserves, even if like many eighteen-year-olds you have never in your life lived in one. Her son pretends to live at another location, goes there regularly to pay the fee and renew his work-permit, hoodwinking the Boer there. I cannot imagine how it is done. Parts of the puzzle are left out in the explanation and I do not like to ask. I can see well enough that it is risky, a matter of time before he and others living surreptitiously in their parental homes will be found out, fined or jailed, and expelled from town, "Endorsed Out"; and for such reasons I have not brought myself to mention their names. Mrs R. now gets up again and crosses over to the wall. She detaches a leaflet that is pinned to a picture-frame and hands it to my cousin who sits back to read it while our hostess tries to talk to us at the

same time about different things. She says to my cousin, "That is the reading matter which that rascal child 'criminal-because-home-dweller' of mine brings back as a trophy from his latest trip to his fee-eating boss-Boer. A Congress leaflet. Oh, red hot African National Congress these boys!" She also keeps up a lively conversation with me. Presently my cousin stretches forward and passes the leaflet to me to read, without making comment, not being politically inclined. (65)

4C. 2. Exercises

1. Keep a journal of important events that happen to you day by day, as suggested on page 153, but this time write everything down in past time. Students have found that keeping such a journal over a period of months has been very useful not only for getting various ideas down on paper but also for practicing various styles of writing day after day.

2. Write your own short story in past time. Use descriptions of places and people. Describe events, using lots of active words, descriptive words, and dialogue. Review Chapter 1 and Appendix A on dialogue if you run into trouble. Make sure that you stay in past time. It is usually wise to write about your own experiences or about events you know quite well.

D. Verbs and "helping verbs": Verb Group 1

Perhaps the most confusing aspect of English verbs is the spelling of verbs after "helping verbs" (often called "auxiliaries"). Helping verbs are words like "have," "had," "is," and "was." For example, note the helping verbs in the underlined words below.

> It was Bessie Smith, through her tone and her cadence, who helped me to dig back to the way I myself must have spoken when I was a pickaninny, and to remember the things I had heard and seen and felt. I had buried them very deep. I had never listened to Bessie Smith in America (in the same way that, for years, I would not touch watermelon), but in Europe she helped to reconcile me to being a "nigger."
> (James Baldwin, "The Discovery of What it Means to Be an American") (10b)

The verb group

Each underlined group of verbs above is called a "verb group." A VERB GROUP CONSISTS OF ONE OR MORE HELPING VERBS PLUS A MAIN VERB.

VERB GROUPS (taken from previous excerpt)

HELPING VERBS	MAIN VERBS
a. must have	spoken
b. had	heard
c. had	seen
d. had	felt
e. had	buried
f. had	listened

There are two kinds of verb groups.
VERB GROUP 1 is discussed now.
VERB GROUP 2 is discussed on pages 181-187.

Verb group 1

Look once again at the sentence by James Baldwin.

> It was Bessie Smith, through her tone and her cadence, who helped me to dig back to the way I myself must have spoken when I was a pickaninny.... (10b)

Notice the "SPOKEN" is one way to spell "SPEAK" in the past form. Indeed, there are TWO WAYS TO FORM THE PAST OF THE VERB "SPEAK." Also note the two ways to form the past of the verb "see."

SIMPLE PAST	VERB GROUP 1
I spoke quickly.	I must have spoken quickly.
I saw him.	I had seen him.
I saw him.	I have seen him.

Here are helping Verbs for Verb Group 1.

As shown on page 156, "SAW" is the SIMPLE PAST form of the verb "SEE." On the other hand, "SEEN" is a form of the verb that is found in VERB GROUP 1. In other words, "SEEN" is usually found after the following helping verbs:

CHART 23. Helping Verbs for Verb Group 1

**Helping Verbs
for Verb Group 1**

am	I <u>am seen</u> on television every Friday.
is	He <u>is seen</u> on television every Friday.
are	You <u>are seen</u> by a large audience.
was	He <u>was seen</u> on television.
were	They <u>were seen</u> at the demonstration.
being[*]	He <u>is being seen</u> for advice.
be	You <u>will be seen</u> by a staff of experts.
been	She <u>has been seen</u> by everyone now.
have	They <u>have seen</u> the movie already.
has	He <u>has seen</u> everything.
having	<u>Having seen</u> all he wanted, he went home.
had	He <u>had seen</u> the show already.
get[†]	They might <u>get shot</u> if they do that.
gets[†]	What if he <u>gets shot</u>.
getting[†]	I am afraid of <u>getting shot</u>.
got[†]	I <u>got shot</u> in the arm.
gotten[†]	We did not know who <u>had gotten shot</u>.

[*]Avoid "being" as much as possible.
[†]Avoid all forms of "get" as a helping verb as much as possible. Note that "seen" would be much more awkward than "shot" if we tried to use the main verb "seen" with the forms of the helping form "get."

Spelling the Verb 169

In short, after the words "am," "is," "have," "has," etc., a particular form of the main verb is needed. Compare the simple past with Verb Group 1.

SIMPLE PAST

I <u>wrote</u> it.
He <u>went</u> home.
They <u>froze</u> last night.
He <u>chose</u> not to go.

VERB GROUP 1

It <u>was written</u>.
He <u>has gone</u> home.
They <u>were frozen</u> by the time they arrived.
He <u>had been chosen</u> to chair the meeting.

How do you spell main verbs for Verb Group 1?

1. Regular verbs. Add "ED" to present form—same word as the simple past form.

PRESENT	SIMPLE PAST	VERB GROUP 1
call	callED	(he was) callED
help	helpED	(he was) helpED
marry	marrIED	(he was) marrIED

2. Irregular Verbs. The spelling for the main verbs has to be memorized. See Chart 25 for a full list.

PRESENT	SIMPLE PAST	VERB GROUP 1
eat	ate	(he has) eatEN
throw	thrEw	(he has) throwN
write	wrOte	(he has) eatEN

Descriptive words that look like verbs: Spell them the same way as the main verb for verb group 1

As discussed on page 70, descriptive words that look like verbs are spelled the same way as the main verb in Verb Group 1. So, in the following excerpt, the underlined descriptive words are spelled according to the guidelines given in Chart 25.

Held in bondage, <u>stripped</u> of his culture, <u>denied</u> family life for centuries, <u>made</u> to labor for others, the Negro tried to learn to live the life of the New World in an atmosphere of rejection and hate.

(Richard Wright, *White Man, Listen!*) (143)

CHART 24. Summary of Simple Past Time and Verb Group 1

Simple Past

Add "ED" to present form of verb. See p. 55

Memorize list of irregular verbs.

He <u>married</u> her.
He <u>wrote</u> the essay.

Verb Group 1

Helping Verbs

am	was	have*	had	(being)†	[get(s)]	(got)
is	were	has		be†	(getting)	(gotten)
are		having		been†		

PLUS

Main Verb for Verb Group 1:
(See Chart 25.)

He <u>got married</u> last week.
He <u>has written</u> the essay.

---

*Do not confuse "have" with "of." "Of" is not a helping verb. (See page 196.)
†The distinction between "he <u>is</u> happy" ("he is happy <u>right now</u>") and "he <u>be</u> happy" ("he is happy <u>continuously</u>") is not made in college writing. "Is" tends to mean both "right now" and "continuously" (which keeps the definition of "is" somewhat vague). "Be," "being," and "been" are generally used with another helping verb in college writing: "he <u>will be</u> happy," "he <u>wants to be</u> happy," "he <u>has been</u> happy for a long time."

CHART 25. Some Important Verbs in Present, Past, and Verb Group 1

Add your own verbs to the list. See p. 328 for dictionary guide to looking up verb spelling.

Regular Verbs

Present	Simple Past	Verb Group 1 (Has*) Plus Main Verb
agree	agreed	(has) agreed
analyze (analyse)	analyzed (analysed)	(has) analyzed (analysed)
argue	argued	(has) argued
arrive	arrived	(has) arrived
ask	asked	(has) asked
attempt	attempted	(has) attempted
call	called	(has) called
decide	decided	(has) decided
describe	described	(has) described
help	helped	(has) helped
increase	increased	(has) increased
look	looked	(has) looked
need	needed	(has) needed
organize	organized	(has) organized
receive	received	(has) received
reply	replied	(has) replied
study	studied	(has) studied
suppress	suppressed	(has) suppressed

_____   _____   _____

_____   _____   _____

_____   _____   _____

_____   _____   _____

*See Chart 23 or 24 for list of other helping verbs.

Regular Verbs

Present	Simple Past	Verb Group 1 (Has*) Plus Main Verb
_____	_____	_____
_____	_____	_____
_____	_____	_____
_____	_____	_____
_____	_____	_____

Irregular Verbs

Present	Simple Past	Verb Group 1 (Has*) Plus Main Verb

(Present and Verb Group 1 are the same.)

| become | became | (has) become |
| come | came | (has) come |

Present	Simple Past	Verb Group 1 (Has*) Plus Main Verb

(All three forms are different.)

| do | did | (has) done |
| go | went | (has) gone |

Present	Simple Past	Verb Group 1 (Has*) Plus Main Verb

(Verb Group 1 ends with "n.")

am (are, is)	was (were)	(has) been
give	gave	(has) given
grow	grew	(has) grown
know	knew	(has) known
lie (down)	lay	(has) lain[†]
see	saw	(has) seen
show	showed	(has) shown
take	took	(has) taken
write	wrote	(has) written

*See Chart 23 or 24 for list of other helping verbs.
[†]"Lie" and "lay" are discussed on page 195.

Irregular Verbs

Present	Simple Past	Verb Group 1 (Has*) Plus Main Verb
_____	_____	_____
_____	_____	_____
_____	_____	_____
_____	_____	_____
_____	_____	_____

Present	Simple Past	Verb Group 1 (Has*) Plus Main Verb
(Past and Verb Group 1 are the same.)		
bring	brought	(has) brought
deal	dealt	(has) dealt
fight	fought	(has) fought
have (has)	had	(has) had
lead	led	(has) led
lay (me down)	laid	(has) laid †
make	made	(has) made
occur	occurred	(has) occurred
say	said	(has) said
spend	spent	(has) spent
stand	stood	(has) stood
_____	_____	_____
_____	_____	_____
_____	_____	_____
_____	_____	_____

Present	Simple Past	Verb Group 1 (Has*) Plus Main Verb
(All three are the same.)		
cut	cut	(has) cut
hit	hit	(has) hit
put	put	(has) put

*See Chart 23 or 24 for list of other helping verbs.
†"Lay" and "lie" are discussed on page 195.

4D. 1. Exercises

Underline Verb Group 1 in the following excerpts, paying particular attention to how its forms are used to show various kinds of time.

Example
He had written those words in a room in Philadelphia when he was thirty-three. (16)

1. Sometimes during the night or stillness of day, a voice would be heard singing the brave song. (118)

2. Had she remained hidden and allowed them to finish their argument, one would have prevailed over the other, and there would have been either no life or no death. (124)

3. At the period of which I write, no railroad had come to Troy. If a traveler, accustomed to the bustling life of cities, could have ridden through Troy on a summer day, he might easily have fancied himself in a deserted village. (28)

4. He tried to advance, but now his legs formed an irremediable part of the block that had slid down on them. He no longer even felt them. He felt only the asphyxia. (13)

5. But the missionaries had not as yet penetrated into the hills, though they sent a number of disciples to work there. (99)

6. After the beer has arrived the senior representative on the girl's side rises and says, "We have called all of you on the male side together that you may share in eating the food which your child has hoed." (29)

7. The conscience of a race is the gift of its individuals who see, evaluate, record.... We create the race by creating ourselves and then to our great astonishment we will have created something far more important: We will have created a culture. (43)

8. Each agent was given control over a certain number of savages drawn from the wild tribes but armed with firearms. One or more of these was placed in each village to ensure that the villagers should do their task. These are the men who are called "Capitas," or head-men in the accounts, and who are the actual, though not moral, perpetrators of so many horrible deeds. (103)

9. I had been in Paris a couple of years before any of this became clear to me. When it did, I, like many a writer before me upon the discovery that his props have all been knocked out from under him, suffered a species of breakdown and was carried off to the mountains of Switzerland. There, in that absolutely alabaster landscape, armed with two Bessie Smith records and a typewriter, I began to try to re-create the life that I had first known as a child and from which I had spent so many years in flight.

It was Bessie Smith, through her tone and her cadence, who helped me to dig back to the way I myself must have spoken when I was a pickaninny, and to remember the things I had heard and seen and felt. I had buried them very deep. I had never listened to Bessie Smith in America (in the same way that, for years, I would not touch watermelon), but in Europe she helped to reconcile me to being a "nigger." (10b)

4D. 2. Exercises: Editing for Verb Group 1

Look for Verb Group 1 and descriptive words that look like verbs in the following excerpts and change the spelling of the main verb or descriptive word, or add the helping verb when necessary, in order to put the excerpts back into college writing. Make all changes directly in the sentences as if you were editing a paper. If an excerpt does not need to be changed, put a check (√) next to its number. Look only for the main verbs in Verb Group 1 using the guidelines given on pages 167-173. Do not edit for anything else. (See page 2 for how to use the "Answer" Section.)

Example

Douglas was pelt*ed*~with eggs and~*thrown* ~~threw~~ down steps; but he stood his ground and took his knocks. (16)

1. As we are warnt, the new grouping will be effected "under the leadership of the Ivory Coast." (115)

2. The river was call Honia, which meant cure, or bring-back-to-life. (99)

3. From my classroom window I have seeing fall turn into winter, and winter to spring. Nothing in this block ever changes, except the seasons. (58)

4. When he had finish selling he went on his way and came to an open glade where he saw a very large and very fierce elephant. Now that elephant seen him! (27)

5. Their few forces are dissipate and waste and the chances of achieving their objective are thus reduce. (86)

6. This was the building where Mr. Lawson had kill a man for peeing in the hall. I remembered being afraid to go downstairs the morning after Mr. Lawson had bust that man's head with a baseball bat. (22)

7. In the southern regions which have been longest expose to the influence of Western civilization, the foundation for the contemporary élite pattern first developed from what may be call the "old-established families." (117)

8. Even though black Americans had live through hundreds of years of slavery, this major difference, the role of the arts in life, carried over to a great degree; everyone participated at home, church, parties, and gatherings. (25)

9. I was always rather amuse to find that separate robing-rooms had been set aside for me in the Johannesburg and Pretoria Supreme Courts—I suppose I might have contaminate my colleagues if I had donned my gown and wig in their presence. (104)

10. In doing so, we will be merely following the natural demands of our culture. These demands be suppress in the larger (white) culture, but, nonetheless, be foun in our music and in our spiritual and moral philosophy. (120)

11. I had gone in the house for bread and butter and coming out I heard a steady unfamiliar drone. It was unlike anything I had ever hear before. I tried to place the sound. It was no use. It was a sensation like that I had when searching for my father's watch, heard ticking unseen in a room. It made me feel as though I forgotten to perform some task that my mother had order . . . then I located it, overhead. (42)

12. I pressed my face against the window, watching the earth come closer; soon we were just above the tops of trees. I could not suppress the thought that this earth had acquir its color from the blood that had drip down from these trees. My mind was fill with the image of a black man, younger than I, perhaps, or my own age, hanging from a tree, while white men watched him and cut his sex from him with a knife. (10e)

13. For the first time in her life somebody had called her "madam." She had been standing, bewilder but unafraid, while innumerable Red Caps appropriated piece after piece of the baggage array on the platform. (46)

14. I have often spoke of the role of underdeveloped nations in the building of the international community. Because the Negro Africans have keeped a sense of brotherhood and dialogue, because they are inspire by religions that preach love, and, above all, because they be living those religions, they can propose positive solutions for the construction of the international as well as the national community. (115)

15. In fact, the bus is getting ready to leave the Pentagon. A driver has got on—to many cheers—and a wire gate is close across the front to protect the chauffeur from attack by any prisoners while he is driving. There are also bars across each window. (Obviously Mailer has had the fantasy of bending the bars and making his escape, and has decide not to—it would certainly make him famous for too little.) (82)

16. Thin pieces of wood shall be plac underneath. There will be a row of loops on either side made of string. The bark of the cliff rose, shredded and rub fine, will be use under the child for a bed. (51)

17. They went up to St. Nicholas Avenue on the bus and climbed to the top

floor of an apartment house. A fat, light-complexion woman with black hair and sleepy eyes, clad in flaming red lounging pajamas, let them into an apartment filled with people getting drunk. (62)

18. Sun-tortured shingles lay on the roofs like decks of water-soaked cards spreaded out to dry. The houses consisted of two square rooms join together by a common floor and roof with a porch in between. As we passed we could look through to the fields beyond. (43)

19. I am without land because the white minority taken a lion's share of my country and force me to occupy poverty-stricken reserves, overpopulated and overstockt. We are ravaged by starvation and disease because our country's wealth is not share by all sections of the population. (84)

20. She has a wasted, dead-leaf appearance. Her body, as scrawny and gnarled as a string bean, seemed less than nothing in the ocean of fray and fade petticoats that surrounded her. These hung an inch or two above the tops of her heavy unlace shoes and showed little grotesque piles where the stockings fallen down from her negligible legs. (20)

E. Verb group 2: the verb ending in "ing"

(Review Part D before going on.)

Verb Group 2 consists of helping verbs PLUS a main verb ending in "ING." For example, Verb Group 2 is underlined below:

> This meant that sorrow was present—either a brave <u>was going</u> on the warpath and expected to die, or else a family <u>was looking</u> for the death of some member of it.
> (Chief Standing Bear, *The Land of the Spotted Eagle*) (118)

Comparison of verb groups 1 and 2

VERB GROUP 1	VERB GROUP 2
He <u>has gone</u> on the warpath.	He <u>was going</u> on the warpath.
A family <u>has looked</u> for him.	A family <u>was looking</u> for him.

The spelling for the main verb for verb group 2: Add "ing" to the present form of the verb (except for "being")[2]

Main verbs for Verb Group 2 end in "ING." There are NO EXCEPTIONS. In other words, whenever you are forming Verb Group 2, your main verb will NOT end in "EN" or "IN." IT WILL ALWAYS END IN "ING." So, even though one may not pronounce the "g", it is always there in the spelling.

PRONOUNCED	SPELLED
go-in	going
play-in	playing
cutt-in	cutting

Usually, you just add "ing" to the present form of the verb.

PRESENT	VERB GROUP 2
act	(I am) actING
bring	(I am) bringING
build	(I am) buildING
study	(I am) studyING

But when the present form ends in "e", you drop the "e" before adding "ing."

freeze	(I am) freezING
love	(I am) lovING
write	(I am) writING

A few verbs double the final letter before adding "ing."

hit	(I am) hittING
fit	(I am) fittING
rob	(I am) robbING
sit	(I am) sittING

[2] Add "ING" to "be," the main verb in the infinitive form (see "infinitive" in index).

The helping verbs for verb group 2

Just as there are specific helping verbs that come before Verb Group 1, so there are helping verbs for Verb Group 2. Sometimes the helping verbs for both groups are the same, and then you have to decide what meaning you want. "I am shot in the leg" has a very different meaning from "I am shooting at the leg." The first sentence uses Verb Group 1; the second uses Verb Group 2.

CHART 26. Helping Verbs for Verb Group 2

Helping Verbs for Verb Group 2

am	I am writing a story.
is	He is writing a story.
are	You are writing a story.
was	He was writing a story.
were	They were writing stories.
be	They will be writing it all down.
been	He has been writing all weekend.
get*	I hope to get writing by Tuesday.
gets*	He is good when he gets going.
getting*	I have trouble getting the car going.
got*	I got it going.
gotten*	I had just gotten the car going when it began to rain.
keep	It is sometimes difficult to keep writing.
keeps	He keeps me writing for an hour.
keeping	He was keeping me writing for an hour.
kept	I kept writing for an hour.

*Avoid all forms of "get" as a helping verb as much as possible.

CHART 27. Summary for Verbs and Verb Groups

Simple Past

Add "ED" to present form. See page 155.

Memorize list of irregular verbs.

He <u>married</u> her.
He <u>wrote</u> the essays.

Verb Group 1

Helping Verbs

am	was	have	being*	[get(s)]
is	were	has	be*	(getting)
are		having	been*	(got)
		had		(gotten)

PLUS

Main Verb for Verb Group 1
See Chart 25.

He <u>got</u> married.
He <u>has written</u> the essay.

Verb Group 2

Helping Verbs

am	was	be*	[get(s)]	keep(s)
is	were	been*	(getting)	keeping
are			(got)	kept
			(gotten)	

PLUS

Main Verb for Verb Group 2
See Chart 28.

He <u>is marrying</u> her.
He <u>kept</u> on <u>writing</u>.

---

*See Chart 24 for note on "be," "been," and "being."

CHART 28. Final List of Important Verbs

Add your own verbs to the list. See p. 328 for dictionary guide to looking up verb spelling.

Fill in present, simple past, and verb group 1 (see Chart 25).

Regular Verbs

Present	Simple Past	Verb Group 1 (Has*) Plus Main Verb	Verb Group 2 (Am*) Plus Main Verb
agree	agreed	(has) agreed	(am) agreeing
_____	_____	_____	(am) analyzing (analysing)
_____	_____	_____	(am) arguing
_____	_____	_____	(am) arriving
_____	_____	_____	(am) asking
_____	_____	_____	(am) attempting
_____	_____	_____	(am) calling
_____	_____	_____	(am) deciding
_____	_____	_____	(am) describing
_____	_____	_____	(am) helping
_____	_____	_____	(am) increasing
_____	_____	_____	(am) looking
_____	_____	_____	(am) needing

*See Chart 27 for a list of other helping verbs.

Spelling the Verb

Regular Verbs

Present	Simple Past	Verb Group 1 (Has*) Plus Main Verb	Verb Group 2 (Am*) Plus Main Verb
_____	_____	_____	(am) organizing
_____	_____	_____	(am) receiving
_____	_____	_____	(am) replying
_____	_____	_____	(am) studying
_____	_____	_____	(am) suppressing
_____	_____	_____	_____
_____	_____	_____	_____
_____	_____	_____	_____
_____	_____	_____	_____
_____	_____	_____	_____
_____	_____	_____	_____
_____	_____	_____	_____

Irregular Verbs

Present	Simple Past	Verb Group 1 (Has*) Plus Main Verb	Verb Group 2 (Am*) Plus Main Verb
_____	_____	_____	(am) becoming
_____	_____	_____	(am) coming

*See Chart 27 for a list of other helping verbs.

Irregular Verbs

Present	Simple Past	Verb Group 1 (Has*) Plus Main Verb	Verb Group 2 (Am*) Plus Main Verb
_____	_____	_____	(am) doing
_____	_____	_____	(am) going

Irregular Verbs

Present	Simple Past	Verb Group 1 (Has*) Plus Main Verb	Verb Group 2 (Am*) Plus Main Verb
_____	_____	_____	(am) being
_____	_____	_____	(am) giving
_____	_____	_____	(am) growing
_____	_____	_____	(am) knowing
_____	_____	_____	(am) lying (down)†
_____	_____	_____	(am) seeing
_____	_____	_____	(am) showing
_____	_____	_____	(am) taking
_____	_____	_____	(am) writing
_____	_____	_____	_____
_____	_____	_____	_____
_____	_____	_____	_____
_____	_____	_____	_____
_____	_____	_____	_____

*See Chart 27 for a list of other helping verbs.
†"Lay" and "lie" are discussed on page 195.

Irregular Verbs

Present	Simple Past	Verb Group 1 (Has*) Plus Main Verb	Verb Group 2 (Am*) Plus Main Verb
_____	_____	_____	(am) bringing
_____	_____	_____	(am) dealing
_____	_____	_____	(am) fighting
_____	_____	_____	(am) leading
_____	_____	_____	(am) laying (an egg)†
_____	_____	_____	(am) making
_____	_____	_____	(am) occurring
_____	_____	_____	(am) saying
_____	_____	_____	(am) spending
_____	_____	_____	(am) standing

Irregular Verbs

Present	Simple Past	Verb Group 1 (Has*) Plus Main Verb	Verb Group 2 (Am*) Plus Main Verb
_____	_____	_____	(am) cutting
_____	_____	_____	(am) hitting
_____	_____	_____	(am) putting

*See Chart 27 for a list of other helping verbs.
†"Lay" and "lie" are discussed on page 195.

4E. 1. Exercises

Underline Verb Group 2 in the following excerpts, paying particular attention to how its forms are used to show various kinds of time.

Example
Now we will open your ears, and also your throat, for there is something that has been choking you and we will also give you the water that shall wash down all the troubles in your throat. (55)

1. The grocery store which gave us credit is still there, and there can be no doubt that it is still giving credit. (10c)

2. He was drowning in a solid, dark river. He stopped moving, stopped the useless struggle. The torment slowly changed into an inexplicable delight. (13)

3. Times were hard in the world. Everywhere there were beings who were eating people. One day a dark rain cloud was seen resting on top of To'ol'i. (51)

4. My mother and Mrs. Caldwell were sitting on the divider between their two roofs talking to Sonny's grandmother, Mrs. Taylor. Mrs. Caldwell was holding Elizabeth's baby, a boy, while Lil Robert, five, and David, three, played at her feet. (89)

5. Sterling was going downtown to high school, grumbling that all the white kids wore better clothes than he did and had long pants while he was still knocking about in his knickers. (89)

6. Liberals have been telling us these long bad years to work for a world where people are equal and our efforts in this direction have not bettered our lives

materially, nor is it probable that they will make the conditions under which Sadika worked in that South African farm disappear. (102)

7. Traveling to remote villages by boat and truck, trained technicians are now offering bush country West African children far better health care than their parents or grandparents ever received. Large medical centers and bush dispensaries alike are attracting parents as never before, and their children are receiving regular examinations and treatment which may substantially cut the youngsters' staggering sickness- and death-rate. (3)

8. The sun has been beating on the bus and it is as uncomfortably warm as a small Southern bus depot on an Indian summer afternoon, which is what the faces outside might suggest, if not for the Pentagon walls. And a battle has been taking place, even if no sign of it seems to be reaching here—except, gloomy thought, the battle cannot be going too well, for there is not the remotest sign of panic in this rear area. (82)

4E. 2. Exercises: Editing for Verb Group 2

Look for Verb Group 2 in the following excerpts and change the spelling of the main verb or add the helping verb when necessary in order to put the excerpts back into college writing. Make all changes directly in the sentences as if you were editing a paper. If an excerpt does not need to be changed, put a check (√) next to its number. Look only for the main verbs in Verb Group 2 using the guidelines given on pages 181-187. Do not edit for anything else. (See page 2 for how to use the "Answer" Section.)

Example
Now we will open your ears, and also your throat, for there is something that ‸choking you and we will also give you the water that shall wash down all the troubles in your throat. (55)
(insertion above caret: *has been*)

1. And I don't even light the torch to see where the cockroaches are climb on me. (112)

2. As the sun was setten we started up the boardwalk towards his house, with out wet bathing trunks on under our trousers. (9)

3. We were passin a collection of shacks and log cabins now, bleached white and warped by the weather. (43)

4. I am compelled to use this type of terminology because of the nature of the application I am now made. (84)

5. She was wantin the word that would free her of this nightmare; but he would not give it to her. (140)

6. So now Angola has seven political groups that share the same objective—the independence of Angola—but they are all work for it in different ways. (86)

7. He heard Bessie's clothes rustling in the darkness and he knew that she was pullen off her coat. Soon she would be laying here beside him. He waited for her. (140)

8. The third day it reached well beyond the middle, and the fourth day the rain enveloped the entire mountain and falling at its base. (51)

9. I could still see blood all over the hall. This was the building where somebody was always shootin out the windows in the hall. They were usually shootin at Johnny D., and they usually missed. (22)

10. And Waiyaki thrust out his arms and wanted to hold the moon close to his breast because he was sure she was listen and he wanted her cold breath near him. (99)

11. We are not goin to throw stones at the police or do anything that is going to obstruct the police. Any person who does all these things shall be dealt with by the police of course and we, as an organization, shall further deal with him. Nobody is carring money, knives, or any dangerous weapon with himself tomorrow. (72)

12. Now I am perfectly aware that there are other slums in which white men are foughting for their lives, and mainly losing. I know that blood is also flown through those streets and that the human damage there is incalculable. People continually pointing out to me the wretchedness of white people in order to console me for the wretchedness of blacks. But an itemized account of the American failure does not console me and it should not console anyone else. That

hundreds of thousands of white people are liveing, in effect, no better than the "niggers" is not a fact to be regarded with complacency. The social and moral bankruptcy suggested by this fact is of the bitterest, most terrifying kind. (10c)

F. "Lay" and "lie" as verbs
   "Suppose_d to" and "use_d to"
   "would ha_ve," "could ha_ve," and "should ha_ve"

"Lay" and "lie" cause a lot of confusion, even among the most accomplished of writers. Actually, there is a very simple way to remember the difference:

1. "LAY" always has a "receiver," someone or something receiving the action. An easy expression to remember is:

   Now I lay me down to sleep. . . .

Notice that "me" is the receiver of the action in this prayer.

2. "LIE" (meaning to "lie down on a bed") never has a receiver. A common expression to help you remember how to use the word "lie" is:

   He usually lies down on the job.
                  or
   I want to lie down.

3. "LIE" (meaning to tell a false story) also never has a receiver, but the various spellings of the verb are different from those of the first two.

4. A summary of the various spellings of the three verbs follows:

CHART 29. Spelling of "Lay" and "Lie"

Present	Simple Past	Verb Group 1	Verb Group 2
a. lay (me down)	laid (me down)	(has) laid (me down)	(am) laying (me down)
b. lie (down)	lay (down)	(has) lain (down)	(am) lying (down)
c. lie (to someone)	lied	(has) lied	(am) lying

"Supposed to" and "used to"

You are supposed to put a "d" at the end of "supposeD to," and "useD to," even though you are not used to hearing the "d" pronounced.

Because the "T" on "To" slurs into the "D" of "supposed" and "used," people often forget to put the "D" in. However, if you tend to get red circles around these words when your essays are returned to you by your instructor, it would be a good practice to skim your essays before handing them in to see if you have the "D." There is no other solution. You have to edit your essays (if you feel it is necessary) in order to catch the missing "D."

"Would have," "could have," and "should have"

There is no "of" in "would have."

Because speakers generally slur the word "have" in "would have," "should have," and "could have," you usually hear "would of," "should of," and "could of."

The "have" in "would have," etc., is a helping verb for Verb Group 2 (see page 182). The word "of" does not appear anywhere in the list of helping verbs (see page 183). So, although your ear tells you to write the word "of," the "acceptable" word is always "have."

4F. Exercises: Editing

Look for uses of "lay" and "lie" and spelling of "used to," "supposed to," "could have," etc., in the following excerpts and change the spellings when necessary in order to put the excerpts back into college writing. Make all changes directly in the sentences as if you were editing a paper. If an excerpt does not need to be changed, put a check (√) next to its number. Look only for the words covered in Part F, using the guidelines given on pages 195-196. Do not edit for anything else. (See page 2 for how to use the "Answer" Section.)

Example
Now I lie[lay] me down to sleep.

1. I never knew what significance I'm suppose to attach to these factors. (32)

2. He lifted her and lied her on the bed. (140)

3. I was very thirsty, and that must of been what woke me. (48)

4. He placed the two pillows near the window, so that when he lay down the window would be just above his head. (140)

5. "I think anyone but a doctor would have fainted. I should of liked to have fainted...." (48)

6. He had been rewarded for marrying a girl nobody in his right mind would of married. (132)

7. Sun-tortured shingles laid on the roofs like decks of water-soaked cards spread out to dry. (43)

8. There was a broad river to reflect those lights, which would have made their nighttime winkings very pretty indeed. (132)

9. I was about eleven years old at the time and use to stay with my godmother, Eulalie Echo, who spoiled me and gave me a little freedom. (79)

10. When Conchis had advised me to go back and marry Alison he must of known she was dead; Lily must have known she was dead. (48)

11. The urge to do violence against the stranger lies just below the surface in the individual who has such an emotional reaction. (116)

12. If Billy had had to guess as to the source, he would of said that there was a vampire bat hanging upside down on the wall behind him. (132)

13. There is a housing project standing now where the house in which we grew up once stood, and one of those stunted city trees is snarling where our doorway use to be. (10c)

14. Maude and her sister Rebecca and me were lain on the rise of the roof looking over the edge and chewing tar, which was suppose to keep your teeth white. (89)

15. In the night we laid awake, knowing each other awake yet afraid to talk. I felt her hand feel out for mine. We lied for a while without talking. Then she spoke. (48)

16. When he was outside, he picked up one of the weights he had bought to keep himself in condition and laid down with it. Laying on his back, he held the weight at arm's length for quite a long time. (122)

G. Complications of noun-verb pair agreement

As outlined on pages 142-149, the basic "rule" for noun-verb pair agreement is as follows: IF YOU CAN CHANGE THE NOUN TO "HE," "SHE," OR "IT," AND THE VERB FORM IS PRESENT, ADD S TO THE VERB.

SINGULAR		PLURAL
he, she, it, that, this } IS		we, you, they, these, those } ARE
he, she, it, that, this } TAKES		we, you, they, these, those } TAKE

But there are times when the noun of the noun-verb pair is not right next to the verb. In these cases, it is most useful to look at the verb and ask, "who is doing it?" For example, in the following sentence the verb is "sings." Who is doing the singing? The hill is not doing the singing; the fool is doing the singing. Therefore, the "fool" is the noun of the noun-verb pair: "the fool sings." The words "on the hill" have to be disregarded when deciding what noun belongs to the pair. The words in brackets in the sentences below are not included in the noun-verb pair.

The split noun-verb pair

NOUN	VERB
Singular: The fool [on the hill]	sings his song.
Plural: The fools [on the hill]	sing their song.

Double noun = plural noun

NOUN AND NOUN	VERB
Plural: The owl and the pussycat	go to sea.

Group noun = singular noun[3]

GROUP NOUN		VERB
Singular: The group		is here.
Singular: The group } [of students] {		is here.
Singular: The class		is here.

---

[3] A group noun is considered PLURAL when the elements within the group are considered as individuals. See the excerpt by Nyerere, P. 373. He discusses a group of families, but he means families as individual units, all of whom "*have decided . . . and are discussing.*"

"Either ... or": THE NOUN CLOSEST TO THE VERB IS PART OF THE NOUN-VERB PAIR.

> Singular: Either the children or the teacher is right.
> Plural: Either the teacher or the children are right.
> Singular: Either Grace or John is right.

Special pronouns are singular (memorize these)

PRONOUN	SINGULAR VERB
Anyone	
Anybody	
Anything	
Each person	
Each of the people	
Each man and woman	
Every	
Every person	
Every man and woman	
Everyone	LIKES
Everybody	
Everything	
Either	
Neither	
Nobody	
Nothing	
One	
One of the people	
Someone	
Somebody*	

Names of academic subjects are singular (they end in "ICS")

NOUN	VERB
Athletics	is my next class.
Genetics	is an important subject.

H. "There is" or "there are"? "Here is" or "here are"?

For "who is" and "who are," see pages 259-260.

When a sentence begins with the word "there," the NOUN-VERB PAIR is usually BACKWARDS. The noun usually comes AFTER the verb:

```
      V    N
There is a party tomorrow night.

       V  N
There's a party tomorrow night.

        V        N
There are three parties tomorrow night.
```

*For example, "Somebody up there likes me."

SO YOU HAVE TO LOOK FOR THE NOUN IN ORDER TO DECIDE IF YOU NEED A SINGULAR OR PLURAL VERB.

      V   N
Here is the ticket.

     V   N
Here's the ticket.

      V   N
Here are the tickets.

The word "here" can refer to a location. If other words which show location are used instead of "here," you can also have a backwards noun-verb pair:

      V   N
Here are the tickets.

            V   N
On the table are the tickets.

It is not the <u>table</u> that belongs to the noun-verb pair, but the <u>tickets</u>.

4G, H. Exercises: Editing for Noun-Verb Agreement

Look for noun-verb pairs in the following excerpts and change the spelling of any verb that does not agree with its noun in the noun-verb pair in order to put the excerpts back into college writing. Make all changes directly in the sentences as if you were editing a paper. If an excerpt does not need to be changed, put a check (√) next to its number. Look only for noun-verb agreement, using the guidelines given on pages 199-201. Do not edit for anything else. (See page 2 for how to use the "Answer" Section.)

Example

There ~~was~~ were riots and other disorders and young toughs came charging to the platform. . . . (16)

1. There was footsteps on the road. Three men were walking slowly along it. (48)

2. Neither white nor Negro middle-class society offer a way out for the Negro masses. (44)

3. There has been little peace in Africa in our time. (81)

4. Miss Dietrich had taught Nancy Lee how to paint spring, people, and a breeze on what were only a plain white piece of paper from the supply closet. (63)

5. Michele had a fever and the apartment was cold and I was out of work again and there was three pounds of fatty white hamburger meat on the table. (53)

6. The Bantu have known since time immemorial that the sun do not move round the earth, but that the earth move round the sun. (96)

7. The Universal Declaration of Human Rights provide that all men are equal before the law and are entitled, without discrimination, to equal protection before the law. (84)

8. There are no sizable bloc of people of wealth, education, and gentility in existence yet. There are only individuals who are recognized by their positions and achievements and whose status extend to their immediate families. (117)

9. Everyone from the President to the Panthers are using the phrase "Power to the People," but unless the people show initiative and some real follow-through, it's just a slogan. Our kids are our most valuable asset and the education they receive are our most important task. (147)

10. At the present time there is three universities in Ghana. The University of Ghana, which is located in the capital city, Accra, train its students in the "liberal arts." The University of Science and Technology in Kumasi are where the pupils specialize in scientific subjects and research. (3)

11. Let me return for a moment to the foundation of the arts in Africa. The arts were part of the total complex of life; there were no audience and everyone participated in the dance and musical expression in some way. (25)

12. The Sioux, my own people, have a great tradition of conflict. We were the only nation ever to annihilate the United States Cavalry three times in succession. (36)

13. For about a week my relations with my father was virtually nonexistent—on the surface, at any rate. Underneath, things were building up to a climax: the powder train were laid, and it needed only a tiny spark to touch it off. (17)

14. Branson County, North Carolina, is in a sequestered district of one of the staidest and most conservative States of the Union. Society in Branson County is almost primitive in its simplicity. Most of the white people owns the farms they till, and even before the war there was no very wealthy families to force their neighbors, by comparison, into the category of "poor whites." (28)

15. Weakness, frailty, cowardice, and effeminacy is, among other attributes, associated with the Mind. Strength, brute power, force, virility, and physical beauty are associated with the Body. Thus the upper classes or Omnipotent Administrators, is perennially associated with physical weakness, decay, underdeveloped bodies, effeminacy, sexual impotence, and frigidity. Virility, strength, and power are associated with the lower classes, the Supermasculine Menials. (32)

16. We set aside increasing amounts of money every year for our publicity campaign and more people is now aware that any month in Kenya is a holiday month and that all tourists, whether wealthy or not, is always welcome.

Having referred earlier to our game conservation policy, it is necessary to mention that these policies are decided after facts is made available to us by research workers. Both the National Parks and the Game Department pursues an active research policy, again assisted by overseas friends, and already there exist a nucleus around which a strong game research investigation is being developed. (6)

I. Two words in one: Contractions—Where to put the apostrophe

There are two major types of contractions.
1. The pronoun-verb pair[2] becomes one word—e.g., he is = he's.
2. The word "not" is combined with the verb—e.g., do not = don't.

The pronoun-verb pair becomes <u>one</u> word

The following words can be combined with a verb to make a contraction:

I	we	there
you	you	
he		
she	they	
it		
that		
who		

Usually you remove the <u>first</u> letter or the <u>first two</u> letters of the verb when combining the <u>verb</u> with the <u>pronoun</u>: put the apostrophe in the place of these letters. In Chart 30, the letters that will be removed are in capitals.

[2] Same as noun-verb pair. See page 8.

CHART 30. Pronoun-Verb Pair Contractions

One Letter Removed

Singular			Plural		
I Am	=	I'm	we Are*	=	we're
you Are*	=	you're	you Are*	=	you're
he Is	=	he's	they Are*	=	they're
she Is	=	she's	who Are*	=	who're
it Is	=	it's			
that Is	=	that's	(there are = no contraction)		
who Is	=	who's			
there Is	=	there's			

*Notice the starred word "are." Because the word "are" is difficult to pronounce after the words "you," "we," and "they," people usually slur the pronoun and the verb "are" together. The result is that "are" as a <u>separate word</u> is quite rare in <u>spoken</u> language. However, you should be aware of its existence in <u>written</u> language, for it will help you to know where the words "you're," "we're," and "they're" come from. Also note that "are" is the plural form of "is": "John <u>is</u> here," "John and Helen <u>are</u> here." See page 147. See page 233 for discussion of the difference between "their," "they're," and "there," and between "your" and "you're."

Two Letters Removed

Singular

I WIll	=	I'll
you WIll	=	you'll
he WIll	=	he'll
she WIll	=	she'll
it WIll	=	it'll
who WIll	=	who'll
I HAve	=	I've
you HAve	=	you've
he HAs	=	he's
she HAs	=	she's
it HAs	=	it's
that HAs	=	that's
who HAs	=	who's
what HAs	=	what's

Plural

we WIll	=	we'll
you WIll	=	you'll
they WIll	=	they'll
who WIll	=	who'll
we HAve	=	we've
you HAve	=	you've
they HAve	=	they've

Four Letters Removed

Singular

I WOULd	=	I'd
you WOULd	=	you'd
he WOULd	=	he'd
she WOULd	=	she'd
who WOULd	=	who'd

Plural

we WOULd	=	we'd
you WOULd	=	you'd
they WOULd	=	they'd
who WOULd	=	who'd

The word <u>NOT</u> is combined with the verb

The following verbs usually can be combined with the word "not" to make one word:

are	can	will
is	could	would
was	do	should
has	does	
have	did	
had		

Usually the "o" in "not" is removed and replaced with an apostrophe. As with pronoun-verb pairs, the letter or letters that are removed are shown in capitals.

CHART 31. Contractions for Verbs Combined with "not"

are nOt	=	aren't	canNOt*	=	can't
is nOt	=	isn't	do nOt	=	don't
was nOt	=	wasn't	does nOt	=	doesn't
has nOt	=	hasn't	did nOt	=	didn't
have nOt	=	haven't	wILL not	=	won't†
had nOt	=	hadn't			
			could nOt	=	couldn't
			should nOt	=	shouldn't
			would nOt	=	wouldn't

*Notice that <u>two</u> letters are removed.
†Notice that the word really changes altogether.

For more on contractions and editing exercises, see Chapter 5, Part E, pages 237-238, and the cumulative editing at the end of Chapter 5, page 239.

J. Verbs, and how they express time

The English verb system is extremely complicated and vague. The verbs and helping verbs change in spelling according to WHEN the action is happening, but unlike some other languages, English remains not very precise in its use of verbs to express time.

Therefore, it is not to your advantage to learn all the various ways to express verbs through "rules." If you want this kind of approach, you are best off with one of the current textbooks of English usage and grammar.

But if you want to get a <u>feel</u> for how authors use various verbs and helping verbs to express fine distinctions in TIME, the following excerpts are worth studying. The verbs, helping verbs, and words that express time are underlined. Note especially how the authors use "have" and "had" in excerpts (b) and (c). The helping verb "have" is often used before the main verb to express time JUST BEFORE THE <u>PRESENT</u>: it happened JUST BEFORE everything else in the passage. The helping verb "had" usually helps to express time JUST BEFORE THE <u>PAST</u>: It also happened JUST BEFORE everything else in the passage. Thus notice the difference between "have been decreased" in excerpt (b), and "had told" in excerpt (c). Also note how you can make a prediction of the future even though you are writing about the past. The helping verb "would" is often used before the main verb to express a prediction made in the past. See "would keep" in excerpt (d). Regular future is expressed with the helping verb "will." See excerpt (a).

a. Present and Prediction (future)

White people <u>cannot</u> [present], in the generality, <u>be taken</u> [present] as models of how to live. Rather the man <u>is</u> [present] himself in sore need of new standards, which <u>will release</u> [prediction: future] him from his confusion and place him once again in fruitful communion with the depths of his own being.

(James Baldwin, *The Fire Next Time*) (8)

b. Present and Just Before the Present

At a time when heart transplant operations <u>are being performed</u> [present] with ever-increasing frequency elsewhere, large numbers of West African children <u>are</u> [present] still <u>dying</u> [present] of a relatively simple inflammation of the intestine called dysentery. While the dangers of trachoma, an eye disease, <u>have been</u> [just before the present] greatly <u>decreased</u>, and the condition <u>is diagnosed</u> [present] and <u>treated</u> [present] routinely in other areas, it <u>is</u> [present] still an everyday recurrence that <u>threatens</u> [present] the eyesight of many girls and boys in West Africa.

(Alfred Allotey Acquaye, *The Children of West Africa*) (3)

c. Past and Just Before the Past

But she <u>felt</u> [past] his lips on her forehead, soft and very gentle. He <u>drew</u> [past] away. When she <u>opened</u> [past] her eyes he <u>was looking</u> [past] at her with a little smile and he <u>seemed</u> [past] very tired. Someone at the party <u>had told</u> [just before the past] her that he <u>hadn't slept</u> [just before the past] for two days. What <u>struck</u> [past] her <u>was</u> [past] the innocence of the kiss, innocence, yes, and a kind of gratitude. For what, she <u>had asked</u> [just before the past] herself in the mirror, for what?

(John A. Williams, *The Man Who Cried I Am*) (136)

d. Past, Just Before the Past and a Prediction (of the future) Made in the Past.

I already knew [past] what Natalia felt [past] inside. I knew [past] something about her; that she had been [just before the past] lonely for a long time. I already knew [past] that. We had been [just before the past] together many times; but always the shadow of Tunilo kept [past] us apart. We felt [past] that his blistered hands came [past] between us and carried [past] Natalia away so that she would keep [prediction in the past] on nursing him; and we knew [past] that it would always be [prediction in the past] like that as long as she lived [past].

(Juan Rulfo, "Talpa") (133)

4J. Exercises

1. Find a short story that you like and change it into a different time. If the short story is in past time, change it into the present, and vice versa. There is no need to copy the story over; simply pencil the new verbs right into the text.

2. Write a prediction.
a. For the future.
b. Start in past time and predict what <u>would</u> happen. (See excerpt (d), p. 211).

5 Other Uses of S

(For Noun-Verb Pair Agreement, See Chapter 4.)

A. The noun and pronoun: Definitions

Before you can review the other uses of S, you must know the definition of NOUN and PRONOUN. Even if you do know what nouns and pronouns are, review the definitions that this book uses.

A noun is anything you could write an essay about

In the following passage, all nouns are underlined. Stop at each one and notice how it might be discussed in an essay you might write. Some of the nouns in this passage would not be nouns in other passages, but they are BEING USED AS NOUNS in this particular passage. "Giving" and "sense" are such nouns. In addition, some of the words that are not nouns in this passage would be nouns in another passage. In this passage they are used as descriptive words. "Militant" and "short" are such words. "Militant" describes "groups" in this passage, but in another passage, you might be talking about "the militant," something you could write an essay about. Likewise, "short" describes "time." But a "short" is also something you see in the movies before the feature film. In other words, you must see how a word is being used in a sentence before you decide finally whether it is being used as a noun or not.

> Within a very short time, the Panthers and similar militant groups among blacks have succeeded in giving black people something even the late Dr. Martin Luther King, for all his abilities and devotion, never succeeded in giving them: a sense of pride in their own race and heritage.
>
> (Hilary Ng'Wend, "The Panthers: An African's View") (101)

Notice that you could write an essay about any one of the nouns above: time, Panthers, groups, blacks, giving, people, Dr. Martin Luther King, abilities, devotion, sense, pride, race, and heritage.

In addition, nouns can usually be recognized by the words that go before them. In the following passage, all the nouns are nonsense words—words that do not really exist. Yet you can still recognize them as nouns.

> There are lots of zocgags who will hit me on the nobnud with criges as soon as they see me. Big sharp criges rain from every lopnet. And then my rejork has to be

215

mended and I have to wait many zibles for the mufts on my pemmot or scod to heal.

The words in the above passage that told you a noun was coming were:

a. There are lots of
b. the
c. with
d. Big sharp[1]
e. every
f. my
g. many
h. or

Here is the original passage. The nouns are underlined. Look at the words that tell you the noun is coming.

There are lots of <u>people</u> who will hit me on the <u>head</u> with <u>rocks</u> as soon as they see me. Big sharp <u>rocks</u> rain from every <u>side</u>. And then my <u>shirt</u> has to be mended and I have to wait many <u>days</u> for the <u>scabs</u> on my <u>face</u> or <u>knees</u> to heal.
(Juan Rulfo, "Macerio") (112)

The pronoun takes the place of a noun when it is clear what the pronoun means

The following passage has NO PRONOUNS (except the pronoun "this") in it. All the nouns are underlined. Notice how boring and repetitive it is:

Then the <u>mother</u> came back. The <u>mother</u> had a <u>grasshopper</u> for the little <u>children</u>. The <u>mother</u> found the <u>mother's children</u> dead. The <u>mother</u> went to the <u>cardinal</u> and said, "The <u>people</u> on <u>earth</u> treated the <u>mother</u> like this. The <u>people</u> killed all the <u>mother's children</u>."

Now the underlined words show where the author used pronouns so he would not have to repeat words too much. Notice that it is always clear what the pronoun means, what noun it is replacing.

Then the mother came back. <u>She</u> had a grasshopper for the little <u>ones</u>. <u>She</u> found <u>her</u> children dead. <u>She</u> went to the cardinal and said, "The people on earth treated <u>me</u> like <u>this</u>. <u>They</u> killed all <u>my</u> children."
(Morris Edward Opler, "The Adventure with the Whippoorwill") (106)

The following words, then, are the most common pronouns.

---

[1] Most descriptive words come before nouns.

CHART 32. Common Pronouns

Singular (one)			Plural (More Than One)		
Do-er	**Receiver**	**Ownership**	**Do-er**	**Receiver**	**Ownership**
I	(to) me myself	my mine	we	(to) us ourselves	our ours*
you	(to) you yourself	your	you	(to) you yourselves	your yours*
he	(to) him himself	his*			
she	(to) her herself	her hers*	they	(to) them themselves	their theirs*
it	(to) it itself	its*			
this	(to) this		these	(to) them themselves	their theirs*
that	(to) that		those	(to) them themselves	their theirs*
one†	(to) one oneself	one's			
another†	(to) another	another's			
anybody†	(to) anybody	anybody's			
anyone†	(to) anyone	anyone's			
everybody†	(to) everybody	everybody's			
nobody†	(to) nobody	nobody's			
no one†	(to) no one	no one's			
somebody†	(to) somebody	somebody's			
someone†	(to) someone	someone's			
who	(to) whom	whose*	who	(to) whom	whose*
which	(to) which	whose*	which	(to) which	whose*

*Note that there is NO 'S on ownership pronouns until you get to the pronoun "one." Also note that there is NO 'S in "whose." See page 237 for use of "who's."

†These are traditionally called "Indefinite Pronouns." See Index.

218 *The Ends of Words*

The following ownership pronouns NEVER HAVE 'S. ALL THE REST OF THE PRONOUNS AND ALL NOUNS NEED 'S TO SHOW OWNERSHIP. See pages 231-232.

                yours   ours
                his   yours
                hers

                                      theirs
                its
                whose   whose

ALL OTHER OWNERSHIP WORDS HAVE 'S.

                one's coat
                each other's coat
                Barbara's coat

5A. Exercises

1. Underline all the nouns you can find in several newspaper and magazine articles. Make a list of the words that tell you a noun is coming.

2. Underline all the pronouns you can find in several newspaper and magazine articles. Add to the list in Chart 32.

Other Uses of S 221

B. The difference between S̲ and 'S̲

General guidelines (for specific guidelines, see Parts C, D, and E) (for summary of S̲, 'S̲ and S̲', see Chart 35, page 243)

For plural nouns, add S̲

ONE NOUN	ADD S̲		PLURAL NOUN (MORE THAN ONE)
cat	+ s̲	=	cats (several cats) The c̲a̲t̲s̲ are hungry.
house	+ s̲	=	houses (several houses) The h̲o̲u̲s̲e̲s̲ are rent-controlled.
sister	+ s̲	=	sisters (several sisters) The s̲i̲s̲t̲e̲r̲s̲ often sing together.

(For plural noun guidelines, see Part C, page 223.)

For ownership, add 'S̲ to a̲l̲l̲ nouns and s̲o̲m̲e̲ pronouns

NOUN	ADD 'S̲		OWNERSHIP WORD
cat	+ 's̲	=	cat's (owned by the cat) The c̲a̲t̲'̲s̲ tail is long.
sister	+ 's̲	=	sister's (owned by the sister) I used my s̲i̲s̲t̲e̲r̲'̲s̲ notebook.
Helen	+ 's̲	=	Helen's (owned by Helen) I used H̲e̲l̲e̲n̲'̲s̲ notebook.
everyone	+ 's̲	=	everyone's (owned by everyone) I used e̲v̲e̲r̲y̲o̲n̲e̲'̲s̲ notebooks.

(For ownership guidelines, see Part D, page 231.)

For ownership for s̲o̲m̲e̲ pronouns, add S̲

PRONOUN	ADD S̲		OWNERSHIP PRONOUN
your	+ s̲	=	yours The book is y̲o̲u̲r̲s̲.
her	+ s̲	=	hers The book is h̲e̲r̲s̲.
it	+ s̲	=	its I̲t̲s̲ wing is broken.

222 *The Ends of Words*

our	+	s	=	ours
				The book is ours.
their	+	s	=	theirs
				The book is theirs.

(For ownership pronoun guidelines, see Part D, page 231. For complete list, see Chart 32.)

For two words in one, 'S often means "is"

NOUN OR PRONOUN		ADD 'S		TWO WORDS IN ONE
it	+	's	=	it's (it is)
				It's a bird.
sister	+	's	=	sister's (sister is)
				The sister's in trouble.[2]
everyone	+	's	=	everyone's (everyone is)[2]
				Everyone's here now.

(For differences between "its" and "it's", "whose" and "who's", etc, see Part E, page 237.)

Remember: 'S does not make words plural[3]

'S means "of the."

The horse's mouth = The mouth of the horse

The man's eyes = The eyes of the man

In Spanish, "del" means "of the" or 'S. In college writing, use the second translation as much as possible.

El nombre del hijo es Juan.
(1) The name of the son is John.
(2) The son's name is John.

S means more than one. (For special plurals, see page 224.)

I love horses.
He had three sons.

---

[2] Notice that this same spelling could be used to show ownership: "the sister's speech was good." You have to look at how the word is being used to decide which meaning you want. Generally in more formal college writing it is advisable not to use 'S to mean "is" after a noun. Use the words, "the sister is in trouble" as opposed to "the sister's in trouble." The same is true of pronouns like "everyone." Avoid using 'S to mean "is" as much as possible.

[3] Exception: If you are talking about letters or numbers, you can use 'S for plural: "Mind your P's and Q's."

C. Plural nouns

How to make nouns plural (more than one)

For most nouns, add <u>S</u>.

SINGULAR	PLURAL
sister	sisterS
brother	brotherS
joy	joyS
knuckle	knuckleS
list	listS
mind	mindS

When "Y" is a sound by itself, change it to "IES."

family	sounds like:	(fam-il-<u>ee</u>)	familIES
duty	sounds like:	(dut-<u>ee</u>)	dutIES
controversy			controversIES

(Compare with "joy" above)

When the plural will add an extra sound (syllable) to the noun, add "ES."

box	boxES	sounds like:	(box-ez)
flash	flashES	sounds like:	(flash-ez)
match	matchES	sounds like:	(match-ez)

Sometimes nouns ending in "F" or "FE" change to "VES" in plural.

leaf	leaVES
life	liVES
knife	kniVES
wife	wiVES

Other nouns ending in "F" are regular.

gulf	gulfS
belief	beliefS (Compare with <u>verb</u> "believe")

Some nouns form the plural by adding "EN."

child	childrEN
ox	oxEN

Sometimes the letters <u>inside</u> the noun change.

fOOt	fEEt
tOOth	tEEth
mOUse	mIce
mAn	mEn
womAn	womEn

Some nouns are exactly the same in singular and plural.

one fish	two fish
one sheep	two sheep
one series	two series

And finally, the plurals of some nouns just have to be memorized.

crisis	crisEs
thesis	thesEs
hypothesis	hypothesEs
datum	datA
stimulus	stimulI
person	people (or persons)

It is also useful to know when a plural is coming

What follows is a list of words that tell you that a plural noun is likely to come afterward.

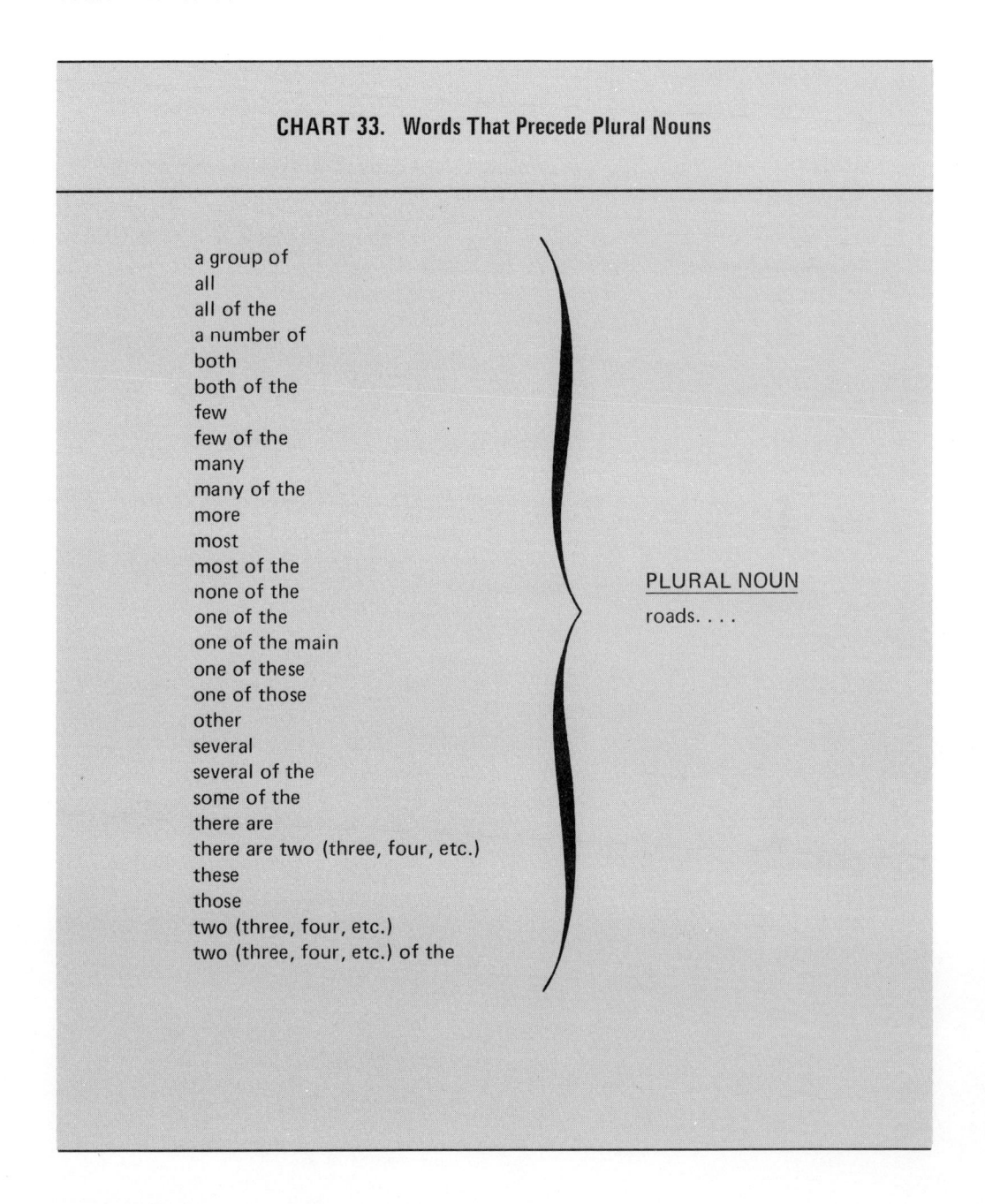

CHART 33. Words That Precede Plural Nouns

---

a group of
all
all of the
a number of
both
both of the
few
few of the
many
many of the
more
most
most of the
none of the
one of the
one of the main
one of these
one of those
other
several
several of the
some of the
there are
there are two (three, four, etc.)
these
those
two (three, four, etc.)
two (three, four, etc.) of the

} PLURAL NOUN

roads. . . .

In the following passage, notice the words that introduce the underlined plural nouns:

> It provides for smaller classroom situations and two <u>teachers</u> instead of one to deal with these <u>problems</u>. However, the overwhelming number of <u>problems</u> facing the black children are those[4] inherent in their blackness, or those[4] directly related to their blackness.
>
> (Jim Haskins, *Diary of a Harlem Schoolteacher*) (58)

Words that tell you nouns are coming never change in spelling for plural (exception: "this," "these," and "that," "those")

In Spanish, and in several other languages, the word that comes before or after the noun changes its spelling as the noun changes its spelling. For example, note the changes in spelling for the Spanish word "the."

	SINGULAR	PLURAL
English:	<u>the</u> song	<u>the</u> song<u>s</u>
Spanish:	<u>la</u> cancion	<u>las</u> cancione<u>s</u>

In English, the word "the" does not change its spelling. Even in plural, there is no <u>S</u> on "the." But in Spanish, "la" becomes "laS" in plural.

In fact, in Spanish, if the noun is plural, ALL THE WORDS WHICH DESCRIBE THAT NOUN become plural also:

	SINGULAR	PLURAL
English:	the white house	the white house<u>s</u>
Spanish:	la casa blanca	las casas blanca<u>s</u>
English:	an interesting book	interesting book<u>s</u>
Spanish:	un libro interesante	libros interesante<u>s</u>

But in English, the descriptive words never change in spelling: "interesting" can be singular <u>or</u> plural.

THERE ARE TWO EXCEPTIONS:

	SINGULAR	PLURAL
	this book	th<u>ese</u> book<u>s</u>
	that book	th<u>ose</u> book<u>s</u>

---

[4] Notice that the word "those" does not always introduce a noun. Like many other pronouns, "these" and "those" can take the place of a noun.

5C. 1. Exercises: Editing for Plural Nouns

Look for plural nouns in the following excerpts and change the spelling when necessary. Remember that there is only ONE case in which you add 'S to a noun to make it plural. See page 222 (note). Make all changes directly in the sentences as if you were editing a paper. If an excerpt does not need to be changed, put a check (√) next to its number. Look only for plural nouns, using the guidelines given on pages 223-226. Do not edit for anything else. (See page 2 for how to use the "Answer" Section.)

Example
Both would climb out of their narrow prisons on ladder's of words; both would climb steep mountain and walk lonely path's; and both would grapple with the revolutionary implications in Thomas Jefferson's word's. (16)

1. White peoples cannot, in the generality, be taken as models of how to live. (8)

2. Gudatrigakwitl left the people all kind's of dance's. (74)

3. The human beans also passed canteens, which guards would fill with water. (132)

4. Ten's of thousand's of American shuffled eastward, their hand clasped on top of their heads. (132)

5. She had two big can of soup for the American's. . . .She had stacks of loave's of black bread, too. (132)

6. The maternal uncle accompanies him to his new home but gives him no further advice and instructions', lest his mind be confused trying to hold in his head so many thing. (29)

7. His eyes were filled with the white blur moving toward him in the shadows of the room. Again Mary's body heaved and he held the pillow in a grip that took all of his strength. For a long time he felt the sharp pain of her fingernail's biting into his wrist's. The white blur was still. (140)

8. The village elders taught them the traditional do's and don't's of their own tribal society, and how to survive in the jungle (if that was where they lived) or the desert, swamp or forest. (3)

9. There were riot's and other disorder's and young toughs came charging to the platform, screaming, "Kill the nigger," "Get the god-damned nigger." Douglas's was pelted with eggs and thrown down stepes; but he stood his ground and took his knock's. (16)

10. White's moved through the ghetto like maggots' on a carcass: cops, social worker's, schoolteachers, bill collectores, the supervisor's and collectors of the syndicate, the owner's of taverns, furniture store's, currency exchanges, television stores'. (52)

11. In these place life, and its possibility, has been distorted almost identically. And the distortion is as old as its sources: the fear, frustration, and hatred that Negroe's have always been heir to in America. It is just that in the citys, which were once the black man's twentieth-century "Jordan," *promise* is a dying bitch with rotting eye's. And the stink of her dying is a deadly killing fume. (69)

5C. 2. Exercises: Editing for Plural Nouns and Words That Tell You a Noun Is Coming

Look for plural nouns and words that tell you a noun is coming in the following excerpts and change spelling when necessary (remember that almost all descriptive words do NOT change in spelling when the noun is plural, see page 226), in order to put the excerpts back into college writing. Make all changes directly in the sentences as if you were editing a paper. If an excerpt does not need to be changed, put a check (√) next to its number. Look only for plural nouns and words that tell you a noun is coming, using the guidelines given on pages 223-226. Do not edit for anything else. (See page 2 for how to use the "Answer" Section.)

1. But put on your crown, my Queen, and we will build a New City on this ruins. (32)

2. "Are yours friends, masters and acquaintance's enjoying the best of health?" (77)

3. On theirs heads were headdresses with wide edges that reached beyond theirs faces and shaded them. (2)

4. This streets stretch from one end of America to the other and connect like a maze from which very few can fully escape. (69)

5. When I was at work, up in the Roseland Men's room, I just couldn't keep still. My shine rag popped with the rhythm of those greats band rocking the ballroom. (83)

6. She could see the old woman in her picture (really her grandmother in the South) lifting her head to the brightes stars on the flag in these distance. (63)

7. But now they seem to have trapped you into coming to these forest by giving you a good meal of porridge and chicken, as if you were a traveler or guest. (70)

8. The departure of theses student has astonished right-thinking Angolan circle's, because alls Angolan's settled outside Angola are considered foreigners in thes eye's of the Lisbon Government. (86)

9. Youths of good and courteous ways within theirs own mother's community always married quickly because their maternals uncle's lost no time in arranging betrothal for them. (29)

10. But there was a solitude to this work that had never been present in the old slaves times. The huges plantations fields had manys slaves, and they sang together. (68)

11. This prevailings attitudes put the Negro on the defensive, for he had to defend his person and his humanity. All of this permeated the American theater and American life as long as the syndicate reigned. This prevailings attitudes were to send Negroes fleeing toward a community where they might find a measure of safety. These time's were to see the Negro expelled from the Broadway theater. (91)

D. Ownership (and the difference between "their," "they're," and "there" and between "your" and "you're.")

For nouns, 'S generally shows ownership

As outlined on page 221, 'S means ownership when added to a noun.

| the girl's book | = | the book of the girl |
| Carol's book | = | the book of Carol |

When more than one person owns something, add S'

| the girls' book | = | the book of the girls |

But when the plural noun has a special spelling for plural (see list, page 224), show ownership by adding 'S

PLURAL OWNERSHIP NOUNS

REGULAR SPELLING OF PLURAL NOUN: ADD S'	SPECIAL SPELLING OF PLURAL NOUN: ADD 'S
the girls' books	the children's books
the brothers' voices	the men's voices
the citizens' power	the people's power

Ownership pronouns

Some ownership pronouns do NOT need 'S because the ownership is already shown in the spelling. The word "my," for example, already shows ownership.

| my records | = | the records that belong to me. |
| his records | = | the records that belong to him. |

Ownership pronouns are listed in Chart 32, page 217.

Other ownership pronouns need 'S

someone's records = the records that belong to someone.

CHART 34. Summary of Ownership

	Singular	Plural
Nouns: **Regular** **Spelling**	student's country's box's Paula's	students' countries' boxes' Paula's and Jim's
Nouns: **Special** **Spelling**	child's mouse's	children's mice's
Pronouns with Ownership Already in the Spelling	my mine your yours[†] his her hers[†] its[†]	our ours[†] your yours[†] their[*] theirs[†]
Pronouns That Add 'S to Show Ownership	one's another's somebody's everybody's	

[*]See p. 233 for the difference between "their," "they're," and "there."
[†]NO 'S!

The difference between "their," "they're," and "there"

Their = ownership

Their land was taken away.

They're = "they are" (a contraction; see page 207)

They're going to take back the land = They are going to take back the land.

There has two major meanings.
1. A place (Take the "t" off of "there," and you are left with the word "here," which can also mean a place.)

She pointed over there.
We will go there later.

2. Introductory word to make a smooth sentence (see also page 200)

There is a reason to be angry.
There are two reasons to be angry.

The difference between "your" and "you're"

Your = ownership

Your land was taken away.

You're = "you are" (a contraction; see page 207)

You're going to take back the land = You are going to take back the land.

5D. Exercises: Editing for Ownership Nouns and Pronouns

Look for ownership nouns and pronouns in the following excerpts and change the spelling when necessary in order to put the excerpts back into college writing. Make all changes directly in the sentences as if you were editing a paper. If an excerpt does not need to be changed, put a check (√) next to its number. Look only for ownership nouns and pronouns, using the guidelines given on pages 231-233. Do not edit for anything else. (See page 2 for how to use the "Answer" Section.)

Example

The car was now purring through the paved streets of town, and, for a moment, he was three blocks from his father's undertaking establishment! (138)

1. But let us also remember that even a black man's government can go wrong. (98)

2. "The white mans' Heaven," sings a Black Muslim minister, "is the black man's Hell." (8)

3. The slum is the villain then—not it's inhabitants. (116)

4. One drew in all ones breath and tightened ones fist and pulled the small body against the heavens, stretching, straining all the muscles in the legs to make—one giant step. (56)

5. When the "probationer's" maternal uncles arrive they gather together with the girls legal representatives and exchange formal greetings. (29)

6. I make no threat when I say that unless these wrongs are remedied without delay, we might well find that even plain talk before the countrys Courts is too timid a method to draw attention to ours grievances. (84)

7. Neither her brief seventy year's journey through life nor her long two days' travel northward had dimmed the live brightness of her eyes, which, for all there bewilderment, had accurately selected hers own treasures out of the row of luggage and guarded them vigilantly. (46)

8. I suppose this was why I asked her to marry me: to give mineself something to be moored to. Perhaps this was why, in Spain, she decided that she wanted to marry me. But people can't, unhappily, invent their mooring posts, there lovers and there friends, anymore than they can invent they're parent's. Life gives these and also takes them away and the great difficulty is to say Yes to life. (9)

9. It is a peculiar sensation, this double-consciousness, this sense of always looking at one's self through the eyes of others, of measuring ones soul by the tape of a world that looks on in amused contempt and pity. (40)

10. The drum, or tom-tom, is Africa's most traditional musical instrument, and the "talking drums" of West Africa are known far and wide, for there use in signaling and communication. (96)

11. Billy covered hi's head with his blanket again. He always covered his head when hi's mother came to see him in the mental ward—always got much sicker until she went away. (132)

12. My father fought with all the fury of a wild beast wounded by the hunters first shot: all the neighbors came out of there houses to watch. From all sides voices were raised exhorting me to get out while I could. "What are you waiting for, you young fool?" (17)

E. Two words in one (contractions): the difference between "its" and "it's"; the difference between "whose" and "who's"

As outlined on pages 217, 218 and 221, "ITS" is an ownership pronoun. But when do you use "IT'S"?

> It's dreadful when there's no one to moan to.
> (William N. Gass, *We Have Not the Right Life*) (50)

WHOLE THOUGHT	FRAGMENT (See p. 20)
It's dreadful	when there's no one to moan to.

The above sentence contains a whole thought. But where is the noun-verb pair? The fragment also has a noun-verb pair, but where is it?

Since the pronoun "IT" is used like a noun, we can call it the noun of the noun-verb pair (or it is part of the pronoun verb pair).

The verb of the noun-verb pair is 'S.

'S = IS

Thus the sentence above could be written:

N V   V   N
It is dreadful when there is no one to moan to.[5]

Comparison of meanings

OWNERSHIP WORDS	'S = IS
His head is spinning.	He's spinning. = He is spinning.
Its eyes are glowing.	It's a bird! = It is a bird!
Whose book is this?	Who's here? = Who is here?
Theirs: The book is theirs.	There's no one here. = There is no one here.[5]
John's book is here.	John's here.[6] = John is here.

A list of two words in one

And because 'S can mean "IS" in a particular sentence, here is a list of commonly used words that might be used with 'S to mean "IS." However, keep in mind that in the most formal of college writing, using 'S to mean "IS" is not generally acceptable. Make sure you know your professor's attitude—and your attitude toward him—when you edit your essays.

---

[5] Technically "no one" is the pronoun of the pronoun-verb pair. "There" is an introductory word to make the sentence smooth (see page 200).

[6] Avoid this use of 'S in college writing.

TWO WORDS IN ONE	MEANING	ILLUSTRATIVE SENTENCE
who's	who is	Who's next in line?
what's	what is	What's playing tonight?
when's	when is	When's the best time to call?
how's	how is	How's it going?
it's	it is	It's three o'clock.
he's	he is	He's a cool guy.
she's	she is	She's a good speaker.
that's	that is	That's the way!
there's	there is	There's someone at the door.
here's	here is	Here's your hat.

5E. Exercises: Editing for Contractions

Review Chapter 4, Part I on contractions before doing this exercise.

Look for contractions and words confused with contractions in the following excerpts and change the spelling when necessary in order to put the excerpts back into college writing. Make all changes directly in the sentences as if you were editing a paper. If an excerpt does not need to be changed, put a check (√) next to its number. Look only for contractions and words confused with contractions, using the guidelines given on pages 207-209 and 237-238. Do not edit for anything else. (See page 2 for how to use the "Answer" Section.)

Example
It's not my shame but yours. (16)

1. He don't mind the smell of mustard gas and roses. (132)

2. "Ma," he called softly. "Your still there?" (141)

3. Felipa stays alone in the kitchen cooking food for the three of us. Since I've known her, that's all she doe's. (112)

4. Its dreadful when theres no one to moan to. (50)

5. That's the way that spider was. (106)

6. People arn't supposed to look back. Im certainly not going to do it anymore. (132)

7. He didn't look like a soldier at all. He looked like a filthy flamingo. (132)

8. One guy I knew really *was* shot in Dresden for taking a teapot that wasn't his. (132)

9. He said there wasnt a man there who wouldnt gladly die for those ideals. (132)

10. "You're lawyer is wearing sneakers," said the last of the prisoners. (82)

11. I had determined that I would'nt fight, that it would be better to keep cool and wait until a time when I could hurt someone I really want'ed to hurt. (48)

12. After she has eaten, she makes two little piles with her hands, one for Felipa, the other for me. But sometimes Felipa doesn't feel like eating and then the two little piles are for me. Thats why I love Felipa, because I'm always hungry and I never get filled up—never, not even when I eat up her food. (112)

13. For where does one run to when his already in the promised land? (22)

14. Sons and daughters of Africa—there is a choice before us. We are either slaves or free men—thats all. (72)

15. The writer is meeting in Europe people who are not American, who's sense of reality is entirely different from his own. (10b)

16. Here's a white man, swinging in Africa with a white woman. And you're down in Georgia, not knowing any better. You really believe there's a white man whose king of the jungle. (18)

17. Black people have influenced every field of knowledge taught in schools from literature to engineering, and it's up to the schools to "unbleach" their courses and let their students know about this. (145)

18. Blood has a good flavor too, although it is'nt really like the flavor of Felipa's milk—Thats why I always live shut up in my house—so they wont throw

rocks at me. As soon as they feed me I lock myself in my room and bar the door so my sins won't find me out, because its dark. (112)

19. But you never really stop believing in Santa Claus. When Momma is gone and you're Santa Claus you can't accept not being able to give. Maybe that's why honest people steal at Christmas time. Christmas is'nt right unless you give. (53)

20. But we were far more cheerful than anything Iv'e said might indicate and none of the above seemed to matter very much at the time. (10a)

21. At first you tell yourself that it's all a dirty joke, or that its due to the "political situation." But deep down you come to suspect that your yourself to blame, and you stand naked and shivering before the millions of eyes who look through you unseeingly. (43)

22. Educated people, of any color, are so extremely rare that it is unquestionably one of the first tasks of a nation to open all of it's schools to all of it's citizens. But the dispute has actually nothing to do with education, as some among the eminently uneducated know. (10e)

23. "You know what I say to people when I hear they're writing anti-war books?"

"No. What *do* you say, Harrison Starr?"

"I say, 'Why dont you write and anti-*glacier* book instead?'" (132)

24. "But its mad. Its like putting a girl in a convent till your ready to marry her. . . . We have to be free. We haven't got a choice."

"Do'nt get upset. Please do'nt get upset."

"Weve got to see how things go."

There was a silence.

"I was thinking of coming back here tomorrow night. That's all."

"I'll write. Every day."

"Yes." (48)

CHART 35. Summary Chart of S, 'S, and S'

	S	'S	S'
Singular Ownership Nouns		sister's dog's lady's man's John's	
Singular Ownership Pronouns	his hers (It is hers)* yours (It is yours)*	one's somebody's another's everybody's	
Plural Ownership Nouns		(When there is a special plural spelling) men's children's sheep's (the sheep's coat)	(Regular plural spelling) sisters' ladies' dogs'
Plural Ownership Pronouns	ours yours theirs (It is theirs)*		
Plural nouns	sisters dogs ladies	(signs, symbols, numbers) ABC's #'s 5's P's $'s 34's Q's	
Two Words in One— Pronouns 'S = Is		(Avoid in formal writing) it's = it is he's = he is who's = who is what's = what is	
Two Words in One— Nouns 'S = Is		(Avoid in formal writing) sheep's = sheep is (The sheep's in the meadow) John's = John is	

*But, "It is her book"; "It is your book"—no S at all.

Cumulative Editing for Chapter 5

Look for all words covered in Chapter 5 in the following excerpts and change spelling when necessary in order to put the excerpts back into college writing. Make all changes directly in the sentences as if you were editing a paper. If an excerpt does not need to be changed, put a check (√) next to its number. Look only for words ending in S, 'S, and S' and for other contractions and ownership words, using the guidelines given on pages 215-243. Do not edit for anything else. (See page 2 for how to use the "Answer" Section.)

1. They wore garments made in the shape of a man's body. And the sandal's on theirs feet were truly unusual. (2)

2. Horny Sy, one of Jimmys gang members, can't let well enough alone when the boys' jump a woman and drag her into a lot; he has to go back for seconds and discovers that it's his mother underneath him. (23)

3. He started to kick out with he's foots to move what was under his leg's. He only started because he didn't have any legs' to kick with. Somewhere just below his hip joints they had cut both of hi's leg off. (129)

4. I hastily ran over in my mind the few rudiments of boxing I had learnt from my friends in college; but when the moment came, I could'nt bring mineself to hit him, and gave ground rapidly. (17)

5. Do you remember that period? Father's used to take they're children to school as they might lead sheep into a slaughter-house. Tiny tots would turn up from backwood villages thirty or forty miles up-country, shepherded by there parent's, to be put on the books of some school, it didnt matter which. (17)

6. The first men to walk the earth were not like the peoples of today. They all looked exactly alike—golden-eyed, hairless, with skin as red as Africas plain's.

In these day's they're were no black-skinned or dark brown people, no Pygmies, no Bushmen, no Hottentot's, no long-bearded Arabi, no white man. The splitting up of humanity into different races came much later, through the wickedness of men theirselves. (96)

7. I wanted her to know that I recognized that we were both Negroes. "What is your last name?" I inquired. "Alma will do," she stated simply. She let me know that I was a guest and should stay in my place and she would stay in her's. And that set the tone of my relationship with all of the servant. (26)

8. Nancy Lee was proud of being American, a Negro American with blood out of Africa a long time ago, too many generation back to count. But her parents had taught her the beauties of Africa, it's strength, it's song, it's mighty rivers, it's early smelting of iron, it's building of the pyramids, and it's ancient and important civilizations. (63)

9. Negroe's in these country—and Negroe's do not, strictly or legally speaking, exist in any other—are taught really to despise theirself's from the moment there eyes open on the world. (8)

10. And it's up to black parents to insist upon it. Theres more to taking care of our kids education than attending a special auditorium meeting to celebrate Negro History Week with a student sketch. Parents have to stay on top of what their children are being taught and they should organize to help influence teachers' and administrator's. (147)

11. Our's is a continent in revolution against oppression. And peace and revolution make uneasy bedfellows. There can be no peace until the forces of oppression are overthrown. (81)

12. Now we will open your ear's, and also you're throat, for there is something that has been choking you and we will also give you the water that shall wash down all the trouble's in your throat. We shall hope that after thes your mind will recover it's cheerfulness'. (55)

13. Those day, mineself, I thought I would die unless I had a hat with the emblem Stetson in it and some Edwin Clapp shoe. But Nert and Nonny and many of them wouldn't wear readymades shoes. They wore what they called the St. Louis Flat's and the Chicago Flat's, made with cork soles and without heels and with gambler designs on the toes. Later on, some of them made arrangements' to have some kind of electric-lights bulbs in the toes of their shoes with a battery in they're pockets, so when they would get around some jane that was kind of simple and thought they could make her, as they call making um, why they'd press a button in there pocket and light up the little-bitty bulb in the toe of their shoes and that jane was claimed. It's really the fact. (79)

14. The majority accepted these idea. In truth, the stranger must have been very strange, since these kindes peoples could not know that in the big citie's the scribe's role is played by the lawyer and the faith healer's, I think, by the doctor. Distance permits such differencs. (88)

15. And so it is with me. Without light I am not only invisible, but formless as well; and to be unaware of one's form is to live a death. I myself, after existing some twenty year, did not become alive until I discovered my invisibility. (43)

16. And they rode animals with longes ears that looked like bull's but were not. To the faces of this animals were tied leather thongs with which they guided them. On thes backs of the animals were seats on which they sat. A leather thong hung from each side of the animal. Into this they pushed their foots and balanced themselfs. And, in front of him, with one hands on it, each mans carried a piece of wood into which was worked a round piece of iron. And, miracle of miracles, the face of each man was almost completely covered with hair so that only the nose and eye's and forehead showed. And the'se were white. (2)

SECTION THREE

When Ideas Become Complicated

As an adult writer who is learning how to edit your own work, you may find that your ideas are often far more complicated than your ability to express them in college writing. And the more complicated an idea is, the more likely it is that you will run into college writing "problems." Of course you do not want to make your ideas LESS complex by using simple sentences. Instead, you might find a way to preserve the complexity of your ideas and still present them in college writing. The next two chapters are devoted to the trouble adult writers find when expressing complex ideas. Chapter 6 deals with the pronoun difficulties that usually arise when many ideas are expressed at the same time. Chapter 7 deals with those sentences English instructors often call "awkward." "Awkward" is a catch-all word that teaches you absolutely nothing. Why is a sentence "awkward"? How do you change it so it is not "awkward"? Chapter 7 cannot possibly deal with all "problem" areas, but it covers the more common cases. Finally, Chapter 8 provides an overview of what you need to know about introductory paragraphs, internal paragraphs, and the organization of short essays.

6 Special Pronoun Traps

Review the discussion of pronouns on pages 216-218 before going on.

A. The pronoun with the double meaning

As discussed on page 216, pronouns can be very useful little words. For example, note how effectively John A. Williams uses pronouns in the following excerpt.
(Pronouns are underlined.)

> She had smiled. Obviously he had asked somebody to tell him how to ask for a kiss. The dust of Africa hadn't remained on him long; he adjusted very quickly. And she had thought that he might kiss her and had decided that she would let him.
> (John A. Williams, *The Man Who Cried I Am*) (136)

Even though Williams doesn't name the people, it is clear who is doing what.

However, notice what happens when a pronoun seems to have more than one meaning, when it is not clear which word the pronoun is replacing:

> Joanne told Louise that she was going to run the meeting.

Who does the writer mean by "she"? Joanne or Louise? In order to make it perfectly clear WHO IS GOING TO RUN THE MEETING, the writer might change the sentence to:

> Joanne asked Louise to run the meeting.

> OR

> Joanne found out that Louise was supposed to run the meeting, so she told her.

> OR

> Joanne said to Louise, "You are going to run the meeting."

Here is another example of a pronoun whose meaning is not clear:

> The group decided to extend the meeting, which created some new problems.

It is not really clear what created the problems. Is it the decision or the meeting? A clearer sentence might be:

> The group's decision to extend the meeting created some new problems.

By far the most frequent trouble makers are the words "that" and "this."

251

252 *When Ideas Become Complicated*

> One group is working on day-care centers and the other is planning street plays. <u>That</u> is the most important aspect of the new organization.

Although one could probably take a good guess at the meaning of the word "that," the writer should avoid even the slightest confusion by rewriting the sentence:

> Two groups are involved in the most important aspects of the new organization. One group is working on day-care centers and the other is planning street plays.

B. The pronoun with no meaning: Make sure each pronoun really renames something

In the following sentence, note how the underlined pronoun does not seem to rename anything earlier in the sentence.

> The United States is probably the richest nation in the world, yet <u>they</u> do not have enough money to help the poor.

Who are the people meant by "they"? Although we can most certainly guess, the writer would strengthen his point considerably if he <u>named</u> those who mismanage American money:

> The United States is probably the richest nation in the world, yet the <u>people in power</u> do not have enough money to help the poor.
>
> **OR**
>
> The United States is probably the richest nation in the world, yet the <u>government</u> does not have enough money to help the poor.

C. Is the pronoun singular or plural? Is the pronoun "him" or "you"? (Pronoun reference)

When a writer is expressing complicated ideas, it often happens that he forgets what went on at the beginning of his sentence. For example, he may begin his sentence talking about ONE PERSON, and end up talking about MORE THAN ONE PERSON. Or, he may start a sentence talking about YOU and end up talking about HIM.

Keep the amount of people the same

> If <u>a person</u> is to survive in society, <u>they</u> must live by the rules society enforces.

Here the writer begins by talking about ONE PERSON, and ends up talking about MORE THAN ONE PERSON. In editing, he might change the sentence to:

> If <u>a person</u> is to survive in society, <u>he</u> must live by the rules society enforces.

In this next sentence, the same thing happens:

> One must not forget his <u>next-door neighbor</u>, who maintains many of the old traditions of <u>their</u> household.

Here the writer starts talking about ONE NEIGHBOR and ends up discussing MANY NEIGHBORS. He might change his sentence to:

One must not forget his <u>next-door neighbor</u>, who maintains many of the old traditions of <u>his</u> household.

Keep the <u>kind</u> of people the same

In the following sentence, the writer starts by discussing YOU and ends up discussing A MAN.

It does not matter what <u>you</u> decide to do with <u>your</u> life; if <u>a man</u> does not like what <u>he</u> is doing, <u>he</u> can change.

He might change this sentence to:

It does not matter what <u>he</u> decides to do with <u>his</u> life; if <u>a man</u> does not like what <u>he</u> is doing, <u>he</u> can change.

Now the whole sentence talks about HIM. Or, the writer might change the sentence this way:

It does not matter what <u>you</u> decide to do with <u>your</u> life; if <u>you</u> do not like what <u>you</u> are doing, <u>you</u> can change.

Now the whole sentence talks to YOU.

A person is a person, not a thing

The words "which" and "that" usually refer to THINGS. The words "who" and "whom" usually refer to PEOPLE. So, when there might be confusion, avoid "the person <u>that</u>" or "the person <u>which</u>." Use "the person <u>who</u>."

CONFUSING:

Monsona Quintana is an emaciated countrywoman of my land <u>that</u> has given birth seventeen times. . . .

CLEAR:

Monsona Quintana is an emaciated countrywoman of my land <u>who</u> has given birth seventeen times. . . .
(Emilio Belaval, "El Nino Morado de Monsona Quintana") (14)

6C. Exercises: Editing for Pronoun Reference

Look for pronouns in the following excerpts and change those that switch the amount or kind of people or things in the middle of a sentence or paragraph in order to put the excerpts back into college writing. Make all changes directly in the sentences as if you were editing a paper. If an excerpt does not need to be changed, put a check (√) next to its number. Look only for pronoun switches, using the guidelines given on pages 252-253. Do not edit for anything else. (See page 2 for how to use the "Answer" Section.)

Example

The Government should act. ~~They~~ It must deal firmly with anyone who is found exploiting racial, tribal or religious differences. (98)

1. If some do not like what I say, let him be. (74)

2. He was conscious of himself as a frail object which had to protect itself against a pending threat of annihilation. (141)

3. Many Negroes who were sharecroppers, or who managed to purchase one of the tiny farms that dotted the less fertile lands of the South, worked in their fields alone or with his family. (68)

4. Today most of these dancers are old, but you need only the whisper of encouragement to bring forth the powerful dances of your youth. (111)

5. "Well, yes, my son, if one doesn't give up the ghost in the process, they are hardened and strengthened and tempered by suffering, like iron in the fire. (77)

6. Does one sit down, as did Mrs. Wells, and contemplate moving to another community—at considerable expense and inconvenience—so that their children can spend more time with people who look like her, and avoid all contact with those who might challenge her or make him feel inferior? (64)

7. The University of Ghana, which is located in the capital city, Accra, trains their students in the "liberal arts." (3)

8. Despair sits on this country in most places like a charm, but there is a special gray death that loiters in the streets of an urban Negro slum. And the men who walk those streets, tracing and retracing your steps to some hopeless job or a pitiful rooming house or apartment or furnished room, sometimes stagger under the weight of that gray, humiliated because it is not even "real." (69)

9. In prison, those things withheld from and denied to the prisoner become precisely what they want most of all, of course. (32)

10. Arriving at the village, they came to the "talking-place," where the men are in the habit of gathering, sewing mats and doing one's various work in the sun. (29)

11. After several months spent at my hotel in convalescence, I realized once and for all that Paris is not a French city but an international center in which human beings are grouped solely according to one's intellectual affinities. (77)

12. The white man is in love with the past, with dead things and soon they will become one. They are in love with the past because it is in the past that they really exist. (67)

13. In such cases whites are interested parties. . . . It is improper and against the elementary principle of justice to entrust whites with cases involving the denial by him of basic rights to the African people. . . . (84)

14. And so long as I am leader of the Party I am not going to allow any stupid people to come here to disrupt the country because of their ideologies. If I discover him here in Zambia, he will go away by the fastest plane. Please, please, please, Mr. Capitalism and Mr. Communism, remain here but cooperate with us. (71)

15. *All* things are God's. And were Christ to return to earth today, he would be leading the boycotts. He would be signing the petitions. He would stand up and oppose the politicians who come to Harlem once every four years during an election year and then shut your eyes and your hearts to the pleas of desperately poor and deprived people. Christ would have walked in Selma, He would have marched in Washington, and He would have lived in Harlem. "For where two or three are gathered together in my name, there am I in the midst of them." (110)

16. In fact, many of the same intellectuals who are the connoisseurs of African art and lovers of African music and dancing experience feelings of shame or revulsion when he contemplates the social systems that produced these specific, highly valued aspects of the cultures. For instance, he can accept psychologically Benin's art, but not their "customs." (39)

17. He had written these words in a room in Philadelphia when he was thirty-three. Now, in another room, in another age, fifty years to the date after the signing of the Declaration of Independence, Thomas Jefferson, the sage of Monticello, the architect, the philosopher, the humanitarian, lay dying in a house filled with rare books and old slaves. All his life, you had wrestled with the awful presence of your slaves and the noble sound of your words and you had gone

down in defeat. You were not a small man and so your defeat gives no man joy. In you was the strength and the weakness of America. You died on July 4, 1826, and went to your grave, borne by slaves. (16)

D. "Which is" or "which are"? "Who is" or "who are"?

(Review pages 141-149 before going on.)

As discussed on pages 141-143 the noun in the noun-verb pair tells you when to put an S at the end of the verb.

SINGULAR (ONE)

John LikeS animals.

PLURAL (MORE THAN ONE)

John and Helen like animals.

In the same way, when the pronoun takes the place of a noun, you must decide whether the pronoun is singular or plural and then add an S to the singular verb.

SINGULAR

He likeS animals.

PLURAL

They like animals.

But the word "he" is obviously singular, and the word "they" is obviously plural.

What do you do with the pronoun that does not tell you in its spelling whether it is singular or plural? Take the pronoun "which," for example. Here is an example of "which is":

And I look at my body, which is under sentence of death.
(James Baldwin, *Giovanni's Room*) (9)

Here is a similar sentence with "which are."

And I look at the bodies, which are under sentence of death.

How do you tell which verb to use? Do you use "which is" or "which are"? If you are in doubt, you can cover with your finger all the words causing confusion—including the word "which," in order to see which noun is "under sentence of death." The brackets indicate which word(s) to cover:

And I look at my body, [which] is under sentence of death.

And I look at the bodies, [which] are under sentence of death.

Study the examples of verbs after the word "who." Do you want a singular verb with an S at the end or a plural verb?

SINGULAR VERB

Then Godmother is the one [who] dishes out food to us.
(Juan Rulfo, "Macerio") (112)

PLURAL VERB

I believe that armed struggle is the only solution for people [who] are fighting for freedom, and I act according to his belief.
(Martin Ebon, *Che: The Making of a Legend*) (41)

Here are some examples with other verbs.

SINGULAR VERB

If we can liken life, for a moment, to a furnace, then freedom is the fire [which] burns away illusion.
(James Baldwin, "Nobody Knows My Name: A Letter from the South") (10e)

... It is the worship [of these artifacts, these dead things, that] is finally evil.
(LeRoi Jones, "American Sexual Reference: Black Male") (67)

PLURAL VERB

All travelers to my city should ride the elevated trains [that] race along the back ways of Chicago.
(Lorraine Hansberry, *To Be Young, Gifted and Black*) (56)

But now black is beautiful and black is proud. There are relatively few people, [white or black, who] do not recognize what has happened.
(Shirley Chisholm, "Racism and Anti-Feminism") (30)

ALWAYS WORK BACKWARDS FROM THE WORD "WHO" OR "WHICH" OR "THAT" TO DECIDE WHAT NOUN IS REALLY DOING THE ACTION. In the first sentence, you can take out the word "which" to see that fire burns. In other words, you have to look at words before the word "which" to see what is doing the burning. In the next sentence, you have to decide what "is finally evil". The "dead things" are not evil; it is the worship of the dead things that is evil; The worship is evil. In the third, the trains race. And in the last, few people do not recognize "what has happened."

Special Pronoun Traps 261

6D. Exercises: Editing for Verbs after "Who," "Which," or "That"

Look for verbs that appear in fragments (usually after "who," "which," or "that"), in the following excerpts and change the spelling to those verbs using the "bracket" method in order to put the excerpts back into college writing. Make all changes directly in the sentences as if you were editing a paper. If an excerpt does not need to be changed, put a check (√) next to its number. Look only for verbs that appear in fragments, using the guidelines given on pages 259-260. Do not edit for anything else. (See page 2 for how to use the "Answer" Section.)

Example

The Government should act. It must deal firmly with anyone who ~~are~~ [is] found exploiting racial, tribal, or religious differences. (98)

1. The Godmother is the one who dish out food to us. (112)

2. I asked him, "What sort of people are these who waits at table?" (1)

3. The new day which is already at hand must find us firm, prudent, and resolute. (45)

4. Among other dances which speaks of the past are those done by the warriors. (111)

5. Every Sunday, people who have left the block take the lonely ride back, dragging their increasingly discontented children with them. (10c)

6. Those who defies God pay the penalty and perish. (71)

7. The black artist must construct models which corresponds to his own reality. (120)

8. While the dangers of trachoma, an eye disease, have been greatly decreased, and the condition is diagnosed and treated routinely in other areas, it is

still an everyday recurrence that threaten the eyesight of many girls and boys in West Africa. (3)

9. In order to destroy this myth of race superiority, the Pan-Africanist Congress has drawn up an unfolding program which start tomorrow and ends up in 1963 with the realization of the United States of Africa. (72)

10. Getting it together for the black church may mean providing education programs and facilities that is uniquely related to the black experience. (135)

11. First of all, we know that of all the peoples who forms the heterogenous yet almost completely homogenous mass that makes up the United States population, Negroes are the only descendants of people who was not happy to come here. The African was brought to this country in bondage and remained in bondage more than two hundred and fifty years. But most of the black people who was freed from formal slavery in 1865 *were not* Africans. They were Americans. And whether or not we choose to characterize the post-Emancipation existence of Negroes in the United States as "freedom," we must still appreciate the idea that a group of people who became familiar with the mores, attitudes, language, and other culture references of this country while being enslaved by it cannot be seen as analogous to peoples who moves toward complete assimilation of these same mores by *choice*, even though these peoples are also despised by the "natives" of the country as "furriners." (68)

12. Let me give one example of the kind of leadership which are needed. Suppose a group of families have decided to start a cooperative farm and village, and are discussing where to build their houses. The problem is whether to build on a hill or down in the valley; and the argument is about the ease of getting

water versus the danger of flooding. A good leader who is a member of this group may argue that it is better to build on a hill and face the drudgery of carrying the water until they can afford a pump and pipes; but let us suppose that despite all his efforts the general opinion is to build near the water's edge. What should he do? (105)

13. One may object—possibly—that this puts the matter somewhat too simply, but the song is true, and it has been true for as long as white men have ruled the world. The Africans put it another way: When the white man came to Africa, the white man had the Bible and the African had the land, but now it is the white man who are being, reluctantly and bloodily, separated from the land, and the African who are still attempting to digest or to vomit up the Bible. (8)

14. Once locked out, one will never again be forced to encounter in the eyes of a stranger who love him the impenetrable truth concerning the stranger, oneself, who is loved. (11)

15. After the Egyptian and Indian, the Greek and Roman, the Teuton and Mongolian, the Negro is a sort of seventh son, born with a veil, and gifted with second-sight in this American world—a world which yield him no true self-consciousness, but only let him see himself through the revelation of the other world. (40)

16. It is traditional Americanism for the white racist power structure to brand all who work uncompromisingly for black liberation and social justice as extremists. (19)

17. The people who have managed to get off this block has only got as far as a more respectable ghetto. (10c)

7 What the Word "Awkward" Usually Means

A. Equal or balanced ideas (parallel construction)

Usually, when you are writing a sentence that states more than one idea, you find yourself using the word "and." This is especially true when you are writing a series:

I gave the leaflets to

| PROFESSORS |,| STUDENTS |,| and | PEOPLE in the community.

Because the three things are all <u>people,</u> they are said to be the same kinds of things. Thus the word "and" is a kind of equality word. It adds together things of the same type. The same is true in the next sentence:

The group began to build consciousness among the people through

| LEAFLETTING |,| PUTTING up posters |,| and | generally TALKING to people in the community and hospital.[1]

The first "and" in the above sentence holds together three ACTIVITIES. Note that the three activities are all expressed in the same way. The words are all "balanced," "equalized" or "parallel." HERE IS THE SAME SENTENCE, BUT NOW IT IS <u>NOT</u> EQUALIZED:

The group began to build consciousness among the people through

| LEAFLETTING |,| PUTTING up posters | and | generally TALKED to people in the community and hospital.

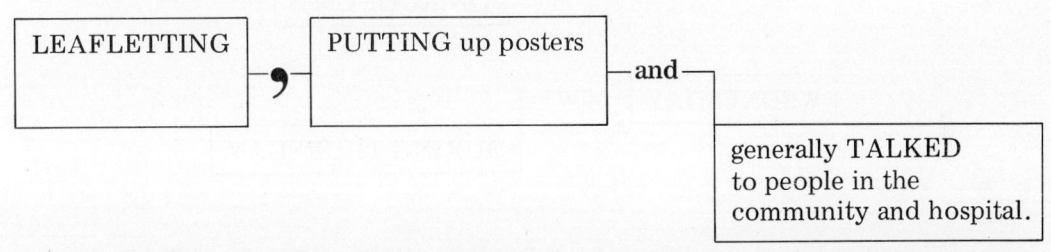

[1] Cleo Silvers and Danny Argote, Think Lincoln Committee, "Think Lincoln," *Palante*; Latin Revolutionary News Service; Young Lords Party. Vol. 2, No. 11 (September 11, 1970), page 2.

Now the three activities are not being expressed in the same way. The first two activities are expressed with verb-like words ending in "ing": "leafletting" and "putting." The third activity is expressed with a true verb, "talked." Indeed, you do not need to know grammar: the first two activities SOUND the same, while the third sounds different. Such a sentence is considered NOT BALANCED OR EQUALIZED, or NOT PARALLEL, or "AWKWARD" in college language.

"And" is an equal sign or balance word

All words joined together by "and" are usually equal in some way

The following sentences from *Palante* provide various examples of "good parallel construction" or "good equalizing."

> The brothers and sisters who took to the STREETS AND ROOFTOPS WEDNESDAY AND THURSDAY REALIZE who our enemy is AND HAVE BEEN FIGHTING for control of the streets.[2]

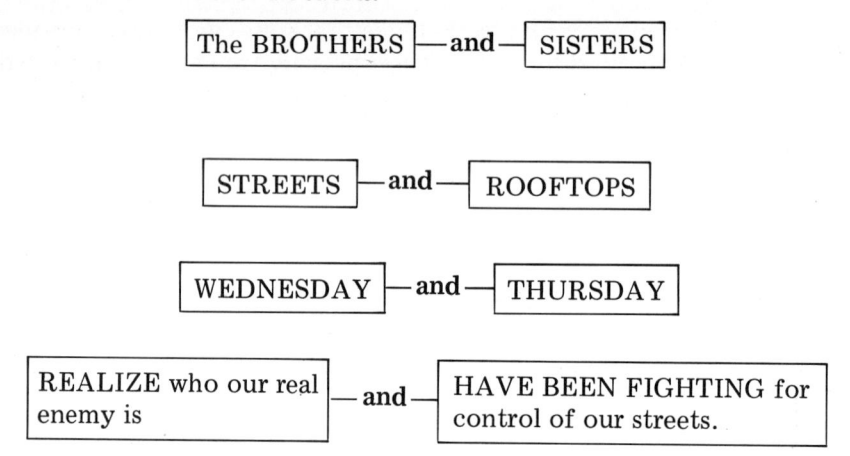

| The BROTHERS | —and— | SISTERS |

| STREETS | —and— | ROOFTOPS |

| WEDNESDAY | —and— | THURSDAY |

| REALIZE who our real enemy is | —and— | HAVE BEEN FIGHTING for control of our streets. |

Here is the same sentence, but now it is NOT EQUALIZED:

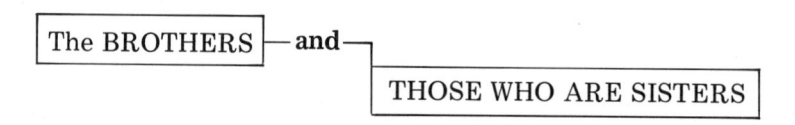

| The BROTHERS | —and—
| | THOSE WHO ARE SISTERS |

who took to the

| STREETS | —and—
| | ON ROOFTOPS |

| WEDNESDAY | —and—
| | DURING THURSDAY |

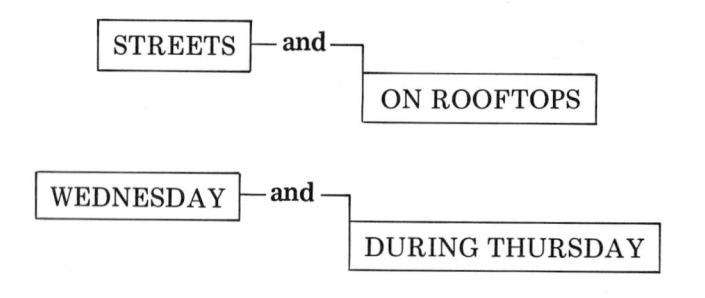

[2] Ministry of Information, Young Lords Party, "South Bronx Rebellion," *Palante*; Latin Revolutionary News Service; Young Lords Party. Vol. 2, No. 11 (September 11, 1970), page 2.

What the Word "Awkward" Usually Means 267

```
┌─────────────────────┐
│ REALIZE who our real│──and──┐
│ enemy is            │       │
└─────────────────────┘       │
                      ┌───────────────────────┐
                      │ WHO WERE FIGHTING for │
                      │ control of our streets.│
                      └───────────────────────┘
```

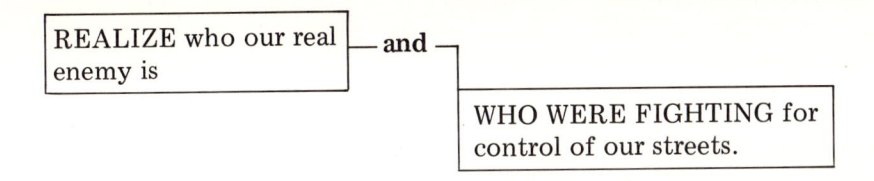

When we attend the PUBLIC SCHOOLS of the United States AND the COLONIAL SCHOOLS of Puerto Rico, we are taught THAT GEORGE WASHINGTON IS THE FATHER OF "OUR COUNTRY," THAT THE FOURTH OF JULY IS "OUR" NATIONAL INDEPENDENCE DAY, THAT ABRAHAM LINCOLN FREED "OUR" SLAVES, AND [THAT] THE U.S. NATIONAL ANTHEM IS SUPPOSED TO MAKE US FEEL PATRIOTIC. They indoctrinate us this way even though RAMON EMETERIO IS "EL PADRE DE LA PATRIA," EL GRITO DE LARES, SEPTEMBER 23, 1868, IS OUR NATIONAL INDEPENDENCE DAY, AND LA BORINQUEÑA IS OUR NATIONAL ANTHEM.[3]

When we attend

```
┌──────────────────┐         ┌──────────────────┐
│ THE PUBLIC SCHOOLS│         │ THE COLONIAL SCHOOLS│
│ OF THE UNITED    │──and──  │ OF PUERTO RICO,  │
│ STATES           │         │                  │
└──────────────────┘         └──────────────────┘
```

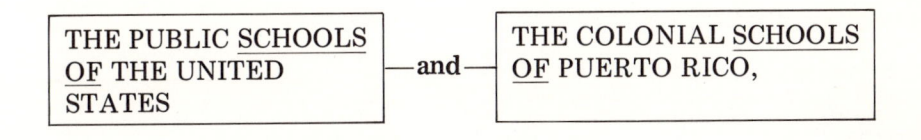

We are taught

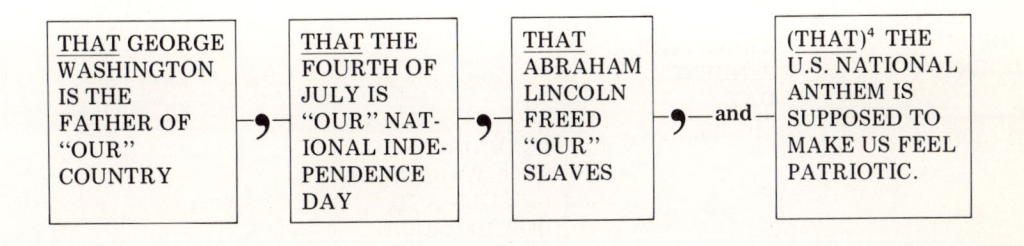

```
┌───────────┐   ┌───────────┐   ┌───────────┐   ┌───────────┐
│THAT GEORGE│   │THAT THE   │   │THAT       │   │(THAT)[4] THE│
│WASHINGTON │   │FOURTH OF  │   │ABRAHAM    │   │U.S. NATIONAL│
│IS THE     │,  │JULY IS    │,  │LINCOLN    │,  │ANTHEM IS  │
│FATHER OF  │   │"OUR" NAT- │   │FREED      │ and│SUPPOSED TO│
│"OUR"      │   │IONAL INDE-│   │"OUR"      │   │MAKE US FEEL│
│COUNTRY    │   │PENDENCE   │   │SLAVES     │   │PATRIOTIC. │
│           │   │DAY        │   │           │   │           │
└───────────┘   └───────────┘   └───────────┘   └───────────┘
```

[3] Aponte, Carlos, Education Lieutenant, Young Lords Party, Bronx Branch, "Padre de la Patria," *Palante*; Latin Revolutionary News Service; Young Lords Party. Vol. 2, No. 11 (September 11, 1970), page 5.
[4] You can leave the word "that" out. See page 21.

They indoctrinate us this way even though

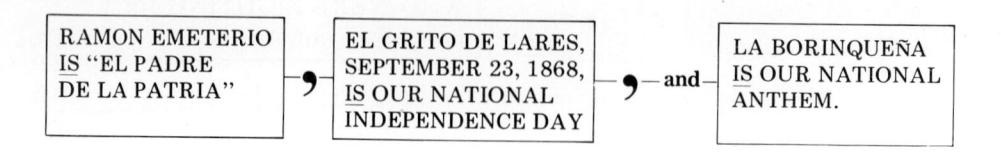

| RAMON EMETERIO IS "EL PADRE DE LA PATRIA" | , | EL GRITO DE LARES, SEPTEMBER 23, 1868, IS OUR NATIONAL INDEPENDENCE DAY | , and | LA BORINQUEÑA IS OUR NATIONAL ANTHEM. |

Here are the same sentences, but now they are NOT EQUALIZED:

When we attend

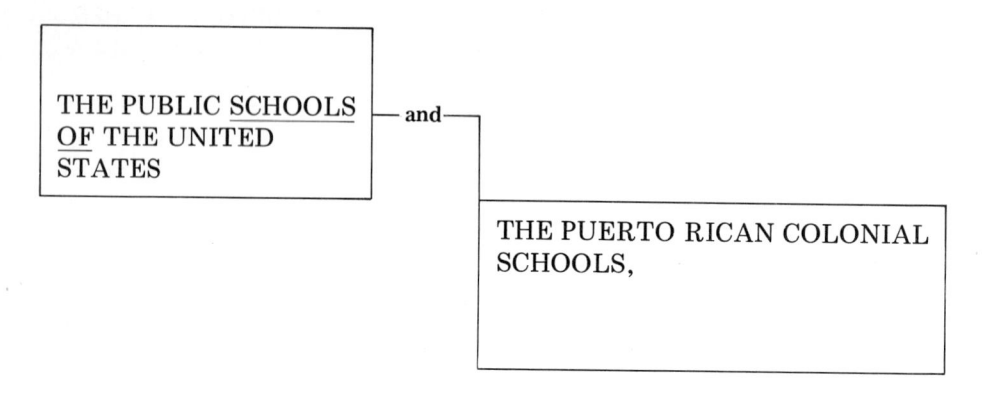

THE PUBLIC SCHOOLS OF THE UNITED STATES —and— THE PUERTO RICAN COLONIAL SCHOOLS,

we are taught

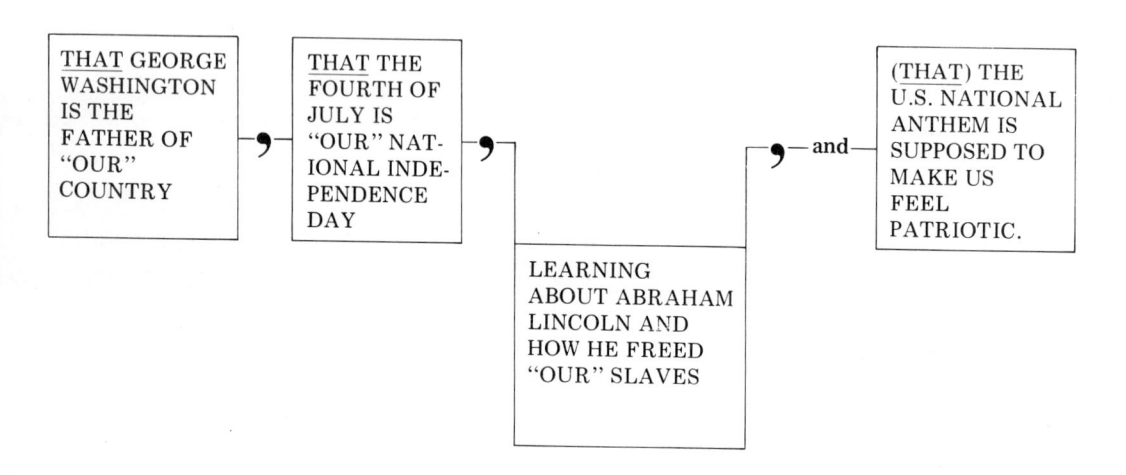

| THAT GEORGE WASHINGTON IS THE FATHER OF "OUR" COUNTRY | , | THAT THE FOURTH OF JULY IS "OUR" NATIONAL INDEPENDENCE DAY | , | LEARNING ABOUT ABRAHAM LINCOLN AND HOW HE FREED "OUR" SLAVES | , and | (THAT) THE U.S. NATIONAL ANTHEM IS SUPPOSED TO MAKE US FEEL PATRIOTIC. |

They indoctrinate us this way even though

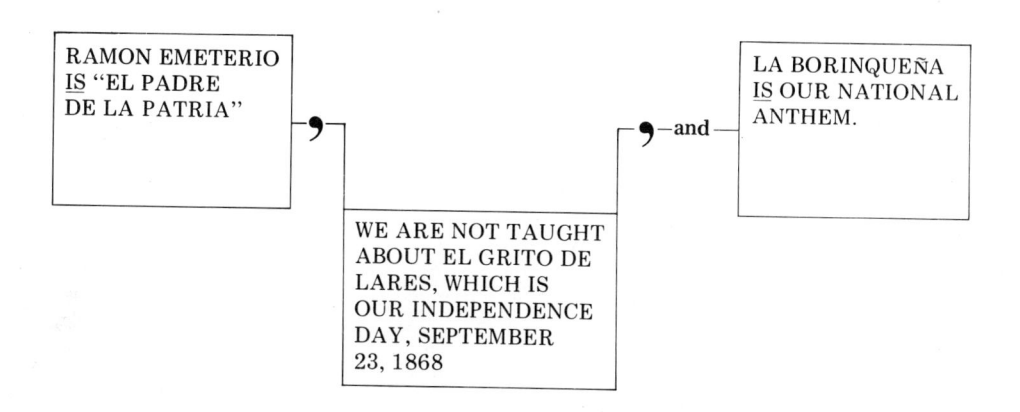

> RAMON EMETERIO IS "EL PADRE DE LA PATRIA" , WE ARE NOT TAUGHT ABOUT EL GRITO DE LARES, WHICH IS OUR INDEPENDENCE DAY, SEPTEMBER 23, 1868 , and LA BORINQUEÑA IS OUR NATIONAL ANTHEM.

Try balancing or equalizing this next sentence:

Why has the United States eliminated our history and trying to convince us from our early youth that we are United States "Americans"?

Here is how the author wrote it:

Why has the United States ELIMINATED our history and TRIED to convince us from our early youth that we are United States "Americans"?[5]

[5] Aponte, op. cit., page 5.

Here are other equalizing or balance words and punctuation marks.

_____ and _____

both _____ and _____

_____ but _____

_____ but also _____

_____ but not _____

not _____ but _____

not only _____ but also _____

_____ or _____

either _____ or _____

either _____ or else _____

neither _____ nor _____

from _____ to _____

whether _____ or _____

_____ yet _____

_____ and yet _____

_____ yet not _____

_____ , _____

_____ ; _____

This meant that sorrow was present—EITHER A BRAVE WAS GOING on the warpath and expected to die, OR ELSE A FAMILY WAS LOOKING for the death of some member of it.
(Chief Standing Bear, *The Land of the Spotted Eagle*) (118)

TO BE A POOR MAN IS hard, BUT TO BE A POOR RACE in a land of dollars IS the very bottom of hardships.
(W.E.B. Dubois, *The Souls of Black Folk*) (40)

For more practice, underline the ideas joined by an equalizing word or words and change the words that are not equal.

In the latter part of the decade we youngsters earned many nickels by climbing through open windows, opening doors and we let neighbors into their apartments.

Everyone desires love but also it is found impossible to believe that he deserves it.

Here is how the authors wrote them:

In the latter part of the decade we youngsters earned many nickels by climbing through open windows, opening doors and letting neighbors into their apartments.
(Loften Mitchel, *Black Drama*) (91)

Everyone desires love, but also finds it impossible to believe that he deserves it.
(James Baldwin, *Tell Me How Long the Train's Been Gone*) (11)

7A. Exercises: Editing for Balanced Ideas

Look for words that tell you balanced ideas are coming in the following excerpts and change any words or groups of words that are not balanced in order to put the excerpts back into college writing. Make all changes directly in the sentences as if you were editing a paper. If an excerpt does not need to be changed, put a check (√) next to its number. Look only for balanced ideas using the guidelines given on pages 265-271. Do not edit for anything else. (See page 2 for how to use the "Answer" Section.)

Examples

a. There was always a border beyond which the Negro could not go, whether musically or ~~in social ways~~ socially. (68)

b. The old shouts and hollers were still their accompaniment for the arduous work of clearing land, planting or ~~to harvest~~ harvesting. (68)

1. The Master swept the ground and having made the plot smooth. The turkey went to the middle of the plot and shook himself. (106)

2. He slammed the door, took a deep breath and walking to the corner where Pete was already shedding his wet clothes. (107)

3. The worker must work for the glory of his handiwork, not simply for pay; the thinker thinks for truth, not for fame. (40)

4. Africa presently is most deeply torn with strife and most bitterly stricken with racial conflict. (81)

5. In the latter part of the decade we youngsters earned many nickels by climbing through open windows, opening doors and let neighbors into their apartments. (91)

6. By deciding neither to give nor receive bribes, and being courageous

enough to expose those with opposite inclinations, they can show a healthy example and to give a good lead in the right direction. (4)

7. Holden's statements show that he wants to stand out amidst all the Angolan leaders, to give the impression that it is his party alone that is fighting at the front and which he alone is leader of the rebellion. But we must analyse the facts. (86)

8. Both would climb out of their narrow prisons on ladders of words; both would climb steep mountains and walk lonely paths; and who would grapple with the revolutionary implications in Thomas Jefferson's words. (16)

9. What are we fighting for: Our overall fight is against imperialism, being in colonialism, and domination. (72)

10. But live you must, and you can either make passive love to your sickness or burn it out and going on to the next conflicting phase. (43)

11. Can anyone honestly and with seriousness suggest that in this type of atmosphere the scales of justice are evenly balanced? (84)

12. They will bring their money; they will die not having found it out. . . . (124)

13. In South Africa complaints are neither freely heard nor do people deeply consider them, let alone speedily reformed, and there is nothing to persuade us that Dr. Verwoerd's government is going to change in the near future. (102)

14. I also, as a Christian and patriot, could not look on while systematic attempts were made, almost in every department of life, to debase the God-factor in man or in setting a limit beyond which the human being in his Black form might not strive to serve his Creator to the best of his ability. (81)

15. He went. There was a cream-colored car outside the house. In the parlor were smoking stands, and knickknack brackets, and a grand piano nobody played. Cora's father smoked cigars, owning a few pieces of stock, went to Florida two weeks every winter, told stories about the "Florida niggers." Cora's mother had the same parted lips Cora had, but who breathed through them heavily as if she were always trying to catch up with herself. She was fat and overdressed. (93)

16. The squad cars moved slowly through the ghetto, stopping here and there to collect their graft. Whores arose, dressed and moving into the unfamiliar sunlight toward a restaurant and eating late afternoon breakfast. (52)

17. Cora sat with her hands in her lap and her fingers which were laced tightly together. Jim smiled at Mr. Hartley's jokes and having a miserable time. And Jim discovered that it was best not to go to anybody's house. (93)

18. All I can say is at this stage in world history I am not a little sick of being bullied, chastised, scourged, and having people spit upon me by white men in Johannesburg, London, or New York, and if I assess the mood of black people correctly, two thirds of the world's colored people are also sick to death of this treatment. (102)

19. This meant that sorrow was present—either a brave was going on the

warpath and expected to die, or else a family which looked for the death of some member of it. The brave song was to fortify one to meet any ordeal bravely and keeping up faltering spirits. (118)

20. I pushed my way to the window, pulled the light cord and hide from myself in the friendly darkness. Easing the noise from the old-time window shade, I pushed up the window and will squeeze my hand through the iron gate my aunt had put in to keep the crooks out. (125)

21. The thoughts pressed on my brain. I grab my face with both hands and squeezed hard, pushing it all out of shape; I pulled out my lips and my face down. The reefer kick was still on, and I could feel the smallness of the room and the neatness of its humble furniture and smelling its credit, which $1.50 a week paid off. I pushed my way to the window, pulled the light cord and hiding from myself in the friendly darkness. Easing the noise from the old-time window shade, I pushed up the window and squeeze my hand through the iron gate my aunt had put in to keep the crooks out. (125)

22. Whereas a middle-class Negro in a northern city may aspire, for instance, to move into Deerfield, Illinois, or moving into other white middle-class communities, and may dine and wine, rubbing shoulders with the whites, in downtown hotels, the masses of Negroes must stay home in the ghettos. Consequently, the lower-class Negro who has the capacity and having motivation for self-improvement must seek it within the Negro community. He cannot afford the luxury of the middle-class make-believe. He knows he is black, but wanting to be self-respecting. He may be poor, but wanting to be decent. (44)

23. I might also mention that in the course of this application I am frequently going to refer to the white man and to people who are white. I want to make it clear that I am not a racialist* and do not support racialism of any kind, because to me racialism is a barbaric thing whether it comes from a black man or a man who is white. (84)

24. Your Worship, I would say the whole life of any thinking African in this country drives him continously to a conflict between his conscience on the one hand and the law on another. . . . The law as it is applied, the law as it has been developed over a long period of history, and especially the law which the Nationalist Government wrote and designed is a law which, in our view, is *immoral, unjust, and cannot be tolerated.* Our consciences dictate that we must protest against it, that we must oppose it, and that attempting to alter it. (84)

25. This picture of the typical new leader of Nigeria applies whether he is premier or being the minister of state, an "honorable" member of the legislature or who is an important parliamentarian, business "tycoon" or labor spokesman, district councilor or senior civil servant, high church dignitary or well-known university professor, being a government corporation chairman or high court judge, lawyer, as a militant politician, or professional man, with variations as a result of individual differences. (117)

---

*"Racialist" is British for "racist." "Racialism" is British for "racism."

B. **When does a question NOT have a question mark after it?**

Direct questions: Use a question mark

When you know something about somebody, you can make a statement about him:

REGULAR SENTENCE PATTERN:

James is coming home.
  N   V

But if you DON'T KNOW about James, you might ask:

DIRECT QUESTION:

Is James coming home?
V   N   V

Notice the change in the order of the noun-verb pair. Also notice that there is a question mark at the end of a direct question.

Indirect questions: No question mark

But now suppose that you are WONDERING about James. You might ask yourself:

INDIRECT QUESTION:

I wonder if James is coming home.
             N   V

Notice that the order of the noun-verb pair is back to "normal." Also notice that there IS NO QUESTION MARK at the end.

Take this last sentence, the indirect question, apart for a moment:

WORDS THAT INTRODUCE INDIRECT QUESTIONS	REGULAR SENTENCE PATTERN
I wonder if[6]	James is coming home.

Notice that the second part of the indirect question is just like the REGULAR SENTENCE PATTERN above: "James is coming home."

There are many combinations of words that introduce the indirect question. Some of them are listed on the following page. ALL ARE FOLLOWED BY A REGULAR SENTENCE PATTERN. NONE HAVE A QUESTION MARK.

---

[6] NOT: I wonder _is_ James coming home?

CHART 36. Words That Introduce Indirect Questions

Words That Introduce Indirect Questions	Regular Sentence Pattern (Noun–Verb)
I wonder if	James is coming home.
I wonder whether (or not)	James is coming home.
I wonder why	James is coming home.
I wonder who	James is.[*]
I wonder what	James will see.[*]
I wonder where	James is going.[*]
I wonder how	James is going to do it.[*]
I am asking if	James is coming home.
I am asking whether (or not)	James is coming home.
I am asking why	James is coming home.
I am asking who	James is.[*]
I am asking what	James will see.[*]
I am asking where	James is going.[*]
I am asking how	James is going to do it.[*]
I question whether (or not)	James is coming home.
I question why	James is coming home.
I am inquiring if	James is coming home.
I am inquiring why	James is coming home.
I want to know if (why, etc.)	James is coming home.
I understand why (who, etc.)	James is coming home.
I do not understand why (who, etc.)	James is coming home.
I am learning whether (or not)	James is coming home.
I doubt whether	James is coming home.
I do not know if (why, etc.)	James is coming home.

*Pay special attention to these statements. They are still in the regular noun-verb order.

MAKE SURE THE TIME OF THE REGULAR STATEMENT MAKES SENSE. What are the differences in meaning between the following?

> I wonder if James is coming home.
> I wonder if James will be coming home.
> I wonder if James came home.
> I wondered if James was coming home. (STAY IN PAST TIME)
> I wondered if James would be coming home. (STAY IN PAST TIME)
> I wondered if James had come home. (STAY IN PAST TIME)

C. What comes after the words: "He said that. . ."? Other indirect statements.

(Review Section B on the indirect question before going on.)

After the word "that"

There are several other introductory words which can sometimes cause "awkward" sentences in college writing. The most confusing ones are variations of the following:

WORDS THAT INTRODUCE INDIRECT STATEMENTS	REGULAR SENTENCE PATTERN
James said that	he would come home.

First, here is the direct quotation:

> James said, "I will come home."

Take careful notice of the quotation marks, and most important, notice that the EXACT WORDS THAT JAMES SAID ARE PLACED WITHIN THE QUOTATION MARKS.

Now take the quotation marks away and INTRODUCE what James said by the words: JAMES SAID THAT. . . .

Now you are talking ABOUT James, but you are NOT QUOTING HIS EXACT WORDS.

CHART 37. Words That Introduce Indirect Statements

Words That Introduce Indirect Statements	Tells What He Said in Different Words Regular Sentence Pattern	
	Noun	Verb
James said (that)*	he	would come home.
James remarked that	he	would come home.
James wrote that	he	would come home.
James told me (that)*	he	would come home.
James promised (that)*	he	would come home.
James thought (that)*	he	would come home.

*The word "that" can be left out.

You can leave the word "that" out

Sometimes you can leave the word "that" out. Use your ear to tell you when you can do this. You are always safe if you put it in, but if you take it out, make sure you still use the INDIRECT STATEMENT. (The indirect statement without the word "that" is underlined).

I did not believe it, and thought [removed THAT] they were telling a lie, so I rang the bell and a waiter came who knew German.

(Salim Bin Abakari, "A Journey to Russia and Siberia in 1896") (1)

[removed THAT] Daddy told him he should have appreciated that nice suit with the long pants he got him from the pawnshop because God knows when he'd get the money to buy him another one.

(Louise Meriwether, *Daddy Was a Numbers Runner*) (89)

There is no comma before the word "that"; There is no comma after the word "that"; There are no quotation marks after the word "that"

Notice the punctuation in the following indirect statement:

And they replied that they too were Muslims.

(Salim Bin Abakari, "A Journey to Russia and Siberia in 1896") (1)

Direct quotations

Use quotation marks ONLY WHEN YOU ARE REPEATING WORD FOR WORD what a person said. See page 323 for excerpt illustrating quotation marks.

Study the direct quotations and indirect statements in the following passage and notice how effectively the combination of the two forms can be.

> They were very surprised at the way I ordered my food and what I wanted to drink, and they asked, "Why don't you eat pork and drink wine?" I told them, "I don't drink wine nor eat pork because I am a Muslim." And they replied that they too were Muslims.
>
> (Salim Bin Abakari, "A Journey to Russia and Siberia in 1896") (1)

7C. 1. Exercises: Editing for Indirect Questions and Statements

Look for indirect questions and statements in the following excerpts and change the word order when necessary in order to put the excerpts back into college writing. Make all changes directly in the sentences as if you were editing a paper. If an excerpt does not need to be changed, put a check (√) next to its number. Look only for indirect questions and statements, using the guidelines given on pages 279-283. Do not edit for anything else. (See page 2 for how to use the "Answer" Section.)

1. The first Indian will announce: that he lives in a one-room shack. (36)

2. Waiyaki often remembered, why was he sent to Siriana. (99)

3. I knew, I had about twenty-five minutes before I was due on stage. (11)

4. They say, a person does get filled up eating, but I know very well that, "I don't even though I eat all they give me." And Felipa knows it too—They say in the street, that I'm crazy because I never stop being hungry. (112)

5. I wonder, could I come down and see you, and we could drink and talk and remember? (132)

6. Billy wondered was there a telephone somewhere? He wanted to call his mother, to tell her he was alive and well. (132)

7. It is a fact that, the Bantu knew that, the earth was not the center of the universe hundreds of years before the white man realized this. (96)

8. I wrote a letter in reply to say, "that I had been expecting her letter, that she was perfectly free." But I tore it up. I realized, that if anything might hurt her, silence would. (48)

9. She also thought, that she was the head of the family, since she had had to manage her mother's funeral, since she had to get a housekeeper for Billy, and all that. (132)

10. He said, he was sure that all the other Americans would do the same. He said, that his primary responsibility now was to make damn well sure that everybody got home safely. (132)

11. When they say, you have no home and no past, call them liars. Recall that you have both past and home. Recall that your past as well as your home, stretches throughout the world.
You could ask where would you find home and find that home is in the music you hear wherever we are? (34)

12. He thought, we were alike. I did not want to think so. I did not want to think, that would my life be like his, or that, my mind would ever grow so pale, so without hard places and sharp, sheer drops. (9)

13. When school closed, she permitted me to go to pick berries at the Strawberry farm. I thought, I could eat up the whole strawberry farm and ate enough to get sick and so returned back home, about a forty-five-mile trip. Then I was convinced that, was the world a little larger than New Orleans. (79)

14. But there are a great many ways of outwitting oblivion, and to ask whether or not is homosexuality natural is really like asking whether or not was it natural for Socrates to swallow hemlock, whether or not was it natural for St. Paul to suffer for the Gospel, whether or not was it natural for the Germans to

send upwards of six million people to an extremely twentieth-century death? (10d)

15. Whites who attempt to help Indians are constantly frustrated by their tragic lack of understanding of Indian people. For Indians always know exactly what position will they take on major issues, how far can they push certain concepts, and when to delay so as to wear out their opponents and eventually get their way. (36)

16. We might also ask, should the members of the guerrilla band be drawn from a certain social class. It has already been said that this social composition ought to be adjusted to that of the zone chosen for the center of operations, which is to say, that the combatant nucleus of the guerrilla army ought to be made up of peasants. (54)

7C. 2. Exercises: Add Indirect Questions and Statements

Finish the following introductions to indirect questions and statements using the guidelines on pages 279-283. Make sure you use the word order discussed on those pages.

1. I wonder how _____

_____

_____

2. I wonder why _____

_____

3. I wonder who _____

_____

4. I wonder what _____

_____

5. I wonder where _____

_____

_____

6. I asked him who _____

_____

_____

7. I want to ask them where _____

_____

_____

290 *When Ideas Become Complicated*

8. They questioned us about whether or not _____
_____
_____

9. Nobody could understand why _____
_____
_____

10. Everybody wants to know why _____
_____
_____

11. The investigator wanted to know who _____
_____
_____

12. We made an investigation into why _____
_____
_____

13. It is hard to tell if _____
_____
_____

14. It is hard to tell why _____
_____
_____

15. They have to learn who _____
_____
_____

16. It is important to analyze why _____

17. He wrote an essay on what _____

18. This discussion will answer the question about where _____

19. It is important to investigate the reasons why _____

20. It is no longer necessary to wonder if _____

21. The text said that _____

22. The people in the crowd remarked that _____

23. The audience was told that _____

When Ideas Become Complicated

24. These people said that _____

_____

_____

25. The critic wrote that _____

_____

_____

26. The steering committee said* _____

_____

_____

27. The speaker then went on to say _____

_____

_____

28. Several sisters told the chairman _____

_____

_____

29. The whole group was promised _____

_____

_____

30. In the analysis, the author said _____

_____

_____

*Note that in sentences 26 through 30 the word "that" has been left out. However, you must still treat the sentence as an indirect statement.

7C. 3. Exercises for Writing Dialogue

Study the excerpt illustrating the use of dialogue in the punctuation appendix, page 323. Also study dialogue in some short stories and novels. Then pick one or more of the following topics (or make up your own) and write dialogue:

1. Write a dialogue between:

a. An old person and a young person.
b. A mother and her son or daughter who is over eighteen.
c. Two children.
d. Two teen-agers.
e. A man and a woman.
f. Two people in a television detective play.

2. Conduct an interview with people in which you ask them their opinions on a topic that interests you. Write the interview up so that it is half in dialogue and half in indirect statements and questions. Incidentally, this is the kind of assignment one sometimes has to do for a sociology course.

D. Other problems with word order

What follows is a summary of the kinds of problems students usually run into with word order—with which words come first in a sentence.

Descriptive words <u>usually</u> come BEFORE the word they describe

Descriptive words are underlined in the following passages:

> His <u>spacious</u> and <u>comfortable</u> house stood on a hill overlooking a <u>beautiful</u> valley.
> (Horace B. Cayton, "A Picnic with Sinclair Lewis") (26)

Notice that the words "spacious" and "comfortable" describe "house"; "beautiful" describes "valley."

> Granny Judith said that in Africa they had very <u>few</u> <u>pretty</u> things, and that they had <u>no</u> <u>red</u> colors in cloth.
> (Julius Lester, *To Be a Slave*) (78)

Here the words "few" and "pretty" describe "things"; "no" and "red" describe "colors."

However, on occasion, descriptive words come AFTER the word they describe, but this word order is rare and is used in order to have variety. Here is an example:

> His house, <u>spacious and comfortable</u>, stood on a hill overlooking a beautiful valley.

Notice that the descriptive words begin and end with commas to indicate that the word order has been changed from the usual pattern.

The other time that a descriptive word usually comes after the noun it describes is in Whole Thought Type 4 (see page 9). Here a verb separates the noun and the descriptive word:

	NOUN	VERB	DESCRIPTIVE WORD
WHOLE THOUGHT TYPE 4	His house	is	spacious
	Life	can be	weird

Here is a final example of how descriptive words might come AFTER the noun they describe:

> The sun would rise <u>spotted</u> and <u>ringed</u> with purple...
> (William H. Gass, "We Have Not the Right Life") (50)

Here "spotted' and "ringed" both describe the "sun." The author might have written:

> The <u>spotted</u> and <u>ringed</u> sun would rise...

but then he would not have been able to include the fact that the sun was "spotted and ringed <u>with purple</u>." That is probably why he put the descriptive words after the words "would rise."

The receiver of the action generally comes AFTER the action word

Turn to page 9, and note the word order for Whole Thought Type 2:

DO-ER	WHAT HE DOES	WHAT HE DOES IT TO
(noun)	(verb)	(receiver)
John	wrote	the speech.

Sometimes a person will try to put the receiver at the beginning of the sentence, and come out with something like this:

The speech, John wrote.

The above is NOT standard college writing word order.

STANDARD WORD ORDER

John wrote the speech.

Here is another example of what can happen to a sentence when the receiver is put first in Whole Thought Type 2:

"AWKWARD" WORD ORDER

The man who came to dinner, I introduced.

STANDARD WORD ORDER

I introduced the man who came to dinner.

DO-ER	WHAT HE DOES	WHAT HE DOES IT TO
I	introduced	the man (who came to dinner).

Sometimes a person will add an unnecessary "it" or "him" to the sentence in order to make it sound as if the sentence is in standard word order again. But compare sentences with the unnecessary "it" or "him" with those that are in more standard word order:

UNNECESSARY "IT"—"AWKWARD" WORD ORDER

The speech, John wrote it.

STANDARD WORD ORDER

John wrote the speech.

UNNECESSARY "HIM"—"AWKWARD" WORD ORDER

The man who came to dinner, I introduced him.

STANDARD WORD ORDER

I introduced the man who came to dinner.

There are other times when the word "it" is unnecessary

UNNECESSARY "IT"—"AWKWARD" WORD ORDER

I think that the poll tax, it is unfair.

STANDARD WORD ORDER

I think that the poll tax is unfair.

UNNECESSARY "IT"—"AWKWARD" WORD ORDER

It had always been pounded into his head, how blacks were dumb and incompetent.

STANDARD WORD ORDER

That blacks were dumb and incompetent had always been pounded into his head.

OR

How blacks were dumb and incompetent had always been pounded into his head.

Starting a sentence with "that"

The last example brings us to another problem area when ideas become complicated. There is a special kind of sentence which is useful for complex ideas, but which is also difficult to put together. This is the sentence in which a whole string of words takes the place of the noun in the noun-verb pair (for noun-verb pair, see Chapter 1). Take the following sentence, for example:

That not enough Puerto Rican literature has been translated into English is a well-known fact.

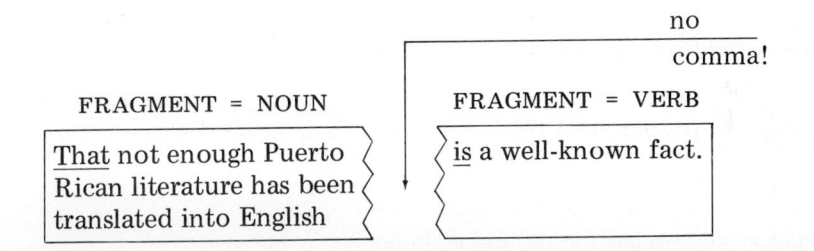

no comma!

FRAGMENT = NOUN

That not enough Puerto Rican literature has been translated into English

FRAGMENT = VERB

is a well-known fact.

This sentence is a whole thought. It consists of a group of words that ACTS LIKE A NOUN and another group of words that ACTS LIKE A VERB. (See also page 66). All the W words that usually introduce a fragment (see page 19) can introduce this kind of sentence, plus the words "how" and "that":

who	where	which	whatever	how
whose	when	whether	whichever	that
what	why	whoever		

FRAGMENT = NOUN	FRAGMENT = VERB
<u>Whose</u> opinion he takes	
<u>What</u> he does	
<u>Where</u> he goes	
<u>When</u> he goes	
<u>Why</u> he goes	
<u>Which</u> road he takes	
<u>Whether</u> he goes or not	is very important to me.
<u>Whoever</u> comes in	
<u>Whatever</u> he does	
<u>Whichever</u> road he takes	<u>no comma!</u>
<u>How</u> he goes	
<u>That</u> he goes	

You are safest starting this kind of sentence with one of the words on the list. Avoid starting with any others—although on occasion other words will also work well.

Putting the essay question into your paper as a topic sentence

Avoid forcing the essay question between words of your own. You are better off making up your own topic sentence. (For fuller discussion, see Chapter 8)

ESSAY QUESTION

Should all students pay for a college education?

TOPIC FORCED INTO YOUR OWN SENTENCE—"AWKWARD" WORD ORDER

Should all students pay for a college education? Is a difficult question to answer.

STANDARD WORD ORDER—MAKE UP YOUR OWN TOPIC SENTENCE

All students should pay for their college education.

OR

No student should have to pay for his college education.

OR

It is not easy to determine if all students should pay for their college education.

Avoid a weak topic sentence in your essay. Do not repeat the essay question and then answer it:

ESSAY QUESTION

Should the government pay for all medical expenses?

"WEAK" TOPIC SENTENCE OF ESSAY

Should the government pay for all medical expenses? I say "Yes."

"STRONG" TOPIC SENTENCE OF ESSAY

The government should pay for all medical expenses.

E. When you leave words out

You will usually know if you tend to leave words out of your essay, because your instructor will put a "caret" (∧) at the place where a word has been omitted. For example, "carets" appear where words have been left out of the following excerpt:

> The two old black folks, sitting quietly side∧side, showed no excitement. In another instant∧car hit∧water∧dropped immediately out∧sight.

Try reading this excerpt out loud and determine what words have been left out. Here is the original passage. The words that were left out are underlined:

> The two old black folks, sitting quietly side <u>by</u> side, showed no excitement. In another instant <u>the</u> car hit <u>the</u> water <u>and</u> dropped immediately out <u>of</u> sight.
> (Arna Bontemps, "A Summer Tragedy") (20)

If leaving words out is one of your "problems," try reading your essays out loud before handing them in. Pronounce every word. Usually there is a pattern to the words that are left out. For example, some people forget to put in the words "the," "and," or "not." Try to determine which words you tend to leave out and check especially for them. By the way, you are more likely to leave words out when you are rushed and nervous about doing a good job. It's like stammering when you have to say something just right. So be especially alert to possible words that have been left out when you know that you are nervous.

It is also easy to leave out the <u>ends of words</u> when you are nervous. See Chapters 4 and 5.

8 Have Faith in the Paragraph As a Unit of Thought. Turning a Paragraph into an Essay.

As discussed on page 10, each whole thought usually expresses at least one idea. However, do not forget that there is a LARGER unit of thought, the paragraph.

A. Definition of a paragraph

A paragraph usually consists of a group of sentences. All the sentences are arranged in an order that adds up to one LARGE IDEA (or sometimes more than one)—the idea of the whole paragraph. Usually ONE sentence in the paragraph summarizes or introduces the LARGE IDEA of the whole paragraph and the other sentences are SMALLER IDEAS that can add up to the LARGE IDEA. Some texts call the summary or introductory sentence of the paragraph the topic sentence.

The topic sentence or LARGE IDEA of the paragraph is underlined in the example that follows. Then there are two SMALLER IDEAS which have something to do with the LARGE IDEA:

> As it happened the dance called "the Charleston" was the one that caught on and spread throughout the world. The Charleston was the spark that ignited dance participation and interest as it had never been in the United States and Europe. I'm sure it surprised most black people during that time as to why the Charleston became so popular.
>
> (Dolores Cayou, "The Origins of Modern Jazz Dance") (25)

B. A paragraph is usually a group of sentences

It is important to remember that you can have a period BETWEEN two ideas even though the two ideas add up to one LARGER IDEA. If you squeeze all ideas into one large sentence you are bound to find yourself with a bunch of run-ons and comma-splices (see Chapter 3), rather than a group of separate sentences which are all about the same topic.

Run-ons and comma-splices

Given all the time and experience of black life in this country, the characteristics mentioned at the beginning of this brief history are still the major characteristics of black dance, the place where these characteristics are holding less true at

301

this point is at its most recently developed level, the stage, the dance in the church remained essentially the same and was done for the same reasons as always this was also true of the social dances of the masses of black Americans, however, with the advent of the traveling shows and the black musical revue (the only one of its kind at that time), the dance was taken out of context for the first time and put on a stage to entertain. Within a few years such dances as the Black Bottom, The Shim Sham Shimmy and the Lindy Hop radically changed the social dance patterns of the entire white community, before that time the dances which were done were the well-known European ones such as the Waltz or derivations of court dances such as Square Dance.

Edited

Given all the time and experience of black life in this country, the characteristics mentioned at the beginning of this brief history are still the major characteristics of black dance. The place where these characteristics are holding less true at this point is at its most recently developed level, the stage. The dance in the church remained essentially the same and was done for the same reasons as always. This was also true of the social dances of the masses of black Americans. However, with the advent of the traveling shows and the black musical revue (the only one of its kind at that time), the dance was taken out of context for the first time and put on a stage to entertain. Within a few years such dances as the Black Bottom, The Shim Sham Shimmy and the Lindy Hop radically changed the social dance patterns of the entire white community. Before that time the dances which were done were the well-known European ones such as the Waltz or derivations of court dances such as Square Dance.

(Dolores Cayou, "The Origin of Modern Jazz Dance") (25)

C. Two major types of paragraphs

1. The paragraph that comes WITHIN a whole essay.
2. The paragraph that comes at THE BEGINNING of a whole essay (see Part E).

D. Paragraphs that come <u>within</u> a whole essay.

There are several good ways to organize this kind of paragraph.

Put the topic sentence first

When the topic sentence comes at the beginning of the paragraph, it usually becomes a kind of promise to the reader that the rest of the paragraph will have something to do with the topic sentence; it is a kind of contract with the reader. In the example that follows, the topic sentence is underlined and each sentence that fulfills the promise of the topic sentence has a number.

<u>This nation was not conceived to be run by a silent majority.</u> (1) It was conceived to further participatory democracy, to be government of, by and for the people, to be a nation of engaged, involved people, whose freedom to speak and write openly was as much a duty as a right. (2) It was conceived to be a nation where dissent would be respected and listened to, even encouraged as a healthy sign

of a flourishing republic. ③ It was a nation conceived to face its faults, not to berate those who raise them.

(Richard G. Hatcher, "The Black City Crisis") (59)

As in the above paragraph, the sentences that follow the topic sentence are often balanced the way ideas are balanced within one sentence (see pages 265-271). The balancing can take on different forms. Numbers refer to the numbered sentences in the paragraph above:

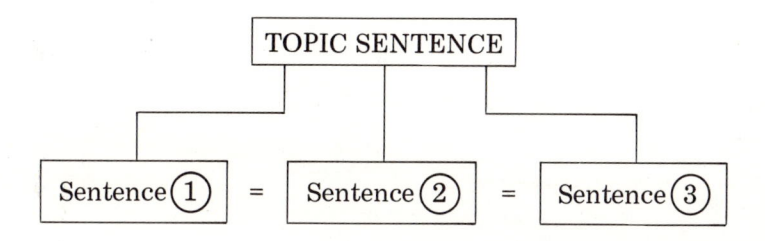

```
              TOPIC SENTENCE
        ┌───────────┼───────────┐
   Sentence ①  =  Sentence ②  =  Sentence ③
```

Here is another paragraph with a topic sentence and balanced sentences.

Years of ghetto revolts speak to the fact that a decade of non-violent protest has not altered ghetto life materially. ① The economic gap between whites and blacks has narrowed only slightly. ② The spate of civil rights and poverty legislation has not substantially closed the gap between white promises and the grim particulars of black existence. ③ More than 40 per cent of the nation's 22 million blacks are still officially classed as poor. ④ Ghetto unemployment is still running at Depression levels and at rates double those for whites. ⑤ Ghetto housing is still a disaster—43 per cent of it substandard and overcrowded. ⑥ Ghetto schools are still more segregated than in 1954 and woefully ill-equipped to educate black children. ⑦ Ghetto blacks are still dying, on the average, seven years earlier than whites. ⑧ There are still rats, the filth, the exploiting merchants, the callous police. ⑨ There is still white society's stubborn refusal to admit that the ghetto it created is a problem it must solve.

(Richard G. Hatcher, "The Black City Crisis") (59)

As shown on page 304, the numbered sentences are all balanced.

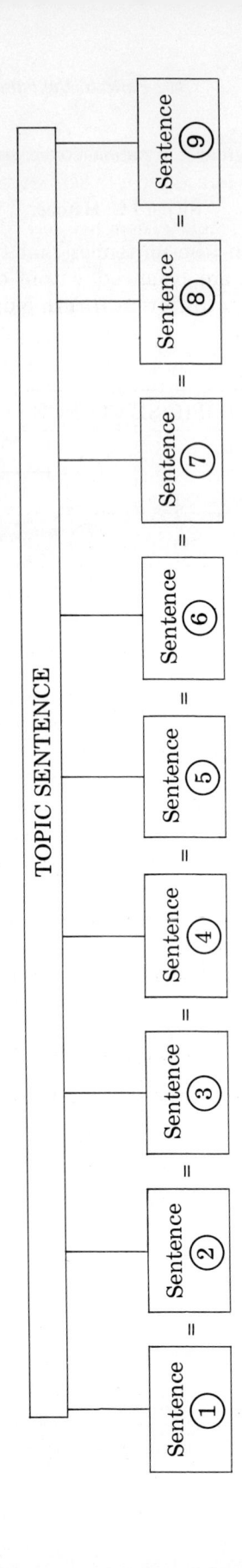

TOPIC SENTENCE

Sentence ① = Sentence ② = Sentence ③ = Sentence ④ = Sentence ⑤ = Sentence ⑥ = Sentence ⑦ = Sentence ⑧ = Sentence ⑨

Sometimes the sentences are organized so that each one is dependent upon the one that came before it. Here the topic sentence is first:

> The New York City school system has developed techniques to handle this problem. though so far as I can tell few teachers benefit and many children are permanently damaged by them. ①A child who cannot conform in a classroom, particularly in a ghetto school, is removed from the classroom, first to the principal's office to run errands, then to the "guidance" counselor, and finally to a special school for the "socially maladjusted," *i.e.*, a "600" school. ②To help the teacher maintain order the child is removed, yet it doesn't help. ③In a classroom and school governed by fear, the removal of one disorderly child merely creates another. ④Fortunately, there are few groups of children so resigned to adult tyranny that they will not generate and covertly encourage one defiant member. ⑤Because of this, it was only with the greatest reluctance that I would resort to a class transfer for a child I was having difficulty with, and it was for the same reason I welcomed other teachers' "problems."
>
> (Herbert Kohl, *36 Children*) (73)

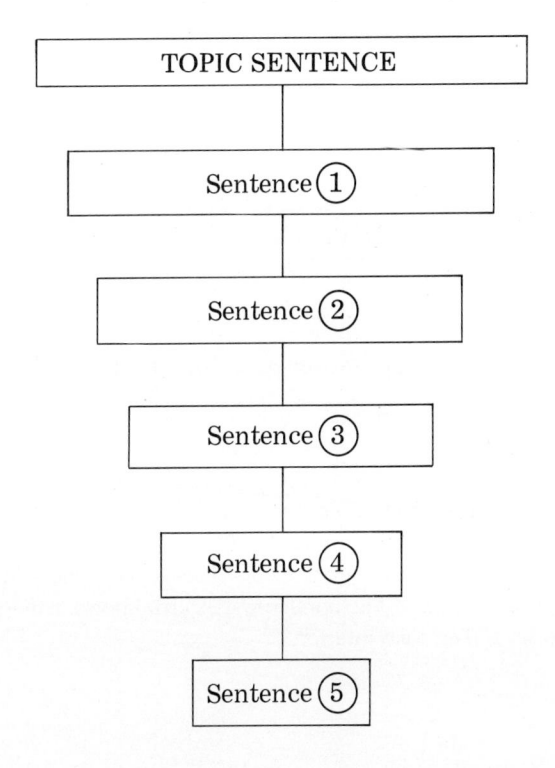

```
          ┌─────────────────────┐
          │   TOPIC SENTENCE    │
          └──────────┬──────────┘
                     │
              ┌──────┴──────┐
              │ Sentence ①  │
              └──────┬──────┘
                     │
              ┌──────┴──────┐
              │ Sentence ②  │
              └──────┬──────┘
                     │
              ┌──────┴──────┐
              │ Sentence ③  │
              └──────┬──────┘
                     │
              ┌──────┴──────┐
              │ Sentence ④  │
              └──────┬──────┘
                     │
              ┌──────┴──────┐
              │ Sentence ⑤  │
              └─────────────┘
```

Or the topic sentence will come <u>at the end</u>:

> ①In Opalousa, Louisiana, a sweet potato cooperative has been created. ②Farm laborers have bought land and are working it jointly and selling the produce for their own benefit. ③Organized by John Zippert, young CORE Task Force worker from New York, the cooperative now has 375 Black farmers. ④The success of this project has caused 15 small white farmers to join the combine.

⑤ The special methods and marketing techniques learned there will be applied in other parts of the country. This is an illustration of Black economic power.[1]

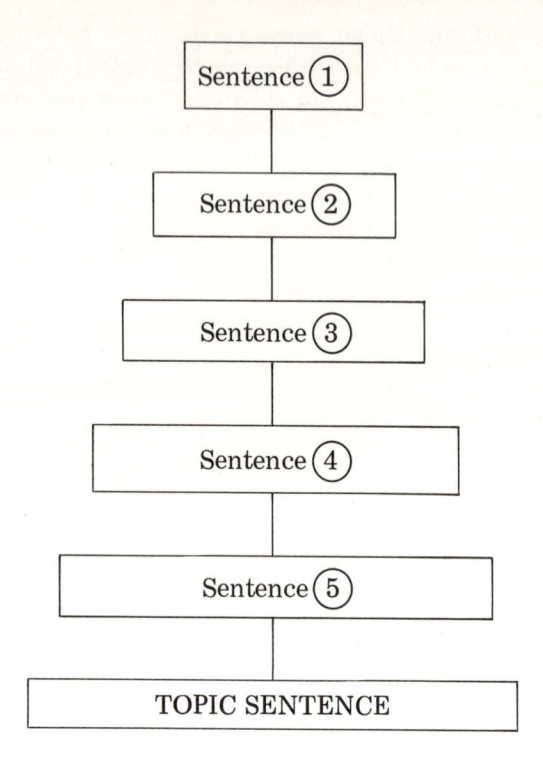

```
        Sentence ①
            |
        Sentence ②
            |
        Sentence ③
            |
        Sentence ④
            |
        Sentence ⑤
            |
       TOPIC SENTENCE
```

Often, you will have a topic sentence in the middle of the paragraph:[2]

① In the resulting color caste system, white people made certain that any wares they allotted to the Negro were inferior. The Caucasian American socialized the black man to internalize and believe all of the many vile things he said about him. ② They encouraged and rewarded behavior and attitudes in Negroes that substantiated their indicting stereotypes. ③ Black men were happy-go-lucky, lazy, stupid, irresponsible, etc. ④ Our mass media disseminated these images with vigor on radio, in movies, etc., and like unrelenting electric shocks conditioned the mind of the Negro to say, "Yes, I am inferior."[3]

---

[1] Floyd B. McKissick, "Programs for Black Power," appearing for the first time in *The Black Power Revolt: A Collection of Essays*, edited by Floyd B. Barbour (Boston: Porter Sargent Publisher, 1968), pp. 179-181.

[2] Because of the importance of the idea about mass media in the last sentence, TWO sentences might add up to the topic of this paragraph: the underlined one and the last one.

[3] Alvin F. Poussaint, "The Negro American, His Self-Image and Integration," *Journal of the National Medical Association*, ed. W. Montague Cobb, Vol. 58 (1968), pp. 419-423, as reprinted in *The Black Power Revolt: A Collection of Essays*, edited by Floyd B. Barbour (Boston: Porter Sargent Publisher, 1968), pp. 94-102.

INTRODUCTION TO TOPIC SENTENCE

```
         ┌──────────────┐
         │ Sentence ①   │
         └──────┬───────┘
                │
      ┌─────────┴──────────┐
      │   TOPIC SENTENCE   │
      └─────────┬──────────┘
                │
         ┌──────┴───────┐
         │ Sentence ②   │
         └──────┬───────┘
                │
            ┌───┴──────────┐
            │ Sentence ③   │
            └──────┬───────┘
                   │
                ┌──┴───────────┐
                │ Sentence ④   │
                └──────────────┘
```

Sometimes the paragraph has an <u>unwritten overall topic</u> which is implied in the details of the individual sentences. For example, the unwritten topic in the following excerpt is slave-ship revolts and the subsequent sentences are all bits of information about slave-ship revolts:

①Most revolts came either at the point of embarkation or between that time and actual sailing. ②Gaston-Martin catalogues several slave revolts on board ships, and says that he discovered fifty references to revolts, or about one every fifteen trips, in his studies of Nantes slaving. ③(Nantes is a French seaport.) ④He adds that there were almost certainly many revolts which were never recorded, and he comments that they were very likely accepted as a normal hazard of the trade. ⑤Some revolts even took place at sea, where the slaves would perish even if they overcame the crew, for they had no idea of how to steer the ships. ⑥Ships' logs record the ferocity of these revolts. ⑦Usually they failed, with only a few slaves and crew members dead; sometimes the death toll went as high as forty or fifty. ⑧Rather than be taken again some blacks drowned themselves. ⑨Many crew members died. ⑩ A few revolts did succeed, in which case the crew was usually massacred, sometimes merely taken captive.

(C.L.R. James, "The Atlantic Slave Trade and Slavery") (66)

E. The opening or introduction paragraph of an essay

Just as the topic sentence of the above paragraphs makes a promise to the reader about what the whole paragraph is going to be about, so, generally, does the opening PARAGRAPH of an essay: it makes a promise to the reader that THE WHOLE ESSAY will discuss a certain topic.

For example, in an essay in which you prove the truth of something, your opening paragraph may state the point to be proven. You make a contract with your reader that you are going to PROVE something. The rest of your essay is really an attempt to make your essay topic STAND UP IN COURT—you must provide evidence for the truth of your essay topic. And the more evidence you can provide, the more your readers will be convinced of the truth of your topic statement.

In another kind of essay, the topic sentence in the opening paragraph states the topic to be discussed. You promise the reader that you will stay on the topic presented in the introduction. Now subsequent paragraphs are pieces of information about the topic, arranged in some logical and interesting order.

In short, the kinds of paragraphs discussed in the preceding pages are really like small essays—with a topic and supporting ideas arranged in an effective order. In fact, often you can turn a paragraph like Hatcher's, pages 302-303, into a small essay. The first sentence can be the topic of the whole essay:

> This nation was not conceived to be run by a silent majority.

This sentence now needs a paragraph of its own, an introductory paragraph. The rest of the sentences might also be turned into paragraphs: each sentence can be the topic sentence of its own paragraph with new sentences added to give more information about each topic sentence.

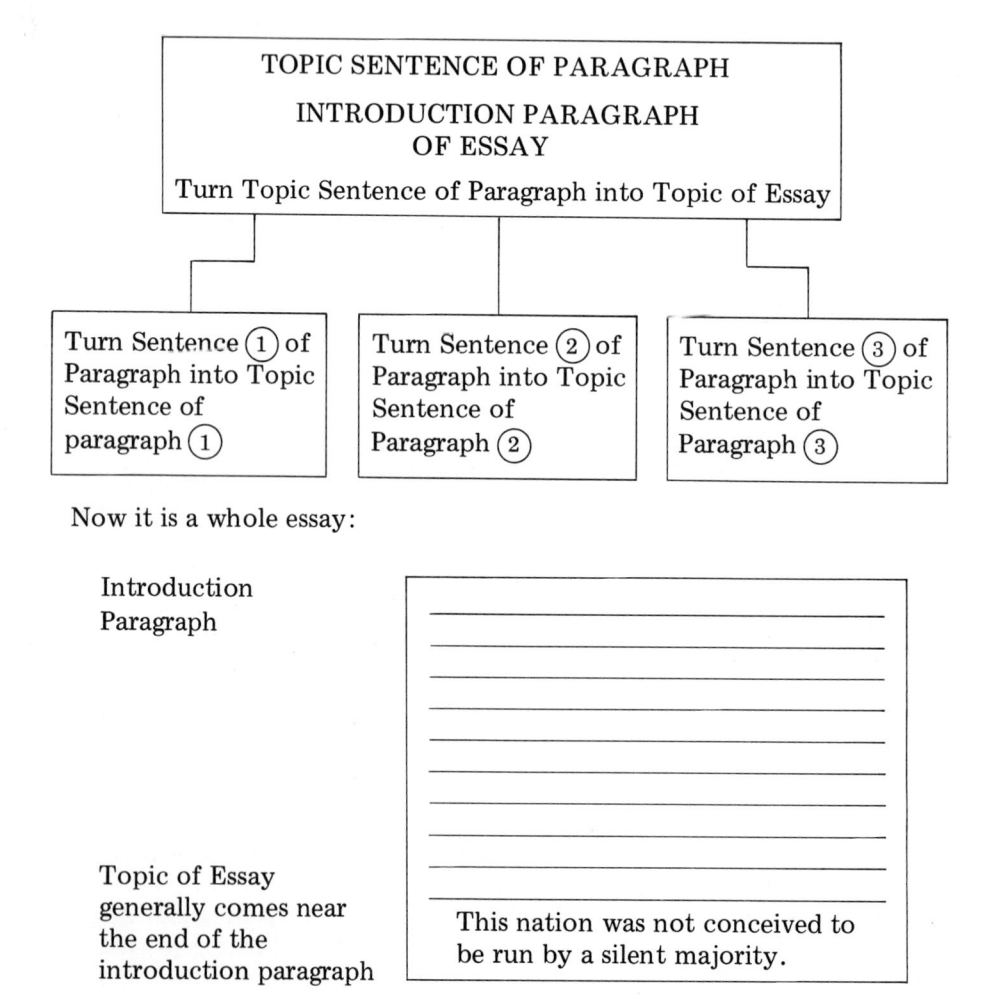

```
                TOPIC SENTENCE OF PARAGRAPH
                  INTRODUCTION PARAGRAPH
                         OF ESSAY
        Turn Topic Sentence of Paragraph into Topic of Essay
```

Turn Sentence ① of Paragraph into Topic Sentence of paragraph ①	Turn Sentence ② of Paragraph into Topic Sentence of Paragraph ②	Turn Sentence ③ of Paragraph into Topic Sentence of Paragraph ③

Now it is a whole essay:

Introduction
Paragraph

Topic of Essay generally comes near the end of the introduction paragraph

> This nation was not conceived to be run by a silent majority.

Internal
Paragraph 1

Topic Sentence

> It was conceived to further participatory democracy, to be government of, by, and for the people, to be a nation of engaged, involved people, whose freedom to speak and write openly was as much a duty as a right.
> _____
> _____
> _____
> _____
> _____
> _____

Sentences in the paragraph that pertain to the topic sentence of the paragraph

Internal
Paragraph 2

Topic Sentence

> It was conceived to be a nation where dissent would be respected and listened to, even encouraged as a healthy sign of a flourishing republic.
> _____
> _____
> _____
> _____
> _____
> _____
> _____
> _____

Sentences in the paragraph that pertain to the topic sentence of the paragraph

Internal or Final
Paragraph 3

Topic Sentence

> It was a nation conceived to face its faults, not to berate those who raise them.
> _____
> _____
> _____
> _____
> _____
> _____
> _____
> _____
> _____
> _____

Sentences in the paragraph that pertain to the topic sentence of the paragraph

This is one of many good methods for converting a paragraph into a whole essay: in essence, Hatcher's paragraph "a" has become an OUTLINE for an entire essay of four paragraphs. Of course, you have to have enough to say about the topic—enough facts—before you can do this.

Ways to begin an essay

It is usually best to put the TOPIC for the WHOLE ESSAY in your first paragraph.

You are best off putting the topic of the essay AT THE END OF THE OPENING PARAGRAPH. If you make it the very first sentence of your essay, you may run into the common problem of saying everything you want to say in one paragraph.

Lead or seduce your reader into the essay with interesting and relevant information or a quotation. Then lead from those sentences right into the essay topic without beating around the bush too much. One method is to state a fact related to the topic and then "turn the corner," so to speak, right into the topic.

Study the following opening to the essay, "Black Power in the International Context." The last sentence in the first paragraph of the essay is the TOPIC OF THE ESSAY:

> The struggle for for black liberation has come to a significant turning point. Currently, the most advanced elements of the Black Power movement are beginning to understand the international implications of the struggle for black liberation. It is becoming increasingly clear that the struggle cannot be contained within the bounds of national life. As a matter of fact, to continue to do so is a tendency that must be strongly fought. <u>The African-American struggle is inextricably linked to the world-wide struggles of oppressed peoples against decadent political and economic systems.</u>[4]

{ LEAD-IN SENTENCES

{ ESSAY TOPIC

The rest of the essay is devoted to how the struggle is "inextricably linked to the world-wide struggles of oppressed peoples against decadent political and economic systems."

Notice that the OPENING paragraph of an essay is usually organized much differently from an INTERNAL paragraph (pages 302-307). The topic sentence of a WHOLE ESSAY is not to be confused with the topic sentence of ONE INTERNAL PARAGRAPH.

Of course this is not the only method of introducing an essay. The best way to find methods is to study an essay anthology. Read through each essay in an effort to determine the topic. Generally the essay topic will appear almost immediately: near, or at the end of the first paragraph, as in the above example.

In the next example, an editorial which appeared in a black newspaper in 1880, the essay topic again appears at the end of the first paragraph. The whole editorial is given. Note how each subsequent paragraph relates to and develops the underlined topic sentence of the essay. This time the lead-in sentences set the stage by describing a recent, relevant event.

---

[4] Lawrence P. Neal, "Black Power in the International Context," appearing for the first time in *The Black Power Revolt: A Collection of Essays*, edited by Floyd B. Barbour (Boston: Porter Sargent Publisher), 1968, 136-146.

BLOOD, BRAND, OR LIBERTY; 1880

Clarksville, Tennessee, was visited last week by a terrible fire. The business portion of the town was burned, leaving a mere shell of suburban residence in place of the great tobacco mart of Tennessee. It is supposed to be the work of incendiaries and the colored people bear the blame. When the city was burning, they gathered in little knots and crowds; discussed the situation, witnessed with a good deal of manifest satisfaction the strenuous efforts to suppress the fire, but would not lend a helping hand, for love or money. We are loath to advocate lawlessness. We deplore the necessity of resorting to arson and rapine but if such things must come, let them come. If the colored people of Clarksville did fire the town, we regret the necessity but not the act. If they had been denied the rights and privileges of men; if, by studied persecution, their hearts have been hardened; if goaded by oppression to desperation they have lost all their interest in and love for their homes; we are proud to see them have the manhood to be the willing witnesses of its destruction.[5]

} LEAD-IN SENTENCES

} ESSAY TOPIC

The colored people of Clarksville were incensed over a multitude of wrongs. Not long ago, a colored man was lynched upon the charge of an attempt at outrage. An attempt, mind you. This is a comprehensive term in the South. It embraces a wink by a colored man at a white girl a half mile off. Such a crime is worthy of lynching, but a beastly attack upon a colored girl by a white man is only a wayward indiscretion. The colored people have stood such discriminations long enough.

The people of Clarksville have broken the ice, God grant it may extend from Virginia to Texas. Still later, a colored man was brutally killed by a policeman, and ever since, the people have given forth mutterings, not loud, but deep.... [President] Hayes has plainly told the colored people they must make peace at any price. We repeat it, but with a different signification—they must make peace at any price. It may cost treasure, it may cost blood, it may cost lives, but make it, be the cost what is may.... The trying scenes of a presidential contest will soon be upon us. We claim no prophetic vision, but we warn the southern whites that they need not expect such one-sided scenes of butchery in future. They will have to make a choice between Blood, the Brand, and Political Liberty.[6]

---

[5] Since the words "they" and "them" do not name the people discussed in the editorial, the last TWO sentences of the first paragraph might validly be called the topic sentences of the essay. In any event, it should always be clear in an essay topic sentence exactly who or what is going to be discussed.

[6] "Blood, Brand, or Liberty; 1880," an editorial reprinted from the *Chicago Conservator*, as it appears in *The Black Power Revolt: A Collection of Essays*, edited by Floyd B. Barbour (Boston: Porter Sargent Publisher, 1968), 50-51.

312 *When Ideas Become Complicated*

In this next essay opening, the author takes two paragraphs to make his introduction:

EDWARD BLYDEN: APOSTLE OF BLACKNESS

The intellectual history of the black movement toward peoplehood must be written. It is one of the foremost tasks of black scholarship. It is a task which falls heavily on the shoulders of the younger black scholars, perhaps those who are now engaged in meaningful black studies programs in kindergarten. } LEAD-IN SENTENCES

When this history is written, it will record no greater chapter than that which describes and analyzes the life, the works and the times of Edward Wilmot Blyden from the time of his birth in the West Indies in 1832 until his death in Sierra Leone in 1912.[7] } ESSAY TOPIC

Very often the TOPIC of an essay appears in the first or second paragraph, but the POINT or MESSAGE (sometimes referred to as the THESIS) of the essay appears in one of the concluding paragraphs. In this next example, the TOPIC sentence appears as the last sentence of the opening paragraph. It raises the question about the relevance of Christianity to black Americans:

BLACK CHRISTIANITY IN THE POST-CHRISTIAN ERA, U.S.A.

Black Americans live in a post-Christian era, an era when the historic domination of the Christian churches is gone, to the extent that the age may not be realistically called "Christian." The Black Church of today, although it looms larger than its ghetto, is challenged by serious alternatives to its faith, honest experiments and outright embrace of other faiths. It is challenged perhaps even more, numerically speaking, by the strange spectre of blacks somehow capable of embracing no religion at all, and joining in the completely secular world view. Having rejected the super-natural, many are nevertheless highly idealistic and deeply committed. They have no confidence in ecclesiastical institutions. } LEAD-IN SENTENCES

Indeed, both kinds of challengers persistently and impressively raise the question of whether Christianity can possibly be a suitable faith for black Americans, now that they have awakened.[8] } ESSAY TOPIC

The rest of the essay discusses the suitability of Christianity, and it isn't until the last paragraph of the essay that the POINT or MESSAGE is stated:

Altogether, then, it is clear that Christianity *can* be a very suitable religion for Afro-Americans, granted the kinds of growth and the styles of working relationships which I   POINT OF ESSAY

---

[7] Andrew Billingsley, "Edward Blyden: Apostle of Blackness," *The Black Scholar*, Vol. II, no. 4 (December, 1970) pp. 3-12.

[8] Henry H. Mitchell, "Black Christianity in the Post-Christian Era, U.S.A.," *The Black Scholar*, Vol. II, no. 4 (December, 1970) pp. 43-49.

have outlined here. Indeed, the Black Christian Church may, with the new styles of ministry, become more relevant to black need than it has ever been. This should be welcome news in the light of the fact that the slow shifts in the tides of culture will guarantee that the Black Church will be here for a long time to come. It should be even more joyous news for church and non-churched when one reviews the very slow progress to all other movements that have attempted to take the place of the church as the preeminent community organization in the black community. In times as crucial as these it is most encouraging to know, if we will but accept it, that we do not have to start from zero to establish a mass based organization that can and will take care of the liberation of blacks. That organization is the Black Christian Church resurrected for life here and now, and assisted to relevance by prophets both within and without the church, who proclaim the kingdom of God and Its justice and righteousness.[9]

In this final example, the topic of the essay is not the last sentence of the opening paragraph: this last sentence expands upon the underlined topic.

UPROOTING RACISM AND RACISTS IN THE UNITED STAGES

In March, 1968, one month before the racist murder of Dr. Martin Luther King, Jr., the President's Commission on Civil Disorders, headed by Illinois Governor Otto Kerner, issued its monumental report charging white racism with responsibility for the degraded conditions of blacks in this country. } LEAD-IN SENTENCE

In the year and a half since the report appeared, white racist hostility toward blacks, particularly among white workers, has increased, not decreased. } ESSAY TOPIC

Polls indicated that today fewer whites believe that blacks are the victims of discrimination, and that, in fact, a growing number of whites believe that blacks are the villains rather than the victims.[10] } EXPANSION OF ESSAY TOPIC

The rest of the essay moves from the rise of white hostility to an analysis of the relationship between economics and racism. When James Boggs returns to the Kerner report at the end of the essay, he makes his POINT by stating that one cannot try to end the racism depicted in the Kerner report "and at the same time maintain the economic and social system." The final paragraphs demonstrate how blacks are best suited to the role of leadership in putting "politics in command of economics." In short, you do not have to give away the message of your essay in the topic sentence, but you must give your reader a foothold, an idea of what the essay is about. Then you can develop ideas around the topic, all of which will

---

[9] Mitchell, p. 49

[10] James Boggs, "Uprooting Racism and Racists in the United States," *Black Scholar*, Vol. 2, No. 2 (October, 1970), pp. 2-10, reprinted from *Racism and the Class Struggle*, published by Monthly Review Press, 1970.

eventually prove the truth of your MESSAGE which may come at the CONCLUSION of your essay.

To summarize, there are two major ways to organize an essay, and both ways include putting the TOPIC in the first or second paragraph.

1. The TOPIC and POINT or MESSAGE appear in the first or second paragraph. See pages 310 and 312.

2. The TOPIC appears in the first or second paragraph, but the POINT or MESSAGE appears towards the end of the essay. See pages 312 and 313.

In both instances, the TOPIC generally comes towards the END of the FIRST or SECOND paragraph, with one or more sentences leading up to it.

Exercises

1. Write an argument in one paragraph. Make the first sentence of your paragraph the topic sentence. Have the other sentences prove the truth of the topic sentence—as if you were in court and your life depended upon convincing the jury.
    IDEAS (You might also try the opposite points of view):
    a. The government should pay for the college education of all students.
    b. The space program should be stopped.
    c. All cars should be banned from large cities.
    d. The community should have control over its hospital services.
    e. Marriage is an outmoded concept.
    f. A woman should pay her own way when she dates a man.
    g. There should be no imprisonment before trial.
    h. There should be day care centers in the colleges.

2. Take one of the argument paragraphs you have written and turn the first sentence into an opening paragraph for a whole essay. Remember that THE TOPIC SENTENCE comes at the END of the opening paragraph. Read opening paragraphs in magazine articles and essays in order to get an idea how various authors start off. Underline the topic of the essay, as if you were going to write it. Do several of these.

3. Take each of the other sentences in your argument paragraph (#1 above) and turn each one into its own paragraph. Make the original sentences the topic sentences for each paragraph. Use the introduction (#2 above) as the introduction for your essay. Make sure that each paragraph in the essay says something about the essay topic. In a sense, the paragraph you wrote for exercise 1 has become an OUTLINE for a whole essay. In this essay the TOPIC and POINT or MESSAGE are in the first paragraph.
    It is also important that each paragraph in your essay somehow relate to the one that came before it. The logical words (see page 121) are very helpful in making the transition from one paragraph to the next. In the end, your whole essay should "hang" or "stick" together (coherence).

4. Write other argument essays using the same method as in #3 above. Thumb through the Bibliographic "Answer" Section and find some ideas that you would like to write about. Have a friend and/or your instructor check your essays for:
    a. The topic sentence of the WHOLE ESSAY: is it towards the END of the opening paragraph or paragraphs?
    b. The other paragraphs: does each one have its own topic sentence? Does each paragraph have something to do with the topic of the essay?
    c. The sentences in each paragraph: do they say something about the topic sentence of that paragraph?
    d. The whole essay: does one paragraph prepare for the next one? Do the paragraphs seem to come in a logical order? Do the paragraphs fulfill the contract with the reader contained in the essay topic sentence? Have you really proven your point?

5. Write an argument essay in which the TOPIC comes in the first or second paragraph and the POINT or MESSAGE comes in the concluding paragraph. Refer back to page 315 for ideas.

APPENDIX A

Punctuation

This section can serve as a review of material covered in the text and as an outline of several punctuation devices not covered in the text. As a review, try to write sentences that fit into the various types outlined on the following pages BEFORE checking the page reference to where you might find an example of the particular punctuation usage. Editing exercises for material covered in this appendix will be found in the Cumulative Editing Section that starts on page 389.

APPENDIX A—PUNCTUATION

		Cross References to Pages in Text
1. Fragments Attached to Whole Thoughts		17-89
a. Whole Thought , Fragment .		22, 31, 39, 51, 60, 66, 71, 77
b. Whole Thought Fragment .		22, 51, 66, 71
c. Whole Thought — Fragment .		22, 31, 39, 51, 60, 66, 71, 77
d. Whole Thought ... Fragment .		22, 31, 39, 51, 60, 66, 71, 77
e. Fragment , Whole Thought .		22, 51, 60, 66, 71
f. Whole , Fragment , Thought .		39, 51, 60, 66, 71
g. Whole Fragment Thought .		32, 51, 77
h. Whole — Fragment — Thought .		
2. Two Whole Thoughts Attached Together		91-137
a. Whole Thought ; Whole Thought .		93, 122

319

320 Appendix A

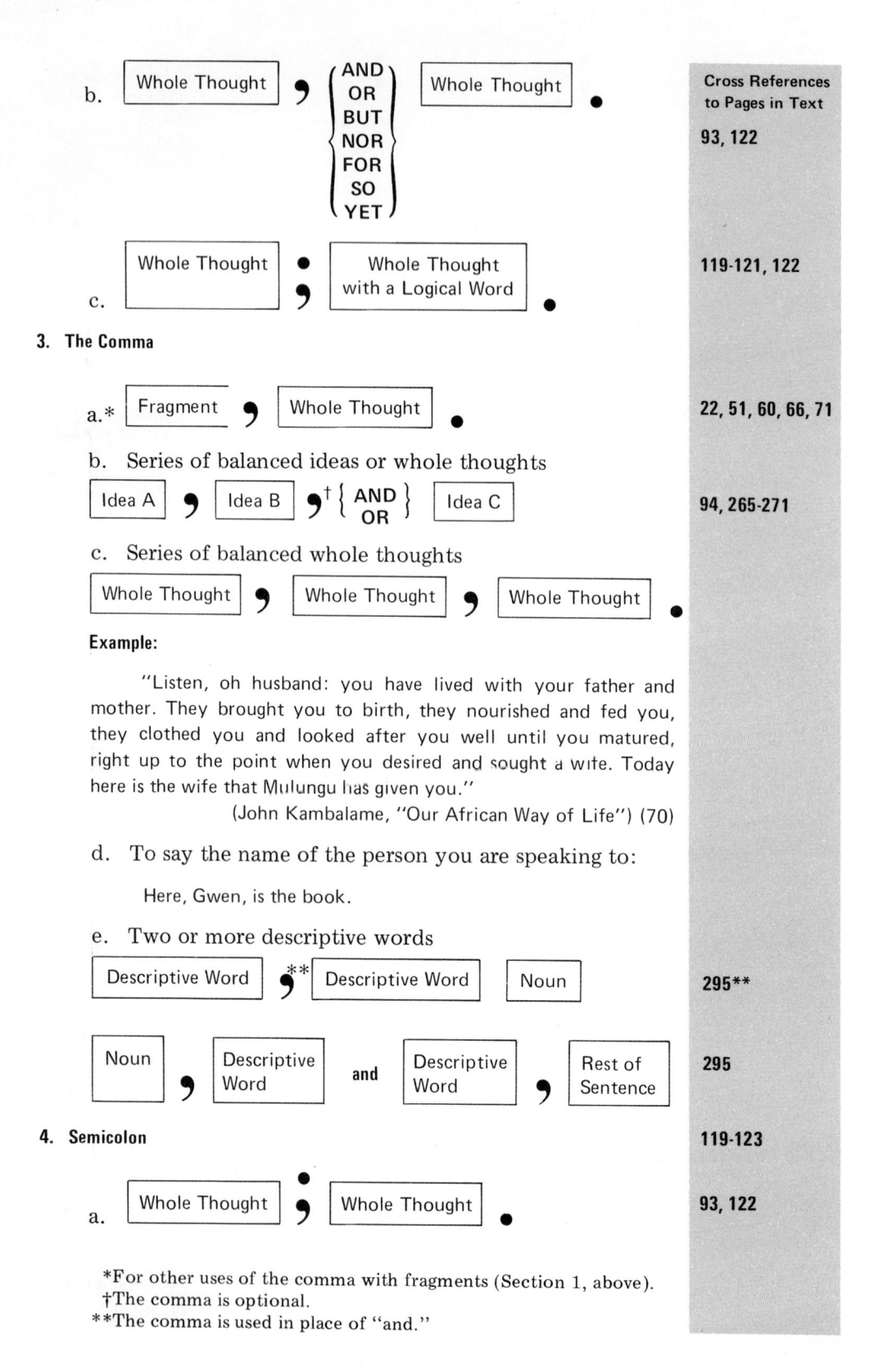

		Cross References to Pages in Text
b.	[Whole Thought] , { AND / OR / BUT / NOR / FOR / SO / YET } [Whole Thought] .	93, 122
c.	[Whole Thought] . [Whole Thought with a Logical Word] .	119-121, 122

3. The Comma

a.*	[Fragment] , [Whole Thought] .	22, 51, 60, 66, 71
b.	Series of balanced ideas or whole thoughts [Idea A] , [Idea B] ,† { AND / OR } [Idea C]	94, 265-271
c.	Series of balanced whole thoughts [Whole Thought] , [Whole Thought] , [Whole Thought] .	

Example:

"Listen, oh husband: you have lived with your father and mother. They brought you to birth, they nourished and fed you, they clothed you and looked after you well until you matured, right up to the point when you desired and sought a wife. Today here is the wife that Mulungu has given you."
        (John Kambalame, "Our African Way of Life") (70)

d. To say the name of the person you are speaking to:

 Here, Gwen, is the book.

e. Two or more descriptive words

[Descriptive Word] ,** [Descriptive Word] [Noun]	295**
[Noun] , [Descriptive Word] and [Descriptive Word] , [Rest of Sentence]	295

4. Semicolon   119-123

a.	[Whole Thought] ; [Whole Thought] .	93, 122

*For other uses of the comma with fragments (Section 1, above).
†The comma is optional.
**The comma is used in place of "and."

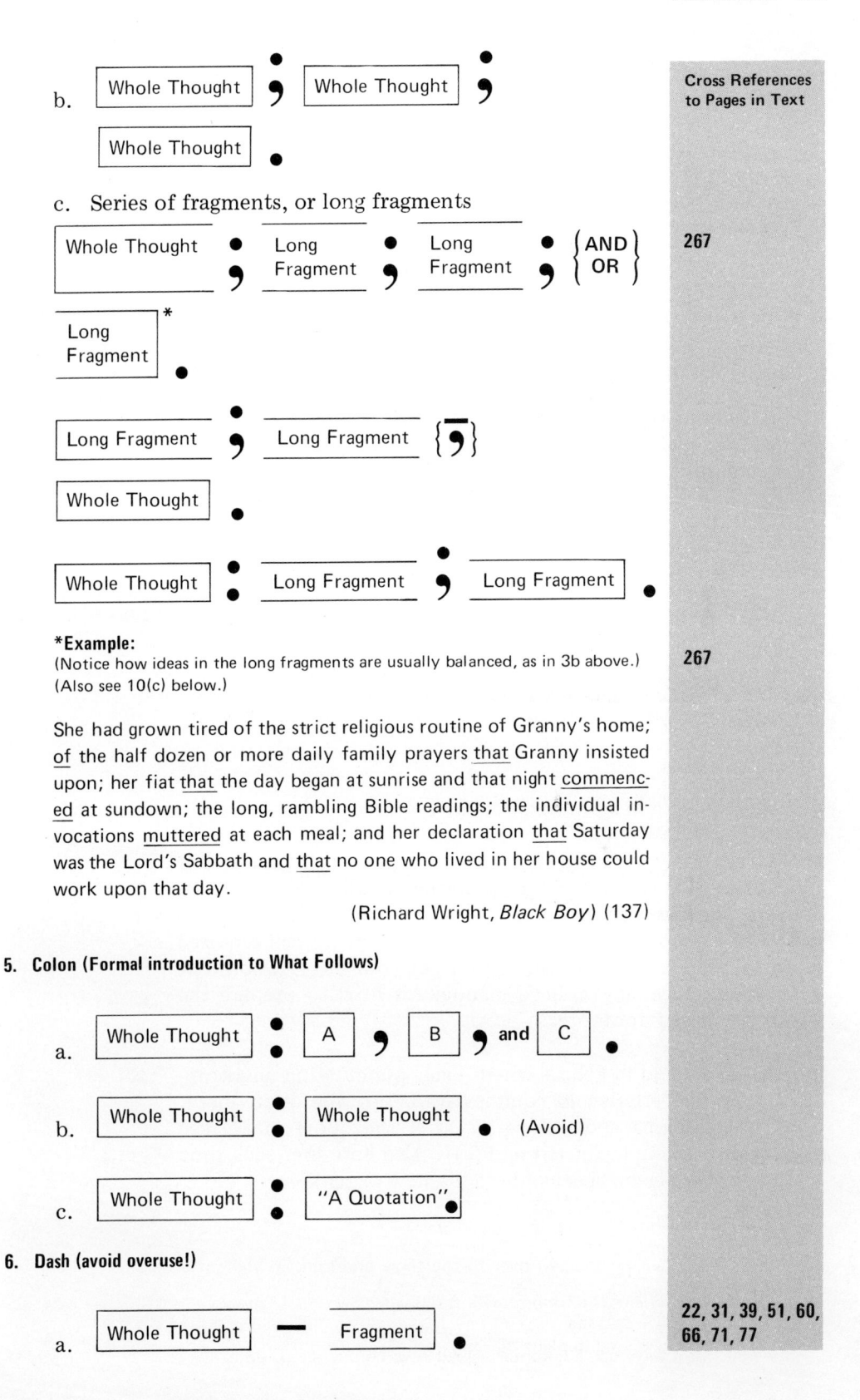

Punctuation 321

b. [Whole Thought] ; [Whole Thought] ;

[Whole Thought] .

c. Series of fragments, or long fragments

[Whole Thought] ; [Long Fragment] ; [Long Fragment] ; {AND / OR}

[Long Fragment]* .

[Long Fragment] ; [Long Fragment] {;}

[Whole Thought] .

[Whole Thought] : [Long Fragment] ; [Long Fragment] .

267

*Example:
(Notice how ideas in the long fragments are usually balanced, as in 3b above.)
(Also see 10(c) below.)

267

She had grown tired of the strict religious routine of Granny's home; of the half dozen or more daily family prayers that Granny insisted upon; her fiat that the day began at sunrise and that night commenced at sundown; the long, rambling Bible readings; the individual invocations muttered at each meal; and her declaration that Saturday was the Lord's Sabbath and that no one who lived in her house could work upon that day.

(Richard Wright, *Black Boy*) (137)

5. **Colon (Formal introduction to What Follows)**

a. [Whole Thought] : [A] , [B] , and [C] .

b. [Whole Thought] : [Whole Thought] . (Avoid)

c. [Whole Thought] : ["A Quotation"] .

6. **Dash (avoid overuse!)**

22, 31, 39, 51, 60, 66, 71, 77

a. [Whole Thought] — [Fragment] .

Cross References to Pages in Text

322 *Appendix A*

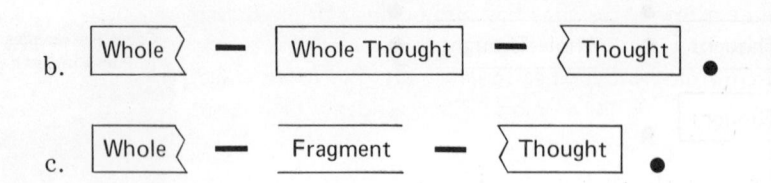

b. ⟨Whole⟩ — |Whole Thought| — ⟩Thought⟨ •

c. ⟨Whole⟩ — Fragment — ⟩Thought⟨ •

7. **Exclamation Point**

   Only use when you want to yell the idea!

8. **Period or Dots**

   a. |Whole thought| •   **8, 10**

   b. Abbreviation: Mr. Mrs.
   c. Use three dots (. . .) to show you left out words while quoting.
   d. Use four dots (. . . .) when words you leave out while quoting come at the end of the quoted sentence.

9. **Question Mark**

   a. Direct question (not for indirect question)   **279**

   Example:

   Is anything being done to help these youngsters?
   (Alfred Acquaye, *Children of West Africa*) (3)

10. **Quotation Marks**

    As a writer and a scholar, you are required to use quotation marks WHENEVER you copy the exact words of another writer. As a scholar you run the risk of getting into legal trouble (for plagiarism) if you do not use quotation marks when you are copying another writer's ideas word for word. Even if you do not copy someone's ideas word for word, you are still required in scholarship to indicate where you got your information. Use a footnote. (See any college manual for how to prepare the various types of footnotes.)

    a. Conversation. Note where each punctuation mark appears: periods and commas are before the quote mark; semicolons and colons are after the quote mark [see also example for (b) and (c)]. Also note that each time a new person speaks, there is a new paragraph.   **281, 283**

    Example:

    And then he stepped over to the table and said:* "Make it a double this time."

    ---

    *You can always use a comma instead of a colon, see p. 283.

Cross References to Pages in Text

A big white man in a dark gray suit, also buying a drink, braved Lee's tight, black scowl. "I'm Ed Jones, I work for a newspaper."

It required a moment for Lee to get the handle to his voice. "I'm Lee Gordon, I work for a union." Then suddenly he grinned and felt better.

"Good. I belong to a union—and work for it, too."

"Well, I—" He started to say that he was not a member of the union but said instead: "I am strictly for the union men."

Ed looked at him curiously. "At least we don't say grace to the wrong people."

Now Lee looked at Ed curiously. But before he could reply, a pleasant-faced young man with a Boston accent and crew haircut, dressed as a college student, spoke up with a smile: "We don't say grace—period."

"Why?" Lee asked, yielding to the impulse to bait the both of them.

"There is no one to say grace to," Ed replied seriously.

"We have not yet discarded the great god Money."

"But we are discarding it."

"And quickly at this moment," Lee said, noting his empty glass.

The young man laughed and bought them drinks. "What is money but a means for its own discard?" he stated more than asked.

"I might point out that religion and materialism are much the same," Lee said.

"How is that?"

(Chester Himes, *Lonely Crusade*) (62)

b. Short quotations from another author.**
c. Any special word that you would probably want to say "so-called" in front of. See the word "civilized" in the following excerpt.**

Example of (b) and (c):
(Also note that this excerpt is an illustration of 4(c) and 6(c) above.)

Practical men always have a measure of distrust for those who, as James Branch Cabell phrased it, have "heard the music from behind the moon"; or those who say, "Our Kingdom is not of this world"; or those who refuse to consider any custom or social usage sacred. But if Africa is to develop truly "civilized" societies, however small— and we must never forget fifth-century Athens—it must eventually produce from within its own bosom such evaluators.

(St. Clair Drake, "An Approach to the Evaluation of African Societies") (39)

d. Titles of:
essays and articles from magazines or newspapers; chapters or sections from a book; short stories, short poems, short plays.
In short, use quotation marks for any title which appears or could appear <u>within</u> a larger book, magazine, or newspaper. UNDERLINE all other titles.

Cross References to Pages in Text

See entries in Bibliographic "Answer" Section. In print, underlined words appear in *italics*.

Example:

> The urge to violence isn't always controlled. <u>The New York Post</u> of March 25, 1957, carries an example under the heading: "We Were Talking in Spanish—and the Words Meant Death."
> (Clarence Senior, *The Puerto Ricans*) (116)

11. Quoting from Another Author

a. Short quotations: use quotation marks (see 10b).
b. Long quotations: indent on BOTH SIDES of your sheet and use NO QUOTATION MARKS. More formal writers often introduce a long quotation with a colon:

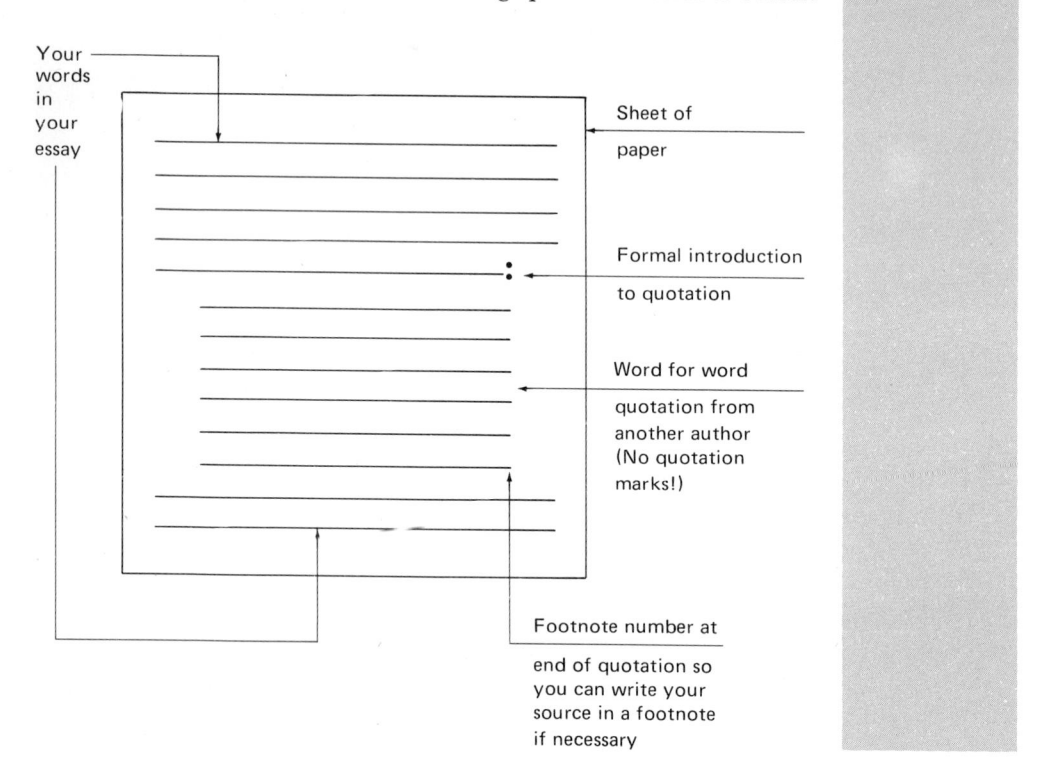

- Your words in your essay
- Sheet of paper
- Formal introduction to quotation
- Word for word quotation from another author (No quotation marks!)
- Footnote number at end of quotation so you can write your source in a footnote if necessary

APPENDIX B

Some Dictionary Guidelines

A good dictionary will give you directions on how to use it. There are some basic features of a dictionary that are especially useful, especially if you are having trouble with spelling the forms of the verb or in finding the right definition for a word. The following guidelines do not cover all that a dictionary can do for you; they cover those aspects which seem to be most relevant to what has been covered in this book.

A word about a pocket dictionary

It is hoped that as a student you lead an active life, and will not always be writing your papers at home next to a large, comprehensive dictionary. You should invest in that large dictionary, but you would be wise to have a pocket one with you at all times, so that when you write your next paper on a park bench, you will be able to look something up. However, that paperback dictionary provides no substitute for what you can get out of a desk copy. In addition, there are unabridged dictionaries (they are the most complete) in your college library.

How do you separate the word?

When you come to the end of a line while writing, and you have to break a word up, the dictionary will show you how to do it. Take the word "semester." When you look this word up to see where to separate it, you will find the following entry:

se · mes · ter

This tells you that the ONLY PLACES YOU CAN SEPARATE this word are where the dots are:

se-
mes-
ter

After looking up a few words, you should discover that words are usually separated at each new sound. Because the word "should," for example, only has one sound, you cannot separate it. Upon looking it up, you will find no dots breaking up the word.

How do you pronounce the word?

This aspect of the English language is one of the more difficult ones, because a dictionary assumes that you have an American accent. If you have another kind

328 *Appendix B*

of accent, you are best off investing in a small guide book for tourists to the United States who speak your native tongue. There you will find hints on how to pronounce basic English words.

In the dictionary, pronunciation is usually shown in parentheses right after the word itself:

se · mes · ter (sə—meś—tẽr)

The accent mark (´) tells you which part of the word to say louder: "seMESter." The special forms of the letter "e" refer to a little list of how to pronounce certain letters (usually vowels) which is generally found on the bottom of every other page in the dictionary. For example, if you are using *Webster's New World Dictionary of the American Language* (New York: The World Publishing Company, 1962), you will see the entry for the word "semester" on page 1324 and a list of how to pronounce certain letters on the bottom of page 1325. There you will find the word "ovẽr." This word tells you that the ẽ in "semestẽr" is pronounced like the "e" in the word "over." Of course, if you do not have an American accent, this will probably be of use to you only when you learn how to pronounce "over" with an American accent. Just to finish the analysis, the upside-down "e" (ə) is also found on the bottom of page 1325. The "ə" is pronounced, according to this list, like the letter "a" in the word "ago."

Where does the word come from?

The explanation in brackets after the pronunciation in parentheses generally tells you where the word came from. Usually a good dictionary will have a list of the abbreviations it uses so you can figure out what is meant by the words in the brackets. Take our word "semester":

se · mes · ter (sə—meś—tẽr) [G.; L. (*cursus*) *semestris*, half-yearly (period) < *sex*, six + *mensis*, month]

After looking up the list of abbreviations and symbols used in *Webster's New World Dictionary*, on page xxxv, you might loosely translate the words in brackets as: The word "semester" came into English from the German, which took it from the Latin. It was a combination of "sex," which means "six" in Latin, and "mensis," which means "month."

How do you spell the forms of the verb?

As was covered on pages 167-187, lots of English verbs have varied spellings, depending upon what verb group you are using. To look up the forms of the verb, consult the FIRST SET OF BRACKETS. A verb entry will usually have two sets of brackets: the first tells you the forms of the verb; the second tells you where the verb came from. Take the word "see," for example.

see (sē), *v. t.* [SAW (sô), SEEN (sēn), SEEING,] [where the word comes from]

This first set of brackets after a verb tells you that:

"saw" is the simple past
"seen" is the form of the verb for verb group 1 (I have seen him).
"seeing" is the form of the verb for verb group 2 (I am seeing him).

If there are only two words in the brackets, the simple past form and the verb group 1 form are the same. For example, look up the word "catch":

catch (*kach*) *v. t.* [CAUGHT (kôt), CATCHING]

Here you are told that you use the word "caught" as the simple past (I caught a cold) and that you use the same word for verb group 1 (I have caught a cold). "Catching," as usual, is the form for verb group 2 (I am catching a cold).

When there are no special spellings given in brackets, the verb is "regular." See pages 155-156, 169, and 181 for how to spell "regular" verbs.

Which definition do you choose?

Generally, a dictionary gives the earliest historical meaning first. But you usually want a more recent meaning or a special shade of meaning, so read through all the definitions before you decide that you know what the word means in context. The author that you are reading may have used the word in a special sense, so you will have to test out various meanings to see which one the author intends.

APPENDIX C

Bibliographic "Answer" Section

References for all excerpts used for illustrations and exercises are listed alphabetically by author. The number before each reference refers to the number found in parentheses after each illustration and exercise. When an "answer" to an altered exercise excerpt is needed, it appears under the author's name, in context—when possible. A double space between paragraphs indicates a new excerpt. For further instructions on how to use the Bibliographic "Answer" Section, see page 2. You are advised to work closely with a dictionary for words you do not know.

1. Abakari, Salim Bin, "A Journey to Russia and Siberia in 1896," English translation in *Swahili Prose Texts*, edited by Lyndon Harries. London: Oxford University Press, 1956, pp. 263-7, as found in *Africa in Prose*, edited by O. R. Dathorne and Willfried Feuser. London: Penguin Books Ltd., 1969, pp. 19-23. (African: East Africa)

And the majority of the waiters in the hotel were not Russian, most of them were Germans or Tartars, and the Tartars are Muslims. They were very surprised at the way I ordered my food and what I wanted to drink, and they asked, "Why don't you eat pork and drink wine?" I told them, "I don't drink wine nor eat pork because I am a Muslim." And they replied that they too were Muslims.

And they said to me, "We are Tartars by tribe, and the Tartars are Muslims." I did not believe it, and thought they were telling a lie, so I rang the bell and a waiter came who knew German. I asked him, "What sort of people are these who wait at table?"

And as for the dirt of their carriages, as many as twenty or thirty loads can be brought into the passenger compartment, but in Europe this is not allowed, for there is a luggage van as well as a passenger compartment. But in Russia they take on loads at every place and they spit in the compartment; it is very dirty, so much so that one cannot eat when traveling with them.

When we arrived in Moscow, we went to the hotel Safleski Bazar, and we stayed six days.

And the old city of Moscow was burned down. The Russians set fire to it themselves on purpose, because of the French when they went to fight there.

2. Abrahams, Peter, *Wild Conquest*. London: Faber and Faber Ltd., 1951. (African: South Africa)

From the hill where he stood, a path skirted the mountain on his right. He took this walking briskly.... It veered sharply right. As he made the turning, he saw two men. They were stranger than any men he had seen in all his life.... They wore garments made in the shape of a man's body. And the sandals on their feet were truly unusual. Not a part of a foot showed. Not a single toe. On their heads were headdresses with wide edges that reached beyond their faces and shaded them. And they rode animals with long ears that looked like bulls but were not. To the faces of these animals were tied leather thongs with which they guided them. On the backs of the animals were seats on which they sat. A leather thong hung from each side of the animal. Into these they pushed their feet and balanced themselves. And, in front of him, with one hand on it, each man carried a piece of wood into which was worked a round piece of iron. And, miracle of miracles, the face of each man was almost completely covered with hair so that only the nose and eyes and forehead showed. And these were white. No, not white, but a redness mixed with white!

3. Acquaye, Alfred Allotey, *Children of West Africa.* ©1968 by Sterling Publishing Co., Inc., N.Y. 10016. Also published by the Oak Tree Press, Ltd., London, 1968. (African: Ghana)

Until recently, the only education most West African village children received was in a bush camp close to home. The village elders taught them the traditional do's and don't's of their own tribal society, and how to survive in the jungle (if that was where they lived) or the desert, swamp or forest. Boys and girls in remote areas learned about hunting, crafts and farming...but little else.

At the present time there are three Universities in Ghana. The University of Ghana, which is located in the capital city, Accra, trains its students in the "liberal arts." The University of Science and Technology in Kumasi is where the pupils specialize in scientific subjects and research.

At a time when heart transplant operations are being performed with ever-increasing frequency elsewhere, large numbers of West African children are still dying of a relatively simple inflammation of the intestine called dysentery. While the dangers of trachoma, an eye disease, have been greatly decreased, and the condition is diagnosed and treated routinely in other areas, it is still an everyday recurrence that threatens the eyesight of many girls and boys in West Africa.
Is anything being done to help these youngsters?

To meet the demand for better hospital care, Mobile Medical Teams have been organised by most of the West African Nations, supported by funds and supplies furnished through the United Nations and its various health and educational branches. Traveling to remote villages by boat and truck, trained technicians are now offering bush country West African children far better health care than their parents or grandparents ever received. Large medical centers and bush dispensaries alike are attracting parents as never before, and their children are receiving regular examinations and treatment which may substantially cut the youngsters' staggering sickness-and death-rate.

At this time of year, even the taxi drivers cooperate to make it an enjoyable occasion. They show extraordinary caution while driving, since the children frequently dart across the street without watching traffic. To show that they are caught up in the spirit of the season, many people go out of their way to offer a ride to the happy boys and girls.

4. Akpan, Ntieyong U., *Epitaph to Indirect Rule—A Discourse on Local Government in Africa.* London: Cassell & Co., Ltd., 1956. (African: Nigeria)

Our local government must not be allowed to develop on a foundation of corruption, which is bound to undermine and may finally destroy the social and political fabric of a whole country.

By deciding neither to give nor receive bribes, and being courageous enough to expose those with opposite inclinations, they can show a healthy example and give a good lead in the right direction.

There are indeed many good men among the councilors; men whose real purpose is to serve the people and not to look for private gains; men who are putting up a fierce battle even within the council walls against all forms of corruption. But they are all too few.

In the former place representatives of this class are elected from among themselves and on the councils are charged with special responsibility for matters affecting native law and custom, which, of course, includes such things as the disposal and alienation of land. The Obong of Calabar, however, though popularly crowned with pomp and splendor a few years ago, does not appear to have any special recognition in his person or office. There is no objection, however, to his being elected by other traditional leaders.

There have been actual cases where bitter conflicts existed between the villagers backing their traditional rulers on the one side and the young councilors with a hardly appreciable number of outside supporters on the other. The conflict sometimes reached a stage where the councilors were ostracized by the whole community or punished with village fines and "excommunication"—which in one case meant the extremely serious step in African custom of refusal by the village to join in burying dead relatives of the councilors—for their lawful performance of council duties. In some cases it was necessary for Government administrative officers to intervene in the interests of law and order.

5. Arreola, Jose Juan, "The Prodigious Milligram," *New Voices of Hispanic America: An Anthology*, edited by Darwin J. Flakoll and Claribel Alegria. Boston: Beacon Press, 1962. (Mexican)

One day the inevitable occurred. As if they had agreed beforehand, six common ants—apparently of the most ordinary sort—arrived at the anthill, each with a strange object which was passed off, amid general anticipation, as a prodigious milligram. Naturally, they did not obtain the honors they had hoped for, but they were excused that same day from all further service and were granted pensions.

6. Ayodo, The Hon. S. O., E.G.H., "Tourist Attractions and the Game Policy," *Harambee Country, A Guide to Kenya*, revised edition of *The Lion and the Lily*, Kenneth Bottom. London: Geoffrey Bles, Ltd., 1970. (African: Kenya)

We set aside increasing amounts of money every year for our publicity campaign and more people are now aware that any month in Kenya is a holiday month and that all tourists, whether wealthy or not, are always welcome.
Having referred earlier to our game conservation policy, it is necessary to mention that these policies are decided after facts are made available to us by research workers. Both the National Parks and the Game Department pursue an active research policy, again assisted by overseas friends, and already there exists a nucleus around which a strong game research investigation is being developed.

7. Baldwin, James, *Another Country*. New York: The Dial Press, Inc., 1960. (Afro-American)

Now, as she walked beside him, trim and oddly elegant in a heavy, dark blue coat, and with her head covered by an old-fashioned and rather theatrical shawl, he saw that both her vanity and her contempt were being swollen by the glances which rested on her as briefly and unforgettably as the touch of a whip.

8. Baldwin, James, *The Fire Next Time*. New York: The Dial Press, Inc., 1962, 1963. Also available from: Dell Publishing Co., Inc., 1963. (Afro-American)

It is certainly sad that the awakening of one's senses should lead to such a merciless judgment of oneself—to say nothing of the effort to arrive at any other—but it is also inevitable that a literal attempt to mortify the flesh should be made among black people like those with whom I grew up.

Negroes in this country—and Negroes do not, strictly or legally speaking, exist in any other—are taught really to despise themselves from the moment their eyes open on the world.

He came to our house once, and afterward my father asked, as he asked about everyone, "Is he a Christian?"—by which he meant "Is he saved?" I really do not know whether my answer came out of innocence or venom, but I said coldly, "No. He's Jewish." My father slammed me across the face with his great palm, and in that moment everything flooded back—all the hatred and all the fear, and the depth of a merciless resolve to kill my father rather than allow my father to kill me—and I knew that all those sermons and tears and all that repentance and rejoicing had changed nothing. I wondered if I was expected to be glad that a friend of mine, or anyone, was to be tormented forever in Hell, and I also thought, suddenly, of the Jews in another Christian nation, Germany. They were not so far from the fiery furnace after all, and my best friend might have been one of them. I told my father, "He's a better Christian than you are," and walked out of the house. The battle between us was in the open, but that was all right; it was almost a relief. A more deadly struggle had begun.

"The white man's Heaven," sings a Black Muslim minister, "is the black man's Hell." One may object—possibly—that this puts the matter somewhat too simply, but the song is true, and it has been true for as long as white men have ruled the world. The Africans put it another way: When the white man came to Africa, the white man had the Bible and the African had the land, but now it is the white man who is being, reluctantly and bloodily, separated from the land, and the African who is still attempting to digest or to vomit up the Bible.

Life is tragic simply because the earth turns and the sun inexorably rises and sets, and one day, for each of us, the sun will go down for the last, last time. Perhaps the whole root of our trouble, the human trouble, is that we will sacrifice all the beauty of our lives, will imprison ourselves in totems, taboos, crosses, blood sacrifices, steeples, mosques, races, armies, flags, nations, in order to deny the fact of death, which is the only fact we have. It seems to me that one ought to rejoice in the fact of death—ought to decide, indeed, to earn one's death by confronting with passion the conundrum of life.

White people cannot, in the generality, be taken as models of how to live. Rather, the man is himself in sore need of new standards, which will release him from his confusion and place him once again in fruitful communion with the depths of his own being.

Years ago, we used to say, "Yes, I'm black, goddammit, and I'm beautiful!"—in defiance, into the void. But now—now—African kings and heroes have come into the world, out of the past, the past that can now be put to the uses of power. And black has become a beautiful color—not because it is loved but because it is feared.

9. Baldwin, James, *Giovanni's Room*. New York: The Dial Press, Inc., 1956. (Afro-American)

And these nights were being acted out under a foreign sky, with no one to watch, no penalties attached—it was this last fact which was our undoing, for nothing is more unbearable once one has it, than freedom. I suppose this was why I asked her to marry me: to give myself something to be moored to. Perhaps this was why, in Spain, she decided that she wanted to marry me. But people can't, unhappily, invent their mooring posts, their lovers and their friends, anymore than they can invent their parents. Life gives these and also takes them away and the great difficulty is to say Yes to life.

I think we had been lying around the beach, swimming a little and watching the near-naked girls pass, whistling at them, and laughing. I am sure that if any of the girls we whistled at that day had shown any signs of responding the ocean would not have been deep enough to drown our shame and terror. But the girls, no doubt, had some intimation of this, possibly from the way we whistled, and they ignored us. As the sun was setting we started up the boardwalk towards his house, with our wet bathing trunks on under our trousers.

He thought we were alike. I did not want to think so. I did not want to think that my life would be like his, or that my mind would ever grow so pale, so without hard places and sharp, sheer drops. He wanted no distance between us, he wanted me to look on him as a man like myself. But I wanted the merciful distance of father and son, which would have permitted me to love him.

Perhaps, as we say in America, I wanted to find myself. This is an interesting phrase, not current as far as I know in the language of any other people, which certainly does not mean what it says but betrays a nagging suspicion that something has been misplaced. I think now that if I had had any intimation that the self I was going to find would turn out to be only the same self from which I had spent so much time in flight, I would have stayed at home.

He stood, insolent and dark and leonine, his elbow leaning on the cash-register, his fingers playing with his chin, looking out at the crowd. It was as though his station were a promontory and we were the sea. Jacques was immediately attracted.

But the silence of the evening, as I wandered home, had nothing to do with that storm, that far-off boy. I simply wondered about the dead because their days had ended and I did not know how I would get through mine.

The body in the mirror forces me to turn and face it. And I look at my body, which is under sentence of death. It is lean, hard, and cold, the incarnation of a mystery. And I do not know what moves in this body, what this body is searching. It is trapped in my mirror as it is trapped in time and it hurries toward revelation.

10a. Baldwin, James, *Nobody Knows My Name: More Notes of a Native Son*. New York: The Dial Press, Inc., 1961. Originally published as "The Black Boy Looks at the White Boy," *Esquire* (May, 1961). (Afro-American)

There is a difference, though, between Norman and myself in that I think he still imagines that he has something to save, whereas I have never had anything to lose. Or, perhaps I ought to put it another way: the thing that most white people imagine that they can salvage from the storm of life is really, in sum, their innocence. It was this commodity precisely which I had to get rid of at once, literally, on pain of death. I am afraid that most of the white people I have ever known impressed me as being in the grip of a weird nostalgia, dreaming of a vanished state of security and order, against which dream, unfailingly and unconsciously, they tested and very often lost their lives. It is a terrible thing to say, but I am afraid that for a very long time the troubles of white people failed to impress me as being real trouble. They put me in mind of children crying because the breast has been taken away. Time and love have modified my tough-boy lack of charity, but the attitude sketched above was my first attitude and I am sure that there is a great deal of it left.

But we were far more cheerful than anything I've said might indicate and none of the above seemed to matter very much at the time. Other things mattered, like walking and talking and drinking and eating, and the way Adele laughed, and the way Norman argued.

Norman came on to America, and I went to Corsica. We wrote each other a few times. I confided to Norman that I was very apprehensive about the reception of *Giovanni's Room*, and he was good enough to write some very encouraging things about it when it came out. The critics had jumped on him with both their left feet when he published *The Deer Park*—which I still had not read—and this created a kind of bond, or strengthened the bond already existing between us. About a year and several overflowing wastebaskets later, I, too, returned to America, not vastly improved by having been out of it, but not knowing where else to go; and one day, while I was sitting dully in my house, Norman called me from Connecticut.

One can never really see into the heart, the mind, the soul of another. Norman is my very good friend, but perhaps I do not really understand him at all, and perhaps everything I have tried to suggest in the foregoing is false. I do not think so, but it may be. One thing, however, I am certain is *not* false, and that is simply the fact of his being a writer, and the incalculable potential he as a writer contains. His work, after all, is all that will be left when the newspapers are yellowed, all the gossip columnists silenced, and all the cocktail parties over, and when Norman and you and I are dead.

10b. Baldwin, James, *Nobody Knows My Name: More Notes of a Native Son.* New York: The Dial Press, Inc., 1961. Originally published as "The Discovery of What It Means to Be an American," *The New York Times Book Review* (January 25, 1959). (Afro-American)

I had been in Paris a couple of years before any of this became clear to me. When it did, I, like many a writer before me upon the discovery that his props have all been knocked out from under him, suffered a species of breakdown and was carried off to the mountains of Switzerland. There, in that absolutely alabaster landscape, armed with two Bessie Smith records and a typewriter, I began to try to re-create the life that I had first known as a child and from which I had spent so many years in flight.
It was Bessie Smith, through her tone and her cadence, who helped me to dig back to the way I myself must have spoken when I was a pickaninny, and to remember the things I had heard and seen and felt. I had buried them very deep. I had never listened to Bessie Smith in America (in the same way that, for years, I would not touch watermelon), but in Europe she helped to reconcile me to being a "nigger."

This perpetual dealing with people very different from myself caused a shattering in me of preconceptions I scarcely knew I held. The writer is meeting in Europe people who are not American, whose sense of reality is entirely different from his own. They may love or hate or admire or fear or envy this country—they see it, in any case, from another point of view, and this forces the writer to reconsider many things he had always taken for granted. This reassessment, which can be very painful, is also very valuable.

Every society is really governed by hidden laws, by unspoken but profound assumptions on the part of the people, and ours is no exception. It is up to the American writer to find out what these laws and assumptions are. In a society much given to smashing taboos without thereby managing to be liberated from them, it will be no easy matter.

10c. Baldwin, James, *Nobody Knows My Name: More Notes of a Native Son.* New York: The Dial Press, Inc., 1961. Originally published as "Fifth Avenue Uptown: A Letter from Harlem," *Esquire* (July, 1960). (Afro-American)

There is a housing project standing now where the house in which we grew up once stood, and one of those stunted city trees is snarling where our doorway used to be. This is on the rehabilitated side of the avenue. The other side of the avenue—for progress takes time—has not been rehabilitated yet and it looks exactly as it looked in the days when we sat with our noses pressed against the windowpane, longing to be allowed to go "across the street." The grocery store which gave us credit is still there, and there can be no doubt that it is still giving credit.

Now I am perfectly aware that there are other slums in which white men are fighting for their lives, and mainly losing. I know that blood is also flowing through those streets and that the human damage there is incalculable. People are continually pointing out to me the wretchedness of white people in order to console me for the wretchedness of blacks. But an itemized account of the American failure does not console me and it should not console anyone else. That hundreds of thousands of white people are living, in effect, no better than the "niggers" is not a fact to be regarded with complacency. The social and moral bankruptcy suggested by this fact is of the bitterest, most terrifying kind.

The people who have managed to get off this block have only got as far as a more respectable ghetto. This respectable ghetto does not even have the advantages of the disreputable one—friends, neighbors, a familiar church, and friendly tradesmen; and it is not, moreover, in the nature of any ghetto to remain respectable long. Every Sunday, people who have left the block take the lonely ride back, dragging their increasingly discontented children with them.

10d. Baldwin, James, *Nobody Knows My Name: More Notes of a Native Son.* New York: The Dial Press, Inc., 1961. Originally published as "Gide As Husband and Homosexual," *The New Leader* (December 13, 1954). (Afro-American)

But there are a great many ways of outwitting oblivion, and to ask whether or not homosexuality is natural is really like asking whether or not it was natural for Socrates to swallow hemlock, whether or not it was natural for St. Paul to suffer for the Gospel, whether or not it was natural for the Germans to send upwards of six million people to an extremely twentieth-century death. It does not seem to me that nature helps us very much when we need illumination in human affairs. I am certainly convinced that it is one of the greatest impulses of mankind to arrive at something higher than a natural state. How to be natural does not seem to me to be a problem—quite the contrary. The great problem is how to be—in the best sense of that kaleidoscopic word—a man.

It is one of the facts of life that there are two sexes, which fact has given the world most of its beauty, cost it not a little of its anguish, and contains the hope and glory of the world. And it is with this fact, which might better perhaps be called a mystery, that every human being born must find some way to live. For, no matter what demons drive them, men cannot live without women and women cannot live without men. And this is what is most clearly conveyed in the agony of Gide's last journal. However little he was able to understand it, or, more important perhaps, take upon himself the responsibility for it, Madeleine kept open for him a kind of door of hope, of possibility, the possibility of entering into communion with another sex. This door, which is the door to life and air and freedom from the tyranny of one's own personality, *must* be kept open, and none feel this more keenly than those on whom the door is perpetually threatening or has already seemed to close.

10e. Baldwin, James, *Nobody Knows My Name: More Notes of a Native Son.* New York: The Dial Press, Inc., 1961, from "Nobody Knows My Name: A Letter from the South," *Partisan Review* (Winter, 1959). (Afro-American)

In the fall of last year, my plane hovered over the rust-red earth of Georgia. I was past thirty, and I had never seen this land before. I pressed my face against the window, watching the earth come closer; soon we were just above the tops of trees. I could not suppress the thought that this earth had acquired its color from the blood that had dripped down from these trees. My mind was filled with the image of a black man, younger than I, perhaps, or my own age, hanging from a tree, while white men watched him and cut his sex from him with a knife.

(We do not trust educated people and rarely, alas, produce them, for we do not trust the independence of mind which alone makes a genuine education possible.) Educated people, of any color, are so extremely rare that it is unquestionably one of the first tasks of a nation to open all of its schools to all of its citizens. But the dispute has actually nothing to do with education, as some among the eminently uneducated know.

Before arriving in Atlanta I had spent several days in Charlotte, North Carolina. This is a bourgeois town, Presbyterian, pretty—if you like towns—and socially so hermetic that it contains scarcely a single decent restaurant. I was told that Negroes there are not even licensed to become electricians or plumbers. I was also told, several times, by white people, that "race relations" there were excellent. I failed to find a single Negro who agreed with this, which is the usual story of "race relations" in this country.

11. Baldwin, James, *Tell Me How Long the Train's Been Gone.* New York: The Dial Press, Inc., 1968. (Afro-American)

I knew I had been working too hard. I had been warned. But I have always worked too hard. I came offstage at the end of the second act. I felt hot and I was having trouble catching my breath. But I knew that I was tired. I went to my dressing room and poured myself a drink and put my feet up. Then I felt better. I knew I had about twenty-five minutes before I was due onstage. I felt very bitterly nauseous and I went to the bathroom but nothing happened. Then I began to be afraid, rather, to sit or lie down again and I poured myself another drink and left my dressing room to stand in the wings. I had begun to sweat and I was freezing cold. The nausea came back, making me feel that my belly was about to rise to the roof of my head. The stage manager looked at me just as I heard my cue. I carried his face onstage with me. It had looked white and horrified and disembodied in the eerie backstage light. I wondered what had frightened him. Then I realized that I was having trouble finding my positions and having trouble hearing lines.

My life, that desperately treacherous labyrinth, seemed for a moment to be opening out behind me; a light seemed to fall where there had been no light before. I began to see myself in others. I began for a moment to apprehend how Christopher must sometimes have felt. Everyone wishes to be loved, but, in the event, nearly no one can bear it. Everyone desires love but also finds it impossible to believe that he deserves it. However great the private disasters to which love may lead, love itself is strikingly and mysteriously impersonal; it is a reality which is not altered by anything one does. Therefore, one does many things, turns the key in the lock over and over again, hoping to be locked out. Once locked out, one will never again be forced to encounter in the eyes of a stranger who loves him the impenetrable truth concerning the stranger, oneself, who is loved. And yet—one would prefer, after all, not to be locked out. One would prefer, merely, that the key unlocked a less stunningly unusual door.

And what did the fire say? Now that I knew that I was going to live, at least for a while, the fire seemed warmer than it ever had before. I sipped my drink, watching that crumbling, shaking, brilliant universe.

12. Baldwin, James, "This Morning, This Evening, So Soon," in *Going to Meet the Man.* New York: The Dial Press, Inc., 1948. (Afro-American)

13. Bastos, Roa Augusto, "The Excavation," *New Voices of Hispanic America: An Anthology*, edited by Darwin J. Flakoll and Claribel Alegria. Boston: Beacon Press, 1962. (Paraguayan)

Suddenly the earth seemed to give way a bit. He clawed in the emptiness. Like a stone, he remained behind, strangling on the air. He tried to advance, but now his legs formed an irremediable part of the block that had slid down on them. He no longer even felt them. He felt only the asphyxia. He was drowning in a solid, dark river. He stopped moving, stopped the useless struggle. The torment slowly changed into an inexplicable delight.

14. Belaval, Emilio, "El Niño Morado de Monsona Quintana," in *Puerto Rico, La Nueva Vida The New life*, edited by Nina Kaiden, Pedro Juan Soto, and Andrew Valdimir. Housing Investment Corporation, 1966. Originally from *Monsona Quintana's Purple Child*, translated by Patricia Valles. (Puerto Rican)

Monsona Quintana is an emaciated countrywoman of my land who has given birth seventeen times; her belly is so stretched that her husband can no longer tell when she is pregnant. Childbearing has devoured the youth of this countrygirl who once had the color of camádula seeds and breasts of a sleepy turtle dove.

15. Benedetti, Mario, "Gloria's Saturday," *New Voices of Hispanic America: An Anthology*, edited by Darwin J. Flakoll and Claribel Alegria. Boston: Beacon Press, 1962. (Uruguayan)

Even before waking, I heard the rain falling. At first I thought it must be six-fifteen in the morning and I should be going to the office.

16. Bennett, Lerone, Jr., *Before the Mayflower*. Chicago: Johnson Publishing Co., Inc., 1961, 1969. (Afro-American)

He had written these words in a room in Philadelphia when he was thirty-three. Now, in another room, in another age, fifty years to the date after the signing of the Declaration of Independence, Thomas Jefferson, the sage of Monticello, the architect, the philosopher, the humanitarian, lay dying in a house filled with rare books and old slaves. All his life, he had wrestled with the awful presense of *his* slaves and the noble sound of *his* words and he had gone down in defeat. He was not a small man and so his defeat gives no man joy. In him was the strength and the weakness of America. He died on July 4, 1826, and went to his grave, borne by slaves.

"Peculiarsome," too, was Frederick Augustus Washington Bailey, a nine-year-old slave in Baltimore, Maryland. Frederick and Abe were two of a kind. Both would climb out of their narrow prisons on ladders of words; both would climb steep mountains and walk lonely paths; and both would grapple with the revolutionary implications in Thomas Jefferson's words.

In these three boys, in their hopes, in their dreams, in their fears, is the whole story of the crisis which reached a climax in a Civil War and the emancipation of four million slaves with a book value of four billion dollars. The crisis was a compound of many things, of machines and turnpikes and railroad tracks; of sin, sex and salvation; of the restless yearnings of poor whites and the volcanic stirrings of poor blacks; of the fear, guilt and anxiety which lay like a slave chain across the American soul.

A major actor in this drama was William Lloyd Garrison, a brilliant young journalist who published the first issue of his famous *Liberator* in 1831. His first editorial sang with indignation.

"I will be as harsh as truth, and as uncompromising as justice. On this subject [slavery] I do not wish to think, to speak, or write, with moderation. No! No! Tell a man whose house is on fire to give a moderate alarm; tell him to moderately rescue his wife from the hands of the ravisher; tell the mother to gradually extricate her babe from the fire into which it has fallen;

but urge me not to use moderation in a cause like the present! I am in earnest—I will not equivocate—I will not excuse—I will not retreat a single inch—AND I WILL BE HEARD."

Crises breed big men. They come forth like diamonds, perfected by the pressures they have been subjected to.

The pioneer Negro abolitionists gave way in the forties to the giants of the movement, Charles Lenox Remond, the first Negro to take the platform as a professional antislavery lecturer; Samuel Ringgold Ward, the eloquent black man who pastored a white church; Henry Highland Garnet, the bitterly brilliant Thomas Paine of the movement; Martin R. Delany, the Harvard man who was the first major Negro nationalist; William Wells Brown, the grandson of Daniel Boone (he said) and the first Negro to write a novel and a play. There were others: the big-souled, God-intoxicated women, Sojourner Truth and Harriet Tubman, and scholars like J. W. C. Pennington, the minister who received a D.D. degree from the University of Heidelberg while he was still a fugitive slave; Alexander Crummell, the erudite Episcopal priest; and James McCune Smith, the New York physician who graduated from the University of Glasgow.

There were riots and other disorders and young toughs came charging to the platform, screaming, "Kill the nigger," "Get the god-damned nigger." Douglass was pelted with eggs and thrown down steps; but he stood his ground and took his knocks.

Listen to Sojourner Truth. She stands on an Indiana platform, braving the taunts of proslavery Northerners. A local doctor rises and says there is some doubt about the sex of the speaker. He asks Sojourner to submit to an inspection by local ladies. The meeting goes up in an uproar; there are shouts, screams, coarse laughs. Sojourner looks out into the audience and shouts: "My breasts have suckled many a white babe, even when they should have been suckling my own." She stabs a bony finger. "Some of those white babes are now grown men, and even though they have suckled my Negro breasts, they are in my opinion far more manly than any of you appear to be." Suddenly, without warning, she rips open the front of her dress. "I will show my breasts," she says, "to the entire congregation. It's not my shame but yours. Here then, see for yourself." Her eyes lock on the face of the doubting doctor and she says quietly, "Do you wish also to suck?"

Henry "Box" Brown escaped from slavery in a box lined with baize. A friend locked him in the box and shipped it from Richmond to Philadelphia. Brown stepped from the box and sang: "I waited patiently for the Lord, and he heard my prayer."

A massacre followed. The enraged white shot down innocent Negroes who smiled and innocent Negroes who did not smile.

17. Beti, Mongo, *Mission to Kala*. Rosica Colin Ltd., 1957. Translated from *Mission Terminée*, Paris: Corrêa, 1957. As found in *Drum Beats: An Anthology of African Writing*, compiled by Ime Ikiddeh, Leeds: Arnold & Son Ltd., 1968. (African: Cameroun Republic)

Do you remember that period? Fathers used to take their children to school as they might lead sheep into a slaughter-house. Tiny tots would turn up from backwood villages thirty or forty miles up-country, shepherded by their parents, to be put on the books of some school, it didn't matter which.

I personally loathed my father, and have continued to do so to a greater or lesser degree according to my age; but I have never ceased to admire the way in which he brought this enterprise to a successful conclusion—in other words, his *style*. Knowing what a passion all his compatriots have for parties and family gatherings—however little like parties the latter may be—he used to invite all his half-brothers and nephews round once a month, and say to them: "I'd like you to help me do a little job. There's plenty of wine laid on this morning; so you can wet your whistles before you go out to work, and finish it up when you're done."

For about a week my relations with my father were virtually nonexistent—on the surface, at any rate. Underneath, things were building up to a climax: the powder train was laid, and it needed only a tiny spark to touch it off.

My tactics remained more or less constant.

My father fought with all the fury of a wild beast wounded by the hunter's first shot: all the neighbors came out of their houses to watch. From all sides voices were raised exhorting me to get out while I could. "What are you waiting for, you young fool?"

I hastily ran over in my mind the few rudiments of boxing I had learnt from my friends in college; but when the moment came, I couldn't bring myself to hit him, and gave ground rapidly.

18. *Black Scholar*, "Muhammad Ali," *The Black Scholar*, Vol. I, No. 8 (June, 1970), pp. 33-34. (Afro-American)

Then they took the title unjustly. I'm supposed to be selling shoe strings and walking around somewhere broke. But I surprised them; I'm doing better.

You only have two kinds of men, those who compromise and those who take a stand. And those who take a stand are those who get the respect.

Here's a white man, swinging in Africa with a white woman. And you're down in Georgia, not knowing any better. You really believe there's a white man who's king of the jungle.

19. *Black Scholar*, "Robert F. Williams," *The Black Scholar*, Vol. I., No. 7 (May, 1970), pp. 3-11. (Afro-American)

Williams: It is traditional Americanism for the white racist power structure to brand all who work uncompromisingly for black liberation and social justice as extremists.

The greatest change has been in the attitudes of blacks, particularly the so-called black bourgeoisie. Many of them have become more conscious of what's going on—they've been forced to—and are more willing to identify with our people. More race pride is especially apparent among our youth, more co-operation and more militancy.

Back then the going thing was what the white man had told them: to turn the other cheek and appeal to the conscience of the white oppressor. I knew that you couldn't do that; you can't appeal to the conscience of a beast, when you're dealing with savages and brutes and tyrants. So this is one major thing that I see. And it is a change that has influenced the black bourgeoisie and the power structure, though the power structure lately has become even more repressive. But in some ways the fact that the black man was no longer passive and would fight caused the power structure to give more attention to the black man.

20. Bontemps, Arna, "A Summer Tragedy," as found in *Anthology of American Negro Literature*, edited by Sylvester C. Watkins. New York: Random House, 1944. (Afro-American)

Her answer was not strong enough to reach him, but presently the old woman came to the door, feeling her way with a stick. She had a wasted, dead-leaf appearance. Her body, as scrawny and gnarled as a string bean, seemed less than nothing in the ocean of frayed and faded petticoats that surrounded her. These hung an inch or two above the tops of her heavy unlaced shoes and showed little grotesque piles where the stockings had fallen down from her negligible legs.

The sun was hot on his head, his collar still pinched his throat, and the Sunday clothes were intolerably hot.

Jeff adjusted the crank and put his weight upon it. The engine came to life with a sputter and bang that rattled the old car from radiator to tail light. Jeff hopped into the seat and put his foot on the accelerator. The sputtering and banging increased. The rattling became more violent. That was good. It was good banging, good sputtering and rattling, and it meant that the aged car was still in running condition. She could be depended on for this trip.

The two old black folks, sitting quietly side by side, showed no excitement. In another instant the car hit the water and dropped immediately out of sight.
A little later it lodged in the mud of a shallow place. One wheel of the crushed and upturned little Ford became visible above the rushing water.

21. Brooks, Gwendolyn, "The Life of Lincoln West," in *Soon, One Morning, New Writing by American Negroes, 1940-1962*, edited by Herbert Hill. New York: Alfred A. Knopf, Inc., 1963, pp. 317-319. (Afro-American)

She tried to be as pleasant with him as with others, but it was difficult. For she was all beauty, all daintiness, all tiny vanilla, with blue eyes and fluffy sun-hair. One afternoon she saw him in the hall looking very bleak against the wall. It was strange because the bell had long since rung and no other child was in sight. Pity flooded her.

But when their more acceptable friends came, were around, they turned their handsome backs on him. He hated himself for responding gratefully to their later "Hi, Linc!"—hated himself for his feeling of well-being when with them, despite—everything.

22. Brown, Claude, *Manchild in the Promised Land*. New York: The Macmillan Company, 1965. (Afro-American)

Going to New York was good-bye to the cotton fields, good-bye to "Massa Charlie," good-bye to the chain gang, and, most of all, good-bye to those sunup-to-sundown working hours. One no longer had to wait to get to heaven to lay his burden down; burdens could be laid down in New York.
So, they came, from all parts of the South, like all the black chillun o' God following the sound of Gabriel's horn on that long-overdue Judgment Day. The Georgians came as soon as they were able to pick train fare off the peach trees. They came from South Carolina where the cotton stalks were bare. The North Carolinians came with tobacco tar beneath their fingernails.

Before the soreness of the cotton fields had left Mama's back, her knees were getting sore from scrubbing "Goldberg's" floor. Nevertheless, she was better off; she had gone from the fire into the frying pan.

The children of these disillusioned colored pioneers inherited the total lot of their parents—the disappointments, the anger. To add to their misery, they had little hope of deliverance. For where does one run to when he's already in the promised land?

This was the building where Mr. Lawson had killed a man for peeing in the hall. I remembered being afraid to go downstairs the morning after Mr. Lawson had busted that man's head with a baseball bat. I could still see blood all over the hall. This was the building where somebody was always shooting out the windows in the hall. They were usually shooting at Johnny D., and they usually missed. This was the building that I loved more than anyplace else in the world. The thought that I would never see this building again scared the hell out of me.

As we headed toward the backyard to hide our books, Danny began to explain the great game of hookey. It sounded like lots of fun to me. Instead of going to school, we would go all over the city stealing, sneak into a movie, or go up on a roof and throw bottles down into the street. Danny suggested that we start the day off by waiting for Mr. Gordon to put out his vegetables; we could steal some sweet potatoes and cook them in the backyard. I was sorry I hadn't started school sooner, because hookey sure was a lot of fun.

We walked back home up the highway. Grandma had her arm around my shoulder, and I had my arm around her waist. That was the only time I ever touched Grandma—and the only time I recall wanting her to touch me and liking her touch. When I saw the house coming at us up the road, I was kind of sad. I looked at Grandma's wrinkled face and liked it. I knew I had fallen in love with that mean old wrinkled lady who, I used to think, had a mouth like a monkey.

23. Cade, Toni, "Book Review," *Liberator*, Vol. 9, No. 4 (April, 1969), p. 19. (Afro-American)

Horny Sy, one of Jimmy's gang members, can't let well enough alone when the boys jump a woman and drag her into a lot; he has to go back for seconds and discovers that it's his mother underneath him.

24. Cade, Toni, "The Children Who Get Cheated," *Redbook*, Vol. 134, No. 3 (1970), p. 156. (Afro-American)

This issue of life-style differences is crucial in education. Consider the traditional lesson of "A Good Diet Consists of the Daily Basic Seven." The white teacher, in speaking of leafy green vegetables, never seems to have heard of collard greens or turnip greens. When she lists the other basic foods, she overlooks beans and rice and other dishes characteristic of the chilren's homes. The children begin to suspect that something is wrong with their mothers' notion of diet. There is nothing wrong at home, necessarily. But something is wrong at school: the white teacher is talking about a white diet only.

The Black child should master standard English—not simply to understand Shakespeare and the classics, but also to be able to understand how he is being and has been manipulated by language. The Louisiana State Voter Application is a better argument for his learning standard English than *Macbeth*. But he should also know his own language first.

25. Cayou, Dolores, "The Origins of Modern Jazz Dance," *The Black Scholar*. Vol. I, No. 8 (June, 1970), p. 30. (Afro-American)

Let me return for a moment to the foundation of the arts in Africa. The arts were part of the total complex of life; there was no audience and everyone participated in the dance and musical expression in some way. Even though black Americans had lived through hundreds of years of slavery, this major difference, the role of the arts in life, carried over to a great degree; everyone participated at home, church, parties, and gatherings.

26. Cayton, Horace R., "A Picnic with Sinclair Lewis," in *Soon, One Morning, New Writing by American Negroes 1940-1962*, edited by Herbert Hill. New York: Alfred A. Knopf, Inc., 1963, pp. 22-35. (Afro-American)

The Lewis estate was large and lovely. His spacious and comfortable house stood on a hill overlooking a beautiful valley. In addition to the main house, there were a couple of small cottages for servants and guests, a large swimming pool, a tennis court, and a farm. The establishment was run by three Negro servants.

Alma was the maid, and Wilson, her husband, the gardener-handy man. They had one small child. Alma was a light-colored, plump, and attractive creole from Louisiana, in her late twenties or early thirties. She seemed to dominate the quiet, easygoing Wilson. She outwardly accepted her position, kept her place, did her work, and demanded and received respect.

She let me know that I was a guest and should stay in my place and she would stay in hers. And that set the tone of my relationship with all of the servants.

There was one more member of the household, Barnaby Conrad, Lewis' secretary. He was an extremely charming and talented young man who had just returned from Spain, where he had been a bullfighter, and was now engaged in writing his first novel.

Lewis was the master of his household—the complete master. I never heard him reprimand anyone or issue an order, but his control was absolute.

Apparently he knew what to do and did it well, as I never saw Lewis talking with him. Meals were served on time—eight o'clock for breakfast, one o'clock for lunch, and seven o'clock for dinner—and were announced by a large gong near the head of the stairs in the living room. I was warned by Barney that everyone was expected to be on time. The household followed Lewis' routine; people fitted into his mold. He was a stubborn man, set in his ways; while living in his home one conformed to his pattern of life.

27. Chadangalara, J. W. M., "Father and Son," in *Our African Way of Life*, Essays by John Kambalame, E. P. Chidzalo, J. W. M. Chadangalara, presented under the Prize Scheme of the International African Institute for the period 1943-44, translated and edited by Cullen Young and Hastings Banda. London: Lutterworth Press, 1946. (African: Malawi)

When he had finished selling he went on his way and came to an open glade where he saw a very large and very fierce elephant. Now that elephant had seen him!

... Quickly he turned and faced the same direction in which it was going, coming behind the elephant, and took his bow. He pierced it in the abdomen and it stood now: looking everywhere without seeing Jumbe and then moving little by little towards a great, upstanding rock. But he moved with it. Coming at the great rock, he climbed hastily up and the elephant never saw him scrambling up to the very top of the rock. "Oho!" and he began to dance and sing a song testifying to his deliverance.

28. Chesnutt, Charles W., "The Sheriff's Children," in *The Wife of His Youth*. Boston: The Cresset Press, 1889, as reprinted in *Forgotten Pages of American Literature*, edited by Gerald W. Haslam. Boston: Houghton Mifflin Company, 1970. (Afro-American)

Branson County, North Carolina, is in a sequestered district of one of the staidest and most conservative States of the Union. Society in Branson County is almost primitive in its simplicity. Most of the white people own the farms they till, and even before the war there were no very wealthy families to force their neighbors, by comparison, into the category of "poor whites."

At the period of which I write, no railroad had come to Troy. If a traveler, accustomed to the bustling life of cities, could have ridden through Troy on a summer day, he might easily have fancied himself in a deserted village. Around him he would have seen weather-beaten houses, innocent of paint, the shingled roofs in many instances covered with a rich growth of moss. Here and there he would have met a razor-backed hog lazily rooting his way along the principal thoroughfare; and more than once he would probably have had to disturb the slumbers of some yellow dog, dozing away the hours in the ardent sunshine, and reluctantly yielding up his place in the middle of the dusty road.

This speech gave tone and direction to the rest of the conversation. Whether the fear of losing the round-shouldered farmer operated to bring about the result or not is immaterial to this narrative; but, at all events, the crowd decided to lynch the Negro. They agreed that this was the least that could be done to avenge the death of their murdered friend, and that it was a becoming way in which to honor his memory. They had some vague notions of the majesty of the law and the rights of the citizen, but in the passion of the moment these sunk into oblivion; a white man had been killed by a Negro.

29. Chidzalo, E. P., "The Choice of a Wife," *Our African Way of Life*, Essays by John Kambalame, E. P. Chidzalo, J. W. M. Chadangalara, presented under the Prize Scheme for the period 1943-44, translated and edited by Cullen Young and Hastings Banda. London: Lutterworth Press, 1946. (African: Malawi)

For this reason it is the responsibility of the mother and father, and even more the responsibility of the maternal uncle, to supervise the life of the young man so that he may be a lover of work with his hands while he has not departed to the village of another group, in marriage.
And he is also taught the ways of courtesy, both to the older folk and among the younger generation themselves. They restrain and forbid ill-temper or impertinence towards both old and young.

In particular they held that if any youth of rude and impertinent ways were to marry, he would cause deep shame to his community. There was no inducement to arrange marriage for such a one since he would surely bring disgrace on the family from which he came. Youths of good and courteous ways within their own mother's community always married quickly because their maternal uncles lost no time in arranging betrothal for them.

The maternal uncle accompanies him to his new home but gives him no further advice and instructions, lest his mind be confused trying to hold in his head so many things.
Arriving at the village, they come to the "talking-place," where the men are in the habit of gathering, sewing mats and doing their various work in the sun. First of all, the maternal uncle of the lad makes contact with him from whom he had asked the girl in betrothal and announces that he has arrived with the lad.

When the "probationer's" maternal uncles arrive they gather together with the girl's legal representatives and exchange formal greetings. In due time the beer is brought to the "talking-place" (where men always hold meetings and where visitors and travelers in a strange village always report their presence), and is poured out for the lad's uncles and other relatives that might be with them on this mission.
After the beer has arrived the senior representative on the girl's side rises and says, "We have called all of you on the male side together that you may share in eating the food which your child has hoed."

30. Chisholm, Shirley, "Racism and Anti-Feminism," *The Black Scholar*, Vol. I, No. 3, 4 (January-February, 1970), pp. 40-45. (Afro-American)

31. Clarke, John Henrik, "Reclaiming the Lost African Heritage," in *Black Fire: An Anthology of Afro-American Writing*, edited by LeRoi Jones and Larry Neal. New York: William Morrow and Company, Inc., 1968. Originally published in *The American Negro Writer and his Roots*, with the permission of the American Society of African Culture. (Afro-American)

For the last three hundred years Africa and its people have been viewed mainly through European eyes and for European reasons. The entire history of Africa will have to be literally rewritten, challenging and reversing the European concept. It is singularly the responsibility of the Negro writer to proclaim and celebrate the fact that his people have in their ancestry rulers who expanded kingdoms into empires and built great and magnificent armies, scholars whose vision of life showed foresight and wisdom, and priests who told of gods that were strong and kind. The American Negro writer should pay particular attention to the Western Sudan (West Africa), his ancestral home.

32. Cleaver, Eldridge, *Soul on Ice*. New York: McGraw-Hill Book Company, 1968. (Afro-American)

Nineteen fifty-four, when I was eighteen years old, is held to be a crucial turning point in the history of the Afro-American—for the U.S.A. as a whole—the year segregation was outlawed by the U.S. Supreme Court. It was also a crucial year for me because on June 18, 1954, I began serving a sentence in state prison for possession of marijuana.

The Supreme Court decision was only one month old when I entered prison, and I do not believe that I had even the vaguest idea of its importance or historical significance. But later, the acrimonious controversy ignited by the end of the separate-but-equal doctrine was to have a profound effect on me. This controversy awakened me to my position in America and I began to form a concept of what it meant to be black in white America.

In prison, those things withheld from and denied to the prisoner become precisely what he wants most of all, of course. Because we were locked up in our cells before darkness fell, I used to lie awake at night racked by painful craving to take a leisurely stroll under the stars, or to go to the beach, to drive a car on a freeway, to grow a beard, or to make love to a woman.

I was very familiar with the Eldridge who came to prison, but that Eldridge no longer exists. And the one I am now is in some ways a stranger to me. You may find this difficult to understand but it is very easy for one in prison to lose his sense of self. And if he has been undergoing all kinds of extreme, involved, and unregulated changes, then he ends up not knowing who he is. Take the point of being attractive to women. You can easily see how a man can lose his arrogance or certainty on that point while in prison! When he's in the free world, he gets constant feedback on how he looks from the number of female heads he turns when he walks down the street. In prison he gets only hate-stares and sour frowns. . . .Individuality is not nourished in prison, neither by the officials nor by the convicts. It is a deep hole out of which to climb.

I'm perfectly aware that I'm in prison, that I'm a Negro, that I've been a rapist, and that I have a Higher Uneducation. I never knew what significance I'm supposed to attach to these factors. But I have a suspicion that, because of these aspects of my character, "free-normal-educated" people rather expect me to be more reserved, penitent, remorseful, and not too quick to shoot off my mouth on certain subjects. But I let them down, disappoint them, make them gape at me in a sort of stupor, as if they're thinking: "You've got your nerve! Don't you realize that you owe a debt to society?"

Weakness, frailty, cowardice, and effeminacy are, among other attributes, associated with the Mind. Strength, brute power, force, virility, and physical beauty are associated with the

Body. Thus the upper classes or Omnipotent Administrators, are perennially associated with physical weakness, decay, underdeveloped bodies, effeminacy, sexual impotence, and frigidity. Virility, strength, and power are associated with the lower classes, the Supermasculine Menials.

But put on your crown, my Queen, and we will build a New City on these ruins.

33. Cruse, Harold, *The Crises of the Negro Intellectual*. New York: William Morrow and Company, Inc., 1967. (Afro-American)

The economic panic brought on by the 1929 Crash also caused cultural panic among the white intellectuals; from the point of view of their own class and creative status, they saw in these events the beginning of the terrible disintegration of Western civilization. Where was American culture going as a result of all this?

34. Dean, Brenda, "And Call Each Place Home," *Onyx*, (1967), p. 26. (Afro-American)

When they say you have no home and no past, call them liars. Recall that you have both past and home. Recall that your past, as well as your home, stretches throughout the world.
You could ask where you would find home and find that home is in the music you hear wherever we are.

35. de Jesus, Carolina Maria, *Child of the Dark: The Diary of Carolina de Jesus*, translated by David St. Clair. New York: E. P. Dutton & Co., 1962. (Brazilian)

I was ill all day. I thought I had a cold. At night my chest pained me. I started to cough. I decided not to go out at night to look for paper. I searched for my son João. He was at Felisberto de Carvalho Street near the market. A bus had knocked a boy into the sidewalk and a crowd gathered. João was in the middle of it all. I poked him a couple of times and within five minutes he was home.

36. Deloria, Vine, Jr., *Custer Died for your Sins: An Indian Manifesto*. New York: Avon Books, 1970. Published there by arrangement with The Macmillan Company. (American Indian: Sioux)

Three books, to my way of thinking, give a good idea of the intangible sense of reality that pervades the Indian people. *When the Legends Die* by Hal Borland gives a good picture of Indian youth. *Little Big Man* by Thomas Berger gives a good idea of Indian attitudes toward life. *Stay Away, Joe*, by Dan Cushman, the favorite of Indian people, gives a humorous but accurate idea of the problems caused by the intersection of two ways of life.

The Sioux, my own people, have a great tradition of conflict. We were the only nation ever to annihilate the United States Cavalry three times in succession.

The first Indian will announce that he lives in a one-room shack.

Whites who attempt to help Indians are constantly frustrated by their tragic lack of understanding of Indian people. For Indians always know exactly what position they will take on major issues, how far they can push certain concepts, and when to delay so as to wear out their opponents and eventually get their way.

37. Dia, Mamadou, *The African Nations and World Solidarity*, translated by Mercer Cook. New York: Frederick A. Praeger, Inc., 1961. First published as

Nations Africaines et Solidarité Mondiale, Presses Universitaires de France, 1960. Also published in London by Thames & Hudson, 1962. (African: Senegal)

Of the earth's inhabitants, 50 per cent do not get the minimum of calories physiologically necessary; 25 per cent lack proteins; 75 per cent are undernourished. In the first group of privileged countries, the mortality rate is 10 per cent and the life expectancy from sixty to seventy years. In the second group, comprising Latin American and a few African and Asian countries, the mortality rate is between 10 and 20 per cent, the life expectancy from forty to sixty years. And finally, in the third group, which includes the greater part of Africa and Asia, the mortality rates vary between 25 and 30 per cent with a life expectancy of thirty to thirty-five years—the life expectancy in European countries at the beginning of the nineteenth century. Thus "the geography of hunger is also the geography of death."* One is amazed that in this century, when men talk so much about social justice and boast so lyrically about the progress of universal solidarity, one-sixth of the global population, composed primarily of white people, possesses 80 per cent of the total income. This fact alone is eloquent enough and excuses us, we think, from multiplying the statistical comparisons that abound in this area and that stress the great disparity in the living standards of men on our planet, at the very moment when, paradoxically, science is rushing out to conquer other planets. How has humanity reached such a degree of imbalance?

*Gabriel Ardant. *Le Monde En Friche*, Paris: Presses Universitaires de France, 1960, page 3.

38. Donoso, Jose, "Denmarker," *New Voices of Hispanic America: An Anthology*, edited by Darwin J. Flakoll and Claribel Alegria. Boston: Beacon Press, 1962. (Chilean)

It was a wide, open night. The wind whipped by, seeking in the emptiness of the plain something in which to entangle itself while it swept the starry sky.

39. Drake, St. Clair, "An Approach to the Evaluation of African Societies," in *Africa Seen by American Negroes.* Dijon, France: Imprimerie Bourguignonne, 1958. (Afro-American)

African and Afro-American intellectuals sometimes unconsciously forget, and always find it painful to consciously accept, the disconcerting fact that many African societies and the cultures that they embody are often viewed with contempt, and sometimes with fascinated horror, by the peoples of Western world, including the black masses of the United States. In fact, many of the same intellectuals who are the connoisseurs of African art and lovers of African music and dancing experience feelings of shame or revulsion when they contemplate the social systems that produced these specific, highly valued aspects of the cultures. For instance they can accept psychologically Benin's art, but not its "customs."

The lot of the evaluative minority will not always be an easy one, just as it has not been an easy one in Western societies. Practical men always have a measure of distrust for those who, as James Branch Cabell phrased it, have "heard the music from behind the moon"; or those who say, "Our Kingdom is not of this world"; or those who refuse to consider any custom or social usage sacred. But if Africa is to develop truly "civilized" societies, however small—and we must never forget fifth-century Athens—it must eventually produce from within its own bosom such evaluators.

40. Dubois, W. E. B., *The Souls of Black Folk: Essays and Sketches.* Chicago: A. C. McClurg & Co., 1903. New York: Fawcett World Library, 1961. (Afro-American)

After the Egyptian and Indian, the Greek and Roman, the Teuton and Mongolian, the Negro is a sort of seventh son, born with a veil, and gifted with second-sight in this American world—a world which yields him no true self-consciousness, but only lets him see himself through the revelation of the other world. It is a peculiar sensation, this double-consciousness, this sense of always looking at one's self through the eyes of others, of measuring one's soul by the tape of a world that looks on in amused contempt and pity. One ever feels his twoness—an American, a Negro; two souls, two thoughts, two unreconciled strivings; two warring ideals in one dark body, whose dogged strength alone keeps it from being torn asunder.

The worker must work for the glory of his handiwork, not simply for pay; the thinker must think for truth, not for fame.

He felt his poverty; without a cent, without a home, without land, tools or savings, he had entered into competition with rich, landed, skilled neighbors. To be a poor man is hard, but to be a poor race in a land of dollars is the very bottom of hardships. He felt the weight of his ignorance—not simply of letters, but of life, of business, of the humanities; the accumulated sloth and shirking and awkwardness of decades and centuries shackled his hands and feet.

41. Ebon, Martin, *Che: The Making of a Legend*. New York: Universe Books, 1969. (German-American)

I believe that armed struggle is the only solution for people who are fighting for freedom, and I act according to his [Che's] belief.

For all his role as commander, Che was often off in a corner either writing or reading. The guerrillas were wordy, too; the Bustos testimony, after his arrest, described his visit with Che in a total of 20,000 words.

42. Ellison, Ralph, "Flying Home," in *Cross Section*, edited by Edwin Seaver. New York: L. B. Fischer, 1944. As found in *Dark Symphony—Negro Literature in America*, edited by James A. Emanuel and Theodore L. Gross. New York: The Free Press, 1968. (Afro-American)

When Todd came to, he saw two faces suspended above him in a sun so hot and blinding that he could not tell if they were black or white. He stirred, feeling a pain that burned as though his whole body had been laid open to the sun which glared into his eyes.

Then one day a strange thing happened. It was spring and for some reason I had been hot and irritable all morning. It was a beautiful spring. I could feel it as I played barefoot in the backyard. Blossoms hung from the thorny black locust trees like clusters of fragrant white grapes. Butterflies flickered in the sunlight above the short new dew-wet grass. I had gone in the house for bread and butter and coming out I heard a steady unfamiliar drone. It was unlike anything I had ever heard before. I tried to place the sound. It was no use. It was a sensation like that I had when searching for my father's watch, heard ticking unseen in a room. It made me feel as though I had forgotten to perform some task that my mother had ordered . . . then I located it, overhead. In the sky, flying quite low and about a hundred yards off was a plane! It came so slowly that it seemed barely to move. My mouth hung wide; my bread and butter fell into the dirt. I wanted to jump up and down and cheer. And when the idea struck I trembled with excitement: "Some little white boy's plane done flew away and all I got to do is stretch out my hands and it'll be mine!" It was a little plane like that at the Fair, flying no higher than the eaves of our roof. Seeing it come steadily forward I felt the world grow warm with promise. I opened the screen and climbed over it and clung there, waiting. I would catch the plane as it came over and swing down fast and run into the house before anyone could see me. Then no one could come to claim the plane. It droned nearer. Then when it hung like a silver cross in the blue directly above me I stretched out my hand and grabbed. It was like sticking my finger through a soap bubble. The plane flew on, as though I had simply blown my breath after it. I grabbed again, frantically, trying to catch the tail. My fingers clutched the air and disappointment surged tight and hard in my throat. Giving one last desperate grasp, I strained forward. My fingers ripped against the screen. I was falling. The ground burst hard against me. I drummed the earth with my heels and when my breath returned, I lay there bawling.

43. Ellison, Ralph, *Invisible Man*. New York: Random House, Inc. 1952. (Afro-American)

And so it is with me. Without light I am not only invisible, but formless as well; and to be unaware of one's form is to live a death. I myself, after existing some twenty years, did not become alive until I discovered my invisibility.

We were passing a collection of shacks and log cabins now, bleached white and warped by the weather. Sun-tortured shingles lay on the roofs like decks of water-soaked cards spread out to dry. The houses consisted of two square rooms joined together by a common floor and roof with a porch in between. As we passed we could look through to the fields beyond.

I stretched out beneath the covers, hearing the springs groan beneath me. The room was cold. I listened to the night sounds of the house. The clock ticked with empty urgency as though trying to catch up with the time. In the street a siren howled.

The conscience of a race is the gift of its individuals who see, evaluate, record.... We create the race by creating ourselves and then to our great astonishment we will have created something far more important: We will have created a culture. Why waste time creating a conscience for something that doesn't exist? For, you see, blood and skin do not think.

I carried my sickness and though for a long time I tried to place it in the outside world, the attempt to write it down shows me that at least half of it lay within me. It came upon me slowly, like that strange disease that affects those black men whom you see turning slowly from black to albino, their pigment disappearing as under the radiation of some cruel, invisible ray.... At first you tell yourself that it's all a dirty joke, or that it's due to the "political situation." But deep down you come to suspect that you're yourself to blame, and you stand naked and shivering before the millions of eyes who look through you unseeingly. *That* is the real soul-sickness, the spear in the side, the drag by the neck through the mob-angry town, the Grand Inquisition, the embrace of the Maiden, the rip in the belly with the guts spilling out, the trip to the chamber with the deadly gas that ends in the oven so hygienically clean—only it's worse because you continue stupidly to live. But live you must, and you can either make passive love to your sickness or burn it out and go on to the next conflicting phase.

44. Essien-Udom, E. U., *Black Nationalism, A Search for an Identity in America*. Chicago: The University of Chicago Press, 1962. Reprinted by Dell Publishing Company, Inc., 1964. (African: Nigeria)

The rise of the Nation of Islam is inseparable from the leadership of Muhammad and the loyalty of a small group of followers who have worked patiently and persistently since about 1932. It is said that his first followers were his mother, his wife, and his six children. This apparently was the nucleus about which the Detroit Temple, which is today one of the most important in the Nation, was organized.

Neither white nor Negro middle-class society offers a way out for the Negro masses. Whereas a middle-class Negro in a northern city may aspire, for instance, to move into

Deerfield, Illinois, or other white middle-class communities, and may dine and wine, rubbing shoulders with the whites, in downtown hotels, the masses of Negroes must stay home in the ghettos. Consequently, the lower-class Negro who has the capacity and motivation for self-improvement must seek it within the Negro community. He cannot afford the luxury of the middle-class make-believe. He knows he is black, but he wants to be self-respecting. He may be poor, but he wants to be decent.

45. Fanon, Frantz, *The Wretched of The Earth*. New York: Grove Press, Inc. 1966. (Martiniquais)

Come, then, comrades; it would be as well to decide at once to change our ways. We must shake off the heavy darkness in which we were plunged, and leave it behind. The new day which is already at hand must find us firm, prudent and resolute.

46. Fisher, Rudolph, "Miss Cynthie," *Story Magazine* (June, 1933). As reprinted in *The Negro Caravan* by permission of Pearl M. Fisher, and as found in *Dark Symphony—Negro Literature in America*, edited by James A. Emanuel and Theodore L. Gross. New York: The Free Press, 1968. (Afro-American)

For the first time in her life somebody had called her "madam." She had been standing, bewildered but unafraid, while innumerable Red Caps appropriated piece after piece of the baggage arrayed on the platform. Neither her brief seventy years' journey through life nor her long two days' travel northward had dimmed the live brightness of her eyes, which, for all their bewilderment, had accurately selected her own treasures out of the row of luggage and guarded them vigilantly.

Miss Cynthie hardly noted that she had been left, so absorbed was she in the spectacle. To her, the theater had always been the antithesis of the church. As the one was the refuge of righteousness, so the other was the stronghold of transgression. But this first scene awakened memories, captured and held her attention by offering a blend of truth and novelty. Having thus baited her interest, the show now proceeded to play it like the trout through swift-flowing waters of wickedness. Resist as it might, her mind was caught and drawn into the impious subsequences.

47. Forsythe, Dennis, "Frantz Fanon: Black Theoretician," *The Black Scholar*, Vol I, No. 5 (March, 1970), pp. 2-10. (Afro-American)

48. Fowles, John, *The Magus*. Boston: Little, Brown and Company, 1965. Reprinted by Dell Publishing Company, Inc., 1968. (English)

"But it's mad. It's like putting a girl in a convent till you're ready to marry her.... We have to be free. We haven't got a choice."
"Don't get upset. Please don't get upset."
"We've got to see how things go."
There was a silence.
"I was thinking of coming back here tomorrow night. That's all."
"I'll write. Every day."
"Yes."

I wrote a letter in reply to say that I had been expecting her letter, that she was perfectly free. But I tore it up. I realized that if anything might hurt her, silence would.

In the night we lay awake, knowing each other awake yet afraid to talk. I felt her hand feel out for mine. We lay for a while without talking. Then she spoke.

Men love war because it allows them to look serious.

"I think anyone but a doctor would have fainted. I should have liked to have fainted...."

There were footsteps on the road. Three men were walking slowly along it.

I was very thirsty, and that must have been what woke me.

When Conchis had advised me to go back and marry Alison he must have known she was dead; Lily must have known she was dead.

I had determined that I wouldn't fight, that it would be better to keep cool and wait until a time when I could hurt someone I really wanted to hurt.

49. Frazier, E. Franklin, *Black Bourgeoisie*. New York: The Macmillan Company, 1957. (Afro-American)

When the Negro masses acquired the right to vote in northern cities, they continued for a while to give their support to the Republican Party, chiefly on sentimental grounds, though there were some good reasons for their sentimental attachment to the Republican Party. The Republican Party was the party of Lincoln; it was the party which had given them their freedom.

50. Gass, William H., "We Have Not The Right Life," *New American Review* #6, (April, 1969), pp. 7-32.

It's dreadful when there's no one to moan to.

51., Goddard, Pliny Earle, "Birth of the White Shell Woman," in *Navajo Texts: Anthropological Papers of The American Museum of Natural History*, Vol. 34, New York, 1933. (American Indian: Navajo)

"The cradle shall be like this. Thin pieces of wood shall be placed underneath. There will be a row of loops on either side made of string. The bark of the cliff rose, shredded and rubbed fine, will be used under the child for a bed." It was a girl. . . .

Times were hard in the world. Everywhere there were beings who were eating people. One day a dark rain cloud was seen resting on top of To'ol'i. The next day the rain was seen to be falling nearly to the middle of the mountain. The third day it reached well beyond the middle, and the fourth day the rain enveloped the entire mountain and was falling at its base.

52. Greenlee, Sam, *The Spook Who Sat By The Door*. New York: Bantam Books, Inc., 1970. Originally published in London by Allison & Busby, 1969. (Afro-American)

Baseballs, footballs, basketballs filled the air in the ghetto, the spherical symbols of a possible escape from the ghetto cage. The junkies stood and sat in the warm sun, their dope-filled blood moving sluggishly in their veins, the ugly world taking on a warm glow, everything soft and pretty prior to their moving through the streets at night looking for loot to support their habit. The winos drank their sweet wine beneath the El tracks, their hoarse voices rising with laughter as the sweet alcohol filled; . . . The squad cars moved slowly through the ghetto, stopping here and there to collect their graft. Whores arose, dressed and moved into the unfamiliar sunlight toward a restaurant and late afternoon breakfast. Whites moved through the ghetto like maggots on a carcass: cops, social workers, schoolteachers, bill collectors, the supervisors and collectors of the syndicate, the owners of taverns, furniture stores, currency exchanges, television stores. The ghetto moved into the streets from the hovels where they had huddled during the winter—where they would stay until the Chicago cold forced them to return to their small smelly rooms for another winter.

53. Gregory, Dick, *Nigger*. New York: Pocket Books, E. P. Dutton, 1964. (Afro-American)

That was a long summer, the summer of 1951. I was waiting for the scholastic record book to come out. In the spring I had won the mile in 4 minutes 28 seconds at the Missouri state meet for Negroes, one of the best high school times of the year, and I could hardly wait to see my name in the book when it came out in the fall.

He came around in front of me, waving the broken bottle in his hand like Humphrey Bogart would do in the movies. There were others in back of him, grinning. He shoved the broken bottle at me, and I put my hand in front of my face. I didn't feel anything, but they started yelling. The soda jerk came flying over the counter like Alan Ladd, and he and Humphrey Bogart threw me out.

Christmas, 1960. Michele had a fever and the apartment was cold and I was out of work again and there were three pounds of fatty white hamburger meat on the table. Poor people are always embarrassed at not having turkey and cranberry sauce for this one day—the same turkey you can't afford in October, the same cranberry sauce they can't afford in May. You try to think that Christmas day is only twenty-four hours long, just like all the days you were satisfied with beans. But you never really stop believing in Santa Claus. When Momma is gone and you're Santa Claus you can't accept not being able to give. Maybe that's why honest people steal at Christmas. Christmas isn't right unless you give.

54. Guevara, Che, *Guerilla Warfare*. New York: Monthly Review Press, 1961. Reprinted in London by Penguin Books, Ltd., 1969. (Argentine)

We might also ask if the members of the guerrilla band should be drawn from a certain social class. It has already been said that this social composition ought to be adjusted to that of the zone chosen for the center of operations, which is to say that the combatant nucleus of the guerrilla army ought to be made up of peasants.

The guerrilla fighter, as we have said, is a soldier who carries his house on his back like a snail; therefore, he must arrange his knapsack in such a way that the smallest quantity of utensils will render the greatest possible service.

55. Hale, Horatio (editor), "The Book of the Younger Nations," in *The Iroquois Book of Rites*. Toronto: University of Toronto Press, 1963, reprinted from 1883 edition, Philadelphia. (American Indian: Iroquois)

Now we will open your ears, and also your throat, for there is something that has been choking you and we will also give you the water that shall wash down all the troubles in your throat. We shall hope that after this your mind will recover its cheerfulness.

56. Hansberry, Lorraine, *To Be Young, Gifted And Black*. New York: The New American Library, Inc., 1970. (Afro-American)

All travelers to my city should ride the elevated trains that race along the back ways of Chicago. The lives you can look into!

One drew in all one's breath and tightened one's fist and pulled the small body against the heavens, stretching, straining all the muscles in the legs to make—one giant step.

57. Hare, Nathan, "Algiers 1969," *The Black Scholar*, Vol. I, No. 1 (November, 1969), pp. 2-10. (Afro-American)

58. Haskins, Jim, *Diary of a Harlem Schoolteacher*. New York: Grove Press, Inc., 1969. (Afro-American)

From my classroom window I have seen fall turn into winter, and winter to spring. Nothing in this block, ever changes, except the seasons.

It provides for smaller classroom situations and two teachers instead of one to deal with these problems. However, the overwhelming number of problems facing the black children are those inherent in their blackness, or those directly related to their blackness.

59. Hatcher, Richard G., "The Black City Crisis," *The Black Scholar*, Vol. I, No. 6 (April, 1970), pp. 54-62. (Afro-American)

60. Hill, Herbert, editor, *Soon, One Morning, New Writing by American Negroes 1940-1962*. New York: Alfred A. Knopf, Inc., 1963.

Negro writing in America has a long history. It begins with *A Narrative of Uncommon Sufferings*, by Britton Hamon, published in 1760, and with Jupiter Hammon, a writer of both prose and poetry, whose first work appeared later in the same year. He was soon followed by Phillis Wheatley, a Massachusetts slave, who was given special privileges by the rather unusual Wheatley family and encouraged to write poetry, for which she had a talent rare for that period. Phillis Wheatley's *Poems on Various Subjects, Religious and Moral* was published in 1773. In 1829, another book of poems appeared, *The Hope of Liberty*, by George Moses Horton, was was freed late in life, as Phillis Wheatley had been.
In the North during this early period, a number of free Negroes were active as writers and journalists in the anti-slavery cause. Their articles and stories frequently appeared in the abolitionist newspaper *Freedom's Journal*, the first Negro newspaper in the United States, which began publishing in 1818. In 1853, James Whitfield, among those whose work often appeared in *Freedom's Journal*, published his *America and Other Poems*.

Brown, who was active in the abolitionist movement, was a serious writer, and after the Civil War he produced several ambitious historical and narrative works which achieved a rather large circulation at the time. He was the first American Negro who devoted his life to literature and the first to earn his living as a writer.

In the novels written by Negro authors after 1890, there occurs a significant change in subject matter, one that Robert Bone describes as "a shift in theme from attacks upon slavery to attacks upon caste." In these novels the principal characters are usually light enough in color to "pass," handsome, worthy, and cultivated, yet suffering from the stigma of membership in what American society regards as an inferior caste.

An early folk tradition based mainly upon Southern rural material has been richly exploited by several generations of Negro writers—as in the dialect stories and poems of Daniel Webster Davis, Paul Lawrence Dunbar, and others. The best and most sophisticated writer in this genre was James Weldon Johnson, as he shows in "God's Trombones" (1927). Johnson, however, is best remembered for his only novel, *The Autobiography of an Ex-Coloured Man*, first published anonymously in 1912 and reprinted many times since.

61. Himes, Chester B., "Excursion in Paradox," *Pinktoes*. New York: G. P. Putnam's Sons and Stein & Day, Inc., 1965, as found in *The Black Experience: An Anthology of American Literature for the 1970's*, edited by Francis E. Kearns. New York: The Viking Press, Inc., 1970. (Afro-American)

Nothing ever goes right. Nothing ever turns out as one has planned. How many times have you heard that said? How many times have you said it? And yet, it is never an expression of cynicism, defeatism or nihilism. It is always a confession of faith.

62. Himes, Chester, *Lonely Crusade*. New York: Alfred A. Knopf, Inc., 1947. (Afro-American)

In the weird green light, frantic people in defiant garb created the illusion of a costume ball. But the workers had come as workers, proudly—the Negroes as Negroes, apologetically—the Jews as Jews, defiantly. Only the two Mexican girls had come in costume—they had come as Castilian Spanish.

"There is no proof for either unless one believes. I wonder how many of you Marxists realize that it is your belief, and not Marx's proof, that has established the truth of materialism."

The dance finished and she went to someone else. Then Mollie took Lee for a dance and they did her special crawl. Between laughs she said: "Everybody is for you, dear."

They went up to St. Nicholas Avenue on the bus and climbed to the top floor of an apartment house. A fat, light-complexioned woman with black hair and sleepy eyes, clad in flaming red lounging pajamas, let them into an apartment filled with people getting drunk.

And this was one thing they could not hang on the nigger, he thought with sharp disdain. The nigger loved his watermelon, even though the white folks ate most of them. And the nigger loved his chicken—what little the white folks left. But everybody got drunk—nigger, white man, gentile, Jew.

63. Hughes, Langston, "One Friday Morning," in *Anthology of American Negro Literature*, edited by Sylvester C. Watkins. New York: Random House, Inc., 1944. (Afro-American)

Nancy Lee Johnson was a colored girl, a few years out of the South. But seldom did her high-school classmates think of her as colored. She was smart, pretty and brown, and fitted in well with the life of the school. She stood high in scholarship, played a swell game of basketball, had taken part in the senior musical in a soft velvety voice, and had never seemed to intrude or stand out except in pleasant ways, so it was seldom even mentioned—her color.

Nancy Lee was proud of being American, a Negro American with blood out of Africa a long time ago, too many generations back to count. But her parents had taught her the beauties of Africa, its strength, its song, its mighty rivers, its early smelting of iron, its building of the pyramids, and its ancient and important civilizations.

Miss Dietrich had taught Nancy Lee how to paint spring, people and a breeze on what was only a plain white piece of paper from the supply closet. But Miss Dietrich had not said make it like any other spring-people-breeze ever seen before. She let it remain Nancy Lee's own. That is how the old Negro woman happened to be there looking at the flag—for in her mind the flag, the spring and the woman formed a kind of triangle holding a dream Nancy Lee wanted to express.

Dreams began to dance through her head, plans and ambitions, beauties she would create for herself, her parents and the Negro people—for Nancy Lee possessed a deep and reverent race pride. She could see the old woman in her picture (really her grandmother in the South) lifting her head to the bright stars on the flag in the distance.

64. Hunter, Charlayne, "How To Tell Your Child About Race," *Essence*, Vol. 1, No. 2 (1970), p. 57. (Afro-American)

Does one sit down, as did Mrs. Wells, and contemplate moving to another community—at considerable expense and inconvenience—so that her child can spend more time with people who look like her, and avoid all contact with those who might challenge her or make her feel inferior?

Once upon a time, Stokely Carmichael believed in an ultimate humanism. But the layers of hatred and injustice in this country deterred him from its pursuit. He left the country, perhaps to try and find it in Africa, or perhaps simply to breathe awhile. The generation behind him has to struggle with that same problem.

65. Jabavu, Noni, "The Ochre People," in *Scenes from a South African Life*. London: John Murray, 1963. (African: South Africa)

If not employed, that is to say, by Europeans, you had to quit, return to the Reserves, even if like many eighteen-year-olds you had never in your life lived in one. Her son pretended to live at another location, went there regularly to pay the fee and renew his work-permit, hoodwinking the Boer there. I could not imagine how it was done. Parts of the puzzle were left out in the explanation and I did not like to ask. I could see well enough that it was risky, a matter of time before he and others living surreptitiously in their parental homes would be found out, fined or jailed, and expelled from town, "Endorsed Out"; and for such reasons I have not brought myself to mention their names. Mrs. R. now got up again and crossed over to the wall. She detached a leaflet that was pinned to a picture-frame and handed it to my cousin who sat back to read it while our hostess tried to talk to us at the same time about different things. She said to my cousin, "That is the reading matter which that rascal child 'criminal-because-home-dweller' of mine brings back as a trophy from his latest trip to his fee-eating boss-Boer. A Congress leaflet. Oh, red hot African National Congress these boys!" She also kept up a lively conversation with me. Presently my cousin stretched forward and passed the leaflet to me to read, without making comment, not being politically inclined.

66. James, C. L. R., "The Atlantic Slave Trade and Slavery: Some Interpretations of Their Significance in the Development of the United States and the Western World," in *Amistad 1*, edited by John A. Williams and Charles F. Harris. New York: Random House, Inc., 1970, pp. 119-164. (Afro-American)

67. Jones, LeRoi, "American Sexual Reference: Black Male," in *Home: Social Essays*. New York, William Morrow and Company, 1966. Originally published in *Cavalier*. (Afro-American)

The white man is in love with the past, with dead things and soon he will become one. He is in love with the past because it is in the past that he really exists. He understands that he cannot possibly exist in the future, or even in the present. For instance with the idea of art, what is done now, in the present, or with presage of some stronger future is always treated shabbily by mainstream white society, for one reason because it makes reference to living humanity, which is always threatening to what is "established." The white man worships the artifact; his museums are full of dead things, artifacts, which at best, can only make reference to life.

68. Jones, LeRoi, *Blues People.* New York: William Morrow and Company, Inc., 1963. (Afro-American)

First of all, we know that of all the peoples who form the heterogenous yet almost completely homogenous mass that makes up the United States population, Negroes are the only descendants of people who were not happy to come here. The African was brought to this country in bondage and remained in bondage more than two hundred and fifty years. But most of the black people who were freed from formal slavery in 1865 *were not* Africans. They were Americans. And whether or not we choose to characterize the post-Emancipation existence of Negroes in the United States as "freedom," we must still appreciate the idea that a group of people who became familiar with the mores, attitudes, language, and other culture references of this country while being enslaved by it cannot be seen as analogous to peoples who move toward complete assimilation of these same mores by *choice*, even though these peoples are also despised by the "natives" of the country as "furriners."

When the first slaves were brought to this country, there was no idea at all of converting them. Africans were thought of as beasts, and there was certainly no idea held among the whites that, somehow, these beasts would benefit by exposure to the Christian God.

Many Negroes who were sharecroppers, or who managed to purchase one of the tiny farms that dotted the less fertile lands of the South, worked in their fields alone or with their families. The old shouts and hollers were still their accompaniment for the arduous work of clearing land, planting, or harvesting crops. But there was a solitude to this work that had never been present in the old slave times. The huge plantation fields had many slaves, and they sang together.

There was always a border beyond which the Negro could not go, whether musically or socially. There was always a possible limitation to any dilution or excession of cultural or spiritual references. The Negro could not ever become white and that was his strength; at some point, always, he could not participate in the dominant tenor of the white man's culture. It was at this juncture that he had to make use of other resources, whether African, subcultural, or hermetic. And it was this boundary, this no man's land, that provided the logic and beauty of his music.

69. Jones, LeRoi, "Cold, Hurt, and Sorrow (Streets of Despair)," in *Home: Social Essays.* New York: William Morrow and Co., Inc., 1966. (Afro-American)

These streets stretch from one end of America to the other and connect like a maze from which very few can fully escape. Despair sits on this country in most places like a charm, but there is a special gray death that loiters in the streets of an urban Negro slum. And the men who walk those streets, tracing and retracing their steps to some hopeless job or a pitiful rooming house or apartment or furnished room, sometimes stagger under the weight of that gray, humiliated because it is not even "real."

In these places life, and its possibility, has been distorted almost identically. And the distortion is as old as its sources; the fear, frustration, and hatred that Negroes have always been heir to in America. It is just that in the cities, which were once the black man's twentieth-century "Jordan," *promise* is a dying bitch with rotting eyes. And the stink of her dying is a deadly killing fume.

70. Kambalame, John, in *Our African Way of Life*, Essays by John Kambalame, E. P. Chidzalo and J. W. M. Chadangalara, translated and edited by Cullen Young and Hastings Banda. London: Lutterworth Press, 1946. (African: Malawi)

Later, and privately, one of the women nudges the young wife, and sidling close to her, asks, "Na Nkoma, have you not gone beyond a moon?" and she immediately takes the meaning of a question and answers quickly, "It is true, O my Mother; I am glad you have asked me, for I myself desired greatly to ask about this but my lips were dry with shyness. I myself know nothing about what is going on in my body."

So, when the day of the ceremonies has come, all assemble at the village and begin song and dance while the beer is being drunk. The parents of the young lad prepare his food, and give him a fowl, that he may eat at his going out from the village. In the morning, at dawn, they cut the lad's hair, give him food, and when this is finished those who are in the dance take some of the drums to the bush and all follow—following, in a crowd, the young lad. At home, the mother remains alone.

But now they seem to have trapped you into coming to this forest by giving you a good meal of porridge and chicken, as if you were a traveler or guest.

Thereafter they indicate the hut where he will sleep and announce to all, "Nyono's child today is a mature young man: he has left off everything of childhood and is as one of yourselves in wisdom." And no one is allowed to call him by the name he had before, even though it be that used as an "avoidance" title among his grown-up relatives.

"Listen, oh husband: you have lived with your father and mother. They brought you to birth, they nourished and fed you, they clothed you and looked after you well until you matured, right up to the point when you desired and sought a wife. Today here is the wife that Mulungu has given you."

71. Kaunda, Kenneth, "Zambia—Independence and Beyond," *The Speeches of Kenneth Kaunda*, edited by Colin Legum. London: Thomas Nelson & Sons Ltd., 1966. Also published by Thomas Nelson & Sons, Camden, N.J. (African: Zambia)

Those who defy God pay the penalty and perish.

To get food we must work hard, too. Now, there is a slackness in the nation—I can feel it—I can smell it—I can sense it—wherever I go people are beginning to lag behind. This is the wrong spirit.

And so long as I am leader of the Party I am not going to allow any stupid people to come here to disrupt the country because of their ideologies. If I discover them here in Zambia, they will go away by the fastest plane. Please, please, please Mr. Capitalism and Mr. Communism, remain here but cooperate with us.

Provoke nothing because you are sensible, dignified, civilized people.

I can't understand a man who says he is civilized, who says he is a Christian, who does not only rebel against the Queen's Government but who condemns the black race—the entire black race in Rhodesia to a place of servitude—and who calls himself a Christian and calls himself a civilized person. What utter nonsense!

I have always led a fighting life, in a struggle which has always had in view the ultimate independence of my people. My struggle has caused me to be called many things—criminal—a wild man—a black mamba—an agitator. Once I was even called a diplomat.

72. Kgosana, Philip, "A Call to Action," in *I Will Still Be Moved: Reports from South Africa*, edited by Marion Friedmann. London: Arthur Barker Ltd., 1963. (African: South Africa)

At this stage of our struggle we have a choice before us. Are we still prepared to be half-human beings in our fatherland or are we prepared to be citizens—men and women in a democratic non-racial South Africa? How long shall we be called, Bantu, Native, Non-European, Non-White, or black . . . Kaffir in our fatherland?

. . . Sons and daughters of Africa—there is a choice before us. We are either slaves or free men—that's all. What are we fighting for: Our overall fight is against imperialism, colonialism and domination. I want to be properly understood here.

That is our fight.
We are not a horde of stupid, barbaric things which will fight against a white man simply because he is white. In order to destroy this myth of race superiority, the Pan-Africanist Congress has drawn up an unfolding program—which starts tomorrow and ends up in 1963 with the realization of the United States of Africa.

We are not going to throw stones at the police or do anything that is going to obstruct the police. Any person who does all these things shall be dealt with by the police of course and we, as an organization, shall further deal with him. Nobody is carrying money, knives or any dangerous weapon with himself tomorrow.

73. Kohl, Herbert, *36 Children*. New York: New American Library, Inc., 1967.

The weight of Harlem and my whiteness and strangeness hung in the air as I droned on, lost in my righteous monologue. The uproar turned into sullen silence.

74. Kroeber, A. L., in "Wishosk Myths," *Journal of American Folklore*, Vol. 18 (1904), as found in *American Indian Prose and Poetry*, edited by Margot Astrov. New York: Capricorn Books, 1962, pp. 272-273. (German-American)

Gudatrigakwitl left the people all kinds of dances. He said: "When there is a festivity, call me. If some do not like what I say, let them be. . . . Whenever you are badly off, call me. I can save you in some way, no matter how great the difficulty. If a man does not call me, I will let him go. . . . "

At first there were no trees nor rivers and no people on the earth. Nothing except ground was visible. There was no ocean. Then Gudatrigakwitl was sorry that it was so. He thought, "How is it that there are no animals?" He looked, but he saw nothing. Then he deliberated. He thought, "I will try. Somebody will live on the earth. But what will he use?" Then he decided to make a boat for him. He made things by joining his hands and spreading them. He used no tools. In this way he made people. The first man was *wat*, the abalone. The first people were not right. They all died. Gudatrigakwitl thought that they were bad. He wanted good people who would have children. At first he wanted every man to have ten lives. When he was an old man he was to become a boy again. Afterwards Gudatrigakwitl found that he could not do this. He gave the people all the game, the fish, and the trees. . . .

Gudatrigakwitl used no sand or earth or sticks to make the people; he merely thought and they existed.

Gudatrigakwitl thought: "When something is alive like a plant, it will not die. It will come up again from the roots and grow again and again. So it will be with men, and animals, and everything alive...."

75. Ladner, Joyce, and Walter W. Stafford, "Black Repression in the Cities," *The Black Scholar* Vol. I, No. 6 (April, 1970), pp. 38-52. (Afro-American)

76. Laye, Camara, *The Dark Child*. New York: Farrar, Straus & Giroux, Inc., 1955. Originally translated from the French by James Kirkup under the title *The African Child*. London and Glasgow: Fontana Books, 1959. Published in French as *L'Enfant Noir* by Librairie Plon, 1954. (African: Guinea)

While I was dancing, my boubou, split from top to bottom at each side, would reveal the brightly-colored silk handkerchief which I had knotted round my loins. I was quite aware of this and did nothing to prevent it; in fact I did all I could to show it off. This was because we each wore a similar handkerchief, more or less colourful, more or less ornate, which we had received from our acknowledged sweetheart. She would make us a present of it for the ceremony, and it was generally taken from her own head. As the handkerchief cannot pass unnoticed, as it is the one personal note that distinguishes the common uniform, and as its design, like its color, makes it easily identified, there is in the wearing of it a kind of public manifestation of a relationship—a purely child-like relationship, it goes without saying—which the present ceremony may break forever, or, as the case may be, transform into something less innocent and more lasting. Now if our so-called sweetheart was in the least pretty and consequently desirable, we would swing our hips with great abandon, the better to make our boubou fly from side to side, and thus show off our handkerchief to greater advantage. At the same time we would keep our ears open to catch anything that might be said about us, about our sweetheart and about our good fortune; but our ears caught very little, for the music was deafening; and there was extraordinary animation in the tightly packed crowds all around the square.

77. Laye, Camara, *A Dream of Africa*, translated from the French by James Kirkup. London: William Collins, Sons & Co., Ltd., 1968. Originally published in French as *Dramouss* by Librairie Plon, 1966. (African: Guinea)

Stretched on a bed of pain, I spent two weeks of misery. Later, when I left the hospital, I had grown skinny, but I was cured, completely cured, of my illness.

After several months spent at my hotel in convalescence, I realized once and for all that Paris is not a French city but an international center in which human beings are grouped solely according to their intellectual affinities.

We heard nothing but bragging and boasting. And already, after this very short time, we had become accustomed to his flow of words, to his way of turning his material wealth into a celebration—wealth acquired honestly or dishonestly (a diamond trafficker is hardly likely to be honest). Our laughter awakened Marie, who soon joined the swarm of my sisters and "little sisters" in the kitchen.

"Are your friends, masters and acquaintances enjoying the best of health?"

"Well, yes, my son, if one doesn't give up the ghost in the process, one is hardened and strengthened and tempered by suffering, like iron in the fire. May the Lord be bountiful unto your friends over there!"

78. Lester, Julius, *To Be A Slave*. New York: The Dial Press, Inc., 1968. (Afro-American)

Granny Judith said that in Africa they had very few pretty things, and that they had no red colors in cloth, In fact, they had no cloth at all. Some strangers with pale faces come [sic] one day and dropped a small piece of red flannel down on the ground. All the black folks grabbed for it. Then a larger piece was dropped a little further on, and on until the river was reached. Then a large piece was dropped in the river and on the other side. . . . Finally, when the ship was reached, they dropped large pieces on the plank and up into the ship till they got as many blacks on board as they wanted. Then the gate was chained up and they could not get back. (Richard Jones Otkin, p. 57)

79. Lomax, Alan, *Mister Jelly Roll: The Fortunes of Jelly Roll Morton, New Orleans Creole and "Inventor of Jazz."* New York: Grosset & Dunlap, Inc., 1950. (American)

I was about eleven years old at the time and used to stay with my godmother, Eulalie Echo, who spoiled me and gave me a little freedom. When school closed, she permitted me to go to pick berries at the strawberry farm. I thought I could eat up the whole strawberry farm and ate enough to get sick and so returned back home, about a forty-five mile trip. Then I was convinced that the world was a little larger than New Orleans.

Those days, myself, I thought I would die unless I had a hat with the emblem Stetson in it and some Edwin Clapp shoes. But Nert and Nonny and many of them wouldn't wear readymade shoes. They wore what they called the St. Louis Flats and the Chicago Flats, made with cork soles and without heels and with gambler designs on the toes. Later on, some of them made arrangements to have some kind of electric-light bulbs in the toes of their shoes with a battery in their pockets, so when they would get around some jane that was kind of simple and thought they could make her, as they call making um, why they'd press a button in their pocket and light up the little-bitty bulb in the toe of their shoes and that jane was claimed. It's really the fact.

When New Years came I waited for my new suit. Uncle's wife was very good at sewing and I believe it was agreed between both uncle and wife to cut down one of uncle's suits. This was done and the suit was presented to me, very much to my disapproval. Uncle was a very fat man, weighing about two hundred and ten pounds. So the suit was tried and did not fit me anywhere. All the kids had holiday clothes but me. I was so peeved at my uncle and his wife that I tried to kill their cat, Bricktop.

80. Long, Richard A., "Race and Scholarship," *Liberator*, Vol. 10. No. 7 (July, 1970), pp. 4-7.

It is easier to be Black than to learn Black; easier to shout than to study; easier to thump than to think.

81. Luthuli, Albert, "The Chief," in *I Will Still be Moved: Reports from South Africa*, edited by Marion Friedmann. London: Arthur Baker Ltd, 1963, pp. 77-81. (African: South Africa)

This contribution is not in any way unique. I did not initiate the struggle to extend the area of human freedom in South Africa: other African patriots—devoted men—did so before me.

I also, as a Christian and patriot, could not look on while systematic attempts were made, almost in every department of life, to debase the God-factor in man or to set a limit beyond which the human being in his Black form might not strive to serve his Creator to the best of his ability.

Africa presently is most deeply torn with strife and most bitterly stricken with racial conflict.

How strange, then, it is that a man of Africa should be here to receive an award given for service to the cause of peace and brotherhood between men.

There has been little peace in Africa in our time.

Ours is a continent in revolution against oppression. And peace and revolution make uneasy bedfellows. There can be no peace until the forces of oppression are overthrown.

Our continent has been carved up by the great powers, alien governments have been forced upon the African people by military conquest and by economic domination, strivings of nationhood and national dignity have been beaten down by force, traditional economies and ancient customs have been disrupted, and human skills and energy have been harnessed for the advantage of our conquerors.

There is a paradox in the fact that Africa qualifies for such an award in its age of turmoil and revolution.

How great is the paradox and how much greater the honor that an award in support of peace and the brotherhood of man should come to one who is a citizen of a country where the brotherhood of man is an illegal doctrine, outlawed, banned, censured, proscribed and prohibited, where the work, talk of campaign for the realization in fact and deed of the brotherhood of man is hazardous, punished with banishment or confinement without trial or imprisonment, where effective democratic channels to peaceful settlement of the race problem have not existed these 300 years, and where White minority power rests on the most heavily armed and equipped military machine in Africa.

This is South Africa.

82. Mailer, Norman, *The Armies of the Night*. New York: The New American Library, Inc., 1968. (Jewish-American)

In fact, the bus is getting ready to leave the Pentagon. A driver has gotten on—to many cheers—and a wire gate is closed across the front to protect the chauffeur from attack by any prisoners while he is driving. There are also bars across each window. (Obviously Mailer has had the fantasy of bending the bars and making his escape, and has decided not to—it would certainly make him famous for too little.) The sun has been beating on the bus and it is as uncomfortably warm as a small Southern bus depot on an Indian summer afternoon, which is what the faces outside might suggest, if not for the Pentagon walls. And a battle has been taking place, even if no sign of it seems to be reaching here—except, gloomy thought, the battle cannot be going too well, for there is not the remotest sign of panic in this rear area.

"Your lawyer is wearing sneakers," said the last of the prisoners.

83. Malcolm X, *The Autobiography of Malcolm X*. New York: The Grove Press, Inc., 1964. (Afro-American)

When I was at work, up in the Roseland men's room, I just couldn't keep still. My shine rag popped with the rhythm of those great bands rocking the ballroom.

84. Mandela, Nelson, "An Outlaw," *I Will Still be Moved: Reports from South Africa*, edited by Marion Friedmann. London: Arthur Baker Ltd., 1963, pp. 46-60. (African: South Africa)

I might also mention that in the course of this application I am frequently going to refer to the white man and to white people. I want to make it clear that I am not a racialist and do not support racialism of any kind, because to me racialism is a barbaric thing whether it comes from a black man or a white man.

I am compelled to use this type of terminology because of the nature of the application I am now making.

A judiciary controlled entirely by whites and enforcing laws enacted by a white Parliament in which we have no representation—laws which in most cases are passed in the face of unanimous opposition from Africans—cannot be regarded as an impartial tribunal in a political trial where an African stands as an accused.

The Universal Declaration of Human Rights provides that all men are equal before the law and are entitled, without discrimination, to equal protection before the law.

Can anyone honestly and seriously suggest that in this type of atomsphere the scales of justice are evenly balanced?

Why is it that no African in the history of this country has ever had the honor of being tried by his own kith and kin, by his own flesh and blood?

I will tell your Worship why: the real purpose of this rigid color bar is to ensure that the justice dispensed by the Courts should conform to the policy of the country however much that policy might be in conflict with the norms of justice accepted in judiciaries thoughout the civilized world.

It reminds me that I am voteless because there is a Parliament in this country that is vote-controlled. I am without land because the white minority has taken a lion's share of my country and forced me to occupy poverty-stricken reserves, overpopulated and overstocked. We are ravaged by starvation and disease because our country's wealth is not shared by all sections of the population.

I make no threat when I say that unless these wrongs are remedied without delay, we might well find that even plain talk before the country's Courts is too timid a method to draw attention to our grievances.

I am charged with inciting people to commit an offence by way of protest against a law, a law which neither I nor any of my people had any say in preparing.

Your Worship, I would say the whole life of any thinking African in this country drives him continuously to a conflict between his conscience on the one hand and the law on another.... The law as it is applied, the law as it has been developed over a long period of history, and especially the law as it is written and designed by the Nationalist Government is a law which, in our view, is *immoral, unjust and intolerable.* Our consciences dictate that we must protest against it, that we must oppose it, and that we must attempt to alter it.

85. Marques, Rene, "Give Us This Day", *New Voices of Hispanic America: An Anthology,* edited by Darwin J. Flakoll and Claribel Alegria. Boston: Beacon Press, 1962. (Puerto Rican)

The tension of his body, readying itself for the shock of revelation, was so great that for a moment he thought he would be torn apart. Panting, sweating, heartsick, dreading to understand, finally unresisting, he accepted the fact: he lived in an age that was not his own.

86. Matumona, Antoine, "Angolan Disunity," *Angola—A Symposium— Views of a Revolt,* translated by S. M. Armstrong. London: Oxford University Press, 1962, pp. 120-129. (African: Angola)

So now Angola has seven political groups that share the same objective—the independence of Angola—but they are all working for it in different ways. Their few forces are dissipated and wasted and the chances of achieving their objective are thus reduced.

This is not a surprise to those who have followed closely the statements of the UPA President. Holden's statements show that he wants to stand out amidst all the Angolan leaders, to give the impression that it is his party alone that is fighting at the front and that he alone is leader of the rebellion. But we must analyse the facts.

All 250 had been found "suspect." Accused of being "activists," hunted like wild animals, persecuted by the PIDE, the famous secret police, they bolted and took refuge in other countries in Europe.

The departure of these students has astonished right-thinking Angolan circles, because all Angolans settled outside Angola are considered foreigners in the eyes of the Lisbon Government.

87. Mayes, Harvey, "On The Steps of the Pentagon," reprinted by permission of the author in *Armies of the Night*, by Norman Mailer. New York: The New American Library, Inc., 1968. (Jewish-American)

One soldier spilled the water from his canteen on the ground in order to add to the discomfort of the female demonstrator at his feet. She cursed him—understandably, I think—and shifted her body. She lost her balance and her shoulder hit the rifle at the soldier's side. He raised the rifle, and with its butt, came down hard on the girl's leg. The girl tried to move back but was not fast enough to avoid the billy-club of a soldier in the second row of troops. At least four times that soldier hit her with all his force, then as she lay covering her head with her arms, thrust his club swordlike between her hands into her face. Two more troops came up and began dragging the girl toward the Pentagon. . . . She twisted her body so we could see her face. But there was no face there: All we saw were some raw skin and blood. We couldn't see even if she was crying—her eyes had filled with the blood pouring down her head. She vomited, and that too was blood. Then they rushed her away.

88. Meneses, Porfiro, "The Little Dark Man," *New Voices of Hispanic America: An Anthology*, edited by Darwin J. Flakoll & Claribel Alegria. Boston: Beacon Press, 1962. (Peruvian)

The majority accepted this idea. In truth, the stranger must have been very strange, since these kind people could not know that in the big cities the scribe's role is played by the lawyer and the faith healer's, I think, by the doctor. Distance permits such differences.

89. Meriwether, Louise, *Daddy Was a Number Runner*. Englewood Cliffs, N.J.: Prentice-Hall, Inc., 1970. (Afro-American)

It was after ten o'clock but too hot to sleep so we were up on the roof searching for a cool breeze. My mother and Mrs. Caldwell were sitting on the divider between their two roofs talking to Sonny's grandmother, Mrs. Taylor. Mrs. Caldwell was holding Elizabeth's baby, a boy, while Lil Robert, five, and David, three, played at her feet.

Maude and her sister Rebecca and me were lying on the rise of the roof looking over the edge and chewing tar, which was supposed to keep your teeth white.

Rebecca was pretty, with those flashing West Indian eyes and a mouth always laughing. She was my good friend, too, although Daddy didn't like me hanging out with her too much because he said she was too old for me. . . .

Sterling was going downtown to high school, grumbling that all the white kids wore better clothes than he did and had long pants while he was still knocking about in his knickers. Daddy told him he should have appreciated that nice suit with the long pants he got him from the pawnshop because God knows when he'd get the money to buy him another one.

We didn't have any money at all, and that was the truth. When we got our relief check each month all we did was take it across the street to Mr. Burnett, the West Indian grocer, and pay him what we owed. This left us with nothing so the next day we started buying on credit again.

One afternoon I went with Daddy to the barber shop on Lenox Avenue to pay off a hit from yesterday because the barber shop had closed early the night before when Daddy got the money. Daddy wasn't staying out most of the night playing poker like he used to but coming home early now, and if James Junior hadn't been cooped up down there in that jail, things would've been nice.

90. Merton, Thomas, "Conjectures of a Guilty Bystander," *Life* (August 5, 1966), pp. 64-73.

In the latter part of the decade we youngsters earned many nickels by climbing through open windows, opening doors and letting neighbors into their apartments.

91. Mitchell, Loften, *Black Drama*. New York: Hawthorn Books, Inc., 1967. (Afro-American)

During its reign the syndicate noted, too, the rising tide of reaction against the Negro. Other business establishments had noted this, too, had taken advantage of it and had thus pushed the Negro back toward slavery.

These prevailing attitudes put the Negro on the defensive, for he had to defend his person and his humanity. All of this permeated the American theater and American life as long as the syndicate reigned. These prevailing attitudes were to send Negroes fleeing toward a community where they might find a measure of safety. These times were to see the Negro expelled from the Broadway theater.

No site in Harlem has as much theatrical meaning as the corner of 132nd Street and Seventh Avenue. Here once stood the Lafayette, previously noted as having been built in 1912 by John Mulonski. Nearby, at 131st Street and Seventh Avenue, stands the stump of the Tree of Hope, donated by that great dancer Bill "Bojangles" Robinson. This Tree of Hope stood outside the Lafayette Theater, and it was so named because, as legend has it, an unemployed actor once lingered beneath the tree, hoping for work. A theatrical manager is said to have approached him and offered him a job. Thereafter, crowds of unemployed actors stood beneath that tree, sometimes blocking the way of passersby.

The theater tomorrow will, therefore, remain much as it is today unless there is a real change in this society. The one hope is that those groups in the ghetto areas—the townships composed of poor whites, Puerto Ricans and Negroes—will create drama as it was intended, as a living instrument that educates, communicates and entertains, an instrument that has a life commitment.

The Negro theater artist is, therefore, going to have to reckon with the fact that he can get a job in the theater if there is one to be gotten. But there are fewer and fewer shows being produced. The Broadway theater has become not only a middle-class one. Foundations have made it clear that all kinds of groups can get money except those in Negro areas. Therefore, the Negro artist and the Negro masses will have to reckon with this, to strike out for themselves.

They break into our houses. They dress the way they want to dress. They thumb their noses at us and they smoke marijuana and have drunken parties, and they tell us to drop dead—all because we, their parents, have lied to ourselves and to them!

This, then, is the importance of black drama. It is hope—hope that in the world's most powerful country a minority that has made undying contributions can make its greatest contribution and redeem the majority. This minority stands at a moment in time, poised, with new, vital allies, demanding to be reckoned with. And the world looks on, waiting, waiting.

92. Mooney, James, "Origin of the Pleiades and the Pine," *Myths of the Cherokees*, 19th Annual Report of the Bureau of American Ethnology. Washington, 1891. (American Indian: Cherokee)

The boys were very angry, and went down to the townhouse saying, "As our mothers treat us that way, let us go where we shall never trouble them any more." They began a dance—some say it was the Feather Dance—and went round and round the townhouse, praying to the spirits to help them. At last their mothers were afraid something was wrong and went out to look for them. They saw the boys still dancing around the townhouse, and as they watched they noticed that their feet were off the earth, and that with every round they rose higher and higher in the air. They ran to get their children, but it was too late, for they were already above the roof of the townhouse—all but one, whose mother managed to pull him down with the gatayû'si pole, but he struck the ground with such a force that he sank into it and the earth close over him.

93. Motley, Willard, "The Almost White Boy," in *Soon, One Morning, New Writing by American Negroes, 1940-1962*. New York: Alfred A. Knopf, Inc., 1963, pp. 390-400. (Afro-American)

He went. There was a cream-colored car outside the house. In the parlor were smoking stands, and knickknack brackets, and a grand piano nobody played. Cora's father smoked cigars, owned a few pieces of stock, went to Florida two weeks every winter, told stories about the "Florida niggers."

Cora sat with her hands in her lap and her fingers laced tightly together. Jim smiled at Mr. Hartley's jokes and had a miserable time. And Jim discovered that it was best not to go to anybody's house.

Jim and Cora went together for four months. And they had an awful time of it. But they were unhappy apart. Yet when they were together their eyes were always accusing each other. Sometimes they seemed to enjoy hurting each other. Jim wouldn't call her up; and he'd be miserable. She wouldn't write to him or would stand him up on a date for Chuck Nelson or Fred Schultz; then she'd be miserable. Something held them apart. And something pulled them together.

"There's nobody here but us," she said. Her fingers unbuttoned the first button on his shirt, the second. Her fingers crept in on his chest, playing with the little hairs there.
"There's nobody here but us," she said, and she ran her fingers inside his shirt, over his shoulders and the back of his neck.

94. Mphahlele, Ezekiel, *The African Image*. London: Faber and Faber, Ltd., 1962. (African: South Africa)

And so the white world still battles for the soul of the African. I think the educated black man, frustrations notwithstanding, will yet emerge tough as tried metal from all this débris of colonial systems the West has thought fit to dump in Africa. How much of all this the African will find of some use in the scrapyard, and how much of his past, is still a big question. The fervent hope of everyone is that, having once recognized each fraud for what it is, he will not try to use it to oppress his own people and others whose genuine goodwill he needs. I personally cannot think of the future of my people in South Africa as something in which the white man does not feature. Whether he likes it or not, our destinies are inseparable. I have seen too much that is good in Western culture—for example, its music, literature and theater—to want to repudiate it. If the white man shuts his eyes to the good that is in my culture, he is the poorer for it and I am one up on him. There is nothing I can do to cure his malady. He has used the labor of my people for three centuries. To this extent he is deeply committed to a cohabitation with us—and that is reducing the relationship to its barest terms. He has no just reason to deny me the political right many other workers in the world enjoy, and the other good things education creates an awareness of and desire for. The white man has detribalized me. He had better go the whole hog. He must know that I'm the personification of the African paradox, detribalized, Westernized, but still African—minus the conflicts.

95. Murray, Pauli, *Proud Shoes*. New York: Harper & Row, Publishers, 1956. (Afro-American)

Reuben started to say something, but Harriet clapped her hand over his mouth and pushed him through the door.

There was nothing subdued about Grandmother. She blurted out exactly what she thought and was afraid of no one. She never called anyone "Marse." She had the Smith pride and refused to regard herself as a slave.

96. Mutwa, Credo Vusa'mazulu. *My People*. London: Anthony Blond, Ltd., 1964. Compiled from *Indaba, My Children* and *Africa is my Witness*, originally published by Clue Crane Books (Pty) Ltd., Johannesburg, and Stanmore Press Ltd., London.

The first men to walk the earth were not like the people of today. They all looked exactly alike—golden-eyed, hairless, with skin as red as Africa's plains. In these days there were no black-skinned or dark brown people, no Pygmies, no Bushmen, no Hottentots, no long-bearded Arabi [sic], no white men. The splitting up of humanity into different races came much later, through the wickedness of men themselves.

The drum, or tom-tom, is Africa's most traditional musical instrument, and the "talking drums" of West Africa are known far and wide, for their use in signaling and communication.

The boy explores further. He is not surprised to find a large hole yawning blackly at him on the side of the depression. Well does he know what it is—a goldmine. He has stumbled across one of the numerous mines operated by the Ma-Hi, with Bantu and Bushman slave labor, more than two thousand years ago. The strange round stones, he now realizes, are grindstones, which were used to crush the rocks in which the sun metal was contained as fine dust and tiny grains. These, he remembers being told, were washed from the crushed rocks with water, and then melted and poured into molds in the shapes of little crosses and discs.

It is a fact that the Bantu knew that the earth was not the center of the universe hundreds of years before the white man realized this. I have seen hundreds of objects, signs, and engravings which, when correctly interpreted, represent the solar system as we know it today—representations which were reproduced thousands of years ago.

The Bantu have known since time immemorial that the sun does not move round the earth, but that the earth moves round the sun.

The black man is a born poet and some of the hymns the Bantu have composed, both in words and tune, are far more suitable than those imported from Europe. When a black man prays, he wants to gesticulate and pray at the top of his voice; he wants to weep before God, or laugh aloud if the occasion is one of happiness. This nature of the Bantu has enabled him to survive pressures that have driven scores of nations to rebellion and war.

97. Ngubane, Jordan K., *An African Explains Apartheid.* London: Pall Mall Press Ltd., 1963. (© Frederick A. Praeger, Inc., 1963) (African: South Africa)

The second republic came into being when the temper of the slave owner was in the middle of its third evolutionary phase. In this situation, the Afrikaner nationalists realized that insisting on their type of justice was very much like supping with the devil, but they accepted the full implications of it and used the longest possible spoon. In the last analysis, however, the attack on the person ultimately involves the destruction of a people. There is no halfway house between fulfillment and extinction, between growth and death. Living is a continuous process of unfolding, whether the subject is the individual or the group. To stop this action is to destroy life; to slow it down is to frustrate creation's purpose for man. Gas chambers, pogroms, and possibly concentration camps are the handiest instruments by which a majority seeks to liquidate a minority. The few, however, cannot use these instruments against the many unless they want to release forces among the many that might in the end destroy the few. Survival is too precious to the Afrikaner nationalist to be risked in adventures that might endanger his own existence. As a result, he uses quite a number of techniques to frustrate life's purpose for the African. The end is always the same—to keep the African in the position of permanent weakness in order to preserve the Boer's pattern of justice, to transform him into a pliable tool in the hands of the Afrikaner nationalists. In this chapter, we shall pick only a few techniques at random to show different aspects of the pattern of "just" laws.

98. Ngugi, James, *The Black Hermit.* London: Heinemann Educational Books, Ltd., 1968. (African: Kenya)

The Government should act. It must deal firmly with anyone who is found exploiting racial, tribal or religious differences. But let us also remember that even a black man's government can go wrong.

99. Ngugi, James, *The River Between.* New York: Humanities Press Inc., 1965. (First published in African Writers Series, 1965.) (African: Kenya)

The river was called Honia, which meant cure, or bring-back-to-life.

But the missionaries had not as yet penetrated into the hills, though they sent a number of disciples to work there.

Waiyaki was often surprised at his father, who in some ways seemed to defy age. His voice, however, thin and tremulous, betrayed him. Waiyaki often remembered why he was sent to Siriana.

Drip! Drip! All along the edge of the corrugated-iron roof. Drip! Drip! All in a line, large determined drops of rain fell on the ground as if they were competing. They made little holes—little basins, scoop-like. Drip! That fat one was transparent and clear. Down it fell into the small basin its sisters had patiently helped to make. It struck the pool of water in the hole and muddy water jumped up, forming an impatient cone-shaped pillar. And all along the ground the cones jumped up, up like soldiers marking time. The grass outside, which for a long time had been scorched and sickly, was now beginning to wake up refreshed. And the rain came down in a fury, the straying thin showers forming a misty cloudiness so you could hardly see a few yards away. The jumping cones were doing it faster and faster. Soon the dripping stopped and was replaced by jets of water from the roof. They carried on the race.

He went out of the hut; he wanted to go to Makuyu to see Kamau, or any other person; a man maybe would understand him, a man to whom he could talk.

The moon was also awake. Her glare was hard and looked brittle. The whole ridge and everything wore a brilliant white. And the little things that in the day appeared ordinary now seemed to be changed into an unearthliness that was both alluring and frightening. Waiyaki listened for voices on the ridge but he could only hear silence. As he moved across the ridge, through small bushes and trees, the silence and the moon's glare seemed to have combined into one mighty force that breathed and had life. Waiyaki wanted to feel at one with the whole creation, with the spirits of his sister and father. He hesitated. Then the oppression in him grew and the desire to talk with someone mounted. The brightness of the moon seemed now soft and tangible and he yielded to her magic. And Waiyaki thrust out his arms and wanted to hold the moon close to his breast because he was sure she was listening and he wanted her cold breath near him. Now his muscles and everything about his body seemed to vibrate with tautness.

It was the vision of a people who could trust one another, who would sit side by side, singing the song of love which harmonized with music from the birds, and all their hearts would beat to the rhythm of the throbbing river. The children would play there, jumping from rock on to rock, splashing the water which reached fathers and mothers sitting in the shade around, talking, watching. Birds sang as they hovered from tree to tree, while farther out in the forest beasts of the land circled around. . . . In the midst of this Nyambura would stand.

100. Ngugi, James. *Weep Not, Child.* London: Heinemann Educational Books, Ltd., 1964. (African: Kenya)

Yet they were white men. They never talked of color; they never talked down to Africans; and they could work closely, joke, and laugh with their black colleagues who came from different tribes. Njoroge at times wished the whole country was like this.

101. Ng'Wend, Hilary, "The Panthers: An African's View," *New York Times*, Vol. cxx, No. 41, 159 (October 2, 1970), p. 35. (African: Kenya)

Within a very short time, the Panthers and similar militant groups among blacks have succeeded in giving black people something even the late Dr. Martin Luther King, for all his abilities and devotion, never succeeded in giving them: a sense of pride in their own race and heritage.

102. Nkosi, Lewis, "Farm Jails," *I Will Still be Moved: Reports from South Africa,* edited by Marion Friedmann. London: Arthur Baker Ltd., 1963. (African: South Africa)

In South Africa complaints are neither freely heard nor deeply considered, let alone speedily reformed, and there is nothing to persaude us that Dr. Verwoerd's government is going to change in the near future. However, since it is obvious that this mad and savage traffic in slave labor has to be stopped, and since it is palpably obvious how white power works in the world today, it takes a superhuman exercise of will not to work and hope for a world where power is in the hands of black people. Liberals have been telling us these long bad years to work for a world where people are equal and our efforts in this direction have not bettered our lives materially, nor is it probable that they will make the conditions under which Sadika worked in that South African farm disappear. Reluctantly, one comes to the conclusion that white people as a group—after all, it is white people as a group who matter—are prepared to respect the rights of black people only when they have the same power that white people have and, further, when they are able to exercise it as dangerously as white people do. My natural inclinations resist this kind of conclusion, but all the facts available repeatedly and inexorably bring me to this conclusion. All I can say is at this stage in world history I am not a little sick of being bullied, chastised, scourged and spat upon by white men in Johannesburg, London or New York, and if

I assess the mood of black people correctly, two thirds of the world's colored people are also sick to death of this treatment.

103. Nkrumah, Kwame, *Challenge of the Congo.* London: Thomas Nelson & Sons Ltd., and New York: International Publishers Co., Inc., 1967. (African: Ghana)

And now, the two thousand agents being in place and eager to enforce the collection of rubber upon very unwilling natives, how did the system intend that they should set about it? The method was as efficient as it was absolutely diabolical. Each agent was given control over a certain number of savages drawn from the wild tribes but armed with firearms. One or more of these was placed in each village to ensure that the villagers should do their task. These are the men who are called "Capitas", or head-men in the accounts, and who are the actual, though not moral, perpetrators of so many horrible deeds. Imagine the nightmare which lay upon each village while this barbarian squatted in the midst of it. Day or night they could never get away from him. He called for palm wine. He called for women. He beat them, mutilated them and shot them down at his pleasure. He enforced public incest in order to amuse himself by the sight. Sometimes they plucked up spirit and killed him. The Belgian Commission records that 142 Capitas had been killed in seven months in a single district. Then came the punitive expedition, and the destruction of the whole community. The more terror the Capita inspired, the more useful he was, the more eagerly the villagers obeyed him, and the more rubber yielded its commission to the agent. When the amount fell off, then the Capita was himself made to feel some of those physical pains which he had inflicted upon others. Often the white agent far exceeded in cruelty the barbarian who carried out his commissions. Often, too, the white man pushed the black aside, and acted himself as torturer and executioner.

104. Nokwe, Duma, "An African Barrister," in *I Will Still be Moved: Reports from South Africa,* edited by Marion Friedmann. London: Arthur Baker Ltd., 1963. (African: South Africa)

I began to have my doubts and now I realize that I was given an education which fitted me for nothing in South Africa.

Inspired by Oliver Tambo I went to Fort Hare—now a Tribal College for Xhosas only—and got my B.Sc. degree, but the best thing that happened to me there was that I met my wife Vuyisuua who was studying for the same degree.

When I left Fort Hare I quickly discovered an engineering degree was not going to help me get work.

"This is the beginning of a new life," I thought. But within three months I found myself battling against obstacles to set up an office, battling to be allowed to accept cases out of Johannesburg, battling to be allowed to make a living.

Newspapers faithfully carried reports of my first case.

I was always rather amused to find that separate robing-rooms had been set aside for me in the Johannesburg and Pretoria Supreme Courts—I suppose I might have contaminated my colleagues if I had donned my gown and wig in their presence.

After I was refused permission under the Group Areas Act to have an office in the Bar Council building in the center of Johannesburg, members of the Council did appeal to the Prime Minister, but nothing ever came of it.

I set up an office in down-town Johannesburg and accepted the fact that I would have a double struggle to get clients in that area of town.

My bitterest moment came when I went to the Bar Council buildings to be introduced to my colleagues. One advocate, who has since stood as a Nationalist candidate for Parliament, looked at my outstretched hand and said: "No money today . . . out."

Today I am bitter and disappointed.

105. Nyerere, Julius K., *Ujamaa—Essays on Socialism.* London: Oxford University Press, 1968. (African: Tanzania)

The foreigner introduced a completely different concept—the concept of land as a marketable commodity. According to this system, a person could claim a piece of land as his own private property whether he intended to use it or not. I could take a few square miles of land, call them "mine," and then go off to the moon. All I had to do to gain living from "my" land was to charge a rent to the people who wanted to use it. If this piece of land was in an urban area I had no need to develop it at all; I could leave it to the fools who were prepared to develop all the other pieces of land surrounding "my" piece, and in doing so automatically to raise the market value of mine. Then I could come down from the moon and demand that these fools pay me through the nose for the high value of "my" land—a value which they themselves had created for me while I was enjoying myself on the moon! Such a system is not only foreign to us, it is completely wrong. Landlords, in a society which recognizes individual ownership of land, can be, and usually are, in the same class as the loiterers I was talking about: the class of parasites.

How many of our students spend their vacations doing a job which could improve people's lives but for which there is no money—jobs like digging an irrigation channel or a drainage ditch for a village, or demonstrating the construction and explaining the benefits of deep-pit latrines, and so on? A small number have done such work in the National Youth Camps or through school-organized, nation-building schemes, but they are the exception rather than the rule.

Let me give one example of the kind of leadership which is needed. Suppose a group of families have decided to start a cooperative farm and village, and are discussing where to build their houses. The problem is whether to build on a hill or down in the valley; and the argument is about the ease of getting water versus the danger of flooding. A good leader who is a member of this group may argue that it is better to build on a hill and face the drudgery of carrying the water until they can afford a pump and pipes; but let us suppose that despite all his efforts the general opinion is to build near the water's edge. What should he do?

106. Opler, Morris Edward, *Myths and Legends of the Lipan Apache Indians.* New York: American Folk-Lore Society, J.J. Augustin Publisher, 1940. (American Indian: Apache)

Then the mother came back. She had a grasshopper for the little ones. She found her children dead. She went to the cardinal and said, "The people on earth treated me like this. They killed all my children." ("The Adventure with the Whippoorwill")

The Master swept the ground and made the plot smooth. The turkey went to the middle of the plot and shook himself. White corn came down. His master swept another little plot clear. The turkey went to the middle of this and shook himself. Yellow corn came down. A third place was cleared in the same manner. The turkey went to the center of it and shook again. This time blue corn fell. The fourth time that a plot was cleared and the turkey shook himself, corn of different colors, blue, white, and red mixed fell. Tobacco fell also. ("The Man Who Floated Down the River in a Log: The Origin of Agriculture")

This big spider could travel through the air, though there was nothing ahead so long as he had his thread behind. It was just like a kite. He could go to a mountain without any trouble. That's the way that spider was. ("Giant Spider")

107. Parks, Gordon, *The Learning Tree.* New York: A Fawcett Crest Book, 1970. Reprinted by arrangement with Harper & Row, Publishers, 1963. (Afro-American)

"Jack?" Her voice was softly urgent and questioning. He slammed the door, took a deep breath and walked to the corner where Pete was already shedding his wet clothes.

108. Petry, Ann, "In Darkness and Confusion," in *Black Voices.* New York: The New American Library, Inc., 1968. Orginally published in *Cross-Section: A Collection of New American Writing,* Edited by Edwin Seaver. New York: Simon and Schuster, Inc., 1947. (Afro-American)

The woman slapped the man across the face. The sound was like a pistol shot, and for an instant William felt his jaw relax. It seemed to him that the block grew quiet and waited. He waited with it. The man grabbed his belt and lashed out at the woman. He watched the belt rise and fall against her brown skin. The woman screamed with the regularity of clockwork. The street came alive again. There was the sound of voices, the rattle of dishes. A baby whined. The woman's voice became a murmur of pain in the background.

109. Poston, Ted, "The Revolt of the Evil Fairies," reprinted by permission of the author in *The Best Short Stories by Negro Writers*, edited by Langston Hughes. Boston: Little, Brown and Company 1967. (Afro-American)

110. Powell, Adam Clayton, "Black Power in the Church," *The Black Scholar.* Vol. 2, No. 4 (December, 1970), pp. 32-34. (Afro-American)

All things are God's. And were Christ to return to earth today, he would be leading the boycotts. He would be signing the petitions. He would stand up and oppose the politicans who come to Harlem once every four years during an election year and then shut their eyes and their hearts to the pleas of desperately poor and deprived people. Christ would have walked in Selma, He would have marched in Washington, and He would have lived in Harlem. "For where two or three are gathered together in my name, there am I in the midst of them."

111. Primus, Pearl E., "African Dance," *Africa Seen by American Negroes.* Dijon, France: Presence Africaine, Imprimerie Bourguignonne, 1958 (Afro-American)

Among other dances which speak of the past, are those done by the warriors. Today most of these dancers are old, but they need only the whisper of encouragement to bring forth the powerful dances of their youth.

112. Rulfo, Juan, "Macerio," in *The Burning Plain and other Stories*, translated by George Schade. Austin: University of Texas Press, 1967, pp. 1-9. (Mexican)

Felipa stays alone in the kitchen cooking food for the three of us. Since I've known her, that's all she does. Washing the dishes is up to me. Carrying in wood for the stove is my job too.

Then Godmother is the one who dishes out food to us. After she has eaten, she makes two little piles with her hands, one for Felipa, the other for me. But sometimes Felipa doesn't feel like eating and then the two little piles are for me. That's why I love Felipa, because I'm always hungry and I never get filled up—never, not even when I eat up her food. They say a person does get filled up eating, but I know very well that I don't even though I eat all they give me. And Felipa knows it too—They say in the street that I'm crazy because I never stop being hungry.

There are lots of people who will hit me on the head with rocks as soon as they see me. Big sharp rocks rain from every side. And then my shirt has to be mended and I have to wait many days for the scabs on my face or knees to heal.

Blood has a good flavor too, although it isn't really like the flavor of Felipa's milk—That's why I always live shut up in my house—so they won't throw rocks at me. As soon as they feed me I lock myself in my room and bar the door so my sins won't find me out, because it's dark.

And I don't even light the torch to see where the cockroaches are climbing on me. Now I keep quiet. I go to bed on my sacks, and as soon as I feel a cockroach walking along my neck with its scratchy feet I give it a slap with my hand and squash it. But I don't light the torch. I'm not going to let my sins catch me off guard with my torch lit looking for cockroaches under my blanket—cockroaches pop like firecrackers when you mash them.

And as long as I find something to eat here in this house I'll stay here.... And nobody will get me out of there, not even Felipa, who is so good to me, or the scapular that Godmother gave to me and that I wear hung around my neck—Now I'm by the sewer waiting for the frogs to come out. And not one has come out all this while I've been talking. If they take much longer to come out I may go to sleep and then there won't be any way to kill them and Godmother won't be able to sleep at all if she hears them singing and she'll get very angry. And then she'll ask one of those strings of saints she has in her room to send the devils after me, to take me off to eternal damnation, right now, without even passing through purgatory, and then I won't be able to see my papa or mamma, because that's where they are—So I just better keep on talking—What I would really like to do is take a few swallows of Felipa's milk, that good milk as sweet as honey that comes from under the hibiscus flowers—

113. Rulfo, Juan "Talpa," in *New Voices of Hispanic America: An Anthology*, edited by Darwin J. Flakoll and Claribel Alegria. Boston: Beacon Press, 1962. (Mexican)

We had been together many times; but always the shadow of Tunilo kept us apart. We felt that his blistered hands came between us and carried Natalia away so that she would keep on nursing him; and we knew that it would always be like that as long as she lived.

114. Salas, Marquez Antonio, "Like God," in *New Voices of Hispanic America: An Anthology*, edited by Darwin J. Flakoll and Claribel Alegria. Boston: Beacon Press, 1962. (Venezuelan)

Since then time has passed, time as long as a river that never stops passing, time as extensive and limitless as the air ... time that is scarcely a second, a brief fluttering of wings, a blow, something that passes, crosses, dampens us inside briefly and then blinds us with a hundred summers together, with a hundred summers weighing on our backs, until it diminishes us to a bit of streaked, reddish earth.

115. Senghor, Léopold Sedar, *On African Socialism*, translated by Mercer Cook. London: The Pall Mall Press Ltd., 1964. © 1961, Editions Présence Africaine; © 1964, Frederick A. Praeger, Inc. (African: Senegal)

Wealth springs from the diversities of countries and persons, from the fact that they complement each other. We shall always remember a truth expressed by Father Teilhard de Chardin: Races are not equal but complementary which is a superior form of equality. Whence the superiority of the feudal over the unitary state.

As we are warned, the new grouping will be effected "under the leadership of the Ivory Coast."

In the Federation of Mali, however, the important thing is that there is no leader-state, but complete solidarity among the member states. In other words, the only leadership belongs to the Federation, to the general interest. Customs receipts and taxes on imports go first to the federal services.

It is now a commonplace fact that the European masses' standard of living has been able to rise only at the expense of the standard of living of the masses in Asia and Africa. The economy of European nations consists fundamentally in selling manufactured products to underdeveloped countries at high prices and buying raw materials from them at the lowest possible cost. I am not talking about the United States of America.

We stand for a middle course, for a democratic socialism, which goes so far as to integrate spiritual values, a socialism which ties in with the old ethical current of the French Socialists. Historically and culturally we belong to this current.

Every republic in Black Africa can take its independence whenever it deems the moment opportune. Nevertheless, the sequels of colonialism remain and we must absorb and transcend them. As for our West African civilization, however charred it may be by the fire of conquest, it is now becoming verdant once again in the springtime of a new era, even before the first shower of Independence.

I have often spoken of the role of underdeveloped nations in the building of the international community. Because the Negro Africans have kept a sense of brotherhood and dialogue, because they are inspired by religions that preach love, and above all, because they live those religions, they can propose positive solutions for the construction of the international as well as the national community.

116. Senior, Clarence, *The Puerto Ricans.* New York: Quadrangle Books, 1961. (Puerto Rican)

The urge to do violence against the stranger lies just below the surface in the individual who has such an emotional reaction. The urge to violence isn't always controlled. *The New York Post* of March 25, 1957, carries an example under the heading: "We Were Talking in Spanish—and the Words Meant Death."

The slum is the villain then—not its inhabitants.

117. Smythe Hugh H., "The African Elite in Nigeria," original source in *Africa Seen by American Negroes.* Dijon, France: Présence Africaine, Imprimerie Bourguignonne, 1958, pp. 71-82. (Afro-American)

There is no sizable bloc of people of wealth, education, and gentility in existence yet. There are only individuals who are recognized by their positions and achievements and whose status extends to their immediate families. Finer residential areas of private homes have not been zoned or established; so well-recognized and accepted communities of upper class Nigerians have yet to come into being.

Elite status is also acquired through personal achievement. In an undeveloped country like Nigeria, where trained people are few and it is difficult to find opportunities for self-advancement (though under both government and private auspices people are now gaining higher education, and better positions), any who manages to make a mark for himself in life is respected. Thus those who have gone on to higher studies, especially abroad, and who have returned to Nigeria, established themselves in a community, and made a success of their careers are automatically accorded élite status, particularly where one's accomplishments get publicized in one way or another.

His conduct in public is controlled to fit the occasion. At social affairs, such as cocktails or dinner parties, he is urbane, smiling, talkative (but not too much so); he carries conversation well and listens, or pretends to, when other persons of importance are speaking. He cultivates foreign contacts at interracial or international affairs, but he is not obvious about it.

This picture of the typical new leader of Nigeria applies whether he is premier or minister of state, an "honorable" member of the legislature or an important parliamentarian, business "tycoon" or labor spokesman, district councilor or senior civil servant, high church dignitary or well-known university professor, government corporation chairman or high court judge, lawyer, militant politician, or professional man, with variations as a result of individual differences.

This portrait of a generalized leadership, however, must not mislead one into thinking there are no basic elements that divide the élite, since in fact, regionalism makes for a certain kind of differentiation. In the southern regions which have been longest exposed to the influence of Western civilization, the foundation for the contemporary élite pattern first developed from what may be called the "old-established families."

118. Chief Standing Bear, from his autobiography, *The Land of the Spotted Eagle*. New York: Houghton Mifflin, 1933, as found in *American Indian Prose and Poetry*, edited by Margot Astrov. New York: Capricorn Books, 1962. (American Indian: Lakota)

Sometimes during the night or stillness of day, a voice would be heard singing the brave song. This meant that sorrow was present—either a brave was going on the warpath and expected to die, or else a family was looking for the death of some member of it. The brave song was to fortify one to meet any ordeal bravely and to keep up faltering spirits. I remember, when we children were on our way to Carlisle School, thinking that we were on way to meet death at the hands of the white people, the older boys sang brave songs, so that we would all meet death according to the code of the Lakota—fearlessly. (47)

119. Staples, Robert, "The Myth of the Black Matriarchy," *The Black Scholar*, Vol. I, No. 3,4 (January-February, 1970), pp. 8-16. (Afro-American)

120. Stewart, James T., "The Development of The Black Revolutionary Artist," in *Black Fire: An Anthology of Afro-American Writing*, edited by LeRoi Jones and Larry Neal. New York: William Morrow and Company, Inc., 1968. (Afro-American)

The black artist must construct models which correspond to his own reality. The models must be non-white. Our models must be consistent with a black style, our natural aesthetic styles, and our moral and spiritual styles. In doing so, we will be merely following the natural demands of our culture. These demands are suppressed in the larger (white) culture, but, nonetheless, are found in our music and in our spiritual and moral philosophy.

The sense in which "revolutionary" is understood is that a revolutionary is against the established order, regime, or culture. The bourgeoisie calls him a revolutionary because he threatens the established way of life—things as they are. They cannot accept change, though change is inevitable. The revolutionary understands change. Change is what it is all about. He is not a revolutionary to his people, to his compatriots, to his comrades. He is instead, a brother. He is a son. She is a sister, a daughter.

The purpose of writing is to enforce the sense we have of the future. The purpose of writing is to enforce the sense we have of responsibility—the responsibility of understanding our roles in the shaping of a new world. After all, experience is development; and development is destruction. The great Indian thinkers had this figured out centuries ago. That is why, in the Hindu religion, the god Siva appears—Siva, the god of destruction.

Black culture implies, indeed engenders, for the black artist another order, another way of looking at things. It is apparent in the music of Giuseppe Logan, for example, that the references are not white or European. But it is jazz and it is firmly rooted in the experiences of black individuals in this country. These references are found also in the work of John Coltrane, Ornette Coleman, Grachan Moncur and Milford Graves.

Art can not apologize out of existence the philosophical ethical position of the artist. After all, the artist is a man in society, and his social attitudes are just as relevant to his art as his aesthetic position. However, the white Western aesthetics is predicated on the idea of separating one from the other—a man's art from his actions. It is this duality that is the most distinguishable feature of Western values.

121. Stokes, Gail, "Black Man, My Man Listen!" in *The Black Woman*, edited by Toni Cade. New York: New American Library, Inc., 1970, pp. 111-112. (Afro-American)

You are dependent, very dependent, upon my proddings, my ideas, my dreams, and at first I am glad that you need me so. I eagerly and happily feed you from the plate of motivation knowing that it is difficult for you to help yourself. But, then at times you cause my arms to grow weary as I work harder straining myself in order to build you up.

122. Stone, Robert, "Porque No Tiene, Porque Le Falta," *New American Review No. 6*. New York: The New American Library, (April, 1969), pp. 198-226. (American)

When he was outside, he picked up one of the weights he had bought to keep himself in condition and lay down with it. Lying on his back, he held the weight at arm's length for quite a long time.

123. Sundiata, Phaon Goldman, "The White Reaction to the Black Assertion," *The Black Scholar*, Vol. I, No. 5 (March, 1970), pp. 11-16. (Afro-American)

124. Teit, James, *Folktales of Salishan and Sahaptin Tribes*, edited by Franz Boas. Lancaster, Pa., 1917.

One said, "It is much better to be dead." And the other said, "It is better to be alive." When they saw her, they stopped talking, and since then people die from time to time. There are always some being born and some dying at the same time, always some living ones and some dead ones. Had she remained hidden and allowed them to finish their argument, one would have prevailed over the other, and there would have been either no life or no death. (Coeur D'Alêne, "The Origin of Death")

125. Thomas, Piri, *Down These Mean Streets.* New York: The New American Library, Inc., 1967, originally published by Alfred A. Knopf, Inc., 1967. (Puerto Rican)

The thoughts pressed on my brain. I grabbed my face with both hands and squeezed hard, pushing it all out of shape; I pulled my lips out and my face down. The reefer kick was still on, and I could feel the smallness of the room and the neatness of its humble furniture and the smell of its credit, which $1.50 a week paid off. I pushed my way to the window, pulled the light chord and hid from myself in the friendly darkness. Easing the noise from the oldtime window shade, I pushed up the window and squeezed my hand through the iron gate my aunt had put in to keep the crooks out. I breathed in the air; it was the same air that I had breathed as a kid.

126. "Tombs 7," " 'Tombs 7' Defense $$ Plea." *Amsterdam News.* Vol. 61, No. 7 (1971), p. 14.

We want to live as decent human beings, free from want, free from abuse, free from inhuman treatment by an enemy, because his cities are besieged by the masses, who themselves are seeking a place in the sun. We must unite now, or die later.

We have have not destroyed anything, nor will we allow ourselves or our people to be destroyed. It has been said that "the urge to destroy is really a creative urge." Well, we are not the "useful idiot" type, nor do we suffer from "Icarus Complexes." We are firm in our resolve that we are innocent of any wrong doing and that our pleas should not go unanswered by the masses. Peace! power through unity!

127. Toomer, Jean, *Cane.* New York: Liveright Publishers, 1951. (Afro-American)

Esther's hair falls in soft curls about her high-cheekboned chalk-white face. Esther's hair would be beautiful if there were more gloss to it. And if her face were not prematurely serious, one would call it pretty. Her cheeks are too flat and dead for a girl of nine. Esther looks like a little white child, starched, frilled, as she walks slowly from her home towards her father's grocery store. She is about to turn in Broad from Maple Street. White and black men loafing on the corner hold no interest for her. Then a strange thing happens. A clean-muscled, magnificent, black-skinned Negro, whom she had heard her father mention as King Barlo, suddenly drops to his knees on a spot called the Spittoon. White men, unaware of him, continue squirting tobacco juice in his direction. The saffron fluid splashes on his face. His smooth black face begins to glisten and to shine. Soon, people notice him, and gather round. His eyes are rapturous upon the heavens. Lips and nostrils quiver. Barlo is in a religious trance. Town folks know it.

Jerky, aflutter, she closes the store and starts home. Folks lazing on store window-sills wonder what on earth can be the matter with Jim Crane's gal, as she passes them. "Come to remember, she always was a little off, a little crazy, I reckon." Esther seeks her own room, and locks the door. Her mind is a pink mesh-bag filled with baby toes.

Karintha is a woman. Men do not know that the soul of her was a growing thing ripened too soon. They will bring their money; they will die not having found it out. . . .

128. Travis, Dempsey J., "The 1971 Homestead Act," *The Black Scholar*, Vol. I, No. 6 (April, 1970), pp. 14-17. (Afro-American)

129. Trumbo, Dalton, *johnny got his gun.* New York: Lyle Stuart Inc., 1970.

He started to kick out with his feet to move what was under his legs. He only started because he didn't have any legs to kick with. Somewhere just below his hip joints they had cut both of his legs off.

130. Turner, Lorenzo D., "African Survivals in the New World with Special Emphasis on the Arts," *Africa Seen by American Negroes*. Dijon, France: Présence Africaine, Imprimerie Bourguignonne, 1958. (Afro-American)

On the other hand, those who have taken the time to acquaint themselves with the history and culture of the Africans know well that many of the slaves brought to the New World were highly intelligent and talented people. Many were not only proficient in their own language and culture but could write in the Arabic language and speak it fluently. Many were from the upper levels of African societies: kings, princes, chiefs of tribes, priests, military experts, artists, and others well versed in their history and folklore. Inter-tribal wars frequently resulted in the enslaving of the conquered ruler and of all his followers and subsequently in their being sold to white slave-traders and being brought to the New World. Moreover, a study of the native culture of West Africa (the home of the large majority of Africans who came to the New World) reveals that the West Africans had a culture comparable to that of any essentially non-literate and non-machine society in the world. They had well organized economic systems, political systems adequate for the effective administration of large kingdoms, a complex social organization, intricate systems of religious belief and practice, a folk literature comparable to that of any other group, as well as music, the dance, and highly developed art forms. African languages (inaccurately called "dialects" by detractors of the Africans) are also comparable to any other languages as vehicles of aesthetic, logical and effective expression; and as more of these languages are written, the more evident this fact is becoming. The late R. E. G. Armattoe, an anthropologist, says that "throughout the whole of the Middle Ages, West Africa had a more solid politico-social organization, attained a greater degree of internal cohesion, and was more conscious of the social function than Europe".*

*R. E. G. Armattoe, "The Golden Age of West African Civilisation" (Londonderry, Northern Ireland; Published for Lomeshie Research Center by the *Londonderry Sentinel*, 1946). pp. 33, 35.

131. Vazquez de Arce, Margot, "The Puerto Rican Landscape," *Puerto Rico, La Nueva Vida The New Life*, edited by Nina Kaiden, Pedro Juan Soto and Andrew Valdimir. New York: Renaissance Editions, 1966. (Puerto Rican)

Our popular music has the sensual monotony of all tropical music and it sounds similar, in the plenas, to Puerto Rican everyday speech. We are sentimental; the senses and the emotions command our spirit. Our hospitality sometimes reaches indiscretion. Having learned empirically through the ages, we lean toward the fatalistic. Our nervous and sensitive temperament make us undecided and mistrustful. We display a free and bantering mirth which is contradicted by the mute nostalgia in our eyes. We ripen early, as tropical fruits do, and soon turn lifeless, as does the orgy of colors in our twilight. In love and face to face with death we keep acting like Spaniards; we go through everyday life with the Negro's tenderness and the parsimony of the Castilian.

132. Vonnegut, Kurt, Jr., *Slaughterhouse-Five Or the Children's Crusade*. New York: A Seymor Lawrence book, Delacorte Press, 1969. Also available from Dell Publishing Co., Inc. ("A Fourth-Generation German-American")

One guy I knew really *was* shot in Dresden for taking a teapot that wasn't his.

"You know what I say to people when I hear they're writing anti-war books?"
"No. What *do* you say, Harrison Starr?"
"I say, 'Why don't you write an anti-*glacier* book instead?'"

I wonder if I could come down and see you, and we could drink and talk and remember.

He doesn't mind the smell of mustard gas and roses.

People aren't supposed to look back. I'm certainly not going to do it anymore.

She also thought that she was the head of the family, since she had had to manage her mother's funeral, since she had to get a housekeeper for Billy, and all that.

He didn't look like a soldier at all. He looked like a filthy flamingo.

Tens of thousands of Americans shuffled eastward, their hands clasped on top of their heads.

The human beings also passed canteens, which guards would fill with water.

Billy wondered if there was a telephone somewhere. He wanted to call his mother, to tell her he was alive and well.

Billy covered his head with his blanket again. He always covered his head when his mother came to see him in the mental ward—always got much sicker until she went away.

He had been rewarded for marrying a girl nobody in his right mind would have married.

If Billy had had to guess as to the source, he would have said that there was a vampire bat hanging upside down on the wall behind him.

He said he was sure that all the other Americans would do the same. He said that his primary responsibility now was to make damn well sure that everybody got home safely.

There was a broad river to reflect those lights, which would have made their nighttime winkings very pretty indeed.

She had two big cans of soup for the Americans. . . . She had stacks of loaves of black bread, too.

He said there wasn't a man there who wouldn't gladly die for those ideals.

133. Warner, Paris, "I Want to Be a Flesh and Blood Man," in *Children of Longing*, edited by Rosa Guy. New York: Bantam Books, Inc., 1970. (Afro-American)

I wanted to be many things. I wanted to be a basketball player. I wanted to be an actor. I wanted to be a writer. I wanted to be a physical education instructor. I became a dope addict.

134. White, Joseph, "Guidelines for Black Psychologists," *The Black Scholar*, Vol. I, no. 5, pp. 52-57. (Afro-American)

135. Williams, A. Cecil, "Black Souls Are Not For Sale," *The Black Scholar*, Vol. 2, No. 4 (December, 1970), pp. 35-42. (Afro-American)

II. GETTING IT TOGETHER

The irony of the church is that young blacks still feel that black ministers have the greatest potential of reaching the people in the community. Yet, because the black churches have not been able to get it together, they are unable to respond to the needs, the claims, and the demands of the people in the communities.

Getting it together for the black church may mean responding to the Black Panther Party by supporting their breakfast for children program.

Getting it together may mean working with welfare recipients to help them move beyond the point of mere survival.

Getting it together for the black church may mean providing public transportation for communities who have none, and who have been unheard and ignored by the power structures in the city.

Getting it together might mean making sure that urban renewal does not mean removal of indigenous people of the black community, and that public housing does not become urban prisons where black people are shuffled as commodities for the conveniences of city planners and profitmongers.

Getting it together may mean providing health clinics in areas in the communities where people would not have to travel unreasonable distances to receive health care.

Getting it together may mean making sure that blacks are participants for full employment in federal, state and city jobs.

Getting it together may mean that food stamp programs and proposals meet the needs of people who are literally starving in cities throughout America, without the dehumanizing and frustrating bureaucracy and red tape imposed by agencies.

Getting it together for the black church may mean providing education programs and facilities that are uniquely related to the black experience.

Getting it together could mean freeing the black sisters with free and efficient daycare centers.

Getting it together may in fact mean confronting the reality of police brutality and inequitable law enforcement.

Getting it together may mean educating oneself to and dealing with the issue critical in the 70's for all third world communities and those who dissent—the issue of political prisoners.

136. Williams, John A. *The Man Who Cried I Am.* New York: The New American Library, Inc., 1968. Originally published by Little, Brown and Company, Boston, 1967. (Afro-American)

She had smiled. Obviously he had asked somebody to tell him how to ask for a kiss. The dust of Africa hadn't remained on him long; he adjusted very quickly. And she had thought that he might kiss her and had decided that she would let him. "Yes," she said, and she had held up her lips, closed her eyes. But she felt his lips on her forehead, soft and very gentle. He drew away. When she opened her eyes he was looking at her with a little smile and he seemed very tired. Someone at the party had told her that he hadn't slept for two days. What struck her was the innocence of the kiss, innocence, yes, and a kind of gratitude. For what, she had asked herself in the mirror, for what?

Early in September, after having Paris largely to themselves during August, the tourists went home. The new Negro expatriates cast about with increasing desperation. Summer was over and so was the first flush of Paris; they had to be set for winter, somewhere, somehow.

He glanced at Margrit. She had spent every available moment in the sun as if, by tanning, she could minimize the difference between them. . . . Minister Q had told him once that the time to take over America was during the summer, beach by beach when all the white folks were laying out in the sun getting blisters trying to look like black people. Margrit was very dark except for her very white ass and the lower parts of her breasts which looked like two lost half moons in search of some sky.

137. Wright, Richard, *Black Boy.* New York: Harper & Row, Publishers, 1945. (Afro-American)

In the immediate neighborhood there were many school children who, in the afternoons, would stop and play en route to their homes; they would leave their books upon the sidewalk and I would thumb through the pages and question them about the baffling black print.

A quarter of a century was to elapse between the time when I saw my father sitting with the strange woman and the time when I was to see him again, standing alone upon the red clay of a Mississippi plantation, a sharecropper, clad in ragged overalls, holding a muddy hoe in his gnarled, veined hands—a quarter of a century during which my mind and consciousness had become so greatly and violently altered that when I tried to talk to him I realized that, though ties of blood made us kin, though I could see a shadow of my face in his face, though there was an echo of my voice in his voice, we were forever strangers, speaking a different language, living on vastly distant planes of reality.

Later that day I rummaged through drawers and found Granny's address; I wrote to her, pleading with her to come and help us. The neighbors nursed my mother day and night, fed us and washed our clothes. I went through the days with a stunned consciousness, unable to believe what had happened. Suppose Granny did not come? I tried not to think of it. She had to come. The utter loneliness was now terrifying. I had been suddenly thrown emotionally upon my own. Within an hour the half-friendly world that I had known had turned cold and hostile. I was too frightened to weep. I was glad that my mother was not dead, but there was the fact that she would be sick for a long, long time, perhaps for the balance of her life. I became morose. Though I was a child, I could no longer feel as a child, could no longer react as a child. The desire for play was gone and I brooded, wondering if Granny would come and help us. I tried not to think of a tomorrow that was neither real nor wanted, for all tomorrows held questions that I could not answer.

The pupils were a docile lot, lacking in that keen sense of rivalry which made the boys and girls who went to public school a crowd in which a boy was tested and weighed, in which he caught a glimpse of what the world was. These boys and girls were will-less, their speech flat, their gestures vague, their personalities devoid of anger, hope, laughter, enthusiasm, passion or despair. I was able to see them with an objectivity that was inconceivable to them. They were claimed wholly by their environment and could imagine no other, whereas I had come from another plane of living, from the swinging doors of saloons, the railroad yard, the roundhouses, the street gangs, the river levees, an orphan home; had shifted from town to town and home to home; had mingled with grownups more than perhaps was good for me. I had to curb my habit of cursing, but not before I had shocked more than half of them and had embarrassed Aunt Addie to helplessness.

It worked as I had planned. When I broke the news of my leaving two days before I left—I was afraid to tell it sooner for fear that I would create hostility on the part of the whites with whom I worked—the boss leaned back in his swivel chair and gave me the longest and most considerate look he had ever given me.

138. Wright, Richard, *The Long Dream*. New York: Doubleday & Co., 1958. (Afro-American)

The white men joked in low tones as the car got under way. Fishbelly stared unseeingly, once more a prey to anxiety. He held himself stiffly, on the verge of hysteria. The fingers of his freed right hand lifted and hovered indecisively in air, moved tremblingly to his lips, then descended to his groin, fumbling. Yes; he was intact; he had not been castrated while he had been unconscious. He sighed, looking about like a sleepwalker, licking his lips with a dry tongue seeing again the vision of Chris's bloody, broken body inert upon the table under the glaring electric bulb. The car was now purring through the paved streets of town, and, for a moment, he was three blocks from his father's undertaking establishment!

139. Wright, Richard, "The Man Who Went to Chicago," in *Eight Men*. Cleveland and New York: Avon, 1961. Originally titled "Early Days in Chicago," which was reprinted in *Eight Men* by permission of Paul R. Reynolds, Inc. Original story was copyrighted in 1945 by L.B. Fischer Publishing Corporation. (Afro-American)

After tramping the streets and pounding on doors to collect premiums, I was dry, strained, too tired to read or write. I hungered for relief and, as a salesman in insurance to many young black girls, I found it.

140. Wright, Richard, *Native Son*. New York: Harper & Row, Publishers, 1966. (Afro-American)

He saw a little girl pick her way through the snow and stop at a corner newsstand; a man hurried out of a drug store and sold the girl a paper. Could he snatch a paper while the man was inside?

He went to the drug store and looked inside at the man leaning against a wall, smoking. Yes. Like this! He reached out and grabbed a paper and in the act of grabbing it he turned and looked at the man who was looking at him, a cigarette slanting whitely across his black chin. Even before he moved from his tracks, he ran; he felt his legs turn, start, then slip in snow. Goddamn! The white world tilted at a sharp angle and the icy wind shot past his face. He fell flat and the crumbs of snow ate coldly at his fingers. He got up, on one knee, then on both; when he was on his feet he turned toward the drug store, still clutching the paper, amazed and angry with himself for having been so clumsy. The drug store door opened. He ran.

She was wanting the word that would free her of this nightmare; but he would not give it to her. No; let her be with him; let somebody be with him now. She caught hold of his coat and he felt her body trembling.

He lifted her and laid her on the bed. Something urged him to leave at once, but he leaned over her, excited, looking at her face in the dim light, not wanting to take his hands from her breasts.

He felt Mary trying to rise and quickly he pushed her head back to the pillow.

He wanted to move from the bed, but was afraid he would stumble over something and Mrs. Dalton would hear him, would know that someone besides Mary was in the room. Frenzy dominated him. He held his hand over her mouth and his head cocked at an angle that enabled him to see Mary and Mrs. Dalton by merely shifting his eyes. Mary mumbled and tried to rise again. Frantically, he caught a corner of the pillow and brought it to her lips. He had to stop her from mumbling, or he would be caught. Mrs. Dalton was moving slowly toward him and he grew tight and full, as though about to explode. Mary's fingernails tore at his hands and he caught the pillow and covered her entire face with it, firmly. Mary's body surged upward and he pushed downward upon the pillow with all of his weight, determined that she must not move or make any sound that would betray him. His eyes were filled with the white blur moving toward him in the shadows of the room. Again Mary's body heaved and he held the pillow in a grip that took all of his strength. For a long time he felt the sharp pain of her fingernails biting into his wrists. The white blur was still.

She obeyed. He placed the two pillows near the window, so that when he lay down the window would be just above his head. He was so cold that his teeth chattered.

He heard Bessie's clothes rustling in the darkness and he knew that she was pulling off her coat. Soon she would be lying here beside him. He waited for her.

She tried to turn from him, but his arm held her tightly; she lay still, whimpering. He heard her sigh, a sigh he knew, for he had heard it many times before; but this time he heard in it a sigh deep down beneath the familiar one, a sigh of resignation, a giving up, a surrender of something more than her body.

141. Wright, Richard, *The Outsider.* **New York: Harper & Row, 1965. (Afro-American)**

"Ma," he called softly. "You're still there?"

He was conscious of himself as a frail object which had to protect itself against a pending threat of annihilation.

142. Wright, Richard, *Uncle Tom's Children.* **New York: Harper & Row, Publishers, 1940. (Afro-American)**

Green slopes lay before him in the blurred dawn. The boat sped on and he saw jagged outlines of tents. Smoke drifted upward. Soldiers moved. Out of the depths of his tired body a prayer rose up in him, a silent prayer. Lawd, save me now! Save me now . . .

She grabbed her dress, got up and stood by the bed, the tips of her fingers touching the wall behind her. A match flared in yellow flame; Silas' face was caught in a circle of light. He was looking downward, staring intently at a white wad of cloth balled in his hand. His black cheeks were hard, set; his lips were tightly pursed. She looked closer; she saw that the white cloth was a man's handkerchief. Silas' fingers loosened; she heard the handkerchief hit the floor softly, damply. The match went out.

"Yuh little bitch!"
Her knees gave. Fear oozed from her throat to her stomach. She moved in the dark toward the door, struggling with the dress, jamming it over her head. She heard the thick skin of Silas' feet swish across the wooden planks.
"Ah got mah raw-hide whip n Ahm takin yut t the barn!"
She ran on tiptoe to the porch and paused, thinking of the baby. She shrank as something whined through the air. A red streak of pain cut across the small of her back and burned its way into her body, deeply.
"Silas!" she screamed.
She grabbed for the post and fell in dust. She screamed again and crawled out of reach.
"Git t the barn, Gawddammit!"
She scrambled up and ran through the dark, hearing the baby cry. Behind her leather thongs hummed and feet whispered swiftly over the dusty ground.

The white man who had gotten out walked over the ground, going to Silas. They faced each other, the white man standing up and Silas sitting down; like two toy men they faced each other. She saw Silas point the whip to the smashed graphophone. The white man looked down and took a quick step backward. The white man's shoulders were bent and he shook his head from left to right. Then Silas got up and they faced each other again; like two dolls, a white doll and a black doll, they faced each other in the valley below. The white man pointed his finger into Silas' face. Then Silas' right arm went up; the whip flashed. The white man turned, bending, flinging his hands to shield his head. Silas' arm rose and fell, rose and fell. She saw the white man crawling in dust, trying to get out of reach. She screamed when she saw the other white man get out of the car and run to Silas. Then all three were on the ground, rolling in dust, grappling for the whip. She clutched the baby and ran. Lawd! Then she stopped, her mouth hanging open. Silas had broken loose and was running toward the house. She knew he was going for his gun.

One of the white men was on the ground. The other was in the car. Silas was aiming again. The car started, running in a cloud of dust. She fell to her knees and hugged the baby close. She heard another shot, but the car was roaring over the top of the southern hill. Fear was gone now. Down the slope she ran. Silas was standing on the porch, holding his gun and looking at the fleeing car. Then she saw him go to the white man lying in dust and stoop over him. He caught one of the man's legs and dragged the body into the middle of the road. Then he turned and came slowly back to the house. She ran, holding the baby, and fell at his feet.

She saw two white men on all fours creeping past the well. One carried a gun and the other a red tin can. When they reached the back steps the one with the tin can crept under the house and crept out again. Then both rose and ran. Shots. One fell. A yell went up. A yellow tongue of fire licked out from under the back steps.

She watched from the hill-slope; the back steps blazed. The white men fired a steady stream of bullets. Black smoke spiraled upward in the sunshine. Shots came from the house. The white men crouched out of sight, behind their cars.
"Make up your mind, nigger!"
"C mon out er burn, yuh black bastard!"
"Yuh think yuhre white now, nigger?"
The shack blazed, flanked on all sides by whirling smoke filled with flying sparks. She heard the distant hiss of flames. White men were crawling on their stomachs. Now and then they stopped, aimed, and fired into the bulging smoke. She looked with a tense numbness; she looked, waiting for Silas to scream, or run out. But the house crackled and blazed, spouting yellow plumes to the blue sky. The white men shot again, sending a hail of bullets into the furious pillars of smoke. And still she could not see Silas running out, or hear his voice calling. Then she jumped, standing. There was a loud crash; the roof caved in. A black chimney loomed amid crumbling wood. Flames roared and black smoke billowed, hiding the house. The white men stood up, no longer afraid. Again she waited for Silas, waited to see him fight his way out, waited to hear his call. Then she breathed a long, slow breath, emptying her lungs. She knew now. Silas had killed as many as he could and stayed on to burn, had stayed without a murmur. She filled her lungs with a quick gasp as the walls fell in; the house was hidden by eager plumes of red. She turned and ran with the baby in her arms, ran blindly across the fields, crying, "Naw, Gawd!"

143. Wright, Richard, *White Man, Listen!* Garden City, N. Y.: Doubleday and Co., 1957. (Afro-American)

Most whites left Europe voluntarily; the American Negro was snatched by force from the organic, warm, tribal culture of Africa, transported across the Atlantic in crowded, stinking ships, and sold into slavery. Held in bondage, stripped of his culture, denied family life for centuries, made to labor for others, the Negro tried to learn to live the life of the New World in an atmosphere of rejection and hate.

Being a Negro has to do with the American scene, with race hate, rejection, ignorance, segregation, discrimination, slavery, murder, fiery crosses, and fear.

Truly, you must now know that the word Negro in America means something not racial or biological, but something purely social, something made in the United States.

The Negro writer had no choice in his subject matter; he could not select his experiences.

144. Yglesias, Jose, "Right On With the Young Lords," *The New York Times Magazine*, Vol. CXIX, No. 41,042 (June 7, 1970), pp. 32-33, 84-86, 88, 90-95.

145. Young Lords Party, Health Ministry, "Lincoln Hospital Must Serve the People!" *Palante;* Latin Revolutionary News Service. Vol. 2 No. 11 (September 11, 1970), p. 3. (Puerto Rican)

Nobody but us is going to worry about our people and whether they live or die—especially not people who live a million miles away and go home to clean, lily-white communities where they don't know what it is to sit hours in hot, dirty rooms waiting to be treated.

146. Young, Cullen, and Hastings Banda editors, *Our African Way of Life,* Essays by John Kambalame, E.P. Chidzalo, J. W. M. Chadangalara. London: Lutterworth Press, 1946.

As another mode of securing a wife, capture or kidnapping is not unknown among the Chewa people. The usual procedure is to waylay the intended bride, along the footpath that leads from the village to the stream, well or garden. The prospective bridegroom always asks one or more of his friends to assist him with the capture. The party hides somewhere along the footpath. In this, the conspirators are aided by a rich and benevolent Nyasaland nature, which erects from the ground a thick shroud of grass to interlace with an equally thick canopy of tree leaves overhead. As the intended victim approaches or comes past the spot where they are hiding, the men break cover and, seizing their prey by the arms and legs, carry her away between them on their shoulders.

147. Young, Whitney M., Jr., "Negro History Week," *Amsterdam News.* Vol. 61, No. 7 (February 13, 1971), p. 14. (Afro-American)

Black people have influenced every field of knowledge taught in schools from literature to engineering, and it's up to the schools to "unbleach" their courses and let their students know about this.

And it's up to black parents to insist upon it. There's more to taking care of our kid's education than attending a special auditorium meeting to celebrate Negro History Week with a student sketch. Parents have to stay on top of what their children are being taught and they should organize to help influence teachers and administrators. . . .

Everyone from the President to the Panthers is using the phrase "Power to the People," but unless the people show initiative and some real follow-through, it's just a slogan. Our kids are our most valuable asset and the education they receive is our most important task. . . .

Black people have fought and struggled for an education since the dim days of slavery, when it was a crime for a black man to be taught to read and write. Blacks like Frederick Douglass would hide away in attics studying copybooks and would trick and tease school boys into teaching them to read. It's been a long hard struggle and it won't be over until all black children get the high quality education that will prepare them for the future.

Final Cumulative Editing

Look for everything covered in the book in the following excerpts and change anything that has to be changed in order to put the excerpts back into college writing. Make all changes directly in the sentences as if you were editing a paper. If an excerpt does not need to be changed, put a check (√) next to its number.
(See page 2 for how to use the "Answer" Section.)

1. "This is the beginning of a new life I thought. (104)

2. One said, "it is much better to be dead. And the other said It is better to be alive (124)

3. It is easier to be Black than to learn Black, easier to shout than to study, easier to thump than to think. (80)

4. And they said to me We are Tartars by tribe, and the Tartars are Muslims (1)

389

5. The sun was hot on his head his collar still pinch his throat the Sunday clothe's was intolerably hot. (20)

6. Now, as she walked beside him, trim and oddly elegant in a heavy, dark blue coat; and with her head cover by an old-fashion and rather theatrical shawl, he saw that both her vanity and her contempt was being swollen by the glance's which rested on her as briefly and unforgettably. As the touch of a whip. (7)

7. The stage manager looked at me. Just as I heard my cue. I carried his face onstage with me, had look white and horrify and disembodied in the eerie backstage light. I wondered, what had frightened him? Then I realized, that: I was haven trouble findin my position's and with hearing lines. (11)

8. I felt very bitterly nauseous and I went to the bathroom but nothing happened, then I begun to be afraid; rather, to sit or lie down again and I poured myself another drink and having left my dressing room. To stand in the wings. I had began to sweat and I was freezing cold. (11)

9. Nancy Lee Johnson was a colored girl; a few year's out of the South. But seldom did her high-school classmate's think of her as colored. She was smart, pretty and brown. And fitted in well with the life of the school. She stood high in scholarship. Played a swell game of basketball, Had taken part in the senior musical in a soft velvety voice. And had never seemed to intrude or stand out except in pleasants ways, so it was seldom even mention. Her color. (63)

10. I was ill all day. I thought, "I had a cold." At night my chest pain me. I start to cough. I decided, not to go out at night to look for paper. I searched for my son João. He was at Felisberto de Carvalho Street near the market. A bus

had knock a boy into the sidewalk and a crowd gather. João was in the middle of it all. I poked him a couple of time's and within fives minute's he was home. (35)

11. He glanct at Margrit, she had spend every available moment in the sun as if, by tanning, she could minimize the difference between them. . . . Minister Q had told him once that the time to take over America was during the summer; beach by beach. When all the white folks was lying out in the sun getting blisters' trying to look like black people. Margrit was very dark except for her very white ass and the lower parts of her breasts. Which looked like two lost half moons in search of some sky. (136)

12. I cant understand a man who say's he is civilized, who say they are Christians, who do not only rebel against the Queen's Government but who condemn the black race—the entire black race in Rhodesia to a place of servitude—and who call hisself a Christian and call hisself a civilize person. What utter nonsense! (71)

13. The crisis were a compound of many things, of machines and turnpike's and railroads tracks'; of sin, sex and salvation; of the restless yearnings of poor whites and the volcanic stirrings of poor blacks; of the fear, guilt and anxiety which lied like a slave chain across the American soul. (16)

14. No site in Harlem has as much theatrical meaning; as the corner of 132nd Street and Seventh Avenue. Here once stood the Lafayette, previously note as having been builded in 1912 by John Mulonski. Nearby, at 131st Street and Seventh Avenue, stands the stump of the Tree of Hope, donated by that great dancer Bill "Bojangles" Robinson. This Tree of Hope stood outside the Lafayette

Theater, and it was so name because, as legend have it, an unemploy actor once lingered beneath the tree, hoping for work. A theatrical manager is said to have approached him and offered him a job. Thereafter, crowds of unemployed actors stood beneath that tree, sometimes blocking the way of passersby. (91)

15. Three books, to my way of thinking, gives a good idea of the intangible sense of reality that pervade the Indian people. When the Legends Die by Hal Borland gives a good picture of Indian youth. "Little Big Man" by Thomas Berger gives a good idea of Indian attitudes toward life. "Stay Away, Joe" By Dan Cushman, the favorite of Indian people, gives a humorous but accurate idea of the problems cause by the intersection of two ways of life. (36)

16. I personally loathed my father, and have continue to do so to a greater or lesser degree according to my age, I have never ceased to admire the way in which he brought this enterprise to a successful conclusion. In other words, his *style*. Knowing what a passion all his compatriots have for parties and family gatherings; however little like parties the latter may be—he used to invite all his half-brothers and nephews round once a month, and say to them: "Id like you to help me do a little job. Theres plenty of wine laid on this morning; so you can wet your whistles before you go out to work, and finishing it up when your done." (17)

17. There is indeed many good men among the councilors; men whose real purpose are to serve the people and not to look for private gains; men who are putting up a fierce battle even within the council walls against all forms of corruption. But they are all too few. (4)

18. The pioneer Negro abolitionist's gave way in the forties' to the giants of the movement, Charles Lenox Remond, the first Negro to take the platform as a professional anti-slavery lecturer; Samuel Ringgold Ward, the eloquent black man who pastored a white church; Henry Highland Garnet, the bitterly brilliant Thomas Paine of the movement; Martin R. Delany, the Harvard man who were the first major Negro nationalist; William Wells Brown, the grandson of Daniel Boone (he said) and the first Negro to write a novel and a play. There were others: the big-souled, God-intoxicated women, Sojourner Truth and Harriet Tubman, and scholars like J. W. C. Pennington, the minister who received a D.D. degree from the University of Heidelberg while he was still a fugitive slave; Alexander Crummell, the erudite Episcopal priest; and James McCune Smith, the New York physician who graduated from the University of Glasgow. (16)

19. When New Year's came. I waited for my new suit. Uncle's wife was very good at sewing and I believe it was agreed between both uncle and wife; to cut down one of uncle's suits, this was done and the suit was presente to me. Very much to my disapproval. Uncle was a very fat man; weighing about two hundred and ten pounds. So the suit was trie and did not fitted me any'where. All the kids had holiday clothes but me, I was so peeved at my uncle and his wife, that, I tried to kill their cat, Bricktop. (79)

20. Drip! Drip! All along the edge of the corrugated iron roof. Drip! Drip! All in a line. Large determine drops of rain fell on the ground. As if they was competing. They made little holes—little basins; scoop-like. Drip! That fat one was transparent and clear. Down it fell. Into the small basin it's sisters had patiently help to make. It struck the pool of water in the hole and muddy water jumpt up, forming impatient cone-shaped pillar. And all along the ground the cones jumped up; up like soldiers marking time. The grass outside; which for a long time had been scorched and sickly, was now beginning to wake up refreshed. And the rain came down in a fury. The straying thines showers forming a misty cloudiness so you could hardly see a few yards away. The jumping cones were doing it faster and faster, soon the dripping stopped and were replace by jets of water from the roof. They carried on the race. (99)

21. It is now a commonplace fact that the European masses' standard of living have bean able to raise only at the expense of the standard of living of the masses' in Asia and Africa. The economy of European nations consist fundamentally in selling manufactured products to underdevelope countries at high prices and then they buy raw materials from them at the lowest possible cost, I am not talking about the United State's of America. (115)

22. Élite status is also acquire through personal achievement. In an undeveloped country like Nigeria. Where trained people are few and it is difficult to find opportunities for self-advancement (though under both government and private auspices people are now gaining higher education, and better positions), any who manages to make a mark for themselves in life are respected. Thus those who has gone on to higher studies, especially abroad, and who have return to Nigeria, established theirselves in a community, and who have made a success of their careers are automatically accorded élite status; particularly where ones accomplishments get publicize in one way or another. (117)

23. All right then says the senior woman when next you bathe with the young woman in the river—then you will answer me your own question!

Later, and privately, one of the women nudges the young wife, and sidling close to her, asks, "Na Nkoma, have you not gone beyond a moon?" and she immediately take the meaning of a question and answer quickly, "It is true, O my Mother, I am glad you have ask me, for I myself desired greatly to ask about this but my lips were dry with shyness. I myself know nothing about what is gone on in my body." (70)

24. There is a paradox in the fact that Africa qualify for such an award in it's age of turmoil and in revolution.

How great is the paradox and how much greater the honor that an award in support of peace and the brotherhood of man should come to one who are citizens of a country where the brotherhood of man is an illegal doctrine outlawed, ban, censure, proscribed and prohibited, where the work, talk of campaign for the realization in fact and deed of the brotherhood of man are hazardous, punish with banishment or confinement without trial or being put in prison, where effective democratic channels to peaceful settlement of the race problem has not existed these 300 years, and where White minority power rest on the most heavily armed and equip military machine in Africa.

This is South Africa. (81)

25. One soldier spilled the water from his canteen on the ground in order to add to the discomfort of the female demonstrator at his feet. She cursed him—understandably, I think; and shifts her body. She loss her balance, her shoulder hit the rifle at the soldiers side. He raise the rifle, and with its butt, came down hard on the girls' leg. The girl tried to move back. But was not fast enough to avoid the billy-club of a soldier in the second row of troops. At least four times that soldier hit her with all his force; then as she lay covering her head with her arms, thrust his club swordlike between her hands into her face. Two more troops came up and began dragging the girl toward the Pentagon. . . . She twisted her body so we could see her face. But there was no face there: All we saw were some raw skin and blood. We could'nt see even if she was crying, her eyes had fill with the blood pouring down her head. She vomited, that too was blood. Then they rushed her away. (87)

26. And so the white world still battles for the soul. Of the African. I think the educated black man, frustrations notwithstanding, will yet emerge tough as tried metal from all this débris of colonial systems the West has thought fit to dump in Africa. How much of all this the African will find of some use in the scrapyard, and how much of their past, are still a big question. The fervent hope of everyone is: that, having once recognized each fraud for what it is; he will not try to use it to oppress his own people and other's whose genuine goodwill they need. I personally can'not think of the future of my people in South Africa as something in which the white man does not feature. Whether he liked it or not; our destinies are inseparable. I have scene too much that is good in Western culture—for example, it's music literature and theater. To want to repudiate it. If the white man shuts his eyes to the good that are in my culture, he is the poorer for it, I am one up on him. There is nothing I can do to cure their malady, he has used the labor of my people for three centuries. To this extent he is deeply committed to a cohabitation with us, that is reducing the relationship to it's barest terms. He has no just reason to deny me the political right many other workers in the world enjoy, and the other good things education creates an awareness of and desire for. The white man has detribalized me, he had better go

the whole hog. He must know that I'm the personification of the African paradox, detribalized, Westernized, but still African. Minus the conflicts. (94)

27. On the other hand, those who has taken the time to acquaint themselves with the history and culture of the Africans know well, that "many of the slaves brought to the New World were highly intelligent and talent people." Many were not only proficient in their own language and culture; but could write in the Arabic language and who were speaking it fluently. Many were from the upper level's of African societies: king's, prince's, chief's of tribe's, priest's, military expert's, artist's, and other's well versed in they're history and folklore. Intertribal wars frequently result in the enslaving of the conquered ruler and all his followers were enslaved and subsequently in there being sold to white slave-traders and were brought to the New World, moreover, a study of the native culture of West Africa (the home of the large majority of Africans who cames to the New World) reveal that the West Africans had a culture comparable to that of any essentially non-literate and non-machine society in the world. They had well organized economic systems. Political systems adequate for the effective administration of large kingdoms. A complex social organization. Intricate systems of religious belief and practice. A folk literature comparable to that of any other group. As well as music, the dance, and highly develope art forms. African languages (inaccurately called "dialects by detractors of the Africans) is also comparable to any other languages as a vehicle of aesthetic, logical and effective expression, as more of this languages are wrote, the more evident this fact is becomin. The late R. E. G. Armattoe, an anthropologist, says that "throughout the whole of the Middle Ages, West Africa had a more solid politico-social organ-

ization, attained a greater degree of internal cohesion, and were more conscious of the social function than Europe." (130)

28. Do NOT change a thing in this excerpt.

Black Beauty, in impotent silence I listened, as if to a symphony of sorrows, to your screams for help, anquished pleas of terror that echo still throughout the Universe and through the mind, a million scattered screams across the painful years that merged into a single sound of pain to haunt and bleed the soul, a white-hot sound to char the brain and blow the fuse of thought, a sound of fangs and teeth sharp to eat the heart, a sound of moving fire, a sound of frozen heat, a sound of licking flames, a fiery-fiery sound, a sound of fire to burn the steel out of my Balls, a sound of Blue fire, a Bluesy sound, the sound of dying, the sound of my woman in pain *the sound of my woman's pain*, THE SOUND OF MY WOMAN CALLING ME, ME, I HEARD HER CALL FOR HELP, I HEARD THAT MOURNFUL SOUND BUT HUNG MY HEAD AND FAILED TO HEED IT, I HEARD MY WOMAN'S CRY, I HEARD MY WOMAN'S SCREAM, I HEARD MY WOMAN BEG THE BEAST FOR MERCY, I HEARD HER BEG FOR ME, I HEARD MY WOMAN DIE, I HEARD THE SOUND OF HER DEATH, A SNAPPING SOUND, A BREAKING SOUND, A SOUND THAT SOUNDED FINAL, THE LAST SOUND, THE ULTIMATE SOUND, THE SOUND OF DEATH, ME, I HEARD, I HEAR IT EVERY DAY, I HEAR HER NOW . . . I HEAR YOU NOW . . . I HEAR YOU. (Eldridge Cleaver, *Soul on Ice*) (32)

Glossary-Index of Terms

This index includes topics covered in the text, definitions and illustrations of terms not discussed in text, cross-references between traditional grammatical terms and topics covered in the text, and abbreviations and symbols generally used by instructors when making comments on a paper.

ACTIVE VOICE. When the noun of the noun-verb pair <u>does</u> the action of the verb, the verb is in <u>active</u> voice. Whole Thoughts Type 1 and Type 2 are in active voice, 9, 11

ADJECTIVE. Describes a noun. *See* Descriptive Words.

ADJECTIVE CLAUSE (ADJECTIVAL CLAUSE). Generally a fragment beginning with a <u>W</u> word, and sometimes with "that," 19

The whole fragment describes a noun. On page 21, the fragment introduced by "which" describes the noun "body."

ADVERB. Tells how, how much, when, why, where, etc. Describes the quality of a verb, adjective, or another adverb. The underlined words below are adverbs. Adverbs usually end in "ly."

The plane flew <u>on</u>, as though I had <u>simply</u> blown my breath after it. I grabbed <u>again</u>, <u>frantically</u>, trying to catch the tail. (42)

(Adverbs describe the verbs they are near.)

He swung the car into the little pencil-mark road and started <u>off</u> toward the river, driving <u>very slowly</u>, <u>very cautiously</u>. (20)

(Adverbs "very" describe adverbs "slowly" and "cautiously.")

Her useless eyes seemed <u>very</u> large, <u>very</u> white in their deep sockets. (20)

(Adverbs "very" describe adjectives "large" and "white.")

ADVERB CLAUSE (ADVERBIAL CLAUSE). Generally a "<u>because</u> I want to" fragment, 17-22

Tells when, gives a reason, sets up a condition, expresses "although," makes a comparison, 19, 20, 21

AGR. *See* Agreement.

AGREEMENT. Noun-verb pair agreement, 141-148, 199-201, 259-260

AMBIGUOUS PRONOUN. The pronoun with the double meaning, 251-252

ANTECEDENT. The noun that a pronoun replaces in a sentence or paragraph, 252

APOSTROPHE. A mark used in place of one or more letters in a word, 207-209, 221-222, 237-238

A mark used to show ownership, 217-218, 221-222, 231-233, 237-238, 243

APPOSITIVE. A word or group of words that <u>renames,</u> 30, 31, 37-39

ARTICLE. "The," "A," and "An" are articles. They introduce nouns. *See* Definite and Indefinite Articles.

AUXILIARIES. Helping Verbs, 167, 168, 170, 181, 182, 183

AWK. Awkward construction, 249, 265-299

BALANCED IDEAS, 265-271

CAP. If this instructor's mark appears next to a word, the first letter should be capitalized.
CASE. See Nominative, Possessive and Objective Case.
CF. Comma Fault. Comma Splice, 11, 91, 91-137
CLAUSE. A group of words with a noun-verb pair. Whole Thought or fragment with noun-verb pair. See, Independent, Dependent, and Subordinate Clauses.
COH. Coherence. The aspect of an essay that makes it flow from one subtopic to another. Logical words are useful in keeping coherence in a paper. ("To cohere" means to stick together.), 121, 315
COLLECTIVE NOUN. A Group Noun. A noun that indicates a group of things. The words "flock" or "class" are collective nouns, 199
COLON (:), 321
COMMA (,), 11, 22, 31, 37, 39, 51, 60, 66, 71, 77, 91, 92, 93, 94, 123
COMMA FAULT. See Comma Splice.
COMMA SPLICE, 11, 91, 91-137
COMMON NOUN. All nouns except proper nouns. The word "man" is a common noun. Unless it comes first in a sentence, start a common noun with a small letter.
COMPARATIVE DEGREE. The descriptive word used to show a comparison between two things. The underlined words below are in the comparative degree. The descriptive word in the comparative degree usually ends in "er" or is preceded by the word "more."
She and my older sister, Louisa, are going out to be girls together. (12)
Her short, thick, graying hair was rougher than usual, almost as rough as my own—later, she would be going to the hairdresser's; she is fairer than I, and better-looking; ... (12)
Nothing was more familiar to them than the sight of a dark boy singing, and there were few things on earth more necessary. (12)
COMPARISON. The change in the spelling of descriptive words according to the degree of the comparison.
See Comparative Degree and Superlative Degree.
COMPLEMENT. Generally the noun after the verb in Whole Thought Type 4, 9, 12
See Subjective Complement.
COMPLEX SENTENCE. A sentence with only one Whole Thought and at least one fragment with a noun-verb pair, 17-32
COMPOUND SENTENCE. A sentence with two or more Whole Thoughts, 10, 91-137
CONJUGATION. A complete list of all the ways a verb can be used, telling all the principal parts, tenses, voices, and moods of that verb when it is paired to each of the six personal pronouns. See any standard foreign language text for an example of a conjugation.
CONJUNCTION. A word used to link two sentence parts together.
See Connective, Subordinating Conjunction, and Coordinating Conjunction.
CONJUNCTIVE ADVERBS. Logical Words. Logical Connectives, 121
CONNECTIVE A word joining one word or word group to another.
See Subordinating Conjunction and Coordinating Conjunction.

CONTRACTION. Two words in one, 207-209, 233, 237-238, 243
   See Apostrophe.
COORDINATING CONJUNCTION. The seven connecting words: "and," "or," "but," "nor," "for," "so," "yet," 93, 320
   The word that attaches two Whole Thoughts to each other, 10
   Also used to attach any two balanced sentence parts together, 270, 265-271
COPULATIVE VERB (COPULA). A Linking Verb. A verb in Whole Thought Type 4, 9, 12
CORRELATIVE CONJUNCTIONS. A pair of connecting words, such as "either . . . or," "not only . . . but," 199, 270
COULD HAVE, 196
CS. Comma Splice, 11, 91, 91-137

D. Diction. If this instructor's mark appears next to a word, check its definition in a dictionary.
   See WW, 325-329
DANGLING CONSTRUCTIONS. Dangling Modifier: When a descriptive word or group of words does not obviously describe something.
   Dangling Participle: An "ing" verb-like word in a word group which does not somehow have a connection with a noun. The "breaking through" fragment can end up being a "dangling participle."
   The underlined fragment below dangles:
   Seeing it come steadily forward the world grew warm with promise.
   To remove the dangling quality of the word group, name the person or thing who is doing the "seeing."
   Seeing it come steadily forward I felt the world grow warmer with promise. (42)
DECLARATIVE SENTENCE. It makes a statement as opposed to asking a question. Compare with Interrogative Sentence.
DECLENSION. The list of the various ways of spelling a particular noun or pronoun in order to summarize the various ways it could be used in a sentence. The declension of pronouns appears on page 217.
DEFINITE ARTICLE. The word "the." It introduces nouns, 215-216
DEGREE. *See* Comparative and Superlative Degree.
DEMONSTRATIVE PRONOUNS. "This," "that," "these," and "those," 217, 226
DEPENDENT CLAUSE. *See* Subordinate Clause.
DESCRIPTIVE WORD. Generally used in this text as the word that describes nouns and pronouns, 295
   Also can be an adverb.
DIRECT DISCOURSE. DIRECT STATEMENT. The original words that a person said, 281-283
   Compare with Indirect Statement.
DIRECT OBJECT. The "what he does it to" of Whole Thought Type 2, 9
   Compare with Indirect Object.
DIRECT QUESTION, 279

ELLIPSIS. The place in a quotation where a word or words have been left out.

Generally indicated by three or four dots, 322

The removed "that" in a sentence is also a form of ellipsis, 21, 29, 267 *(note)*, 282

ESSAY TOPIC, 298-299, 307-316

EXPLETIVE.   When "there" and "it" introduce an <u>inverted</u> noun-verb pair, "there" and "it" are usually expletives. They are used to make a smooth introduction to a sentence when you want to invert the noun-verb pair, 200, 233, 237

The underlined word below is an expletive:

<u>There</u> is a single person on the avenue, a para-trooper walking toward École Militaire. (12)
        noun verb

(A single person is on the avenue.)

Of course <u>it</u> is quite impossible to live on this amount of money without working—but who will hire a half-blind invalid? (12)
        noun   verb

(To live on this amount of money is quite impossible.)

FRAG.   Fragment, 10, 17-89

FUSED SENTENCE.   A run-on construction, 11, 91, 91-137

FUTURE PERFECT TENSE.   Verb groups with the helping verbs "will have." The time is <u>immediately before</u> another action in the future, 209-211

FUTURE TENSE VERB.   The time of the verb is <u>after right now,</u> 141, 209-211

GENDER.   The sex of nouns and pronouns. "Man" and "he" are masculine. "Woman" and "she" are feminine. "It" is neuter.

GERUND.   A verb-like word ending in "ing" which is used like a noun in a sentence. The underlined words below are gerunds:

The <u>sputtering</u> and banging increased. The <u>rattling</u> became more violent. (20)

GROUP NOUN, 199

See Collective Noun

HELPING VERBS.   Verbs used in making a verb group. Any verbs that are used before a main verb. Although not discussed in the verb group chapter, the word "will" in the verb group "will go," for example, is a helping verb for the verb group indicating future time, 167, 168, 170, 181, 182, 183

ID.   Idiom. When you find this instructor's comment on your essay, it means you have used an expression or idiom which is unfamiliar in general American usage.

IMPERATIVE MOOD (MODE).   A verb in a Whole Thought that gives a command. Generally, the noun of the noun-verb pair is not written in the sentence but it is understood to be the pronoun "you," 10 *(note)*

The underlined verb below is in the imperative mood:

<u>Take</u> me to your leader.

INDEFINITE ARTICLE.   The words "a" and "an." They introduce nouns.

INDEFINITE PRONOUN.   Pronouns that do not refer to any particular person or thing. "Any" and "each" are indefinite pronouns, 217

INDEPENDENT CLAUSE.   A Whole Thought. Any group of words with a noun-verb pair that is <u>not</u> a fragment, 8-10

INDICATIVE MOOD (MODE). A verb in a Whole Thought that makes a statement or asks a question.
INDIRECT DISCOURSE. INDIRECT STATEMENT, 281-283
INDIRECT OBJECT. A noun or pronoun in a sentence that receives the action of the verb (as in the direct object), but the thing that receives the action could have had the word "to" or "for" before it. Here is a Whole Thought Type 2 with the direct object underlined:
Helen wrote a <u>letter.</u>
Here is the same Whole Thought Type 2 with an added indirect object underlined twice:
Helen wrote <u><u>Marie</u></u> a <u>letter.</u>
Notice that you can put the word "to" in front of Marie if you change the word order around, and the meaning does not change:
Helen wrote a <u>letter</u> <u>to Marie.</u>
INDIRECT QUESTION, 279-281
INDIRECT STATEMENT, 281-283
INFINITIVE. A verb plus the word "to." Generally introduces the "<u>To be</u> a man" fragment, 65-66
INTENSIVE PRONOUN. Any pronoun with the word "self" attached to it that repeats the previous noun or pronoun for emphasis, 217
"I <u>myself</u> might be interested in speaking at the convention."
INTERJECTION. Generally a one or two word emotional outburst. "Wow!" and "Good grief" are interjections.
INTERROGATIVE PRONOUNS. Words introducing a question. Generally the W words plus "who," "whose," "what," "where," "when," "why," "which," and "how" when they are used to introduce a question, 19
INTERROGATIVE SENTENCE. A sentence that asks a question, 279
INTRANSITIVE VERB. The verb in Whole Thought Types 1 and 4. There are no direct objects ("what he does it to") in a Whole Thought that has an intransitive verb, 9, 11, 12
ITS, 217, 237-238
IT'S, 237

K. When this appears as an instructor's comment on your paper, it means Awkward Construction.

LAY, LIE, 195
LINKING VERB. A verb expressing the idea of "is" or "feels." In Whole Thought Type 4, 9, 14
LOGICAL WORDS. LOGICAL CONNECTIVES, 119-122

MAIN CLAUSE. *See* Independent Clause.
MISPLACED MODIFIER. When the descriptive word or word group does not clearly describe something. The underlined fragment is a misplaced modifier: "Headdresses were on their heads <u>with wide edges</u> that reached beyond their faces and shaded them." The fragment belongs next to the noun "headdresses," which it describes: "On their heads were headdresses <u>with wide edges</u> that reached beyond their faces and shaded them." (2), 251
MODIFIER. A descriptive word or fragment.
MOOD (MODE). *See* Indicative, Imperative, and Subjunctive Moods.

NOMINATIVE ABSOLUTE PHRASE. "The <u>jet breaking</u> through" fragment, 57-60
  The "<u>afraid</u> of his shadow" fragment when it is introduced by a noun, 57 *(note)*, 70
NOMINATIVE CASE. The noun or pronoun in the noun-verb pair, 8
NON-RESTRICTIVE CLAUSE. Any fragment with a noun-verb pair which does have commas before (and after) it. If you took away the fragment, the sentence would still make sense—it would not lose its essential meaning. The underlined word group below is a non-restrictive clause (note what would happen if you removed the clause from the sentence):
  And I look at my body, <u>which is under sentence of death.</u> (9)
  Since the reader already knows whose body is being discussed, the underlined fragment is not essential to define whose body it is; it is "<u>my</u> body." Compare with the restrictive clause where the underlined fragments distinguish exactly who is being discussed. Unlike the non-restrictive clause, the restrictive clauses are <u>absolutely</u> essential in order for the reader to know who is being discussed.
NOUN. Anything you could use as a topic for an essay. Any word in a sentence whose meaning in that sentence indicates it could be discussed as the topic of an essay, 215-216, 221-222, 223-226
NOUN-VERB PAIR. The subject and verb of a Whole Thought. The "do-er" and the "what he does or is or feels" of a Whole Thought, 8, 9
NOUN-VERB PAIR AGREEMENT. When to put <u>s</u> at the end of a verb, 141-148, 199-201, 259-260
NUMBER. Singular (one thing) or plural (more than one thing). Nouns and pronouns can be singular or plural in number, 221, 223-226
  Verbs also can change in spelling for singular and plural, 141-148, 199-201, 259-260

OBJECT. The "what he does it to" of Whole Thought Type 2, 9, 11
OBJECTIVE CASE. An object is in objective case.
OWNERSHIP, 217-218, 221-222, 231-233, 237, 243

P. Punctuation. If a "P" appears in your paper as an instructor's comment, look for a punctuation "problem."
PARAGRAPH. Generally a group of sentences developing a single idea, 301-316
PARALLEL CONSTRUCTION. Balanced Ideas, 265-271
PARTICIPLE. The main verb of a verb group, 167-173, 181-187
  A descriptive word (without the helping verbs) used to describe a noun or pronoun, 169, 295
  The first underlined participle is a main verb from Verb Group 1; the second is from Verb Group 2.
  One wheel of the <u>crushed</u> and upturned little Ford became visible above the <u>rushing</u> water. (20)
  (It is a crushed Ford; there is rushing water.)
PARTICIPIAL PHRASE. The "<u>breaking</u> through," "the <u>jet breaking</u> through," and "<u>afraid</u> of his shadow" fragments are participial phrases; they have participles in them, 49-51, 57-60, 70-72

Glossary-Index of Terms

PARTS OF SPEECH. The traditional parts of speech are: noun, pronoun, verb, adverb, adjective, preposition, conjunction, and interjection.

PASSIVE VOICE. When the noun of the noun-verb pair <u>receives</u> the action of the verb, the verb is in passive voice. The verb in Whole Thought Type 3 is in passive voice, 9, 12

"Passive" is not to be confused with "past," which has to do with <u>time</u>.

PAST PARTICIPLE. The main verb in Verb Group 1. Special spellings of past participles are listed on pages 171-173.

See Participle.

PAST PERFECT TENSE. Verb groups with the helping verb "had." The time is <u>immediately before</u> another action in the past, 167, 168, 170, 209-211

PAST TENSE VERB. The time of the verb is <u>before right now</u>, 141, 155-157, 209-211

PERFECT TENSE. Verb groups with the helping verb "have" or "had" are in perfect tense, 167-173

See Present, Past, and Future Perfect.

PERIOD (.), 7, 322

PERSON. A way of analyzing a pronoun-verb pair to see whether the noun is doing the talking (first person: "<u>I</u> am studying"), being talked to (second person: "<u>You</u> are studying"), or being talked about (third person: "<u>He</u> is studying"), 141-148

A singular third person noun or pronoun in present time has an <u>s</u> at the end of its verb.

PERSONAL PRONOUN. I, my, mine, me; you, your, yours, you; he, his, him, she, her, hers, her; it, its, it. We, our, ours, us; you, your, yours, you; they, their, theirs, them, 216-218

PHRASE. Any unified group of words or fragment that does <u>not</u> have a noun-verb pair, 37-89

"<u>Because of</u> you" is a phrase.

PLURAL. More than one. Usually said of nouns. ("Men" and "books" are plural nouns.), 221, 222 *(note)*, 223-226, 243

PLURAL OWNERSHIP, 231-233, 243

POSSESSIVE CASE. Nouns and pronouns that show ownership, 217-218, 221-222, 231-233, 237, 243

PREDICATE. The verb of the noun-verb pair plus any words after the verb. The second and third columns in Chart 1, page 9, comprise the predicate.

PREDICATE ADJECTIVE. The descriptive word (adjective) after the verb in Whole Thought Type 4 that describes the noun in the noun-verb pair, 9, 12, 295

In Chart 1, page 9, "cheerful" is the predicate adjective describing the "room"; it is a <u>cheerful</u> room.

PREDICATE NOUN. A word after the verb that renames the noun in the noun-verb pair. Found in Whole Thought Type 4, 9, 12

In Chart 1, page 9, "student" renames "Gus"; it puts another label on who Gus is.

PREPOSITION. Words that introduce a "<u>because of</u> you" fragment. Preposition phrases (prepositional phrases) generally end with a noun or pronoun, 76

PRESENT PARTICIPLE. A participle ending in "ing." The main verb in Verb Group 2, 181
See Participle.

PRESENT PERFECT TENSE. Verb groups with the helping verb "have" or "has." The time is immediately before now, 167, 168, 170, 171-173, 209-211

PRESENT TENSE VERB. The time of the verb is right now, 141, 157, 209-211

PRINCIPAL PARTS OF A VERB. The principal parts are the present, past, past participle (main verb of Verb Group 1), and present participle (main verb of Verb Group 2) spellings of any particular verb, 184-187, 195

PROGRESSIVE TENSES. Verb Group 2. Denotes action taking place over a long period of time, 181-187

PRONOUN. A word that takes the place of a noun. Generally it should be clear what noun the pronoun is replacing, 216-218, 251-263

PRONOUN-VERB PAIR, 8, 111-113, 141-148, 207-208

PRONOUN REFERENCE, 252-253

PROPER NOUN. A noun that provides a name. John is a proper noun. Start a proper noun with a capital letter.

QUESTION, DIRECT AND INDIRECT, 279-281

REDUNDANT. When you repeat something unnecessarily in an essay, you are being redundant, 296

REF. Reference. *See* Pronoun Reference.

REFLEXIVE PRONOUN. Any pronoun with the word "self" attached to it that shows that the person acts upon himself, 217
"You must take care of yourself."

RELATIVE PRONOUN. The W words and "that" when they introduce a fragment, 19, 217, 259-260

RESTRICTIVE CLAUSE. Any fragment with a noun-verb pair which does not have commas before and after it. If you took away the fragment, the sentence would lose its essential meaning. The underlined word group below is a restrictive clause (note what would happen if you removed the clause from the sentence):
The enraged whites shot down innocent Negroes who smiled and innocent Negroes who did not smile. (16)
The underlined fragments are absolutely essential to the meaning of the sentence. If we took them away, the sentence would lose an essential aspect of its meaning:
The enraged whites shot down innocent Negroes and innocent Negroes.
Compare with non-restrictive clause.

RO. Run-On Constructions, 11, 91, 91-137

SEMICOLON (;), 91-137, 92, 93, 119, 127, 319, 320

SENTENCE. A Whole Thought with a capital letter at the beginning and a period at the end. Any group of words that has at least one Whole Thought in it, 7 *(note)*, 10

SHIFTS. Pronoun, 252-253
See Tense.

SHOULD HAVE, 196

SIMPLE SENTENCE. A sentence with only one Whole Thought, 10

SINGULAR. Just one. Usually said of nouns. ("Man" and "book" are singular nouns.), 223-224

SP. Spelling. If you see "Sp" as an instructor's comment on your paper, look up the spelling in a dictionary, 139, 325-329

STATE OF BEING VERB. A Linking Verb. The verb in Whole Thought Type 4, 9

SUBJECT. The noun (or pronoun) of the noun-verb pair (or pronoun-verb pair), 8 *(note)*, 9, 111-113

SUBJECTIVE COMPLEMENT. The noun that tells "how or what" a do-er "is or feels." Generally comes after the verb in Whole Thought Type 4, 9, 12

SUBJUNCTIVE MOOD (MODE). A special form of the verb used in expressing wishes or statements that set up conditions for something else to happen. The underlined verbs below are in the subjunctive mood:

I wish I were there now.

If he should be late, call me up.

SUBORDINATE CLAUSE. Any fragment with a noun-verb pair, 17-22, 29-32

SUBORDINATING CONJUNCTION. Usually the words that commonly make fragments—excluding the W words, 19

A word that introduces the "because I want to" fragment to the Whole Thought—excluding the W words, 20-21

SUBSTANTIVE. Any word or word group used in the sentence as a noun, 215-216

SUPERLATIVE DEGREE. The word used to show a comparison between three or more things. The underlined words below are in the superlative degree. The descriptive word in the superlative degree usually ends in "est" or is preceded by the word "most."

Each seems to find the other full of the weirdest and most delightful surprises. (12)

SUPPOSED TO, 196

SYNTAX. Word order, 279-283, 295-298

T. Tense. If you see "T" as an instructor's comment on your paper, you may have shifted the time of the verb in the middle of a sentence or paragraph. Or you may have used a spelling of the verb which confuses your reader about the time the verb is expressing, 209-211

TENSE. The time of the verb: present, past, or future, 141, 209-211

THAT, uses of, 114, 297

THEIR, 231

THERE, 231

THESIS SENTENCE. The topic of an essay expressed in a sentence that usually appears in the introduction, 298-299, 307-316

THEY'RE, 231

TITLES, 323-324

TRANSITIONAL ADVERBS. Logical words, 121

TRANSITIVE VERB. The verb in Whole Thought Types 2 and 3. A Whole Thought that has "what he does it to" in it generally has a transitive verb, 9, 11, 12

USED TO, 196

VERB.   A word expressing an action or the idea of "is" or "feels," 8, 141, 141-213, 209-211
VERB GROUP 1, 167-173
VERB GROUP 2, 181-187
VERBAL.   Verb-like words when they are not used as verbs. Gerunds, participles, and infinitives.
VOICE.   See Active and Passive voice.

WW.   Wrong Word. When this is an instructor's comment in your essay, look up the word in the dictionary to see if you used it according to its definition, 325-329
W WORDS PLUS "THAT."   Can be used to introduce a fragment, 19, 21
WHOLE THOUGHT.   A group of words that is not a fragment. It contains at least one noun-verb pair, 7-12
WHO'S, 237
WHOSE, 217, 237
WORD ORDER, 279-283, 295-299
WOULD HAVE, 196

YOUR, 217, 233
YOU'RE, 207, 233

Instructor's Symbols

¶ Start a new paragraph, 301-316, 322

No ¶ Do not start a new paragraph, 301-316

∿ Switch the letters or words around.

   firts = first

   |Happy|John feels|. = John feels happy.

∧   Add something that has been left out, 139, 299

   f^i rst = add an "i".

   John ∧^feels sad. = add "feels."

// Check your sentence for Balanced Ideas, 265-271